AF527615

THE MOTHER

INDIAN LIVES

A series edited and curated by Ramachandra Guha

Ashoka: Portrait of a Philosopher King by Patrick Olivelle

Sheikh Abdullah: The Caged Lion of Kashmir by Chitralekha Zutshi

Kamaladevi Chattopadhyay: The Art of Freedom by Nico Slate

Forthcoming volumes:

Akshaya Mukul on Jayaprakash Narayan

Aparna Kapadia on Kasturba Gandhi

Richard Jaffe on the Buddha

Srinath Raghavan on Subramanyan Chandrasekhar

Abhishek Kaicker on Anand Ram 'Mukhlis'

Harish Damodaran on Ramkrishna Dalmia

Prashant Kidambi on Bal Gangadhar Tilak

Richard Davis on Rajaraja Chola

Indian Lives has been made possible through the generous support of

Bajaj Auto Ltd and the late Rahul Bajaj

Forbes Marshall

R.G. Manudhane Foundation for Excellence

INDIAN LIVES

THE MOTHER

A Life *of* Sri Aurobindo's Spiritual Collaborator

PETER HEEHS

An Imprint of HarperCollins *Publishers*

First published in India by Fourth Estate 2025
An imprint of HarperCollins *Publishers*
4th Floor, Tower A, Building No. 10, DLF Cyber City,
DLF Phase II, Gurugram, Haryana – 122002
www.harpercollins.co.in

2 4 6 8 10 9 7 5 3 1

P-ISBN: 978-93-6569-154-2
E-ISBN: 978-93-6569-198-6

Typeset in 11.5/15.2 Crimson Text at
HarperCollins *Publishers* India

Printed and bound at
Thomson Press (India) Ltd

This book is produced from independently certified FSC® paper
to ensure responsible forest management.

Contents

Series Editor's Foreword vii

Prologue: Becoming the Mother xi

PART ONE: 1878–1926

1. A Banker's Daughter 3
2. An Artist's Life 31
3. Cosmic Interlude 47
4. Pivotal Years 70
5. India and After 96
6. Exile 107
7. Return 133

PART TWO: 1927–1973

8. The Mother's Creation 153
9. The Ashram and the World 180
10. Alone 207
11. New Directions 233

Epilogue 258

Notes 273

Bibliography 307

Index 325

Series Editor's Foreword

THIS SERIES OF INDIAN LIVES WAS NEVER INTENDED TO BE NARROWLY xenophobic; hence, this book on someone of 'foreign' origin, who first visited India in her thirties, and chose to make it her home only in her forties. The mark she left on our cultural life was deep and enduring enough to make her an eminently worthy candidate for inclusion here. A later volume in this series will feature an equally remarkable figure, from the field of science rather than spirituality, who was born and raised in India but whose best work was done in England and the United States.

Known in India and to Indians simply as 'the Mother', the subject of this book was named, at birth, Blanche Rachel Mirra Alfassa. Her family and friends called her Mirra. Like Mirra, her biographer, Peter Heehs, first came to India when he was young. Like her again, he chose to make this country his home, and has lived here, more or less continuously, for the past five decades. Yet, he has other and even better qualifications to write this book. Heehs is arguably the greatest living authority on the life and thought of Mirra's mentor, Sri Aurobindo. He played a critical role in building and organizing the archives of the Sri Aurobindo Ashram in Pondicherry. And he is also a serious scholar of twentieth-century Indian history.

As narrated by Peter Heehs, Mirra's life before India was unusually interesting, peopled by all sorts of eccentric and enigmatic characters, who came into her world as friends, companions, teachers and mentors. She was born in a family of moderately prosperous Jews from the Middle East: Her paternal grandfather a banker in Turkey, her maternal grandfather a banker in Egypt. Her own parents moved to Paris shortly after they got married. As a child, Mirra grew to love plants as well as tennis (she played the game, off and on, until her seventies). Notably, she had little or no interest in her ancestral faith, perhaps because her parents were determined to assimilate into French society. However, she read widely in her father's well-stocked library of secular texts.

Late-nineteenth-century Paris was the centre of the art world. Mirra herself studied in an art school; Heehs writes of her early paintings that it 'shows great talent in rendering volume and colour'. She married a fellow artist, a Catholic, and had a child by him, running the household while her husband sought to build his career.

Mirra's first exposure to the land she was to make her own seems to have been by attending a talk by a Bengali Theosophist visiting Paris in the year 1900. This prompted her to read the Bhagavad Gita. Soon, she was developing an interest in esoteric religion, joining a circle that published a journal on occultism and called itself 'the Cosmic movement'. Through this group, she met the man who was to become her second husband, the writer Paul Richard.

Both Mirra and Paul divorced their spouses, and married one another. Meanwhile, Mirra was deepening her interest in spiritual matters and keeping what Heehs characterizes as a 'spiritual diary'. Paul Richard had been to Pondicherry by himself in 1910, and briefly met Aurobindo Ghose, then at the beginning of his exile from British India and moving ever more decisively from politics to spirituality. In 1914, Paul returned to Pondicherry with his wife; later, Mirra told friends 'that when she first saw Sri Aurobindo she recognized him at once as the Divine'. Her heart 'overflowed with joy and gratitude; she felt a boundless hope, inexpressible adoration, wordless reverence'.

At Paul's suggestion, he, Mirra and Sri Aurobindo started a monthly journal printed in English and French, dealing with religion and philosophy. However, the First World War broke out soon afterwards, and, within a year, the Richards had to return to France. After a year there, they moved to Japan, apparently at Mirra's suggestion. Here, they met Rabindranath Tagore, who was also there at the time. Mirra did a pencil sketch of the poet, yet a few conversations with him made her conclude (in Heehs's paraphrase) that Tagore was 'elegant and intelligent but without any true spiritual turn'.

In Japan, relations between Paul and Mirra became strained and even distant. In April 1920, the couple managed to return to Pondicherry. Mirra's own reunion with Sri Aurobindo 'was indescribably joyful and spiritually productive'. She was now absolutely convinced that 'my place and my work are near him, in India'. Her husband did not feel that way and returned to France in 1922.

Now, Sri Aurobindo and Mirra became ever closer in a spiritual sense. He believed that she had come to help him complete his own spiritual journey. As Sri Aurobindo now spent more and more of his time alone, meditating, Mirra came forward to guide the sadhana of the disciples and the spiritual life of the community. By 1926, she had become known as 'the Mother'. As the group associated with Sri Aurobindo in Pondicherry steadily grew, with new recruits coming in from across India and the world, it was the Mother who took charge of running the ashram, raising money for buildings, supervising the spiritual instruction of the disciples, and envisioning the larger international community, 'above all creeds, all politics, and all nationalities', that came to be known as Auroville. Busy from morning to night with prayer, consultations, group meetings both spiritual and secular, she now had virtually no time to, or for, herself.

Sri Aurobindo died in 1950, but the Mother herself lived for another twenty-odd years, continuing throughout this period to be the principal organizer, the chief planner and executor of the ashram's varied activities. The narrative of Heehs' book seamlessly blends the life of the individual with the life of the community whose journeys she directed, and with what was happening in the wider world. His evocation of the Parisian society and culture of Mirra's youth is brilliantly done, and when dealing with the Indian years, Heehs adroitly brings in the impact on the Mother and the ashram of the Second World War, the Indian freedom struggle, the coming of Indian independence, the transfer of Pondicherry from

French to Indian hands, and India's wars with its neighbours. With regard to the last, he underlines the Mother's fervent Indian patriotism, with her donating jewellery to the National Defence Fund during the China war of 1962, and, during the war with Pakistan in 1965, sending a message of solidarity and support to Prime Minister Lal Bahadur Shastri.

Heehs appears to have tracked down everything the Mother said or wrote, published or unpublished, in her very long life, as well as more or less everything said or written about the Mother by others. He tells us a great deal about Sri Aurobindo's spiritual pursuits and journey, providing a thorough yet accessible presentation of Sri Aurobindo's path to yoga. The second part of the book is almost a dual biography, of Sri Aurobindo and of the Mother.

Reading Heehs's book, it struck me that there were at least two other Western women whose life bears comparison to that of Mirra/the Mother. One is Swami Vivekananda's associate, Sister Nivedita, originally an Irishwoman named Margaret Noble. The other is Gandhi's 'adopted' daughter, Mira (spelt in the Indian way, with just one 'r'), whose name at birth was Madeleine Slade and whose biological father was a British Admiral. Here, is a trio of noteworthy Western women who became Indian, transformed by their encounters with a visionary male thinker. However, while Nivedita and Mira were disciples and interpreters of their respective Master, the Mother's relationship with Sri Aurobindo was that of a collaborator and colleague as well.

Peter Heehs is too scrupulous a scholar to seek to make such comparisons himself. He focuses on his own subject, on the relationships that moulded *her*, on the social and historical contexts that shaped *her*. In the process, he has given us a work of immense scholarship, that is so richly readable too.

Ramachandra Guha

Prologue
Becoming the Mother

ON 15 AUGUST 1954, WHEN THE PEOPLE OF INDIA WERE CELEBRATING their country's eighth Independence Day, a seventy-six-year-old Frenchwoman named Mirra Alfassa, known to most as the Mother, made a public statement. She wished, she said, 'to mark this day by the expression of a long cherished wish; that of becoming an Indian citizen'. She was, she went on, 'French by birth and early education' but 'Indian by choice and predilection'. For the past thirty-four years she had been living in Pondicherry, a tiny French colony on the southeast coast of India, which, in a few months, would join the Indian Union. When that happened, it would be possible for her to become a Indian citizen, but she did not think rejecting 'one nationality in order to obtain another' was the best solution. Rather, she wished to remain French while becoming Indian as well. She felt there was no antagonism between the culture of her homeland and that of her adopted country: 'On the contrary, they combine very well and complete one another'. Serving both countries would be a way for her to show 'that all the nations are essentially one and meant to express the Divine Unity upon earth through an organised and harmonious diversity'.[1]

The Mother never got her wish to become a dual citizen of India and France. That option did not exist at the time. She remained a

French citizen until her death in 1973 at the age of ninety-five. By then she had lived in India for more than fifty years, having settled in Pondicherry in 1920, six years after her first visit. Before then she had led a fairly conventional life—education, marriage, motherhood, artistic and intellectual activities—but she had a longing for spiritual growth that impelled her to seek out teachers from different parts of the world. In 1914, she met Sri Aurobindo, the Indian revolutionary turned philosopher and yogi, and felt at once he was her destined spiritual guide. After spending the years of the First World War in France and Japan, she returned to India in 1920, rejoined Sri Aurobindo, and became his spiritual collaborator and the Mother of his ashram.

This story has been told in dozens of biographies, all of which treat Mirra's becoming the Mother as the only possible outcome of her birth. I approach the subject from a different standpoint. There are two ways of writing a biography. One is to view the events of the subject's life as inevitable steps leading to a preordained conclusion. The other follows the subject from a fortuitous birth to an always uncertain, always receding outcome. Literary scholars call the first type of biography 'teleological', the second 'contingent'. I will call them 'omega' and 'alpha' biographies.

Authors of omega biographies plot the events of the subject's life the way novelists arrange the episodes of their stories. Authors of traditional novels have a fairly good idea of how things will turn out and what the story will show (love conquers all, crime doesn't pay, life is absurd). As they write, they arrange the incidents to make the ending seem inevitable. In a similar way, writers of omega biographies select and arrange events and circumstances to show how their subjects achieved the fame or notoriety that made their lives worth telling. How did Mohandas Karamchand Gandhi become the Mahatma? How did Napoleone di Buonaparte become emperor of France? How did Theodore Robert Cowell become the serial killer Ted Bundy? Readers of such biographies know the outlines of the story and look for indications of the eventual outcome as the action develops.

If omega biographies are structured like novels, alpha biographies are like diaries. Keepers of diaries record events as they happen, day by day, without knowing what will happen the day after. This mirrors the way we live our lives. We try to influence what will happen in the future—by passing examinations, finding good jobs, marrying the right partners—but we cannot make the course of our lives fit a predetermined pattern. The web of contingencies is too complex.

Omega and alpha biographies never exist in their pure forms. Omega biographers have to record contingent events; alpha biographers know how things will turn out in the end. Every biography is a mixture of the two approaches. Every biographer must decide how much importance to give to the alpha and omega viewpoints.

Biographies of spiritual figures are strongly omega because their followers regard their births as preordained and each event of their lives full of cosmic significance. Some of the Mother's biographers ask: Why was she born in France? The omega answer runs something like this: The Mother embodied the Soul of India but it was necessary for her to be born in France so that she could have all the experiences of the modern West before coming to India and meeting Sri Aurobindo. This destined encounter prepared the way for the creation of a perfect spiritual synthesis of East and West. Accordingly, the Mother chose as her parents two materialists from the West, or rather from the Middle East but destined to go to the West—and so forth. The alpha answer is more straightforward: Mirra Alfassa was born in France because her mother was living in France when she was born.

I take an alpha approach for two reasons. First, there is no shortage of omega biographies of the Mother. Second, I am a historian and not a theologian. Theological arguments are based on scriptural pronouncements, historical arguments on documents. I feel comfortable around documents and am distrustful of scriptures. But I will, just this once, offer a quotation from Sri Aurobindo, who is considered by many to be a modern rishi or seer, and his writings modern scriptures. When one of his disciples asked him why spiritual teachers such as the Buddha, Confucius and himself did ordinary things like getting married, he replied: 'Do you think that Buddha or Confucius or myself were born with a prevision that they or I would take to the spiritual life? So long as one is in the ordinary consciousness, one lives the ordinary life—when the awakening and the new consciousness come, one leaves it—nothing puzzling in that.'[2]

I write on the assumption that Mirra Alfassa was not born with a prevision that she would take to the spiritual life. Her sense of spiritual vocation emerged gradually over the course of five decades. At every moment, she had to deal with the contingencies of a complex life. Like the rest of us, she had no clear knowledge of what would happen next. When I write about what took place at a given moment of her life, I, along with many of my readers, know more of what was in store for her than she did at the time. I ask my readers to put themselves in her place, facing an unknown future each step of the way. In this way, they may get a glimpse of what it was like for Mirra to become the Mother.

PART ONE

1878–1926

1

A Banker's Daughter

1

MIRRA ALFASSA WAS BORN IN FRANCE AND LIVED THERE FOR thirty-six years, but she was not French by birth.[1] Her parents were immigrants from what we now call the Middle East. To understand her cultural background we have to trace the ancestry of her parents and look briefly at the life of the late Ottoman Empire and the French Third Republic.

The name Alfassa is a variant of Alfasi, meaning 'a person from Fas', which in Arabic refers to Fez, Morocco, and in Turkish to the whole country. Some of Mirra's ancestors evidently lived in Morocco, either before or after the expulsion of the Jews from Spain in 1492. These Spanish Jews, known as Sephardim, spread throughout the Mediterranean basin, which, at that time, was dominated by the Ottoman Empire. In the nineteenth century, the Ottoman Turkish cities of Constantinople (now Istanbul), Adrianople (Edirne) and Salonica (Thessaloniki), together with cities in Ottoman Egypt, such as Alexandria and Cairo, had thriving Jewish communities. Among these Ottoman Jews were forebears of Maurice Alfassa and Mathilde Ismalun, Mirra's father and mother.

Maurice's father, Nissim Alfassa, was a banker of Adrianople, with family and business ties to Constantinople. His first wife, née Bianca

Alfassa, gave him two sons: Samuel, born in Constantinople in 1842, and Maurice, born in Adrianople the next year.[2] Bianca died when the boys were very young. Around 1848, Nissim married Rachel Hillel, with whom he had four children, Léon and Jacques, born in Adrianople in 1849 and 1854, and Sara and Mathilde, born in Constantinople in 1855 and 1857. Nissim clearly moved back and forth between his birthplace and Constantinople, but from the mid-1850s until 1878, when he moved to Paris, he seems to have spent most of his time in the Ottoman capital.

Nissim was a devout Jew but he wanted his sons to receive a secular education. There was a secular Jewish school in Adrianople and it is possible that Maurice studied there as a child.[3] When he was older, his parents placed him in a boarding school in Austria, where he learnt German, French and other subjects.[4] By the time he finished his education, he could speak German and French, along with some Italian and Turkish. At home he probably spoke Judeo-Spanish, also called Ladino, which was the lingua franca of Sephardic Jews.

Constantinople was the capital of an empire that stretched east and south through Turkey, Arabia, the Levantine countries and Egypt, then west across North Africa to Tunisia. To the northwest, it controlled most of the Balkan peninsula: Greece, Macedonia, Bulgaria, Bosnia, and parts of Serbia and Romania. The Ottoman Empire had declined in importance since the seventeenth century, when it came close to defeating the Holy Roman Empire at Vienna, but it was still a major player on the world stage and its capital was a centre of international trade, finance and culture. Modernizing slowly under pressure from the West, the Ottoman government experimented with social reform and provided modern educational and public services, especially in the capital.

The condition of Jews in the Ottoman Empire depended on the will of the reigning sultan but they generally were better off than Jews in Eastern Europe, who often were confined to ghettos and subject to sporadic pogroms. Ottoman Jews had long enjoyed the right to regulate their religious affairs. During the reform period, they were placed on the same legal footing as Muslims but were not considered Ottoman citizens. Many sought the protection of foreign governments. In 1862, a group of Constantinople Jews with Italian connections broke away from the city's main Jewish community and sought the protection of King Victor Emmanuel II of Italy. In May of that year, a representative of the king told members of the breakaway group that that the Kingdom of Italy would recognize the community and protect their freedom of faith. (There definitely was some quid pro quo involved in this. Rulers are always in need of money and the Jewish bankers of Constantinople were glad to make loans to those who kept their interests in mind.) The new congregation changed its name to the Comunità Israelitico Straniera di Costantinopoli sotto la Protezione Italiana (Foreign Israelite Community of Constantinople under Italian Protection).[5] Nissim Alfassa became a member. In January 1863, he went before the elders of the community and declared that Maurice had been born to him and his late wife Bianca on 7 July 1843.[6] This opened the way for Maurice to become an Italian subject, greatly facilitating his career. Roughly speaking, it was the nineteenth-century equivalent of an immigrant of doubtful legal status being granted an Italian passport.

In 1865, Nissim, along with Samuel and Maurice, became a member of the Constantinople branch of the Alliance Israélite Universelle (Universal Jewish Alliance), a group founded in Paris in 1860 by liberal European Jews who wished to share their enlightenment with their less educated Ottoman brethren.[7] The president of the Constantinople branch was Abraham-Salomon de Camondo, a prominent banker and philanthropist. Nissim had business ties with the Camondo Bank, looking after its affairs in central Europe.[8] During the 1860s, if not before, he became close to members of the Camondo family in Constantinople. This would have momentous consequences for his family.

Abraham-Salomon de Camondo was one of the richest and most influential men in the Ottoman Empire, creator of a dynasty that won his family the epithet 'the Rothschilds of the East'. Besides being the unofficial banker of the Ottoman sultan, he conducted commercial and financial affairs throughout the Empire and in Europe, and had enormous real estate holdings in Constantinople. For services to Italy (where his ancestors had lived and where he passed several years of his life), he was granted Italian citizenship in 1865. The next year, his only son, Salomon-Raphaël, died. His grandsons, Abraham-Béhor and Nissim de Camondo, took up the reins of the family businesses.

In 1867, Abraham-Béhor celebrated the marriage of his only daughter, Clarisse, with Léon Alfassa, Nissim Alfassa's third son and Maurice Alfassa's half-brother. Two years later, Abraham-Béhor and Nissim de Camondo shifted to Paris, which became the international headquarters of the Camondo Bank. Along with Abraham-Béhor came Léon and Clarisse, who lived with him in his mansion at 7 Rue de Presbourg, a stone's throw from the Arc de Triomphe. Around 1870, Abraham-Béhor and Nissim de Camondo decided to settle in the up-and-coming Plaine-Monceau district and bought plots at 61 and 63 Rue de Monceau. Abraham-Béhor hired one of Paris's best-known architects to design a mansion to be erected at number 61. Work on it was completed in 1875 and Abraham-Béhor, Clarisse, Léon and their five children moved in.[9]

Maurice Alfassa was much slower off the blocks than Léon. In 1873, he turned thirty and had little to show for it. He lacked three things every businessman ought to have: Capital, work experience and a well-off wife. In 1874, he went to Egypt in search of all three. Through the Ottoman Jewish network, he got in touch with Matteo Ismalun, a prominent merchant and banker of Cairo and Alexandria. Matteo and his wife, Mirra,[10] née Pinto, had five children, the youngest of whom, Mathilde, was sixteen, pretty and well-travelled. Her parents had placed her in a Paris boarding school when she was only five, and she shuttled between France and Egypt during her youth. When Maurice Alfassa arrived in Alexandria, Mathilde was there. Her mother presented her to the young man. Charmed, he asked for her hand. Another man was interested but Mirra left the decision to Mathilde, who chose Maurice. The wedding took place in August 1874. Years later, Mirra Ismalun, an irrepressible personality, recalled that the rites were celebrated 'with great pomp in the government palace; the Viceroy and the ministers were present. I wore a magnificent golden robe and everybody found me more beautiful than my daughter. The ceremony was constantly interrupted by the arrival of some high official and on every side people were throwing small gold coins at us.'[11] As generous as she was flamboyant, Mirra marked the occasion by offering a full set of clothes to each of the students in the local Torah school.[12]

Matteo Ismalun earned his fortune partly through trade and partly through private banking. His most important client was Ismail Pasha, the Khedive or Viceroy of Egypt. Although nominally a vassal of the Ottoman sultan, Ismail was the de facto ruler of Egypt, Sudan and neighbouring regions. From his father, he inherited a 44 per cent share in the Suez Canal Company, founded in 1858 by French diplomat and entrepreneur Ferdinand de Lesseps. (In her memoirs, Mirra Ismalun wrote that de Lesseps once came to call on her with a cavalry escort.)[13] Ismail Pasha's moment of glory was the ceremonial opening of the canal on 17 November 1869, with French Empress Eugénie in attendance. (The Ismalun family took part in the grand festivities.)[14] From that point on it was all downhill for Ismail and those associated with him. Falling deeply into debt, he borrowed enormous sums from foreign banks. Matteo Ismalun was the middleman for several of these loans and, doubtless, bore some of the consequences when Ismail defaulted. In 1875, in a desperate effort to stave off bankruptcy, Ismail sold his shares in the Suez Canal Company to the British government. The next year, Britain and France established a system of dual control over Egypt's finances and, in 1879, compelled the sultan to depose Ismail. Three years later, Egypt became a British protectorate.

2

Maurice and Mathilde Alfassa began their married life during this turbulent period. Not long after their wedding, they moved to Constantinople. Here, in July 1875, their first son, Max, was born. He died two months later. The couple returned to Alexandria, where Maurice became a member of a consortium led by Nissim de Camondo that negotiated with the Grand Vizier about building a railway in the Euphrates Valley.[15] This and other projects kept Maurice busy for a year, but soon the financial and political situation in Egypt made it difficult for anyone to do business. Seeing which way the wind was blowing, he decided to move to Paris, where his brothers Samuel and Léon were living. In February or March 1877, he, Mathilde and their infant son Matteo (born in Alexandria in July 1876) boarded a ship for France.[16] A month or two later, they rented a flat at 41 Boulevard Haussmann in Paris.

If Maurice was longing for political stability he had picked the wrong country. Conditions in France during the 1870s were even more chaotic than in Egypt. In September 1870, Emperor Napoleon III surrendered to the invading Germans and was taken prisoner. Empress Eugénie fled to England. In Paris, Republican deputies proclaimed the end of the Second Empire and the beginning of the Third Republic. The French army continued to fight until January 1871, when the German army occupied Paris. A new French government was elected that accepted the humiliating terms set by the Germans. In March, the people of Paris revolted and established a parallel government known as the Paris Commune. After two months of conflict, culminating in the Bloody Week of 21–28 May, when 20,000 Communards were killed, the government crushed the insurrection. There followed several years of political turmoil as Monarchists, Bonapartists and Republicans jostled for power. In May 1877, the conservative President Patrice de MacMahon replaced the Republican Prime Minister with a Monarchist. When Republican deputies protested, MacMahon dissolved the Assembly. New elections were held in October 1877. The Republicans gained a slim majority.

As a newly arrived immigrant, Maurice Alfassa steered clear of politics and kept his mind on business. The same month as the elections, he and his brother-in-law Alfred Ismalun founded a banking firm called Alfassa, Ismalun and Company with offices at 41 Boulevard Haussmann. Maurice and Alfred were the active partners, and Matteo Ismalun, who remained in Egypt, the primary backer and sleeping partner. The purpose of the firm was to carry out 'all banking, arbitration and commission operations, in accordance with the practices of the Paris financial markets'.[17] Meanwhile, Mathilde, who was five months pregnant, settled into her new life.

3

At 10 a.m. on 21 February 1878, in the Alfassas' flat at 41 Boulevard Haussmann, their third child, a girl, was born.[18] It is the custom among Sephardic Jews to name the first daughter after her father's mother. Maurice's mother, Bianca or Blanche, and his stepmother, Rachel, both died young. Mathilde's mother, Mirra, was very much alive. In honour of these ladies, the baby was named Blanche Rachel Mirra Alfassa. Everybody called her Mirra.

Forty-one Boulevard Haussmann had been built eight years earlier as part of the great renewal of Paris ordered by Napoleon III and carried out by the prefect whose name the boulevard bears, Georges-Eugène Haussmann. The Alfassas' flat occupied an entire floor, with five windows looking out on the street. Two or three rooms were set aside for Maurice, Mathilde, the toddler Matteo and the infant Mirra, with another room for the unmarried Alfred. The rest of the flat was the headquarters of Alfassa, Ismalun and Company. The neighbourhood—the Quartier de la Chaussée-d'Antin—was the site of many landmark buildings: The Opéra Garnier, the Grands Magasins du Printemps (an enormous department store), the Church of the Holy Trinity and the Great Synagogue on Rue de la Victoire. Close by was the Sephardic synagogue on Rue Buffault, which the Alfassas attended on major holidays and for marriages of members of their extended family.[19]

Three months after Mirra's birth, the Exposition Universelle of 1878 opened in Paris. This iteration of the World's Fair was a confidence-building exercise for the Third Republic. After its ignominious defeat of 1871 and the political chaos that followed, France was signalling to the world that it was back on its feet. Among the attractions at the Exposition were the newly cast head of the Statue of Liberty, a tethered balloon able to lift fifty people, an art exhibition, a Hall of Machines (with some of Thomas Edison's latest inventions) and an Avenue of Nations displaying the architecture of almost every country in Europe (not Germany, of course), as well as some from the Americas, Asia and Africa. An 'anthropological exhibition' featured 400 Indigenous people, many of them shipped in from France's African colonies. Called the 'Negro village' by visitors and a 'human zoo' by modern scholars, this outrage on humanity drew thousands of sightseers who gawked at the natives whose homelands had recently been annexed by French armies.

Napoleon III had doubled the size of France's overseas empire, gobbling up New Caledonia, Senegal, Algeria and much of Indochina, while holding on to its vestigial settlements in India. The leaders of the Third Republic continued the land grab, but they did so, they claimed, as bringers of enlightenment. 'The superior races,' declared Jules Ferry in the Chamber of Deputies, 'have the duty to civilize the inferior races.' He immediately was challenged by radical deputy Georges Clemenceau, who ridiculed the idea of a 'superior' country making war against the 'inferior races' in order 'to convert them by force to the benefits of civilization'. And who was to say who was inferior? The Germans had said the French were inferior when they invaded their country. Now the French were saying the same thing about the Indians and the Chinese, who were, Clemenceau said, not in need of being civilized by anyone.[20] Despite such objections, most French people came to believe in the righteousness of France's *mission civilisatrice* or civilizing mission and looked on proudly as the Republic enlarged its holdings in Indochina, Africa and the Pacific.

Wealth drained from the colonies helped power the French economy up to the Franco-German war. There was a collapse during the 1870s, followed by a period of growth. At this time, the most dynamic sector of the economy was the finance industry. The government encouraged French and foreign investors to open up banks and trade on the Paris stock exchange. Financiers from around the world flocked to the city to set up operations. Among them were the Camondos, and, on a much smaller scale, the Alfassas and Ismaluns. The competition was intense and the risks great. The company that Maurice and his brother-in-law Albert set up in November 1877 remained in business only until December 1879. Three months later, Maurice and his half-brother Jacques started a new company, J. and M. Alfassa, with Maurice putting up 90 per cent of the capital. At first, the brothers used 41 Boulevard Haussmann as their headquarters, but sometime before May 1880, they moved across the street to number 60. Maurice's family shifted at the same time. The building was almost identical to number 41. The Alfassas' flat was on the mezzanine floor. Here, Maurice, Mathilde, Matteo and Mirra lived until 1887.

J. and M. Alfassa remained afloat for only twenty months. In October 1881, Maurice and Jacques liquidated the company's assets. Two months later, Jacques and two others joined hands with the eldest Alfassa brother, Samuel, to found a new bank called S. Alfassa and Company. They entered the field at a dangerous moment. In January 1882, the Union Générale bank collapsed, triggering a stock market crash. Hundreds of investors were wiped out. Maurice, now on his own, seems to have kept his head above water. If not exactly thriving, he was able to maintain the lifestyle that he and his wife had grown accustomed to.

4

We know very little about the first years of Mirra's life. When she was around five, her parents engaged an English governess for Matteo and her. This lady spoke and read to them in English and French. Mirra was not inclined to learn how to read until the day Matteo brought home a picture book with captions under the pictures. She pointed at one of the captions and asked, 'What does that say?' He told her to read it herself. She said she didn't know how. 'Then learn!' he replied. 'All right,' she said, 'Show me the letters.' Matteo brought her an ABC book, and then, as she recalled seventy years later, she learnt all the letters in two days 'and on the third day I started reading'.[21]

In photographs taken when she was around seven, Mirra comes across as a serious little girl. Her mother used to say she was always very quiet. She spent much of her time at home, with occasional visits to relatives. Sometimes the family went by carriage to the opulent apartment of Samuel Alfassa and his wife, son and daughter, or else to the palatial house on Rue de Monceau where Léon and Clarisse Alfassa lived with their seven children. There, in carpeted rooms filled with eighteenth-century antiques, the business and financial élite of Paris gathered for lavish banquets. What Mirra liked about the place was the collection of ferns at the entrance. She used to spend hours exploring them.[22]

5

While Maurice Alfassa was struggling to get off the ground, Léon was flying high. His father-in-law had given him extensive powers at the Camondo Bank. Diversifying his personal holdings, he became a major shareholder in the *Gaulois* newspaper and the Musée Grévin, Paris's answer to Madame Tussauds. In 1883, he acquired the historic Château de Sucy-en-Brie, where the seventeenth-century aristocrat and writer Madame de Sévigné had passed part of her childhood—the equivalent, let us say, of a Los Angeles investment banker buying a house in Beverly Hills formerly owned by Greta Garbo. Years later, Mirra remarked, with some understatement, that the château was 'a beautiful place'.[23]

Léon was known around Paris as a shrewd speculator who wasn't afraid to take risks. But in April 1885, his luck ran out. He had invested heavily in Egyptian and Turkish bonds using his father-in-law's fortune to leverage his bets. When the market took an unexpected turn, he was left holding the bag. On 4 April, he wrote in desperation to his younger brother Jacques: 'From now on life is impossible for me. My poor children, those innocent, unhappy creatures will soon be orphans. Jacques my old friend be good to them. Intervene on their behalf so that they do not suffer on account of me.'[24] We don't know exactly what Jacques did next but there is reason to believe he transferred money from S. Alfassa and Company to Léon. It is certain at any rate that on 18 April Samuel withdrew Jacques's cheque-writing power. A few weeks later, he dissolved the company.

By this time, news of Léon's downfall had spread across Paris. On 16 April, under the headline 'A Sinister Financier', the *Figaro* reported that the previous day the stock exchange regulators had liquidated Léon's positions, causing him a loss of 6 million francs in Paris and another huge amount in London. There were rumours that he had killed himself, followed by rumours that he had fled to London or Cannes.[25] (In fact, he was holing up at home.) For the next few weeks, l'Affaire Alfassa was a trending topic in Paris, Berlin, Vienna, London and New York. The Camondo Bank revoked Léon's powers, and began the long process of paying back his creditors and salvaging its reputation. It never fully recovered from the blow. Léon himself seems to have regained his footing fairly quickly. The one who suffered most was his wife, Clarisse, who had a nervous breakdown and later lapsed into insanity. It is not clear how much Samuel and Maurice were damaged by their half-brother's recklessness, but given the entanglement of their finances with the Camondos' it is likely they did not emerge from the debacle unscathed. Worse was to come for Maurice. In 1886, the bank branch he was running went bankrupt and he lost most of his money.[26] He was saved by Mathilde, who sold some of her dowry to repay his creditors. She also wrote for help to her mother, Mirra, who came to Paris and used her fortune to support the family.

In 1887, the Alfassas moved into a new apartment at 3 Square du Roule, a three-storey building in a gated enclave off Rue du Faubourg Saint-Honoré. Mirra Ismalun stayed nearby, at 1 Square du Roule.[27] The neighbourhood was upscale but the apartment much smaller than the one at 60 Boulevard Haussmann. Mathilde got used to a reduced style of life but (as a relative later remarked) she always 'remained a "great lady"' and 'was never the bourgeois housewife even when peeling vegetables'.[28] Little Mirra had to change her habits too. Sometimes, when visiting relatives, she and her family went on foot instead of taking a carriage. On one such occasion, the other children laughed at her when they saw her boots were muddy. She didn't say anything, but when she got home she reflected: Well, if they want to act like morons, that's their business. I don't have to feel bad about it.[29]

6

Sometime during 1886, Maurice Alfassa went to Egypt to see what he could do to recoup his fortune. He remained there for several months. That August, Mirra Ismalun, along with her brother Giacomo Pinto, took Mathilde, Matteo, Mirra and some others on a month-long trip to Auvergne, a hilly region in central France known for its hot springs and picturesque scenery. The adults kept the children busy with expeditions, picnics and entertainments. They returned to Paris in mid-September. At home, Matteo applied himself to his studies in preparation for his first year of school. On 5 October, he entered Lycée Condorcet.[30] Although not the most prestigious school in Paris, Condorcet was the lycée of choice for the upwardly mobile bourgeoisie. Among Matteo's classmates was André Tardieu, who would serve as Prime Minister on three occasions between 1929 and 1934. Four years ahead of them was the future novelist Marcel Proust. Maurice returned to Paris from Egypt in February 1887. The children were excited that he brought two caged canaries with him. His wife and mother-in-law were less delighted that he brought little money and few prospects of employment. He resumed his work as a private banker but does not seem to have had much luck in the ruthless world of Parisian finance. It was only with the help of relatives, in particular his wife's mother, that he was able to sustain his family's standard of living.

At school, Matteo applied himself to his Latin, French, German, mathematics and history studies. Thursdays (a free day) were partly for play and partly for tutoring and drawing lessons. Mirra also took lessons from the drawing teacher, Mademoiselle Bricka, but she received no tutoring apart from an occasional writing exercise dictated by her governess, Mademoiselle Suzanne. Mathilde read to the children from books like *Perdus au Milieu de Paris* and *David Copperfield.* At night, before they went to bed, she read them some traditional Jewish prayers.[31]

Summer vacations were from the beginning of August to the end of September. During these months, the Alfassas, along with assorted Ismaluns and Pintos, went to visit watering places and scenic locales. The trip of 1887 was especially memorable: First Germany (Baden-Baden and the Black Forest), then central Switzerland (Interlaken and Lake Thon, Lucerne and its environs), then Évian-les-Bains and other towns on Lake Geneva. In all these places, the children walked, hiked, rowed and played, ate and slept in fancy hotels, and altogether had a great time. At Évian, Mirra was introduced to tennis, which became her favourite sport.[32] Years later, she explained that when she was getting started she preferred to play with older children rather than those her own age. She generally lost, she recalled, but learnt a lot.[33] The next year, the Alfassas, grandmother Mirra and various members of the extended family went again to Auvergne. On 14 August, Mathilde, Mirra, Matteo and Mademoiselle Suzanne walked to the top of Puy de Dôme, an inactive volcano. When not occupied with hiking and games, the children took part in educative activities: Drawing, reading books in French and English, and, for the boys, fencing and botanizing. Matteo was so diligent in his digging that Mirra remarked that he should join the mining service when he got out of college. This made him so angry he cried. For the most part, the two siblings got along well and had a great deal of affection for one another. He sometimes referred to her as *ma chère Mirette*. She looked up to him as an adored older brother but wasn't afraid to pull his leg.[34]

In 1889, on the advice of their doctor, the Alfassas and grandmother Mirra passed their vacation by the sea. Using the Grand Hôtel of Houlgate as their base, they made trips up and down the Normandy coast—to Villers, Cabourg, Dives and Trouville. Mirra and Matteo spent a lot of time on the beach, playing in the sand, walking along the shore, and competing in croquet and tennis matches. When not otherwise occupied, they sketched, painted and read. In the evenings, there was dancing, which Mirra adored. On 25 August, the adults organized a running competition. Mirra took part in the second race for girls aged nine to eleven and came in first, winning a handheld fan as a prize.[35]

7

The Alfassa–Ismalun–Pinto clan was very close-knit. Mirra's brother and cousins were her favourite playmates. Her elders—parents, aunts, uncles, grandparents, great-aunts, great-uncles—wove a cocoon of love and security around her. Looking back years later, she said her mother was 'like an iron bar'.[36] This is somewhat at odds with the impression one gets from Matteo's diary. At age ten, he wrote of her: 'My mother is so sweet and kind, she's just an angel.' As an adult, he sketched her character in a few laudatory paragraphs: Generous by nature, she was gifted with an enormous vitality. Broad-minded, she was free of dogmatic beliefs but driven by deeply rooted moral habits. 'Extremely strong and tenacious' and 'attached to orderly habits', she was 'hard on herself, severe on those she loved', yet able to be 'lenient as a result of her goodness and elevation of thought'. With firmness tempered with love, Mathilde tried to mould her children into models of perfection. She loved them both deeply but there was no doubt which one she preferred: Matteo, she used to tell people, was her *chef-d'œuvre*.[37]

Maurice was more easy-going than Mathilde but not without his contradictions. On the positive side, he was kind, loving and entertaining. 'Could he tell stories!' Mirra recalled many years later. 'I think he read every novel available, all the stories he could find—extraordinary adventure stories, because he loved adventures. When we were kids he used to let us come into his room very early in the morning and, while sitting up in bed, tell us stories from the books he had read—but he told them as if they were his own, as if he'd had extraordinary adventures with outlaws, with wild animals. . . . We enjoyed it tremendously!' By this time, Maurice was on rather bad terms with Mathilde. 'He had a room to himself in our apartment (because my mother could never much tolerate him),' Mirra explained later, 'he had his separate room, and in it he kept a big cage—full of canaries! During the day he would close the windows and let all the canaries loose.' Taking advantage of his father's good nature, Matteo sometimes pushed him too far. Once Mirra stumbled upon Maurice giving her brother a hiding. 'I came in,' she related seven decades later, 'drew myself up to my full height and said, "Papa, if you ever do that again, I'm leaving home."' Maurice got the message. 'He stopped and never did it again.'[38]

Maurice loved to take the children to the circus and other popular shows. In 1889, they had a lot to choose from. That year's Exposition Universelle marked the centennial of the French Revolution and the government pulled out all the stops. Towering above Paris was the new Eiffel Tower, the tallest structure ever built, a symbol of humanity's growing power over nature. As in 1878 there was a Hall of Machines, this time featuring Edison's phonograph and Alexander Graham Bell's telephone. The 'Negro village' that had been such a hit eleven years earlier was repeated. There was also a recreation of a Cairo street, which must have had special appeal for Mirra Ismalun's grandchildren. Most exciting for everyone, children and adults alike, was Buffalo Bill's Wild West show. Matteo and Mirra were thrilled to see the Red Indians, the rodeo riders, the mounted sharpshooters (Annie Oakley included), and Buffalo Bill himself. After the show, Mirra and some of the other children had a talk with a real Indian brave. He told them how to gauge the distance of approaching footsteps by putting one's ear to the ground. Mirra and the others gave it a try.[39]

8

We learn from Matteo's diary that the Alfassas observed the major Jewish holidays with prayers at home and visits to the temple. It is unclear how much religious instruction Mathilde gave to the children. Mirra read bits of the Jewish Bible, which she found tedious except for the stories. She never forgot the parables of Adam and Eve and Jacob and Esau but was rather vague about Moses: As an adult, she once spoke of the prophet's 'twelve' commandments.[40] Matteo studied Hebrew for around a year and learnt a good deal about Judaism from his tutor. In July 1889, he turned thirteen and celebrated his bar mitzvah. The Rue Buffault Synagogue was crowded with members of the extended family. Everyone was delighted when Matteo, clad in traditional attire, recited his Torah passage without a hitch. Mirra, sitting in the ladies' gallery, was very proud, but her mind was on the theatrical show she would put on later that day. Produced, directed and performed by her (with help from family members), it consisted of English and French songs (sung by her), several dance numbers (executed by her and her cousins) and some skits (acted by her and others).[41] At this juncture, at least, Matteo seems to have embraced his Jewish identity. There is nothing to suggest that Mirra ever did. Nowhere in her accessible writings or talks (her childhood letters are not available) did she show any interest in Judaism or even speak of herself as a Jew.[42] Still, she certainly absorbed, consciously and subconsciously, a good deal of Jewish cultural influence.

The Alfassas and members of their extended family referred to themselves as 'Israelites' rather than 'Jews'. In nineteenth-century France, the term *Israélite* was used for Jews who were well assimilated into French life. *Juif*, a term with negative connotations, was used mostly for recent arrivals from Eastern Europe, who kept to themselves and did not speak French.[43] Mirra Ismalun and her daughter Mathilde were well-assimilated Frenchwomen and also observant Jews,[44] Nissim Alfassa less well assimilated and more pious, his son Maurice well assimilated and indifferent to religion. As in many immigrant families, the Alfassas' sense of national identity changed with each generation. During her youth, Mirra Ismalun considered herself Egyptian—she had, after all, been born and raised in Cairo, and spoke only Arabic till she was twenty-one—but later, she identified as French and, just before her death, became a citizen. Her daughter Mathilde was born in Egypt but knew Paris a great deal better than Alexandria and, as an adult, always thought of herself as French. Mathilde's daughter, Mirra, was born in France, spoke French as her mother tongue and considered herself as French as any other young Parisian. The problem for the Alfassas and other French Jews was that many people in the country refused to accept anyone with a Jewish background as authentically French.

In September 1889, in the district where Matteo was going to school, posters appeared announcing that a certain Adolphe Willette was running for the legislative seat of the third ward as the 'anti-Semitic candidate'. One poster showed a moustachioed Gaul, who looks like a model for Asterix, holding up a severed pig's head. Beside him is the slogan: 'It is not a matter of religion. Jews belong to a different race that is hostile to ours. Judaism is the enemy!'[45] Willette was inspired by the writings of Édouard Drumont, a journalist and conspiracy theorist whose *La France Juive* (Jewish France) sold 1,00,000 copies in the nine months after its release in 1886 and remained a bestseller for years thereafter. Drumont's favourite targets were the rich Jews of Paris, among them the Camondos and Léon Alfassa. Seeing Count Moïse de Camondo in his four-horse carriage at the Paris racetrack, Drumont described him as a 'fat Jew who looks like the leader of a band of Abyssinian eunuchs' and a 'Levantine Shylock'. It was men like this who controlled the world's finance and business. They had brought about the crash of the Union Générale bank.

None of them could be trusted because they belonged to the Semitic race, which was fundamentally different than the Aryan race.[46] This was the sort of rhetoric that prepared the way for the anti-Dreyfus agitation, which Drumont helped launch a few years later.

Despite the persistence of antisemitism and xenophobia in France, the doors of the country remained open to people from diverse backgrounds. For some time, Maurice had been doing what was necessary to obtain French citizenship. Probably the spur for getting this done was the need to normalize Matteo's situation. Maurice and Mathilde wanted him to attend one of Paris's Grands Écoles, its prestigious state-run institutes of higher learning, and eventually enter government service. The naturalization process was onerous. Maurice got a copy of his retrospective Italian birth certificate, made a declaration explaining why Mathilde had no birth certificate, and filed these and other documents at the local police headquarters. The last hurdle was cleared in July 1889, but it was not till the next year that the Ministry of Justice forwarded the file with Maurice's case and those of sixty-five others to the President of the Republic, who signed it on 28 August.[47] Maurice, Mathilde, Matteo and Mirra were now French citizens.

9

Sometime around 1890, Maurice and Mathilde decided it was time to give Mirra some formal education.[48] There was no question of sending her to a lycée for girls. The best families didn't do that sort of thing. Instead they enrolled her in a *cours pour jeunes filles*: A private school for young ladies. In all likelihood, the one they chose was the *cours* of Madame Evelart-Deleury at 54 Rue du Faubourg Saint-Honoré.[49] The advertisements the proprietor placed in the Paris Directory touted the school's 'complete course of education for children and young girls'. The youngest studied 'general education', 'living languages' and the 'decorative arts'. Older girls learnt various subjects taught by university professors, had lessons in drawing and singing, and sessions of gymnastics and dance. Those with a flair for music studied under the 'eminent teacher' Auguste Mercadier, who gave classes in music theory, harmony, transposition and accompaniment.[50] Whether or not Madame Evelart-Deleury's was the *cours* Mirra attended, the instruction she received was along these lines. Together with French, modern languages, history, geography, music and art, she learnt acting, elocution and the social graces.

Mirra studied in her *cours* until at least 1893. A French composition she wrote that year is the first direct evidence we have of the workings of her mind. Her teacher—a tiresome old man, she later recalled—set her a moral theme to write on. Her response was a story she called 'The Path of Later On'. It begins with a young traveller 'walking briskly along, happily breathing the pure morning air'. Coming to a crossroads he takes the path that seems easiest. After a while, he hears a voice saying, 'Turn back, turn back, you are not on the right road,' but he goes ahead, enjoying the pleasures of the moment. More voices are heard: 'Poor fool, can't you see you are heading to your ruin?' The traveller ignores them and walks on. The path becomes a dusty road that seems to go on forever. The landscape becomes menacing. Voices cry: 'Flee this place; go back to the crossroads.' 'Tomorrow,' the traveller replies. Things go from bad to worse. A castle looms ahead. The traveller brushes against it and it crumbles to dust. The ghosts of Desolation, Despair and Disgust with Life rear up and drive the traveller towards a bottomless abyss. 'After a supreme struggle he falls—from his bed.' A student who had put off doing his homework had fallen asleep and had a nightmare. Now he can see that the path was the Path of Later On, the road, the Road of Tomorrow, and the building the Castle of Nothing at All. He has learnt his lesson: Never put off until tomorrow what can be done today. Mirra's teacher was impressed by her story and gave her full marks.[51] When she showed it to her mother, Mathilde doubtless was glad to see that her daughter had internalized some of her good advice.

After leaving the *cours,* Mirra spent much of her time at home. There was little there to keep her busy. She continued to take art and music lessons but lacked mental stimulation. Her father had a library with more than 800 volumes. She decided to read them all. It took her more than a year, she later said, and when she got to the end she was still unsatisfied.[52] It seems never to have occurred to her mother that she deserved more academic training. All Mathilde's attention was on her son's education and career. Between 1893 and 1896, Matteo slogged away in Condorcet's upper classes, preparing himself for the entrance examination of the École Polytechnique, the state-run engineering school that was one of the surest routes to a career in the higher reaches of government service. He failed on his first attempt in 1895. The next year he redoubled his efforts, working day and night on his mathematics. His family hired a tutor to help him. Sometimes Mirra sat in on their classes. Once when Matteo was puzzling over a problem, Mirra came up with the answer. The tutor seems to have told Mathilde that it was Mirra rather than Matteo who should be taking the examination—a good joke since the school was not open to girls.[53] This anecdote shows she was quick on the uptake but underlines the fact that the only way she could study high-school subjects was to look over her brother's shoulder. Matteo sat for the entrance exam again in June 1896. Four months later, he and his family were delighted to learn that he had passed.

10

Mirra continued to take art classes with Mademoiselle Bricka. Now an advanced student, she gave lessons to the younger girls. Then, in the mid-1890s, her parents enrolled her in the Académie Julian, a well-known Paris art school.[54] The proprietor, Rodolphe Julian, had several studios in Paris, four of them reserved for women. The one Mirra went to was located at 5 Rue de Berri, just off the Avenue des Champs-Élysées. Conveniently for her, it was just a ten-minute walk from Square du Roule. The maîtres, or masters, associated with the Rue de Berri studio were William-Adolphe Bouguereau and Gabriel Ferrier, both of them big names in the Academic School that dominated the Paris art world. Most critics as well as the gallery-going public regarded Academic 'history painting' as the supreme form of art. The biggest hits at the yearly art salons were enormous canvasses by Bouguereau and his peers depicting figures from classical history or Greco-Roman myth striking heroic or seductive poses. Detractors of the style called it 'fireman art' because the helmets on the heads of many of the heroic figures resembled those worn by Paris firemen. Impressionism, the school regarded today as the pinnacle of late-nineteenth-century French art, was still a marginal trend. Even 'the most audacious of the young artists' who frequented Julian's in the late 1880s, wrote one of them, Maurice Denis, had 'virtually no knowledge of the great movement of art that under the name of Impressionism had just revolutionized the art of painting'.[55] The masters of that movement—Édouard Manet, Edgar Degas, Claude Monet, Pierre-Auguste Renoir—rebelled against the Academic style and were often turned away by the official salons. Mocked by professional critics, they were patronized by a handful of connoisseurs, among them Léon Alfassa's brother-in-law Isaac de Camondo, who built an extensive collection of paintings by Manet, Degas, Monet, Renoir and Alfred Sisley.

Mirra may have seen some Impressionist works in Isaac de Camondo's residence and almost certainly admired a Monet owned by Isaac's cousin Hortense Ellissen, with whose children she used to play. She later said that Impressionist paintings gave her 'great aesthetic joy'.[56] The training she received at Julian's, however, was totally uninfluenced by Impressionism or any other modern trend. The techniques of perspective, proportion and chiaroscuro that she and her classmates learnt had been passed down from artist to artist since the time of the Renaissance. Once a week, Bouguereau or Ferrier stopped by to criticize the students' efforts. Most of the time, they worked under the eye of a senior student, known as the *massière*, who provided the materials and set the weekly subject for the students to copy—a plaster cast or still-life arrangement or a model's face or figure.[57] Mirra was among the youngest in her class and, as she later recalled, was more serious than the other students, who spent a lot of their time gossiping, quarrelling and fooling around. They called her the Sphinx and left her alone, but when they needed someone to settle their quarrels, it was to her they turned. Mirra was never afraid to speak up, even if it meant tangling with adults. Once, the *massière* mentioned that Julian's wife had threatened to fire her. Mirra went to the lady and asked why. She said it was none of Mirra's business. Mirra grabbed her hand and gave it a hard squeeze. This was enough, she reported years later, to make Madame Julian change her mind.[58]

The studio offered weekly painting competitions. Sometimes Mirra paid the entrance fee and submitted a work. Once, she won first prize for a still-life study: An arrangement of fruit and a ceramic jar on a table. The painting, which survives, shows real talent in rendering volume and colour. We also have some portrait studies from 1895 and 1897. These are less successful: The brushwork is good, but the modelling of the faces is unconvincing. Still, her juvenile paintings make it clear that she was on her way to becoming an accomplished artist in the traditional mould.

In 1896 and 1897, Mirra made three appearances in the Paris cultural sphere. From July to October 1896, two of her works—a painting and a drawing—were displayed in the Musée de Versailles as part of an art exhibition organized by the Society of the Friends of the Arts of the Seine-and-Oise Department. The next year, the society, of which she was now a member, showed two of her paintings, for which she was awarded a third-prize medal. In June 1897, she participated in a concert at the Petite Salle Pleyel that featured works by the young Romanian prodigy George Enescu, with the composer in attendance. The programme consisted of a sonata for violin and piano, a piano solo, two pieces for cello, and a quintet for piano and strings. During the intermission, Mademoiselle Mirra Alfassa recited poems by Georges de Porto-Riche and Victor Hugo. A critic writing for the *Gazette de France* called her performance 'charming'.[59]

11

We have passed over some important events we must take up now. In February 1896, Mirra turned eighteen. It was time for her family to find her a husband. Grandmother Mirra took the matter in hand. She was acquainted with a successful portrait painter named Henri Georges Morisset, whose clientele included minor foreign royalty. Henri Georges had a son named François Henri, who had studied at the École des Beaux-Arts and was beginning to make a name for himself in the Paris art world. It seemed to Mirra Ismalun that young Henri (as he was known) would make the perfect match for young Mirra. The fact that the families were of different religions (the Morissets were Catholic) complicated matters a little, but it was not an insurmountable obstacle. Indeed, given the rise of antisemitism in France, it may have struck Mirra Ismalun as a good idea to find a non-Jewish husband for her granddaughter. However that may be, she arranged a meeting between Mirra and Henri in the summer of 1896. Henri was smitten. After a well-chaperoned courtship, the two announced their engagement in July or August 1897. Together with Matteo, they took a trip to Auvergne, where a wealthy relative, John Hakim de Medici, threw a party in their honour. There were strolling musicians playing mandolins and singing love songs, and course after course of delicious food.[60] On 4 August, Henri wrote to his *maître*, the Symbolist painter Gustave Moreau, that from the moment 'chance or perhaps I should say Providence' had placed Mirra on his path, it was clear to him that he and she 'were destined for one another'.[61] In writing this, Henri seems to have been touched by the muse of poetry. The families went about the business of marriage in a prosaic manner. Lawyers for the Alfassas and the Morissets drew up a *contrat de mariage* (prenuptial agreement), itemizing the silverware, crockery, furniture, artworks and so forth that the couple would be bringing to their new household.

On 13 October 1897, Mirra and Henri were married.[62] In accordance with French law, they first signed the register at the town hall of the 8th arrondissement. Later the same day, they had a small religious ceremony in the nearby Church of the Holy Trinity. Owing to technicalities arising from the couple's 'disparity of worship', the priest pronounced the nuptial blessing in the church's sacristy rather than the nave. The next day there was a reception, with relatives and friends in attendance. Afterwards the couple went to Beaugency, a small town on the Loire, where Henri's father, Henri Georges, lived with his daughters Blanche and Henriette. Suffering from amnesia as the result of a stroke, Henri Georges had been unable to attend the wedding.[63] Henri and Mirra stayed in Beaugency for a few days, then returned to Paris.

We have no idea what was going through Mirra's mind while all this was happening. Up to this point she never had much to do with men or boys outside her extended family. As a result, she was rather naïve. Years later, she recalled that when she was twelve or thirteen she strolled into a room in her grandmother's place and found two of her cousins canoodling: The girl was sitting on the boy's lap and they were 'kissing each other very vigorously'. Mirra couldn't figure out what was going on.[64] As she grew up, she sometimes thought about love and when she was around eighteen she wrote a little book (now lost) on the subject. Seventy years later, she could recall its outlines: 'It was the story of a woman who . . . felt a need to manifest love, a marvellously beautiful love', but found only heartbreak. She was able to overcome her sorrow by realizing that 'personal things had to be overcome by the will to realize something more essential and universal'. This was, she later reflected, her 'first attempt to emerge from the exclusively personal viewpoint' into a broader, universal viewpoint that would enable her to overcome her personal limitations.[65]

12

Mirra was now an adult. During her childhood and adolescence, she had led a privileged and happy life. Supported by a large and loving extended family, she never felt any material or affective need. Her parents, despite their financial ups and downs, were sufficiently wealthy that they could provide her with everything they thought a young lady might require. This included a good general education, with special emphasis on languages, art and music, and long summer vacations in beautiful places. Her brother considered himself her protector and was always ready to help. Her grandmother found her a suitable husband and eased her transition into married life. There were some gaps in this idyll that her family overlooked. Mirra certainly would have liked to receive a more rigorous education. She probably was not anxious to get married at nineteen. More generally, no one in the family took into account what was going on inside her. This may have been Mirra's fault, because she never spoke to anyone about her inner life.

Most of what we know about Mirra's inner life from her childhood until she was twenty-eight comes from remarks she made while talking with students and disciples when she was between forty-two and ninety-four and had assumed another identity, as the Mother. For a biographer, these remarks are somewhat problematic. To begin with, they deal with things that happened as long as eighty-five years before she spoke. Her memory even in advanced age was good, but she herself admitted she could not remember dates, only circumstances. She also had trouble pinpointing her age when specific experiences took place.[66] This makes it difficult to establish a timeline of her inner life. Secondly, inner experiences are impossible to verify using biographical documents. The experiencer's oral or written accounts are documents, of course, but they are not, for the most part, subject to the sort of scrutiny serious biographers give all pieces of evidence that come their way. This leaves a lot of room for misinterpretation. Thirdly, when the Mother spoke about her inner life she was addressing listeners who were much younger than her, and eager for enlightenment and entertainment. She told them stories about her early experiences with the idea of inspiring them to make their own spiritual efforts. Retrospective stories of a person's early life almost always take the form of teleological narratives: Events follow one another in apparently natural order, leading to a preordained conclusion. I said in the Prologue I would try to avoid 'omega' accounts of this sort. But without such accounts we would know nothing about the Mother's inner life. I therefore will cite or paraphrase a number of written and oral accounts of her inner experiences. First, however, I will examine a simple case to show how difficult it is to handle such material.

When she was around eleven, Mirra went walking in the Fontainebleau Forest with some of her friends. While there, something strange happened that she spoke about later on at least three occasions. To one devoted follower, she said that while she was walking her 'foot slipped and she began to fall down' but 'felt somebody supporting her in a lap, as it were, and slowly bringing her down'. When she reached the rocky path below 'she was standing safely on her two feet'. In other accounts she gave more details: She and some friends were playing tag on a hillside. She ran ahead not knowing there was an overhang in front with a drop of 10 feet or more. She flew over the edge. As she fell, it seemed to her that she was moving very slowly, as if someone or something was holding her up and then placing her softly on the ground. The other children ran down. She got up and said, 'It's nothing.'[67]

We can break down this anecdote into four components: (1) Mirra was playing in the Fontainebleau Forest with friends, (2) she fell from a height, (3) she had an unusual experience while falling, (4) she was uninjured. All this can be accepted as fact. What remains unclear is the nature of the experience she had while she fell. In all her accounts she said she felt she was being supported; in two of them, that she was moving very slowly as she fell. Many years later an occultist told her that there are winged beings—guardian angels—who help people in need. Thinking back on her Fontainebleau experience, she concluded it was a being of this sort who supported her as she fell. She did not mention this supernatural intervention when she told the story to two people close to her, but they got the hint. The first one later wrote that the incident was an example of how Mirra 'during her childhood . . . was conscious of a more than human force behind her and often entering her body and working there in a supernormal way'. The second one introduced this and similar anecdotes by saying that even 'when she was quite small' Mirra 'already had inner experiences'.[68]

Mirra certainly had many inner experiences during her childhood and afterwards. Sometimes she spoke about them to others. It is legitimate for biographers to quote from or paraphrase such accounts and I will do so often in the chapters that follow. It is not legitimate for biographers to speak with feigned authority about their subjects' inner states or to make expansive generalizations about them. I will refrain from doing this. For the most part, I will let the Mother speak for herself. If it seems helpful, I will compare her accounts with those of other people who have had similar experiences. Returning to the Fontainebleau incident, it is worth noting that time-bending experiences while falling or during accidents are not uncommon and they often leave a deep impression on those who have them.[69] People speak about such experiences in different ways. Few, if any, mention winged guardian angels. The Mother herself did not invoke such beings for almost twenty years. When she had the experience, it all seemed natural to her. When she landed on her feet, she just thought: 'No, accidents can't happen to me.'[70]

More than once, while speaking of her early experiences, the Mother said she did not think of them in spiritual or supernatural terms when they happened. 'When I was a child,' she said in 1970, 'I knew nothing about spiritual things. My family lived in a completely materialistic atmosphere.' In the light of what we know about her religious upbringing, we have to re-examine this statement. Among the older members of her family, only her father was 'materialistic'. Her grandparents, many of her aunts and uncles, and her mother were conventionally religious. The Mother was aware of this but did not think this sort of religiosity had anything to do with spirituality. Later, she realized that her lack of religious background actually helped her out: 'I was given all experiences without my having *any* knowledge of what it was all about,' she said on one occasion, 'my mind was completely—how to explain?—blank.'[71] Viewing her experiences without preconceptions, she did not try to force them into a conventionally religious mould. Later, when she became curious about spiritual and occult things, and studied the systems of spiritual and occult thinkers, she grew convinced of the spiritual and occult bases of her experiences. From this point on, when she spoke of her inner life, she framed it in spiritual or occult terms, using phrases like 'descent of force' and 'recollections of past births' that never entered her mind when her early experiences took place.

Having laid out these caveats, I will look at a few of Mirra's childhood experiences. When she was around five, she sometimes felt a light and a force above her head. 'It was a very pleasant sensation,' she later explained, 'something very strong, very luminous.' Not knowing what it was—she made it clear when speaking about it later that she 'didn't understand anything, didn't know anything'—she thought, not abstractly but 'as a child can think', that the force that was above her 'was sure to do great things'.[72] At around the same age, she became aware of the influences inside and outside her that made her think and act in one way or another and tried to gain control over them: 'It is a rather unpleasant sensation to feel yourself pulled by the strings and made to do things whether you like it or not,' she told a group of children in 1953. 'At the age of five it began to seem quite intolerable to me and I looked for a way to make it different.'[73]

On two or three occasions, things that Mirra saw triggered feelings of reliving past events. When she was eight or ten, she and Matteo were taken to the Louvre. When they reached the Egyptian galleries, Mirra stood transfixed before a showcase displaying articles used by Queen Hatshepsut. The toilet case and comb 'appeared to be strangely familiar'.[74] On a darker note, when she was fifteen, she had a frightening experience in the Doge's Palace in Venice. The tour included a visit to cells where prisoners were kept before they were put to death. On the walls were graffiti scratched by the prisoners. Looking at one graffito, Mirra had the feeling that she had written it herself. Suddenly she 'had the sensation of people entering, catching hold of me . . . then the sensation of being lifted and thrown out through the window. Well, naturally, fifteen years old, you understand! I said to my mother, "Let's get out of here!"'[75] These incidents are invariably presented by her biographers as recollections of past lives. Perhaps they were, but Mirra did not see them as such at the time: The possibility of reincarnation had never occurred to her.

By the time she reached her teens, Mirra was acutely sensitive to music. Once, while attending a wedding in Paris's Great Synagogue, she listened as the organist played a piece by the French composer Camille Saint-Saëns. She was gazing at one of the windows, feeling uplifted by the music, when suddenly 'through the window came a flash like a bolt of lightning'. It entered her and she had the feeling 'of becoming vast and all-powerful'. This feeling lasted for days. On another occasion, she attended a concert where the celebrated Belgian violinist Eugène Ysaÿe was giving a performance of Beethoven's violin concerto. The orchestra played the opening passage, Ysaÿe raised his bow and with the first notes 'it was as if my head suddenly opened and I was thrown into a splendour . . . For more than an hour I was in a beatific state.' When she had these experiences, she felt them as powerful responses to beautiful music. When she spoke about them later, she explained them in esoteric terms. The flash she felt while listening to Saint-Saëns was 'an entity from the past that entered into me as a result of the aspiration that came from the music'. Beethoven's musical genius, which had somehow remained in form, 'reincarnated' itself in Ysaÿe.[76]

Young Mirra had a vivid and lucid dream life. She developed the ability to continue her dreams from one night to the next. 'It's a most pleasant way of passing the nights,' she told some young listeners in 1956.

'You begin a story, then, when it's time to wake up, you put a full stop after the last sentence and come back into your body. And then the next night you start again, find the page where you left off and resume the story.' When she was around thirteen, she had a particularly remarkable series of dreams she wrote about in her diary twenty-five years later: 'For nearly a year, as soon as I went to bed each evening, it seemed to me that I left my body and rose straight above the house, then above the city, very high.' She was wearing a long golden robe and, as she rose, the robe spread out 'to form a kind of immense roof over the city'. The people in the city gathered under the robe and 'as soon as they touched it, they were comforted or healed'.[77]

In 1920, Mirra summarized her early spiritual development in an article she wrote for an Indian magazine. Asked by the editor how she had become conscious of a mission she was meant to fulfil on earth, she replied it was as if she was 'born with it, and following the growth of the mind and brain, the precision and completeness of this consciousness grew also'. Between the ages of eleven and thirteen, 'a series of psychic and spiritual experiences revealed to me not only the existence of God but man's possibility of uniting with Him, of realising Him integrally in consciousness and action, of manifesting Him upon earth in a life divine'.[78] How she conceived of 'God' at the time is unclear. Looking back on this period of her life years later, she explained that the only God she knew about was the remote, all-powerful God of Judaism, and she rejected Him completely.[79]

2

An Artist's Life

1

NOT LONG AFTER THEIR MARRIAGE, HENRI AND MIRRA MOVED INTO a flat at 15 Rue Lemercier that Mathilde had found and fitted out for them.[1] Located at the edge of the Batignolles district, a favourite haunt of artists and writers, Rue Lemercier combined bourgeois respectability with a touch of the offbeat. Number 15 had a private garden where Henri built a studio. Its roof came up to the level of the couple's first-floor flat, to which it was connected by a footbridge. The flat itself had several rooms, furnished with an eye for elegance and comfort. Henri's two unmarried sisters stayed with him when they were in Paris, but they spent most of their time in Beaugency, where they looked after their incapacitated father. The younger Henri, who turned twenty-eight in April 1898, was now the sole breadwinner of the family.

In August, he had another mouth to feed. On the twenty-third, Mirra gave birth to a son, André. It was a difficult delivery, mismanaged by the attending physician, and she suffered from uterine pains for some time. In the days following the boy's birth, she felt an incredibly close link with him. It was 'as if a piece of her flesh had been removed and put at a distance' and she could feel what he was feeling as if it was happening in her.[2] This intimacy was short-lived. Soon after his birth, André was sent to the Morissets' place in Beaugency where a wet nurse was engaged for him.[3] This practice was extremely common among upper- and middle-class families in nineteenth-century France.[4] Among the reasons for it was a belief that the highest ideal of womanhood excluded the down-to-earth functions of the mother. As the philosopher Louis de Bonald wrote towards the middle of the century: 'Breastfeeding is too animal a function for a lady of quality.'[5] We find an echo of this attitude in a remark made by a character in a play Mirra wrote many years later. A friend of the protagonist reminds her 'how distasteful you used to find everything that displayed human animality' and how she used to say, 'Let us not be mammals.'[6]

In Beaugency André was looked after by Henri's sisters. He and Mirra came down from Paris when they could. During one visit, when André was a few months old, a series of photographs was taken. They show a formally dressed Mirra with the baby in her lap or in a pram. In some of the shots Blanche, Henriette and others stand around the child and her like sentinels.

In Paris, Mirra saw less and less of her brother and parents. Matteo graduated from the École Polytechnique in 1898. While a student, he decided he could best serve his country by joining the colonial service. In October 1898, the President of the Republic signed his appointment as an assistant commissioner in the Colonial Office.[7] He moved into a flat on Boulevard Saint-Michel. His mother moved in with him. When, a year later, he left France on his first overseas assignment, as a second-class commissioner in New Caledonia, Mathilde went along. The two stayed together in a little house by the sea. One does not know what Matteo's colleagues thought about this arrangement but they found him a competent worker. Matteo and Mathilde returned from New Caledonia in September 1901. Mirra and Henri went to Marseille to receive them. Arriving on the same ship was an army officer named Julian Brossé, who had struck up a friendship with Matteo. He was met by his parents and sister, Éva. The two families mingled. Matteo and Éva got to talking. Four years later, they were married. That marked the end of Matteo's day-in-day-out relationship with his mother. Once he got married,

Mirra quipped years later, Mathilde 'really couldn't continue to follow him around any longer'.[8] Maurice Alfassa remained at 3 Square du Roule for a while after Mathilde, Matteo and Mirra departed. By 1899, he was living in a small flat on Rue de la Néva. He now listed his profession as *rentier,* which meant he was living off what was left of his investments. He and Mirra rarely met.

2

For several years after her marriage, Mirra's life revolved around her husband's. Henri began slowly to establish himself in the overcrowded, highly competitive Paris art world. His CV was impeccable. After studying under his father and at the École des Arts Décoratifs, he spent some time at the Académie Julian (six or seven years before Mirra was enrolled there), working under Bouguereau and Tony Robert-Fleury. Passing the examination for the École des Beaux-Arts, he entered the illustrious institution in March 1889. Here, his teachers were Gustave Moreau and Jules-Élie Delaunay. After leaving the École, he continued to work under Moreau, at the time one of the best-known artists in Paris. In 1891, two of Henri's paintings were selected by the hanging committee of the Salon des Artistes Français. He exhibited at this Salon until 1897, but attracted little notice. In 1898, he was elected an associate member of the new, increasingly important Société Nationale des Beaux-Arts. The Salon of the Société Nationale (known informally as the Salon des Beaux-Arts) was held each year in an enormous hall on the Champ de Mars. More than 3,000 works by several hundred artists were displayed. It was hard for newcomers to make their mark. The 1898 jury accepted two of Henri's paintings. He was delighted when the prominent critic Raymond Bouyer devoted a few lines to them.[9]

3

Between 1898 and 1906, Mirra lived an artist's life in the centre of the artistic universe. Paris was the hub of European culture, pre-eminent in art and literature, prominent in music and theatre, the showcase of fashion and the playground of the rich. Emerging from the Long Depression of 1873–96, France was entering a period of prosperity that would last until the start of the First World War. Looking back on this era a half-century later, people labelled it nostalgically La Belle Époque (the Beautiful Era). It was a time of optimism and expansion. Technological advances (electric street lights, the metro, tramways, the automobile) made urban life more convenient and more enjoyable. Department stores like Printemps and the Galeries Lafayette offered the latest clothing, shoes, accessories, cosmetics, perfumes and more. All sorts of entertainments competed for clientele: Theatre, opera, music halls, vaudeville and, from 1895, cinematographic films. After an evening out, people crowded into cafés where they talked, laughed and forgot for a moment the punishing pace of modern life.

The charms of the Belle Époque have been celebrated endlessly by novelists, filmmakers and popular historians. The period's sinister side has received less attention. The wealth of the upper classes was made possible by the exploitation of overseas colonies and impoverished workers at home. The refinement of artistic and literary salons was overshadowed by hyper-nationalism and antisemitism. (The artists Renoir and Degas and the writers Edmond de Goncourt and Alphonse Daudet were all famous for their hatred of Jews.) In 1894, the Jewish military officer Alfred Dreyfus was falsely accused of treason, convicted by a secret tribunal and sentenced to life imprisonment on Devil's Island. The issue split France, with the army, right-wing nationalists and the Church condemning Dreyfus (and through him all Jews) and liberals supporting him. The turmoil reached its acme in 1898. On 13 January, Émile Zola published his famous open letter *J'Accuse*, denouncing the government for its role in the affair. There followed weeks of antisemitic rioting in Paris and other parts of the country. 'In France to-day,' a writer noted in the *Atlantic Monthly*, 'it is perilous to be a Jew.'[10] In February, Zola was put on trial for libel, convicted, but acquitted on appeal. Arraigned by a military court, he crossed the Channel to England, where he remained in exile for over a year. This made a tremendous impression on twenty-year-old Mirra: 'Once he reached England,' she recalled sixty-seven years later, 'he said, "It doesn't matter, Truth is on the march." It caused great uproar.'[11] Zola's trial brought the details of the Dreyfus case before the public for the first time. The officer was recalled to France, reconvicted, pardoned and eventually rehabilitated. In 1899, the Radical Party came to power and controlled French politics for more than a decade. Among its accomplishments was the establishment of *laïcité* or secularism in public institutions. Catholics, Protestants and Jews were now equal before the law, but antisemitism still flourished on every level of society.

4

'I mingled with all the great artists of that period,' the Mother once said, referring to the years before and after the 1900 Exposition Universelle. The artists she knew were looked upon as 'the authoritative figures in the artistic realm' and she was like 'a little sister' to them.[12] A hundred and twenty years later, this statement has to be placed in its historical context. Henri and Mirra knew a great many artists, some of whom had excellent reputations at the time but few of whom are counted today among the 'authoritative figures' of that era.[13] Popular histories of art treat the period between 1890 and 1905 as a trough between the great wave of Impressionism that came before it and the great wave of Modernism that followed. By the time of the Exposition Universelle, the surviving Impressionists had their own circles of clients and rarely exhibited publicly. The early Post-Impressionists—Paul Cézanne, Paul Gauguin, Vincent van Gogh—stayed away from the capital and exhibited, if at all, at the Salon des Indépendants. Henri and Mirra may have been on nodding terms with some of the younger Post-Impressionists, such as Henri Matisse, Édouard Vuillard and Pierre Bonnard, but the artists they were close to are now mostly forgotten. One of their best friends was Abel Faivre, an illustrator and caricaturist who also painted portraits that were exhibited at the Salon des Beaux-Arts. They probably also socialized with artists Henri knew from his days at the École des Beaux-Arts and Moreau's studio, such as Raoul du Gardier and Jules Besson. Another, far more famous artist whom Mirra met at least once was the sculptor Auguste Rodin. 'He was magnificent,' she recalled many years later. 'He had a faun's head—like a Greek faun. He was short, quite stocky' with 'shrewd eyes' and an ironic sense of humour. One day, while the two of them were chatting, he asked Mirra a question: 'How can one prevent two women from being jealous of one other?' It seems that when he went away for a day or two, he covered his clay maquettes with damp cloths so they would not dry up. It was his wife's responsibility to spray the cloths with water each morning. His mistress resented the fact that he had given this job to his wife, and, after her rival had finished spraying the cloths, she did it all over again. 'And so,' Rodin told Mirra, 'the result is that when I come back from my trip, all my sculptures are disintegrating!' Mirra remarked, quite reasonably, that he should tell one or the other that she alone should do the work. The sculptor 'pulled at the little hair that was left on his head and said, "But then there would be a knife fight!"'[14]

In 1898, the priest of the Church of Saint James of Pau, in southwest France, invited Henri to paint four murals in the apse of his church. He and Mirra spent several weeks in Pau working on this commission. The murals represent four episodes in the life of Saint James: His vocation, preaching, martyrdom and the Battle of Clavijo, in which his apparition led the Christian army to victory over the Moors. Mirra, who could not climb the scaffold (she was pregnant with André), worked mainly on the dead and dying Moors at the bottom of the mural. The priest was happy with the overall result. 'When he looked at the paintings,' Mirra later related, 'he tapped Morisset on the shoulder—Morisset was an unbeliever—and said, in his Southern accent, "Say what you like, you know Our Lord; otherwise you could not have painted like that!"'[15] When Mirra and Henri returned to Paris, they both exhibited paintings at the Versailles salon where her works had appeared the two previous years. The organizers awarded her a silver medal. In the catalogue, she is listed as Madame Mirra Alfassa-Morisset.[16] This was the first and last time she would use her married name when she exhibited her works.

Mirra completed few paintings between 1899 and 1902. This may have been due, at least in part, to ill health. Along with uterine discomfort, she had to deal with the pain of a floating kidney, and unspecified liver and stomach complaints. Once, she was confined to her room for several months. She made it an occasion for developing her mental powers: 'I was in a room and at one end there was another little room and at the end of the little room there was a sort of bridge' leading to the roof of the studio. 'I wanted to go and see what was happening in the studio, because I was feeling bored in my room. So I stayed very quiet, closed my eyes and sent out my consciousness, little by little, little by little, little by little . . . . At first you make use of your imagination and then it becomes a fact.'[17]

Henri's works continued to appear in the annual Salon des Beaux-Arts. At the 1900 Exposition Universelle, his entries won him a bronze medal. The next year, he was awarded a travel grant by the Société des Artistes Français, which he used to go to Venice. While there, he did some studies for a predictable *Serenade on the Grand Canal*, one of nine works he exhibited at the salon of 1902. Mirra accompanied him to Venice, exploring the city and getting herself photographed feeding the pigeons in the Piazza San Marco. The couple also passed some time in the home of a friend of Mirra's mother on Lake Garda. Years later, Mirra could still remember the beauty of the countryside, a display of improvised dance, and a remarkable meal of couscous and summer squash. It was probably during this visit to Italy that she wandered into a church and, finding no one around, sat down at the organ and began to play. When she finished, she was surprised to hear the sound of applause behind her. Some townspeople had come in to listen and were enthusiastic in their appreciation.[18]

Some of Henri's paintings of the years between 1900 and 1902 give a glimpse of how he and his wife spent their leisure time. *À la Fête de Neuilly* shows an elegantly dressed Mirra getting down from a carriage at the entrance to the summer festival at Neuilly-sur-Seine, a posh Paris suburb. A gentleman in formal attire offers her his hand. Above is a colourful canopy; to the right, an array of lanterns. *Terrasse de Café (Place Clichy)* shows the evening crowd at the Café Wepler, a short walk from the Morissets' place on Rue Lemercier. In the background, we see the busy street: Labourers with shovels on their shoulders, people-watching pedestrians, a man dressed up like a Spanish dancer. In the foreground, sits a lady with her back to the viewer. It is easy to imagine her as Mirra, a solitary figure observing the bustle around her with a detached air.

In 1901 or 1902, when André was three or four, his parents brought him from Beaugency to Paris. This was always a difficult moment for wet-nursed children: They had to get over their attachment to their nurse and 'milk-siblings', and get to know their parents.[19] So far, André's aunts had been his primary caregivers. Now Mirra took on this role. For the next few years, she lived the life of a stay-at-home mother. At the time, this was a novel way of bringing up children in France. According to the historian Emmanuelle Romanet, 'The model of the *mère au foyer* who took care of her own children did not become the normal way of doing things until the twentieth century.'[20] Henri's paintings of this period record Mirra's motherly interactions with her son: Teaching him to read, giving him a gentle scolding, joining with her sisters-in-law to do a ring-dance around him.

Even after 1902, André spent a good amount of time with his aunts in Beaugency. While there, he looked forward to his parents' visits, not least because they drove down in their Richard Brazier automobile, which could do all of 30 kilometres an hour. They kept a pair of bicycles in the back in case they had a breakdown. These came in handy on their first trip south, when the car's steering mechanism failed 100 kilometres north of Beaugency. The Morissets left the car with the local blacksmith, explored the area on their bicycles, spent the night with a hospitable baker and continued on their way the next morning.[21]

Around 1902, after a break of three or four years, Mirra began to paint regularly again. In April 1903, the Salon des Beaux-Arts accepted two of her works. At the same salon, Henri exhibited six paintings, two of which were reproduced in the catalogue. Two months later, *Fémina* magazine printed a photograph showing Blanche and Henriette, 'expert craftswomen and skilful embroiderers' who were 'sisters of the excellent painter Morisset'. Next to them, 'palette in hand', was 'their sister-in-law Madame Morisset', who was herself 'an artist of considerable talent'.[22] In 1904, Henri and Mirra both exhibited paintings at the Salon des Beaux-Arts and also sent works to the United States for display at the St Louis World's Fair.

Most of Mirra's paintings of this period are quiet interior scenes. She seems to have had a special fondness for the rooms of friends and acquaintances: The studios of painters Abel Faivre and Charles Duvent, the entrance hall of the Manoir de Cantepie in Normandy, the sitting room of the composer Camille Erlanger (husband of her childhood friend 'Becca' Hillel-Manoach, a granddaughter of Rebecca de Camondo). *La Console*, a painting of a console table that Mirra exhibited at the 1905 salon, was mentioned by several critics and reproduced in the catalogue. So was Henri's *Le Modèle*, a study of a female nude, which attracted special praise from the critic Eugène Hoffman, who admired Henri's masterful handling of light effects.[23]

In the beginning of 1905, Raymond Bouyer published a sumptuously illustrated essay on Henri's work in *L'Art Décoratif*, a monthly journal. Morisset was not attracted by fleeting trends, he wrote. 'Before the hour of style and snobbishness, he chose intimacy.' This word had a double meaning for the critic. First, Morisset was a member of the school known as Intimism. Second, he took many of his subjects from his intimate domestic life: André sitting on the floor playing with his toys, Mirra pouring a cup of tea. The artist's family, the critic wrote, was a formative influence on his work: 'Married, a father, supported by a partner who gracefully wields the brush and two sisters [whose embroideries] are precious works of art', Morisset 'found at home the intimate and natural fusion of art and life'.[24] Bouyer's cavalier treatment of Mirra's art was typical of critics of the period. The reviewers who mentioned her paintings at salons and exhibitions strung her name together with those of other female artists, giving them all a polite, patronizing nod. It was fine for women to 'wield the brush' but their place, after all, was in the home and not the studio.

5

Unlike Realism and Impressionism, which had well-defined aims and adherents, Intimism was a loose collection of artists whose only common characteristic was an interest in the expressive possibilities of interior scenes. In February 1905, the owner of Galerie Henry Graves put together an exhibition of works by twenty painters that he called 'the First Group Exhibition of the Intimists (Painters of Interiors)'. Most of the artists—Morisset, Maurice Lobre, Henry Caro-Delvaille, Richard E. Miller and others—were fairly traditional in their approach, but there were also a few—Matisse, Vuillard, Bonnard—who were working on more experimental lines. The show opened on 25 February 1905 and attracted a good deal of attention. The reviewers were impressed especially by the works of Morisset, Lobre and Caro-Delvaille. Louis Vauxcelles, one of the best-known critics of the day, noted Morisset's penchant for 'scenes of happy maternity' but preferred his more tightly composed *Young Woman with a Flower*. Charles Méré, later an important screenwriter and director, praised Morisset's 'impeccable drawing'. An anonymous reviewer in *Le Pays* said that the paintings of Vuillard, Matisse and some others were 'well crafted', but Morisset's displayed a 'richer style'.[25]

One review of the exhibition appeared in the cultural journal *Les Tendances Nouvelles* (New Tendencies) with the name 'M. Almyre'—a pseudonym for Mirra Alfassa.[26] This was her first foray into art criticism and she tried to take a balanced view: Although drawn instinctively to Lobre, she could still find something of value in Vuillard. It was wrong to look for qualities one admires in one artist in other artists. As long as each develops his or her qualities with persistence and sincerity, the results are bound to be worthwhile. Still, 'a broad eclecticism does not prevent us from going voluntarily toward those who seem to us to unite in their work the greatest number of realized qualities'. For 'M. Almyre', the artist who did this best was Morisset. His work was 'remarkable as a whole and in each particular painting'.[27]

Mirra's review was published in the March 1905 issue of *Les Tendances Nouvelles*. In the same issue appeared a speech by the writer Gustave Hue announcing the creation of two artistic and intellectual societies: The Groupe Idéa and the Union Internationale des Beaux-Arts et des Lettres (International Union of Fine Arts and Letters). The purpose of Idéa, Hue said, was 'to gather artists together around the ideas they share'. He went on: 'All reality conceals an idea that is its soul, so to speak. The role of the artist is to release that idea . . . and transcribe it in his work.' Hue disapproved of the 'bohemian' currents that had begun to show themselves in European art. True artists did not turn their backs on nature, he said; rather, they tried 'to penetrate into its very soul'. The members of Idéa would form the core of the International Union of Fine Arts and Letters, which would hold its first congress in the near future.[28]

Over the next two years Mirra and Henri were closely associated with the two new groups. Idéa's first meeting was held in their apartment on 25 February. Among those present were Roger Marx, a leading art critic, Félix Bracquemond, a well-known printmaker, and his wife, Marie Bracquemond, a painter who had exhibited with the Impressionists between 1879 and 1886. The other twenty-two attendees are less well known. Several were members of Mirra's and Henri's families. At the third meeting, the members resolved that Idéa should be 'a place of support, assistance, and evolution, to amplify the faculties of understanding and creation and enhance the possibilities of individual and collective happiness'. The first original paper was not presented until the seventh meeting. As summer approached, the attendance dwindled.[29]

After several months of preparation, the first congress of the International Union of Fine Arts and Letters took place in August 1905. Wishing to break the Parisian monopoly on cultural events, the organizers decided to hold it in Angers, a mid-size city in western France that was the hometown of the editor of *Les Tendances Nouvelles,* now the official organ of the International Union. Along with sessions for speeches and discussions, the congress included a small salon that featured paintings by Henri and Mirra. (They themselves were on vacation and did not attend.) The only critic who covered the exhibition, a local writer named René-Noël Raimbault, noted in *Les Tendances Nouvelles* that it would be hard for Morisset 'to put more art and more mastery' into his nude studies. Madame Alfassa's *Console,* he added, glowed 'with a soft, intimate light'.[30]

Mirra's career as an art critic for *Les Tendances Nouvelles* was short-lived. After publishing three restrained pieces, she was shifted to the journal's 'Home and Dress' department. She responded by writing a brilliant three-part article on the aesthetic aspects of clothing.[31] This was her last contribution. Idéa continued to meet in the apartments of its members: Roger Marx, the Bracquemonds, and most frequently the Morissets. It appears to have been a genteel organization, with polite discussions followed by the adoption of well-phrased resolutions. There is no evidence it had any impact on the artistic or intellectual life of Paris. It did, however, provide Mirra with a model for the intellectual and spiritual groups she would found in later years.

6

The Paris newspaper *Gil Blas* headed its piece on the 1905 congress of the International Union of Fine Arts and Letters: 'Yet Another Group'.[32] There were, in fact, a multitude of art collectives in Paris at the end of the nineteenth and beginning of the twentieth centuries. The more significant ones did not, like the International Union, list big names like Rodin as honorary presidents or noblewomen such as Princess Gagarin-Sturdza as members of the committee of honour. They were loose groupings of artists who met in cafés and studios rather than sitting rooms and lecture halls. One of them was the Nabis, consisting of Paul Sérusier, Vuillard, Bonnard and several others, who worked together between 1889 and 1900, and remained in touch afterwards. Influenced by Paul Gauguin and Japanese woodblock prints, the Nabis used solid colours and stylized forms to break free from the strict imitation of nature. Another group, inspired by Cézanne and van Gogh, and led by Matisse and André Derain, was interested in the expressive power of the formal elements of their paintings—colour, line, form, texture—rather than the things depicted. All of these artists avoided the two official salons, exhibiting instead in the Salon des Indépendants and the Salon d'Automne, which had no bureaucratic juries.

Matisse and his friends first made a splash at the Salon des Indépendants of March–April 1905. The critic Vauxcelles was unsettled by the audacity of these 'vehement disciples of Cézanne', especially their leader, Matisse. He could appreciate the artist's still lifes and landscapes, but when it came to *Luxe, Calme et Volupté*, an enormous pointillist experiment, he had to draw the line. 'Why this foray into pointillist theory?' he asked the artist. 'Your magnificent gifts, in which will and intuitive sensation are measured and balanced, are too great for you to lose yourself in a seeking that is sincere, I know, but hostile to your true nature.'[33]

Mirra, who at the time was still associated with *Les Tendances Nouvelles*, also was unsettled by what she saw at the Indépendants. Rather than writing a review, she offered some general observations. Anyone who claimed to be an artist had to possess 'a true or original perception of light, colour, form, or values, along with the ability to transcribe these qualities, either spontaneously or by following the laws of harmonious composition'. Above all, the painting had to charm the eye. So long as an artist was able to do this, the door 'was open to every sort of talent'. All styles were good as long as they were 'truly pictorial'. She knew that people were saying all sorts of things about this particular salon: 'Some spoke of it with deep contempt, others praised it to the heavens.' Salon-goers should make up their own minds. 'Go and see this exhibition,' she concluded. 'You certainly will find the experience agreeable and useful.'[34]

Historians remember the 1905 Salon des Indépendants as the opening salvo of an artistic revolution. The full barrage came at the Salon d'Automne seven months later. The most talked-about painting at the exhibition was Matisse's *Lady with a Hat*, a portrait of his wife. The composition of the picture is fairly conventional: Madame Matisse gives the viewer a sidelong look, a big ornate hat on her head. But the colours are wild and unrealistic: The hat is a jumble of blues, oranges and greens, the face and neck modelled in green and orange, the background an assemblage of patches of mauve, green, yellow, blue and orange. For Matisse, it was the interrelationship of these elements and not the appearance of the sitter that was the subject of the painting. This was lost on visitors to the Salon, most of whom simply stared and laughed. Even the critic Vauxcelles was puzzled. Comparing the works of Matisse and his friends to a nearby neoclassical sculpture, he said it was as if a bust by Donatello was surrounded by wild animals (*fauves*). The public loved the gibe and, from this point on, Matisse and his *confrères* were known as the Fauves. Their works of 1905 mark the beginning of Modernism in painting.

Henri, Mirra and their friends detested Modernism in general and Matisse's Fauvist art in particular. One of them came up with a story about how he produced his works. It goes something like this: Matisse was a talented artist but he had trouble selling his paintings and as a result could not pay his bills. One day, a dealer came to his studio and asked if he had something to sell. Nothing Matisse showed him caught his eye. Then he noticed an odd piece of canvas that Matisse used for wiping his palette knife after scraping paint off the palette. 'Magnificent,' the dealer cried. 'I'll take it.' Matisse was too hungry to object. The 'painting' sold and the dealer encouraged the artist to give him more. Soon Matisse was the talk of the town.[35] This story tells us nothing about Matisse and much about the feelings of the artists in Morisset's circle.[36] Matisse and his friends received more press coverage in the month after the Salon d'Automne than Morisset and his friends had the previous twenty years. Gallerists approached them. Buyers snapped up their works. This acceptance opened the way to more daring forms of experimentation: Cubism, Futurism, Expressionism. Soon, the whole ecosystem of the art world changed, and Morisset and his friends were left high and dry.

At the end of 1905, nobody knew this was the course that modern art would take. The hold of conventional figurative painting on the market seemed secure. The gallery that hosted the first Intimist exhibition decided to organize another. It opened in February 1906. Most of the works were by traditionalists such as Morisset, Caro-Delvaille and Miller, this time joined by Madame Mirra Alfassa. There also were some paintings by experimentalists like Vuillard and Bonnard. (Matisse and the other Fauves were exhibiting in Brussels.) As in 1905, the critics gave most of their attention to the traditionalists. Étienne Charles, writing in *La Liberté*, was attracted by the nudes of Morisset and Miller, and had a good word for Madame Alfassa's *Petites Notes*. An anonymous reviewer in the *Voltaire* loved Miller's *Figure Nue*, thought Morisset's and Caro-Delvaille's paintings were fine, and mentioned Madame Alfassa in passing. As for Vuillard, his outlines were badly drawn and his forms unclear. Bonnard escaped his notice. This shows, if nothing else, the unpredictability of artistic reputation. Morisset and Caro-Delvaille are now known only to a few specialists. Vuillard and Bonnard are ranked among the most important painters of the early twentieth century. Their works are displayed in museums throughout the world and sell for millions of dollars.

The second Intimist show of February 1906 was the last significant exhibition Mirra took part in.[37] She continued to draw and paint but, as we will see in the next chapter, her interests were moving in another direction. Looking back on her artistic life more than fifty years later, she remarked, with perhaps excessive modesty: 'I was a perfectly ordinary artist.' She never tried to compare herself with the other painters in her circle in terms of technical ability. On the other hand, she felt she was far ahead of them 'in terms of consciousness—observation, experience, study'.[38] And increasingly understanding the workings of consciousness was what mattered to her.

7

During her late teens and early twenties, Mirra felt 'an intense need to *know*'. She had been having inner experiences for several years, but owing to her surroundings she 'never had the chance to receive the intellectual knowledge that would have given me the sense of it all'. In the Rue Lemercier building lived a number of Catholics who were very convinced about their faith. One day, after talking with them, Mirra mused: 'They're lucky, these people who are born into a religion and believe without questioning! How easy! You just have to believe!' Then she saw what she was thinking and gave herself a scolding: 'You're getting lazy!'[39] For the most part, she was left to her own devices, but whenever she chanced upon a book or person that gave her 'a little clue', a hint that if she tried this or that, a path would open before her, she rushed in 'like a cyclone'.[40]

In 1900, she got a clue from a visitor from India. On 24 June, Gyanendra Nath Chakravarti, a member of the Theosophical Society, gave a talk in Paris on 'Spirituality and Psychism'. Mirra apparently was in the audience when Chakravarti explained that people in India did not give the name 'yogi' to those who chased after supernatural powers but only those who 'studied the inner laws of being' and moulded their lives 'according to the dictates of the God within'. To bring one's whole nature 'into obedience to the God within' was 'the root of all true Yoga and all true religion'.[41] At some point Mirra had a private talk with Chakravarti. He suggested she read the Bhagavad Gita, keeping in mind that Krishna is 'the symbol of the immanent God, the God within'. This idea of an inner Divinity 'ever present in the innermost depths of our heart' (as Chakravarti put it) was a revelation to Mirra. Up to this point, she had never connected her inner life with religion or with God. As she read a translation of the Gita with Chakravarti's hint in mind, she began to understand what the 'God within' might mean.[42]

In her 1920 summary of her inner life, Mirra wrote that after the experiences of her early teens, she received, while asleep, 'a practical discipline' from 'several teachers'. Later, 'as the interior and exterior development proceeded', her contacts with one of those teachers 'became more clear and frequent'. After reading the Gita, she began to call this teacher 'Krishna' and felt she would meet him someday in her waking life.[43]

3

Cosmic Interlude

1

TOWARDS THE END OF 1904, MATTEO INTRODUCED MIRRA TO AN OLD school friend of his named Louis Moyse. Under the pseudonym Louis Thémanlys, Moyse had published a book on social theory and contributed some essays on the philosophy of art to *Les Tendances Nouvelles.* His latest passion was occultism. He was in touch with a teacher of esoteric lore known as Max Theon, who lived in Tlemcen, Algeria. Theon was connected with a journal called *La Revue Cosmique* (The Cosmic Review), which published essays and symbolic narratives presenting the doctrines of the Philosophie Cosmique or Cosmic Philosophy. Thémanlys gave Mirra some copies of the *Revue.* She read them and was thrilled. The journal announced that its aim was 'to show psycho-intellectual man that his origin is divine, that he carries divinity in himself, that his mission is to manifest it'. Here was the idea of the inner divine that was guiding her reading of the Gita presented in French by a living teacher. 'It was a revelation!' she later recalled. 'In a few minutes I understood everything. . . . It gave me the contact immediately.'[1] Around the beginning of 1905, she wrote a letter to Theon telling him of her interest. He replied on 15 January encouraging her to take part in his work.[2]

Up to this point, Mirra knew nothing about occultism even though Paris had been a centre of occult thought and practice for five decades. During the 1850s, a lapsed priest named Alphonse Louis Constant published, under the pseudonym Éliphas Lévi, a series of books on the theory and practice of 'high magic', a blanket term covering Kabbalah, necromancy, sacred geometry and other 'traditional' disciplines, which he claimed were the basis of all religions, philosophies and science.[3] His works opened the way for a flood of writings on esoteric subjects that lasted until the First World War, and had a major impact on contemporary literature, art, music and popular thought. In his books, Lévi popularized the new term *occultisme*, which quickly entered English and other languages.

Occultism covers a large number of systems that differ greatly in subject matter and approach but have some common features. All are said to be secret (this is the sense of the Latin *occultus*), traditional, comprehensive and the source of special powers: Each body of traditional knowledge claims to have been passed down from ancient times by masters to initiated disciples. Each accounts for everything in the supernatural and natural worlds: 'As above, so below'. Each enables the perfected master to influence the normal workings of nature. As a historian, I am agnostic about such claims. I examine occultism as an influential strand of late-nineteenth- and early-twentieth-century discourse, one that Mirra was closely connected with.

Theon and his wife played a small but significant role in the *fin de siècle* occult revival in England and France. Between January 1905 and April 1908, they were the central figures in Mirra's life. She corresponded with them throughout this period, met them twice in Paris, and twice went to Algeria to spend time with them. Before we examine her relationship with them, we have to get some idea of who they were. This is hard to do because the established narrative of their lives does not align with factual data in historical records. The narrative, in brief, goes like this: Born in Russia or Poland, Theon was initiated into Kabbalah, spent some time in Egypt (where he met Madame Blavatsky, co-founder of the Theosophical Society), went on to India, where he learnt Sanskrit and studied the Vedas, and finally settled in England, where he began his public work, which was to bring the Cosmic teachings to humanity. In England, he met and married an English or Irish poetess, who shared his interests and aptitudes. Like him, she was a master of many languages and adept in the occult arts.[4] This narrative remained unquestioned until the 1990s, when scholars began to uncover archival material bearing on the Theons' lives.[5] The account that follows is based on this material.

2

The man Mirra knew as Theon was born in Warsaw, Russian Poland, on 12 June 1850, the son of a rabbi named Yehudah Leib Bimstein. The boy's Hebrew forenames were Eliezer Mordechai, but, for most of his early life, he was known as Maximillian or Max Bimstein. Sometime around 1870, young Max went to London to seek his fortune. He got a job as a cigar salesman and, in June 1873, was married to a twenty-year-old woman named Rachel Goldberg in an orthodox ceremony at London's Great Synagogue. We know nothing further about his life until November 1877, when he was arrested under the Coinage Act. According to court records and newspaper accounts, he tried twice on the same day in the same shop on Oxford Street to use diminished gold coins to pay for purchases. The second time, the shopkeeper called a constable, who took Bimstein and his accomplice, a young woman named Eve Lyons, into custody. Lyons, who claimed to be Bimstein's fiancée, was later released. Bimstein was charged with diminishing the coins and trying to pass them off as good. After spending a month in jail, he was tried at the Old Bailey and acquitted on both counts. The Crown was unable to prove that he was the one who clipped the coins or had known they were light when he tried to pass them.[6]

After this misadventure, Bimstein dropped out of sight for four years. The census return of 1881 and the London directory of 1882 show him living and working as a cigarette maker at 28 Dean Street, Soho. The records give no indication that he was living with the woman he had married in 1873 or the one who claimed to be his fiancée in 1877. But he was not destined to live alone. On 21 March 1885, he was married in the

Westminster Register Office to a woman who gave her name as Mary Chrystine Woodroffe Ware.[7]

Mary Ware was born in June 1839 in Sutton Coutenay, a village on the Thames, a few kilometres south of Oxford. Drawn to the religious life, she became a nun at a convent in the village of Claydon, near Ipswich, around 1860. By 1881, she had become the Mother Superior of the convent. It was an unconventional foundation, which passed through a series of controversies while she was there. Some were centred around her unorthodox views, which included a belief in spiritualism. Eventually, the priest of the convent's church denied her Holy Communion. In 1882 or 1883, she left the convent and settled in London.

The esoteric scene in late Victorian England was every bit as lively as the Belle Époque version across the Channel. Mesmerizers, mediums and ceremonial magicians vied for the attention of the public. The Theosophical Society and other groups enrolled hundreds of members. The subcultures of occultism, literature and art intermingled. Edward Bulwer-Lytton and Maria Corelli published blockbuster novels on occult themes. Poets like Dante Gabriel Rossetti and painters like James McNeill Whistler brought the aura of occultism into their work. Mary Ware, whose literary and theatrical impulses had been stifled in the convent, plunged into this vibrant milieu. In 1884, under the Spenserian name 'Una', she began lecturing on psychology, transmigration and other 'advanced' topics at the Universal Philosophic Society, a discussion group in Hampstead. In April, she advertised herself in a theatrical newspaper as a 'Novelist, Dramatic Artist, Playwright, Poetess, Essayist and Lecturer' who was ready to write poems and plays to order, and had a novel in the works. A couple of months later, she announced that a play written by her would soon be produced. Before rehearsals began in earnest, she gave a series of 'Sibylline lectures' and several speeches on esoteric topics in Camden Town. On 4 September 1884, her play *Alta, or Right against Might* was performed in New Cross with her in the lead female role. The only reviewer who covered the show called it 'radically bad', adding: '"Una", who represented the heroine, should be counselled never to attempt to tread the stage again as an actress.'[8]

After this disappointing debut, Una resumed her career as a lecturer on arcane subjects. Summaries of her talks were published in *Medium and Daybreak*, Britain's leading spiritualist review. Soon, she ran afoul of the journal's editor, who opposed her belief that the beings evoked in séances were not actual spirits of the dead. Denied space in the columns of the journal, she continued to lecture in various London halls. We can get some idea of her interests at this time by perusing the 1884 pamphlet *Sayings of the Sibyl Alta Una*, by Una, High Priestess of Pan, the Light God and Eros. Here, she speaks of her nine lives on earth, and offers practical suggestions regarding forms of government, education and human relations. 'Women,' she writes, 'should be taught that their chief glory is to be the rest giver of him whom they have chosen so that . . . he may attain to new heights of wisdom, love and power.'[9] It was around this time she met Max Bimstein.

Towards the end of 1884, an announcement appeared in a new translation of a Hermetic text inviting 'students of the Occult Sciences, searchers after truth, and Theosophists who may have been disappointed in their expectations of Sublime Wisdom dispensed by HINDOO MAHATMAS' to apply for membership in an occult brotherhood. Communications were to be addressed to 'Theon', care of the publisher.[10] This was the first time Max Bimstein used that name. (From this point on, I will refer to him as 'Theon' and to Mary Ware as 'Madame Theon'.)[11] The occult group Theon was connected with was the Hermetic Brotherhood of Luxor, always shortened to the HB of L. It was the creation of a Scottish violin-maker and writer named Peter Davidson, a tradesman from Yorkshire known as Thomas Burgoyne, and Theon. According to Davidson, the HB of L was the current manifestation of an 'ever-existent and ancient Order'. In 1873 (two years before the founding of the Theosophical Society), an adept of this order, normally resident in Tibet, went to England in search of a neophyte. Meeting Theon, he put him to the test and then instructed him in sacred lore. When Theon became an adept himself, he asked permission to establish an 'exterior Circle' to prepare aspirants for initiation.[12] In real-life terms, this circle was the occult brotherhood that advertised itself at the end of 1884. Its aim, according to its promotional material, was to propagate European rather than Oriental forms of occultism, and offer practical as well as theoretical teachings. The practical side included the use of magic mirrors and sex-magic rituals.[13]

The HB of L charged for membership and products but the sums realized were not enough to pay the office-holders' bills. In July 1885, three months after his marriage, Theon began to run monthly classified advertisements in *Medium and Daybreak*: 'THEON, THE EASTERN PSYCHIC HEALER, cures all diseases. Consultation by appointment.' Two months later, apparently on Davidson's advice, he printed a notice in the *Occult Magazine* declaring that Theon of the HB of L was not the same as Theon, the Eastern Psychic Healer who advertised in *Medium and Daybreak*. This statement was not true. The address of Theon the Psychic Healer was the same as the address that Theon of the HB of L put on his marriage certificate.[14]

Between the end of 1884 and the middle of 1886, the HB of L attracted a small number of adherents, some of whom were also members of the Theosophical Society. At first, relations between the two groups were cordial. Then, early in 1886, a Theosophist named A.W. Ayton discovered that Thomas Burgoyne, secretary of the HB of L, was actually an ex-convict named Thomas Dalton, who had served time for mail fraud in Leeds three years earlier. Faced with exposure, Dalton and Davidson decamped to the United States in March 1886. The same month, Theon and his wife crossed over to France. Passing quickly through Paris, they spent a year and a half in the south, then set sail for Algeria. With them was Teresa, a former novice in Mother Mary's convent who was their disciple and secretary.

3

This factual account of the Theons' early lives differs greatly from the largely fictitious narrative I presented at the end of the first section. To give a few examples: There is no reason to believe that Theon was initiated into Kabbalah before being sent to England on a mission to enlighten humanity.[15] Like other European Jews of the period, he was drawn to London because it offered security (England emancipated its Jews in 1858) and economic opportunity. There are no grounds for believing that he went to Egypt or India. He certainly never met Madame Blavatsky.[16] Neither he nor his wife had a good command of French, much less of Sanskrit. We do not know whether they created these fabrications themselves or went along with things that other people imagined, or both. At any rate, the stories that took shape around them have little basis in fact and the factual account of their lives is at odds with their reputation as master occultists. Should we then dismiss them as impostors? Our interest here is not with the Theons themselves but with the teachings they gave to Mirra. These came in two forms: Written works published in the *Revue Cosmique* and *Tradition Cosmique,* and oral teachings of practical occultism. The published writings are remarkable in their extent and variety. Theon took up and continued the Cosmic Myth devised by the first editor of the two periodicals. Madame Theon created a fantasy universe filled with sages, heroes and women with secret knowledge. (Had she been born a century later and received a better education, she might have given J.R.R. Tolkien a run for his money.) On the negative side, the Theons' writings are notably obscure and often pretentious. They do, however, contain fragments of occult wisdom deriving from old traditions such as Neoplatonism, Gnosticism, Hermeticism and Kabbalah. When Mirra read the Cosmic publications, she absorbed ideas from these traditions, which she later incorporated into her own metaphysical synthesis. The Theons' oral teachings included methods of inner practice, such as guided meditation, which she later developed and applied in her work with others. Even if the teachers were not models of integrity and their teachings not all they claimed to be, they provided Mirra with a platform for further development.

4

In March 1888, the Theons settled in Tlemcen, a town lying at the foot of the Atlas Mountains. Besides being a centre of agriculture and commerce, Tlemcen was a place of pilgrimage, with notable mosques, a famous Sufi shrine and an old Jewish cemetery. When France invaded Algeria, the town was a hub of resistance, but eventually it succumbed along with the rest of the country. Hundreds of thousands of French settlers flooded Algeria, which, after 1848, was administered as an integral part of France. Old towns like Tlemcen took on a French provincial look, with European-style town halls, post offices, courthouses, army barracks and prisons. Little is known about the Theons' lives between 1888 and 1898. They published nothing, except an occasional piece in local newspapers. Then, in December 1898, Theon managed to place an article in an esoteric journal of Paris. This helped him get his foot in the door of the crowded world of French occultism.

At that time, the occult revival was in full swing in Paris. Dozens of writers published articles and books on magic, alchemy, Kabbalah, Rosicrucianism, Spiritism, magnetism and other esoteric sub-disciplines. A favourite meeting place of the Paris occult crowd was the Librairie de l'Art Indépendant (Bookshop of Independent Art), opened by the bookseller and publisher Edmond Bailly in 1889. The shop was a magnet for the avant-garde of *fin de siècle* France: Poets Stéphane Mallarmé and Paul Verlaine, composers Claude Debussy and Erik Satie, artists Odilon Redon and Félicien Rops.[17] All of them were interested in things occult and their works helped popularize esoteric themes among the general public. This paralleled developments in other parts of Europe. The Theosophical Society had branches in Great Britain, Ireland and the Continent (not to mention the United States and India), and published a wide array of books and journals that influenced writers such as William Butler Yeats, James Joyce and Algernon Blackwood, and artists such as Hilma af Klint, Wassily Kandinsky and Piet Mondrian.

In France, Theosophy was just one among many occult groups that clamoured for attention. By the mid-1890s, Bailly and other Paris publishers were bringing out dozens of journals to cater to the esoteric boom. The one that accepted Theon's first piece was the *Journal du Magnétisme et de la Psychologie*, which was devoted to the study of magnetism in the quasi-scientific sense popularized by Franz Mesmer at the end of the eighteenth century. Mesmer believed there was an invisible fluid or force in all living beings that he called 'animal magnetism'. A skilled 'magnetizer' could direct this force to cure disease or bring about other physical effects. To Theon, magnetism, or as he preferred to call it, *pathétisme,* was much more than this. In its 'highest sense', he wrote in February 1899, it was a universal force that, when channelled by an experienced magnetizer (typically a man) to a suitable 'sensitive' (typically a woman), would foster the 'development of the passive sensitive to the highest perfection of which she is capable in all the states of her being'.[18]

Theon contributed a dozen pieces to the *Journal du Magnétisme.*[19] In them, he presented the theoretical basis of his philosophy and stated the goal of his practice, which was, in brief, 'to regain a lost dominion, of which the crown is immortality on earth'.[20] In the October 1899 issue, he published his first major work, a book-length critique of the doctrines of Allan Kardec, the founder of Spiritism. A popular French version of Anglo-American spiritualism, Spiritism had become an organized church, and had thousands of adherents in Europe and the Americas. It was set to dominate an international congress of spiritualists to be held in Paris in 1900 and the faithful were not amused by Theon's comments. They issued a statement in the December issue of the *Journal* saying that his critique 'had no value whatsoever'.[21] After this, the journal's publisher refused to print Theon's articles, though he did run two instalments of a 'psychic novel' and a 'vision' written by his wife.

At least one reader of the *Journal du Magnétisme* found value in the Theons' work. In August 1900, Albert Faucheux, who published under the anagrammatic pseudonym F.-Ch. Barlet, made a trip to Tlemcen to speak with them.[22] Barlet was an important node in the Paris occult network. An early member of the French Theosophical Society, he later founded, along with the well-known writers Papus, Stanislas de Guaita and Joséphin Péladan, the Independent Group of Esoteric Studies. Still later, he joined the Kabbalistic Order of the Rosy Cross, was elected a bishop of the Gnostic Church and became a member of the supreme council of the Martinist Order. The proliferation of such groups was due in part to conflicts among their members. No sooner was a group founded than it became riven by doctrinal and personal disputes. At the end of 1900, Barlet was looking for a fresh outlet. He proposed to the Theons that they join with him in founding a new organization that would publish its own journal. They said they were interested. On his return to Paris, Barlet announced that a monthly called the *Revue Cosmique* would be launched with himself as editor. It would publish studies of ancient traditions and esoteric teachings, 'placed on a rational basis and in harmony with the modern interpretation of sacred texts'.[23]

The first issue of the *Revue Cosmique* came out in January 1901. None of the articles were signed. The mark of their authenticity was the Cosmic symbol, a hexagram formed by two intersecting triangles with a square enclosing a lotus in the middle. Barlet, who had been studying sacred geometry for years, explained that the two triangles represented 'a double movement, descending from God to the Universe by Man, ascending from the Universe to the Spirit by man'.[24] This was the central idea of the Cosmic Philosophy, which Barlet developed at enormous length in the first two volumes of the *Revue*. He also published 'ancient texts'—in fact, original works by Madame Theon written in what might be called the fantasy-philosophic style—as well as shorter works of fiction, essays, and a section of questions and answers. Like most other esoteric doctrines, the Cosmic Philosophy claimed to be the original Tradition underlying all religions, philosophies and sciences. It is clear, however, that it owed a great deal to Judaism (including Kabbalah), Gnosticism and Christianity. Reliance on different sources led to a rift between Barlet, who favoured Christianity, and Theon who, though steeped in the Jewish tradition, wanted the journal to stand above all religions. As a result of this and other conflicts, Barlet resigned his editorship towards the end of 1902. The *Revue* limped on for another few months before ceasing publication with the issue of March 1903.[25]

Ten months later, after a successful fundraising drive, the *Revue Cosmique* was reborn. The name of the editorial director now was given as Aia Aziz, an Arabic pseudonym for Max Bimstein/Theon.[26] Thanking the journal's supporters, he restated its objects: Showing the élite of humanity how their capacities could be developed; reminding them that they carried the divine within themselves; lifting undeveloped humanity out of its fallen state; restoring the original Wisdom Tradition through a union of science and theology; and demonstrating that death is a temporary error and that the true state of the human being is 'Integral Immortality'.[27] In the new series of the *Revue* there was less philosophy (this had been Barlet's strong suit) and more literature (Madame Theon's forte). She continued to produce 'unpublished studies from ancient sources' and added original symbolic narratives such as 'The Visions of the Royal Neophyte'. More accessible were essays on miscellaneous topics such as fatalism, astrology and auras. During the same period, the Theons issued the first two volumes of another publication, the *Tradition Cosmique*. Weighing in at more than 700 pages, these tomes present *The Cosmic Drama*, a modern Gnostic Gospel written in faux-mythic French. Neither the *Tradition* nor the *Revue* offered much in the way of practical methods to help readers reach the goal of integral immortality but there was enough in them to hold Mirra's interest.

5

During the first part of 1905, Mirra studied the Cosmic material that Thémanlys gave her and exchanged letters with the Theons, but she had a number of other concerns. André was now six and needed a lot of looking after. There were meetings of the Idéa group, often in the Morissets' apartment. The first Intimist exhibition was held in February and March. After this, she and Henri had to finish the works they planned to exhibit at the Beaux-Arts Salon in April. Only after the salon opened could she give her attention to other things.

Towards the end of April, Mirra wrote to the Theons saying she would like to help them bring out the third volume of the *Tradition Cosmique*. A week or so later, they sent her the first sign of initiation into the Cosmic fellowship.[28] Like all founders of movements, the Theons required three things: Workers, publicity and money. They seem to have guessed that Mirra could help them in all three ways.

In one of her letters to Mirra, Madame Theon asked about her artistic interests. A month or two later, she brought out an 'Unpublished Study from an Ancient Source on Art and Genius' in the *Revue*. The piece is in the form of a dialogue between Thulepenth and Mureh. (Madame Theon loved to invent pseudo-archaic names for her characters, some of which echoed the names of living people.) The first part of the dialogue is fairly straightforward: Thulepenth says that the artist must 'apply the rules of science and art' to 'manifest the idea in the reality'. The proper subject for painters and sculptors is the idealized human form, which can evoke in the mind of evolved sensitives the veiled divinity manifest in humanity. Later, Thulepenth goes more deeply into the Cosmic Philosophy: 'Those who work for the Restoration [of the original perfection] are all embellishers of form.' They must express the beauty of physical forms and, through them, 'the nervous, psychic, and mental individualities' until at last the 'First Emanation' is revealed. Then, as if addressing Mirra directly, Thulepenth exclaims: 'Devote yourself to this noble work, my child, with joy and zeal, persistence and perseverance.' Your 'lofty mission' is to be 'an educator and glorifier of form'.[29]

The 'Unpublished Study' appeared in the July 1905 issue of the *Revue Cosmique.* Towards the end of that month, Mirra, Henri and presumably André as well went to Normandy for two months. They stayed in a rented house in Bernières-sur-Mer, a seaside village a few kilometres from Courseulles-sur-Mer, where their friend Louis Thémanlys had a home. Thémanlys arrived in August after giving a talk at the Angers Congress of the International Union of Fine Arts and Letters. He spent his time working on a booklet called *Exposé sur le Mouvement Cosmique* (An Account of the Cosmic Movement). When Madame Theon learnt he had finished it, she wrote to Mirra that it 'would be of great use to the *Cause we all love and serve together*'. She also thanked her for her translation of the third part of the *Tradition Cosmique.* The result, she said, was 'full of life and of liveliness'.[30]

Thémanlys's *Exposé* was the first of several attempts by followers of the Theons to give logical form to the chaotic doctrines of the Cosmic Philosophy. The booklet is far from transparent but certainly more accessible than the *Revue* and the *Tradition.* 'No active force can manifest without a receptivity which supports and realizes it,' it begins. To foster this receptivity, 'the guardians of the pure treasure of the integral tradition offer this Cosmic philosophy'. All philosophies and religions have a common origin but all have become impure. The aim of the

Cosmic Philosophy is to filter the waters of the various traditions and return to the original pure source. Here, Thémanlys lapses into the arcane terminology of the *Tradition*: the Causeless Cause, the First Emanation, Elohim, the Great Adversary and Man, the supreme evolutionary being. By means of evolution, Man will arrive at 'terrestrial immortality'. All manifestation is dual, and the active and passive (male and female) aspects are equal. Their union must be based on perfect love. All life is sacred because it is the manifestation of divinity. It follows that there is no evil. All children are born pure and have the right to education. When all humanity has been united, women will cease to be oppressed and there will be no more disharmony, conflict or war.[31]

The Cosmic Philosophy, despite its claims to uniqueness, was far from original. It is easy to identify bits of Jewish, Christian and Gnostic teachings in Thémanlys's *Exposé*. His attempt to harmonize theology and science echoed similar efforts by dozens of late nineteenth- and early-twentieth-century thinkers. It was a period when many had lost faith in organized religion but still yearned for individual and social perfection. The Cosmic Philosophy catered to this need. Mirra was among those who felt it opened the way to personal self-development within a community of like-minded people.

While in Normandy, Mirra and Henri spent much of their time painting. One place where they set up their easels was Trouville-sur-Mer, the seaside town immortalized in the art of Gustave Courbet and Claude Monet, and the fiction of Gustave Flaubert and Marcel Proust. Probably in 1905, Henri drew some sketches of Trouville and started work on paintings he exhibited two years later. The critics loved his evocation of the resort's holiday atmosphere: 'The white and pink of the changing-tents and umbrellas, beaches bathed in a pale, friendly light'.[32] The only work of Mirra's that survives from this period is a study of the garden of Thémanlys's house in Courseulles. It was here she had an experience that encapsulated the spiritual progress she had made over the last few months.

Towards the beginning of 1905, she become aware that there was a 'region' between the physical plane and what the Theons called the *degré physico-nerveux* or 'material vital plane'. If she could find this region, she felt, she could connect the inner and outer parts of her consciousness. She worked on this without success for some time. Then she went to Normandy. One day, while visiting Thémanlys's place, she entered his garden and lay down on the lawn. Then 'suddenly . . . all the life of that region between the subtle physical and the most material vital, which is very living in plants and in Nature, all that region became all at once, suddenly, without any transition, absolutely living, intense, conscious, marvellous.'[33]

Back in Paris, Mirra devoted more and more time to editing the movement's publications. In principle, Thémanlys was in charge, but, as Mirra later recalled, 'he was lazy-minded and didn't want to work'. He passed the job on to Mirra, who took care of everything: Copy-editing, dealing with the printer, correction of proofs and so forth. The Theons' writings presented a variety of difficulties. Madam Theon's stories, Mirra had to admit, were 'almost childish'. Theon's pieces were more substantial but spoiled by his impenetrable terminology: He 'invented all the words for the subtle senses, the inner senses; for each of them he found a word—a dreadful barbarism!'[34] Finally, there was the problem of translation. Teresa made 'all the classic mistakes' when she rendered the Theons' English into French. When she sent her work from Tlemcen to Paris, Mirra had to struggle to make it readable. The results were often hard going. No wonder the *Revue* had few subscribers.

The Theons came to Europe at the end of 1905, spending most of November in Nice. While there, Theon sent Mirra a card in which he addressed her as 'Aliana'. This became her name among members of the Cosmic group. Before returning to Tlemcen, the Theons made a trip to Paris, where they met Mirra and Henri. The visit went well, cementing a relationship that had become central to her life.

The Theons invited the Morissets to visit them in Tlemcen. Mirra and Henri were enthusiastic but there was no chance of their going during the early months of 1906. The second Intimist exhibition was held in February and March. After that Henri had to work on the paintings he planned to exhibit at the Beaux-Arts Salon in April. (Because of the pressure of Cosmic work, Mirra gave up the idea of submitting an entry herself.) A trip to Algeria would strain their budget. Henri remarked, perhaps in jest, that if he got a good price for a painting he was working on, he would use the proceeds to finance their trip. The work in question, entitled *Le Repos*, depicts a voluptuous, fair-skinned nude reclining on her bed. Most of the critics liked it but it did not sell. Mirra and Henri continued to make preparations. In the end, it was decided that she would go first and he would join her later.

Mirra had never travelled alone. It was not the done thing for women of her class. Undeterred, she boarded a ship in Marseille, which reached Oran on the morning of 14 July. The train to Tlemcen departed that afternoon. At first, it chugged through fertile plains as if gliding over 'a multi-coloured tapestry'. As darkness fell, it began to climb the foothills of the Atlas and, an hour before midnight, stopped at Tlemcen's imitation French station. Theon was there to meet her. The two went by car to his home on the outskirts of town, which he called Villa Zarif. Before they entered the house, he turned to her and said: 'Now you are at my mercy. Aren't you afraid?' Mirra looked at him, smiled and said, 'I'm never afraid,' then, touching her heart, 'I have the Divine here.'[35]

The next morning, Mirra had a look around. The house was situated on the top of a hill with a view of the valley below and the mountains to the west and south. The ground floor had a large dining room, some smaller rooms, a kitchen and an enclosed veranda. The bedrooms were upstairs. The household consisted of Theon, his wife, their secretary, Teresa, and an Algerian maid. Theon was a man of middle height, with long, curly hair falling to his shoulders. Madame Theon was short, fat and smiling. Teresa seemed older than her sixty years. After breakfast, Madame Theon sat at her table and began to write. Before the sun got too hot, Theon took Mirra out to the garden and showed her his rose bushes and olive trees.

In biographies of the Mother, Theon is identified as her 'teacher of occultism'. How exactly is occultism taught? Many readers are likely to think of Harry Potter's Hogwarts School. People raised on Indian mythological films will doubtless imagine ashrams where semi-divine rishis reveal the secrets of divine knowledge and power to chosen disciples. According to Claire Thémanlys, who visited Tlemcen with her husband Louis in 1907, Theon imparted his teachings over meals or during walks in the garden or while looking at the star-filled sky. Like Claire, Mirra listened to many such discourses, but, as a 'passive sensitive', she also took part in the guided meditations that Theon called *repos.* She never described these sessions in detail, but we can get some idea of what they were like by looking at a dialogue published over Theon's signature in *Les Tendances Nouvelles.* It is called 'The Gateway of the Palace of Art'. First, the author sets the scene: In a room of the sacred academy, a beautiful sensitive, Aliah, rests on her couch. Next to her sits Aeon, the *pathétiseur* or magnetizer, who holds her hand in his. (The names obviously are substitutes for Aliana and Theon.) Aeon asks Aliah, who is 'sleeping with open eyes', to tell him what she sees. She says she is standing in a forest with different sorts of trees, some of them royal cedars. Aeon asks her to approach the cedar grove and, because he is part of her vision, he guides her down the path. They reach the Gateway of Art. Holding Aeon's hand, Aliah passes through it to the Palace of Art, where she falls silent. Aeon asks her why. She replies: 'My soul is filled to overflowing with joy on account of the magnificence I see.' Then suddenly she begins to weep. Why? he asks. She answers that she has grown aware of the sufferings of humanity. She sees that the children of art and genius, of whom she is one, must suffer more than the rest. Then she finds herself on a silver-coloured cloud, and hears a voice proclaim to the children of art and genius: 'It is up to you to create a new heaven and new earth, to lift up humanity.' Returning to the Palace of Art, Aliah sees pictures and statues that depict 'the Divine manifested in and by the human'.[36]

This description of a *repos* session was imaginary—Theon wrote it before he met Mirra face to face—but it gives a rough idea of how a magnetizer uses a sensitive to explore inner worlds and gain knowledge of secret things. The process was not without its dangers. Mirra once spoke of a narrow escape she had while practicing *repos* with Theon. When the conscious being leaves the body in trance, she explained, it remains attached to its physical base by a sort of cord. Once, while she was voyaging within, her cord was severed and she was unable to come back on her own. Fortunately, she was able to tell Theon and 'he used his power and knowledge to help [her] come back'.[37]

Mirra came to believe that the Theons had extraordinary powers. During the 1950s and 1960s, she related a few incidents that had convinced her that they had achieved some control over the forces of nature. Once, Theon took her to the terrace during a thunderstorm. A bolt of lightning came towards them, then suddenly swerved and struck a tree further off. Mirra asked Theon: 'Did you do that?' He nodded.[38] Mirra often went walking in the countryside around the house, locking her door behind her. When she got back, she invariably found a garland of flowers on her pillow. Who put them in her room, she wondered. One day, Madame Theon asked her, 'Were there no flowers in your room?' Indeed there were, Mirra replied. This was enough to convince her that Madame Theon had used her occult power to materialize the flowers in her room. More striking was an experience involving a floating table. Another day, a man came to the Theons' place and asked some stupid questions. Madame Theon told Mirra, 'Wait and see, we're going to have some fun!' All of them were sitting at some distance from a heavy wooden table. Suddenly (as Mirra related years later), 'the table started moving and with an almost heroic gesture launched an assault on the poor man. . . . Madame Theon hadn't touched it, nobody had touched it. She just concentrated on the table and made it move by means of her vital power.'[39] Claire Thémanlys witnessed a similar incident during her visit to Tlemcen. While sitting at the dinner table, she asked Madame Theon about the reality of mediumistic phenomena. The next moment, the table rose and pressed against the astonished young Frenchwoman. 'The table really likes you,' Madame Theon said, 'but perhaps it's pushing you a bit too much.' The table then returned to its normal place.[40]

Incidents like these fill the literature of occultism, not to mention fantasy novels and films. People accept them or reject them in accordance to their backgrounds and interests. As a historian, I am inclined to compare them with published treatments of related phenomena. When spiritualism came to France in the early 1850s, one of the forms it took was 'table turning' (*tables tourantes*). In darkened rooms, people placed their hands on the tops of tables and summoned a spirit guide. After a while, the tables rocked, lifted and sometimes moved around the room. Soon, everyone in Paris was trying it. Dozens of proponents and detractors—spiritualists, magnetizers, religious leaders, scientists—published books and articles on the subject. After a year or two, the fad tapered off and French furniture stayed solidly on the ground. Nevertheless, until the start of the First World War table turning was part of the repertoire of professional spiritualists—and the acts of professional magicians. The most famous mediums who made tables turn were the Italian Eusapia Palladino and the Canadian-American Mina Crandon. Both convinced a lot of people that the phenomena they produced were genuine but both resorted to trickery at least some of the time and, in the end, both were dismissed as frauds. Scientists who studied the question, the most prominent of whom was the physicist Michael Faraday, concluded that table turning, when not due to chicanery, was the result of involuntary lifting by participants or hypnotic suggestion, or both.

The Mother believed that the Theons' powers were real but she did not think that they had much spiritual value. The most important things she learnt from the teachers were the structure of the human psyche and the presence of the inner divine. The Theons taught that each person is made up of four 'degrees' or levels: The *nervo-physique* or vital-physical (that is, the living body), the *nerveux* or vital (the life-force), the *psychique* or psychic (everything relating to the soul and higher emotions) and the *mental* (everything relating to the mind). These levels interpenetrate, giving rise to composite levels such as the *degré physico-nerveux* or material vital level I mentioned earlier. Madame Theon had the ability to leave her physical body and entering the vital body, leaving that and entering the next degree, and so forth. She showed Mirra how to do this. Under her guidance, Mirra entered and left her various bodies until she reached the stage the Theons called *pathétisme*, where she experienced 'complete unity—unity in something that was the essence of Love'. Beyond this level lay the Formless or, in Cosmic-speak, the *Forme sans forme*.[41]

Mirra studied Theon's occult philosophy with great interest. She read his wife's mythology with indulgence. But what truly attracted her to the Cosmic teachings was the idea of the inner divine: 'I was completely against "God",' she explained in 1971. 'The European notion of God was quite repellent to me.' But when Theon showed her how to contact the divine within, she had 'an absolutely convincing experience'.[42] Looking back from the vantage point of 1964, when she had been practising Indian yoga for fifty years, she said that her sessions with Theon marked the start of her 'conscious yoga'. From this point on, she felt she was under the government of her soul or psychic being and her physical body was 'constantly attuned to the Divine Will'.[43]

6

Henri joined Mirra in Tlemcen on 17 August 1906. His interest in the Cosmic Philosophy was far less intense than hers. He was glad to speak with the Theons about occult things but his main reasons for coming were artistic. He did some preliminary work for paintings he exhibited at the Beaux-Arts Salon five years later. Mirra also did some painting and drawing. Her works from this period include an oil sketch of the Theons' garden and two of Villa Zarif. In one of them, Theon and his huge dog, Little Boy, who was a great friend of Mirra's, make cameo appearances. She also did a pencil sketch of Theon that brings out the power of his eyes. On 13 September, she, Henri, Theon and Teresa went to visit a cork oak forest near Tlemcen. That evening, she and Henri departed for France.[44]

In Paris, Mirra resumed her work in the Cosmic office. She also began to publish her own writings in the *Revue*. On November 1906, she brought out a symbolic narrative entitled 'A Vision'. This and six more Visions that appeared in subsequent issues, along with an eighth that was published posthumously, are the earliest surviving documents in which she recorded her inner experiences close to the time they happened.[45]

In the first Vision, a dreamer awakes just as she is sinking into a luminous sea. In the depths, she feels the presence of 'Him in whom all harmonies reside'. Admitted to a crystalline grotto by the guardian of the gate, she is overwhelmed by lights of different colours. Their source is a luminous being, profoundly asleep on a couch covered with a white duvet. He awakes, silently greets the dreamer, and leads her to the couch. She lies down on the downy whiteness and is penetrated by a tender current of force, which vitalizes every cell of her body. Sinking into a state of beatific repose, she learns many secrets, one of which is this: Wherever there is beauty, wherever there is radiance, wherever there is progress towards perfection, there one finds being in the human form, because the human being is the agent of evolution.[46]

Each of Mirra's Visions recounts a voyage by a dreamer through symbolic landscapes, blazing with vivid colours. Most of them feature three characters: A beautiful young woman, a wise old man and a heroic youth. In one Vision, the dreamer enters a dark cathedral and is shocked to see the religious paraphernalia crumble to dust. On a violet screen, a message appears: 'The Self is your God. You are the living Temple of the Divine Inhabitant.' In another, the dreamer passes successively through scenes of ancient Egypt, ancient India, Celtic Europe and medieval Venice. In the Italian city, the beautiful young woman, who is a fair-haired passive, clings to the old man. He tells her that the time for the Victory has not yet come. She exclaims: 'When we again return to earth we will see the Victory.' In the final Vision, the young woman is seated in a house that closely resembles Villa Zarif. Near her is an old man dressed in a shabby dark robe. The young woman is waiting for someone. The luminous young man arrives. The old man embraces him and his shabby robe turns to gold. Then the young man approaches the young woman. They embrace. He kisses her forehead and she too becomes luminous. He explains: 'This is quite natural on account of the great affinity that unites us.' He then invites the young woman to lie down beside him. Holding one another's hands, they fall asleep. The room fills with a great luminescence.

These fairy-tale-like Visions could be interpreted in many different ways. At the time, Mirra saw them in terms of the Cosmic teachings. (She even, at the end of the last Vision, inserted a Cosmic maxim: 'In the equilibrium of the duality of being lies the victory.'[47]) But there was something more. The Visions left her with an impression, in the background of her consciousness, 'that one day something like this would take place'.[48] The luminous youth of her Visions became a model for the teacher she felt she was destined to meet.

7

By the end of 1906, Mirra was devoting most of her time to the activities of the Cosmic movement. She edited all the issues of the *Revue*, contributed her Visions, translated a novel by Madame Theon into French, and helped the treasurer and office manager look after the financial and practical affairs. In addition, she organized the weekly meetings of the Cosmic group, which now overlapped with Idéa.[49] One evening, the proceedings were disturbed by the arrival of an uninvited visitor. His worn clothes and defensive posture 'made him look like a hunted animal'. Mirra asked him politely: 'May I help you, sir?' He replied 'I have come from Kyiv to see you.' He and his friends had read some Cosmic publications and were impressed that this philosophy 'did not limit itself to theory but encouraged action'. Mirra asked him what sort of action he was involved in. He said: 'I work for the revolution.' He went on to describe the part he and his comrades had played in the 1905 uprising against the Tsarist government. At first, they made some minor gains, 'then collapse came, mowing us down like wheat in a field'. They sought direction in philosophical works, including those of the Cosmic movement. Now, he and a female comrade had come to Paris to prepare for the next stage, reorganizing, writing and printing propaganda leaflets, and contacting people who might help them. Mirra and her friends spoke with him for a while, offering words of encouragement. As he left, they invited him to come to a future meeting. He said he would return, but never did. Harassed by the police, he was forced to return to Russia, where, Mirra reflected, 'perhaps a tragic end awaited him'.[50]

8

Around this time, Theon told the overworked Mirra that he was in touch with someone he hoped would help her out. His name was Paul Richard.[51]

Born in 1874 in Marsillargues, a town near Montpellier, Richard entered a Protestant seminary after finishing his military service and, in 1900, was granted the degree of bachelor of theology. The same year, he married a Dutch woman named Wilhelmina van Oostveen and began to serve as pastor in a Reformed church in Lille. Drawn by the evangelical social movement, he became involved in the running of orphanages and homes for delinquent boys. Faced with the disapproval of his conservative parishioners, he resigned his pastorship in September 1904. The same month, he voyaged to French Guiana to study the condition of convicts on Devil's Island. After returning to France in January 1905, he published his findings in the daily newspaper *Le Siècle.* Around the same time, he took up the study of law, became active in left-wing political groups, and tried to obtain a party endorsement for a seat in the Chamber of Deputies. On top of all this, he developed an interest in occultism. This brought him into contact with people who knew about the Cosmic movement and the Theons. In mid-December, he attended a meeting of the Cosmic group, where he met Mirra and other members.

Theon was interested in attracting writers who could publicize his movement. He took the unusual step of inviting Richard to visit him in Algeria. Intrigued, Richard made the journey, arriving in Tlemcen in the beginning of January 1907 and staying for more than a month. His hosts lived up to their reputation. Theon looked very much the mystical Jewish sage, with his long hair, skull cap and purple robes. He gave the former Protestant pastor some rudimentary lessons in the Kabbalistic reading of the Book of Genesis. Madame Theon said little but seemed to Richard to be 'a really spiritual person with great gifts of intuition'.[52] When he returned to France, Richard wrote to some friends with the fervour of a new convert: 'I have passed 40 days with the most marvellous man in the world. It seems to me that I climbed to the top of a high mountain where my eyes were able to discern the magnificent horizons of which I have dreamed. To be sure throughout history there have been men who have come from on high to manifest the divine force and goodness.'[53] At the time, he evidently thought that Theon was such a man.

While Richard was in Tlemcen, his wife packed her bags and went back to Holland, taking their four children with her. Richard was shaken. Members of the Cosmic group offered him moral support. Soon, he was devoting more and more of his time to their activities. The former preacher's discourses at Cosmic meetings were well received by the audience. (It didn't hurt that he was a tall, attractive man, with an impressive beard.) On 25 April, Mirra wrote to Claire Thémanlys that the turnout at that week's meeting was especially large and 'attentive ears listened to the extremely beautiful words that our friend P.R. so eloquently spoke'.[54] In May, Richard went to Amsterdam to try to reconcile with his wife. She said she would return to him but never did. This left him free to give all his spare time to the Cosmic movement.

For all the effort that Mirra and others put into their meetings and publications, the Cosmic movement never attracted much attention in Paris or anywhere else. The Theons liked to say that their following was small but select. This did not prevent them from promoting themselves whenever and wherever they could. They were especially interested in attracting the 'élite', which meant, in practice, people with money and position. Madame Theon had an English schoolgirl's fascination for the aristocracy, and she and her husband were especially proud about having a few widowed or divorced noblewomen on their roster. To appeal to this high-class clientele, they asked Mirra to move the Paris centre to a new place near the Étoile. She did so towards the beginning of July 1907. A few days later, she left for Tlemcen, where she spent three months with her teachers. Some of the experiences I spoke about earlier must have taken place during this period. On 18 September, Madame Theon went to Italy to find a place for a new headquarters of the Cosmic movement. Mirra stayed back with Theon and Teresa. On 4 October, the three of them left for Algiers, where they boarded a ship for France.[55] When they reached Marseille, Theon and Teresa went to Florence to join Madame Theon while Mirra went north to Paris.

4

Pivotal Years

1

IN PARIS, MIRRA SPENT LITTLE TIME AT 15 RUE LEMERCIER. SHE received her mail at the new Cosmic centre and probably made that her base. In November, she seems to have gone to Beaugency.[1] Presumably, she wanted to spend time with André but she also needed to reflect on her situation and make some plans for the future. Her marriage with Henri had been under stress for more than two years.[2] It had reached a point where separation seemed inevitable. In January 1908, after a failed reconciliation meeting, Henri filed for divorce. On 30 January, Mirra received a summons from the court. She declined to appear or to hire a lawyer.[3]

Divorce became legal in France during the Revolution, was abolished after the restoration of the monarchy and not reinstated until 1884. There was no provision for divorce by mutual consent. One of the spouses had to prove in court that the other was adulterous, physically abusive or morally cruel. Henri based his case on Mirra's self-sufficient behaviour: She had ceased conjugal relations, abandoned the family home and subjected him to *injures graves*—a technical term in French law for words or actions damaging to the honour of a spouse.[4] In particular, Henri wrote through his lawyer, Mirra revolted against his authority, refused to explain her absences and 'created an independent existence for herself'. We do not know Mirra's side of the story since she chose not to answer the charges. Even if she had, it would not have changed the outcome. In divorce cases in patriarchal France, the odds were stacked against women. On 11 March, the court 'pronounced the divorce of the Morisset couple at the request and for the benefit of the husband'. Henri was given custody of André. A lawyer was appointed to oversee the division of property. Mirra would receive maintenance until the liquidation was complete, then nothing. She was obliged to pay all court costs.[5]

It was, to say the least, a trying period for her. In February, while the case was going on, she published an essay in the *Revue Cosmique* entitled 'Courage!': 'You who are weary, dejected, bruised, you who fall, who think perhaps you are defeated,' she began, 'listen to the voice of a friend. . . . She has, like you, crossed many deserts under the burden of the day, she has known thirst and hunger, solitude and abandonment, and, cruellest of all wants, the privations of the heart.' This was the message she had to give: 'Stay strong! Hear the lesson the rising sun brings to the earth with its first rays each morning. It is a lesson of hope, a message of solace. . . . There is no night without dawn, and sunrise prepares itself when darkness is thickest.' Those who have lost all, will regain all, for 'from the worst always comes the best'.[6] Writing this Cosmic pep talk was a way for Mirra to deal with her own sorrows. And the ordeals she had to face were not over.

Theon joined his wife in Italy in the second week of October 1907. In the November issue of the *Revue,* they gave their address as 15 Via Lorenzo il Magnifico, Florence. They hoped to make this the headquarters of an expanding Cosmic movement, but things didn't work out the way they wanted. By the beginning of 1908, they were thinking of moving to France. During this period, their relationship with Mirra cooled. She had planned to join them in Florence but the divorce case kept her in Paris, where she continued to work for the *Revue.* In the meantime, others were currying the Theons' favour and spreading rumours about her. This sort of backbiting was par for the course in occult groups but it took Mirra by surprise. She had devoted three years of her life to the Theons' work. For half of that time, she had, almost single-handedly, brought out the *Revue* and run the Paris centre. Now, Theon was listening to other people's lies. In March, a new recruit, a wealthy widowed baroness, came from Florence to Paris and began bossing her around, supposedly on Theon's orders. Mirra did what she could to accommodate the newcomer but tensions rose.

On 15 March, Theon wrote a curt letter to Mirra asking her to explain herself. He made it clear he would never allow anyone to come between him and her. This was a reference to her relationship with Paul Richard.[7] Since her return from Algeria the previous October, Mirra had grown increasingly close to Paul. He was the only member of the Cosmic group who stood firmly beside her during the turmoil of the last few months. Theon, who had welcomed him into the movement, now felt he was getting in the way. Like most guru figures, he demanded complete obedience. He also, like many other men in his position, took advantage of some of his female followers under the guise of promoting their spiritual welfare. Mirra was not among those who assented to this.[8] He seems to have taken her rejection badly.

In the beginning of April, Theon came to Paris and occupied a flat on Rue de la Pompe. Mirra met him there once. A few days later, he broke off all connection with her.[9] The April issue of the *Revue Cosmique* was the last one she worked on. That month's instalment of a series on the Vedas contained some speculations that may be related to her current predicament: If the All-Powerful and All-Merciful knows all beings, where does suffering come from? 'I have thought deeply about these things,' the writer said, 'but they are hidden from me.'[10]

2

During the summer of 1908, the Theons went to stay with Louis and Claire Thémanlys at their place in Courseulles-sur-Mer. In September, Madame Theon decided to go by herself to the Isle of Jersey, a British dependency off the Normandy coast.[11] During the crossing, she fell mortally ill and died almost immediately after reaching the port of Gorey. Theon was informed and reached Gorey on 11 September. He identified the deceased as 'Miriam Lin Woodroff', a final fictional identity for Mary Ware/Una/Madame Theon.[12] After the funeral, he went back to Courseulles, then to Paris, where he remained for several months. Depressed by his wife's death, he took little interest in the activities of the movement that she, much more than he, had nurtured. The December 1908 issue of the *Revue Cosmique* was the last to appear. After summarizing the seven volumes of the journal, the editor declared that a new phase was beginning. The seeds of the movement had been sown. Now it was time for cultivation, blooming and harvest.[13] This optimism did not last long. In May 1909, Theon went back to Tlemcen, where he remained, isolated and inactive, until his death in 1927. A century later, the huge mass of material that appeared in the *Revue Cosmique* and *Tradition Cosmique* lies unread in specialist libraries and on rarely visited websites. It had few readers even when it was published. The spread and cultural influence of the Cosmic movement never approached that of other occult groups, such as the Theosophical Society or Hermetic Order of the Golden Dawn. Its most important legacy was indirect. During her three-year association with the movement, Mirra absorbed a number of Cosmic ideas that derived from earlier traditions. When she went to India and spoke with Sri Aurobindo, he took up some of these ideas and transformed them into elements of his system of yoga. I will speak more about this later.

3

After her break with Theon in April 1908, Mirra went to live with a friend of hers in a flat at 49 Rue de Lévis, a mostly commercial street in the 17th arrondissement.[14] She knew the area well: To the west were Parc Monceau and Square du Roule, to the east, Rue Lemercier. Money was apparently not a problem. Her grandmother, Mirra, and mother, Mathilde, made sure she had enough to live in reasonable comfort. (Mirra Ismalun died the next year and doubtless left her granddaughter a bequest.) Sometime before the middle of August, Paul Richard moved into a separate flat in the Rue de Lévis building. He was eking out a living as a journalist and lawyer, writing columns for *Le Siècle* and representing the occasional impecunious client at the Court of Appeals. It was, he later wrote, 'a very respectable form of poverty'.[15] Without Mirra's money, he wouldn't have been able to pay his rent.

Mirra and Paul were now a couple but she made it clear from the start that it was not to be a typical intimate relationship. Years later, Paul explained: 'Although Mira had no inhibitions or moral objections about the full exchange of love and creative forces between human beings, she believed that the animal mode of reproduction was only a transitional one and that until new ways of creating life became biologically possible her own motherhood would have to remain spiritual.' In other words: No sex. This was all very well and good, Paul thought, but he 'believed that one should not refuse to share with another human being the joy of creation and the duty of the unborn'. In other words: He wanted sex. The solution was for him to have sexual relations with other women on the side. He did so with Mirra's 'full consent and even encouragement'.[16] She was under no illusions about his motives. He 'had a sexual side that was not at all healthy', she later remarked. 'He had a lot of mental knowledge (a lot, a very strong intelligence) but no spiritual life.'[17]

It was Paul's intellect that attracted Mirra, and the search for intellectual knowledge was the dominant theme of her life over the next six years. After her split with Theon, as she later recalled, she began to develop her mind to its farthest limits, studying all philosophies, juggling all ideas, realizing that all of them are in some sense true, and creating a synthesis.[18] She always regretted not having had the chance to make a thorough study of philosophy, as Matteo had done at school and the Polytechnique. She began to make up for this deficiency while a member of the Cosmic movement. Three years of grappling with the Theons' mythology taught her the value of organized thought. Her editorial labours sharpened her ear for good French prose. In contrast with the Theons' often unintelligible writings, her pieces in the journal were concise and clear. After leaving the movement, Mirra continued her intellectual development; at first, by means of literary collaborations with Paul. She urged him to expand his horizons. Instead of cranking out newspaper articles he should write a book. He agreed and the two began work on *L'Éther Vivant et le Réalisme Supra-nerveux* (The Living Ether and Supra-nervous Realism). Later, they had divergent recollections about the writing. She said it was based on her occult experiences: He simply wrote down what she told him. Paul admitted that Mirra was the driving force behind the book but dismissed it as a mixture of theosophical and spiritualistic notions that 'tended to confuse objective and subjective realities'. *L'Éther Vivant* came out in 1911 and attracted little attention. One of the few reviewers who noticed it said that it had some substance but was written in an unreadably turgid style.[19]

4

We know very little about Mirra's life between the middle of 1908 and the middle of 1910. Her only dated writing from this period, an essay from 1910, suggests it took a long time for the wounds of 1908 to heal. It is called 'Knowing How to Suffer'. 'My heart has suffered and groaned, ready to break beneath a sorrow too heavy, ready to sink beneath a pain too strong,' she began. 'But I have called to thee, divine comforter, I have prayed ardently to thee, and the splendour of thy dazzling light has appeared to me and revived me.' As the light penetrated her being, she 'perceived the path to follow, the benefit that can be drawn from suffering'. She concluded: 'Suffering is not obligatory, much less desirable, but when it comes to us, how useful it can be!'[20] This piece shows Mirra's inner resilience and also marks a change in her relationship with the Divine. For the first time, she addresses the Lord in the second person. In her sorrow, she found she was not alone.

Early in 1910, a colleague of Paul's asked him if he wanted to stand for the French India seat in the Chamber of Deputies in Paris. Paul jumped at the chance. He had long wanted to enter politics and was also interested in visiting India, which he and Mirra regarded as a land of spiritual knowledge. He sailed from Marseille on 25 March and reached Bombay two weeks later. There, he was handed a telegram saying that the party's plans had changed and the ticket had been given to someone else. Undeterred, he continued on to Pondicherry, the capital of French India. At a meeting with local notables, he mentioned his desire to speak with an Indian wise man. They laughed at the idea of finding such a person in Pondicherry. As it happened, however, Aurobindo Ghose, a leader of the Indian revolutionary movement, and also a philosopher and yogi, had recently come to town. Pursued by the British government, he had taken refuge in French territory and was staying incognito in the house of a local sympathizer.

The thirty-seven-year-old Aurobindo had led an eventful life. Born in Calcutta in 1872, he had been sent by his Anglophile father to a convent school in Darjeeling and later to England, where he was educated at St Paul's School, London, and King's College, Cambridge. His father wanted him to enter the Indian Civil Service and Aurobindo passed all the required examinations, but in the end deliberately failed the riding test so he would not have to become a cog in the British imperial machine. Returning to India in 1893, he worked in the administration of the maharaja of Baroda and later became vice principal of the local college. At the same time, he made contact with men who shared his ambition of launching a revolutionary movement. Leaving Baroda for Calcutta in 1906, he became the editor of a newspaper in which he openly declared that the aim of the nationalist movement had to be complete independence. In 1907, he was tried for sedition but acquitted for lack of evidence. The next year, he was arrested along with three dozen others for conspiring to carry out assassinations of British officials. After a year-long trial, he was acquitted. (The active leaders of the group, among them his brother Barindra Kumar, were sentenced to death, later commuted to transportation for life.)

During his imprisonment, Aurobindo spent most of his time in meditation and had a series of inner experiences that changed his outlook on life. From now on, his main preoccupations were studying and writing about Indian scriptures, and practising meditation and other yogic disciplines. After his release from jail, he resumed his political journalism, and in 1910, was charged with sedition again. This time, he decided to seek refuge in French India and went secretly to Pondicherry, reaching the town in April 1910, just days before the arrival of Paul Richard.

Some of the people Richard met in Pondicherry were in touch with Aurobindo and arranged a meeting between the two.[21] They talked, among other things, about Indian politics and Aurobindo's precarious position in Pondicherry. Richard told Aurobindo about his and Mirra's spiritual interests, and showed him some occult symbols. Aurobindo said he was familiar with the Indian ones.[22] Richard asked him for a photograph, which Aurobindo gave him. A day or two later, Richard went to Madras, where he met Annie Besant, the head of the Theosophical Society, and saw the designated messiah, J. Krishnamurti, playing tennis. When he got back to Paris, he showed Aurobindo's photograph to Mirra. She was not bowled over. Years later, she admitted: 'I can't say that when I saw that photograph I felt, "It's him!"'—that is, the figure she had seen in her visions. 'I had the impression he was a very interesting man, that's all.'[23]

5

While Paul was in India, Mirra shifted their belongings to a new house at 9 Rue du Val-de-Grâce, a pleasant little building at the far end of a large enclosed courtyard. Downstairs, there was a kitchen, a living room, a bathroom and a room Mirra used as a studio. Behind the kitchen was a dining room, which opened onto a veranda. Upstairs was a bedroom and minuscule bathroom. One wall of the studio was lined with bookshelves holding 3,000 volumes, among them Mirra's copies of the *Revue Cosmique* and *Tradition Cosmique*, which she still treasured.

Sometime earlier, Paul's wife had sued him for divorce. The judgment was delivered in May 1910. As the offending party, he lost the right to live with his children except when they were on vacation.[24] His and Mirra's domestic situation was now highly unorthodox: Two divorced people living in the same house without being married. Mirra's true friends took this in stride but some of her acquaintances made sure she knew they disapproved. Decades later, in an informal talk, she asked her interlocutor to imagine a woman with many friends. Suddenly, 'owing to a series of circumstances, she finds herself socially ostracized, because she went off with another man, or was living with someone without being officially married, all those social things that have no value in themselves'. Her so-called friends—not the ones who really loved her but her social acquaintances, people who used to smile warmly when they passed her on the street—began 'looking the other way and walking straight ahead without giving her a glance'. Some of them even whispered: 'She's a fallen woman!' Mirra—for the woman in the story clearly was her—said to herself, 'Oh, so *that's* where they are!'[25]

Mathilde Alfassa did not think ill of her daughter—she herself was separated from her husband—but still she was upset over Mirra's living arrangements. She pleaded with her to marry her partner as soon as possible.[26] (A divorced person could not remarry for ten months after the date of the divorce.) Mirra had no wish to go through the whole procedure again, but for the sake of her mother and to help out Paul, who, by marrying, would regain the right to see his children, she went ahead. The two were married on 5 May 1911, in the town hall of the 12th arrondissement.

6

Among the people Mirra and Paul received at 9 Rue du Val-de-Grâce was the scholar and traveller Alexandra David-Neel. Mirra first saw her when she gave a talk on Buddhism in Paris towards the end of 1910.[27] David-Neel was far from being a starry-eyed Western convert to an Eastern religion. For more than a decade, she had been insisting that Buddhism, as practised by most of its adherents, was a corruption of the original doctrine of Gautama Buddha. Buddhism was not a religion but an analytical philosophy. The most important Buddhist teachers did not propound a 'nebulous mysticism' but offered 'a rigorously logical method, a constant appeal to our reason'.[28] After the talk, a mutual acquaintance introduced David-Neel to Mirra. Not knowing the sort of person she was, Mirra gushed out: 'Oh, Madame, while you were speaking I saw Buddha there'—in a circle of blue light beside her shoulder. David-Neel was furious. 'That's impossible,' she growled. 'Buddha is in nirvana.'[29] After this awkward beginning, the two women found they had a lot in common. Mirra invited Alexandra to dinner and, on 19 December, she paid the first of many visits to the Richards' home.[30] There, Mirra and Paul learnt something about her unconventional life.

Louise Eugénie Alexandrine Marie David was born in Saint-Mandé, a suburb of Paris, in 1868. When she was six, her parents settled in Brussels. Educated in a convent school, she was a pious Catholic during her youth. Later, she joined the Unitarian church before rejecting Christianity altogether. In 1892, she went to London, where she frequented esoteric groups and became an active member of the Theosophical Society. Around the same time, she joined the Freemasons and associated with anarchist thinkers. As a young woman, she had trained as a singer, and performed in Belgium and France. Between 1894 and 1900, she tried to make a living as a professional performer, touring Indochina, France, Belgium, Greece and Tunisia, coming in contact with the demimonde of performers, impresarios and hangers-on. While in Tunis, she met a French engineer, Philippe Néel, whom she married in 1904.[31] She had as little regard for the institution of matrimony as Mirra, but she too discovered that it was hard for an independent woman to forego the social legitimacy offered by marriage. David-Neel and her husband had a stormy relationship, and spent little time together.

From the early 1890s, David-Neel had begun to write articles on a variety of subjects—Buddhism (which she had encountered in Vietnam), yoga (which she had encountered in India), and contemporary life in China and Korea, along with speculative works on human society. In 1890, she published her first book, *Pour la Vie* (For Life), an anarchist-flavoured social manifesto. This was followed nine years later by a scholarly study of the Chinese philosophers Mozi and Yang Zhu, whom she presented as early materialists and socialists. Her approach to Buddhism was similar. In *Le Modernisme Bouddhiste et le Bouddhisme du Bouddha* (Buddhist Modernism and the Buddhism of the Buddha), published in 1911, she wrote that Buddhism was above all an intellectual doctrine, which 'based its moral edifice on the brains of its adepts'. Even its mystical side was 'supported by a mental education conceived in an absolutely rational sense'.[32]

David-Neel went to the Richards' place on Christmas day 1910 for a group reading, on New Year's Eve for a 'philosophical meditation', and a dozen times over the next two months for evening discussions or dinner. Together with Mirra, she attended the Théâtre de l'Odéon and strolled in the Bois de Boulogne. There they watched the early French flying machines trying to get off the ground: 'O look, Alexandra,' Mirra would cry. 'This time it rose 4 or 5 metres into the air!' Alexandra, ever the sceptic, retorted: 'Do you think it was really that much?' Mirra, ten years younger than her new friend, was fascinated by her tales of travel in Asia and impressed by her knowledge of Eastern religions. Alexandra was struck by Mirra's intelligence, her gentleness and her 'tendency to self-effacement'. She once was surprised to hear her speak of the 'veiled' role women should play. Still, she could see that beneath her calm exterior, Mirra 'concealed a great deal of energy'.[33]

In the beginning of 1911, Alexandra's relationship with her husband was passing through an especially turbulent phase. To ease the, tension he suggested she take a trip abroad. She accepted and in August departed for India. After spending three months in Ceylon, where she met Buddhist leaders such as Anagarika Dharmapala, she arrived in south India in mid-November. On her way to the headquarters of the Theosophical Society in Madras, she stopped in Pondicherry, where she spoke with Aurobindo Ghose. Later, she wrote that he belonged 'to that uncommon category that I so much admire, the reasonable mystics. I am truly grateful to the friends [the Richards] who advised me to visit this man. He thinks, with such clarity, there is such lucidness in his reasoning, such lustre in his eyes, that he leaves one with the impression of having contemplated the genius of India such as one dreams it to be after reading the noblest pages of Hindu philosophy.'[34]

When David-Neel reached Madras, she was met not by representatives of the Theosophical Society but by the chief of police. He wanted to know about her dealings with Aurobindo, whom the British still looked upon as a dangerous revolutionary. Eventually, she was able to convince them that her interests were purely philosophical. In Madras, she learnt that the thirteenth Dalai Lama, the religious and political leader of Tibet, was living in exile in Kalimpong in northern India. She decided to go meet him but her motives were not religious. 'To come home with a study of Lamaism written after meeting the Dalai Lama—that would be a fabulous piece of orientalist research!' she wrote to her husband. After spending the winter in Calcutta, she went north to Kalimpong and, in April 1912, was granted an audience with the Dalai Lama. Ushered into this presence, she offered him a scarf (as she had been instructed to do) and received his benediction (which she could have done without). Afterwards, the two talked about various things through an interpreter. 'He seems quite cheerful,' she wrote to her husband the next day. 'Clearly he's not an idiot but neither is he an intellectual as we understand the term.' Two months later, in Sikkim, she met His Holiness again. This time, they spoke about Mahayana philosophy. Before leaving Sikkim, she wrote a letter to Mirra, which unfortunately has not survived. Did she tell her friend, as she had told her husband, that she did not like 'the sort of Buddhist Catholicism' that the 'Tibetan Pope' presided over?[35] David-Neel later became famous as an expert on Tibetan Buddhism but she never got over her dislike of religious pomp and ceremony.

7

In September 1911, Mirra and Paul went on holiday to Cluses, a town at the foot of the French Alps. With them were Paul's elder children, Jacques and Hélène, aged ten and eight. They didn't take to Mirra, whom they found affected and remote. (They complained she wore a veil even while walking in the mountains.[36]) This was the last occasion they and Mirra spent time together. On 21 September, Mirra wrote a postcard to her friend Johannes Hohlenberg, a Danish artist, in which she recalled their philosophical conversations in Paris and encouraged him in his spiritual endeavours.[37] In closing, she mentioned that she and Paul would soon return to Paris.

The commercial failure of *L'Éther Vivant* meant that Paul had to resume his journalism to help pay the bills. He pronounced himself an expert on foreign affairs and contributed hundreds of articles to the liberal daily *L'Aurore.* He also gave as much time as he could to his and Mirra's next book, a work of speculative theology called *Les Dieux* (The Gods). Its purpose, Mirra wrote to David-Neel that November, was to help men and women break the cords that bound them to the gods. Mirra thought that her friend, as a non-theistic Buddhist, would respond well to this. She herself was much taken by Buddhism at the time. She told David-Neel that Paul found her words 'so impregnated with Buddhism' that 'he used to call [her] a Buddhist'.[38]

André, who could visit his mother freely now that she and Paul were married, used to see them working together at 9 Rue du Val-de-Grâce: 'After lunch, specially when the weather was bad, we went to the studio. Paul Richard stretched on a couch, lit his pipe, and they started working. That is, my mother wrote in her own handwriting what he dictated. I could not help but notice that Mother was rectifying most of Paul's dictation.'[39] Mirra's collaboration with Paul was one of several sorts of intellectual work she was involved in at this time. Towards the end of 1911, she joined the Union de Pensée Féminine (Union for Feminine Thought), a group founded by the feminist thinker and educator Lydie Martial. Its aim was 'to realize and express the particularity of feminine thought, the complement of masculine thought', and to prepare women for the full 'exercise of their freedom, their duties, and their rights'.[40] Mirra felt comfortable with Martial's gradualist approach to the 'woman question', an issue that generated much debate, and much masculine discomfort, during the Belle Époque. Between December 1911 and April 1912, she gave a half-dozen talks to members of the union. In one, she seconded Martial's idea 'that it would be wrong for women to want to think in the same way as men', for if they did they would be in danger 'of losing their own qualities, that is, profound intuition and practical deduction, without acquiring those of their masculine counterparts, that is, logical reasoning and the capacity of analysis and synthesis'. The mental role of women was not to speculate on the metaphysical causes of phenomena 'but to draw practical conclusions from these phenomena'.[41]

Mirra's primary interest was not 'feminine thought' but the process of thought in general. When we look within, she said in one talk, we become aware of a 'whole stream of incoherent thoughts'. If we observe them closely, we notice that some thoughts 'are stronger and more tenacious than the others'. 'Look at one of these ideas,' she suggested. 'Ask yourself why you have this opinion on that subject rather than another.' The answer will almost always be the same: 'Because it is the opinion prevalent in your environment.' To escape this social contagion (as psychologists now call it), 'we must take these ideas one after another and analyse them by calling on all our common sense, all our reason, our highest sense of equity; we must weigh them in the balance of our acquired knowledge and accumulated experience, and then try to align them with one another, to establish harmony among them'.[42]

In her talks, Mirra sometimes referred to God or the Divine but her tone was not religious. Instead, she urged her listeners to practise self-discipline. This comes out clearly in a series of presentations she gave to a circle of friends that met weekly between May and July 1912 'with the aim of gaining self-knowledge and self-mastery'. This was the fourth discussion group she was associated with in Paris—after Idéa, the Cosmic centre and the Union for Feminine Thought—and, by now, she knew how to make the meetings productive. At the end of each session, the members decided on a topic to be discussed the following week. At home, they reflected on the topic and perhaps wrote down some ideas. Mirra, who was the lynchpin of the group, crafted her presentations in well-structured prose. Speaking on the theme 'What is the psychological difficulty I can best study by means of experience?' she focused on 'excessive sensitivity'. People who had this problem (and she admitted she was one) found it difficult 'not to watch [themselves] acting, feeling and thinking, and this results in a lack of spontaneity that approaches insincerity'. To get over this problem, she said 'we must understand that if our sensitivity puts us in contact with all human sufferings, we must at the same time be sufficiently vigilant and discerning to dissolve these sufferings as they come', seeing that at root 'they are purely imaginary'.[43] Speaking on the topic 'What is the most useful work to be done at the present time', she outlined an ambitious programme of personal and social development: The first step was for people 'to become conscious of the divine Presence in themselves and of their identity with it'; the next, to individualize higher states of being and to tap unseen universal forces; the third, to 'speak again to the world the eternal word in a new form adapted to its present mentality', and finally 'to establish an ideal society in a propitious spot for the flowering of the new race'.[44]

In the last of this series of talks, delivered on 2 July, Mirra spoke about human relationships. Using the terminology of the Cosmic movement, she said that people could meet one another on four different levels: Physical, vital, psychic and mental. Only a 'few rare beings' were 'close to us in all four modes of existence at the same time'. These were our friends in the true sense of the word. More important than our relations with other human beings was our relationship with the inner Godhead. When we become one with it, 'we become one with all in their depth' and 'it is through It and by It that we must come into contact with all beings'.[45]

Later in July, Mirra and Paul went to Normandy for a brief vacation. Photographs taken at the Trouville beach show the two of them on a tennis court. Mirra, wearing flat black shoes, an ankle-length skirt and a full-sleeved blouse, looks intent as she moves towards the ball and swings her racket.

8

In her talks on thought, Mirra recommended self-observation and self-analysis. In her spiritual diary, which she began to keep around this time, she framed her observations and inner aspirations as a conversation with the Divine. In the first available extract, dated 2 November 1912, she wrote:

> It has taken me several weeks to learn that the reason for this written meditation, its justification, lies in the very fact of addressing it daily to Thee. In this way I shall put into material shape each day a little of the conversation I have so often with Thee. . . . By turning towards Thee, by immersing myself in Thy light at the moment when I consider these things, little by little I shall see them more like what they really are,—until the day when, having made myself one in identity with

> Thee, I shall no more have anything to say to Thee, for then I shall be Thou.

The language, which is that of French (and English) translations of the Bible, now sounds dated, but the sincerity of Mirra's effort at consecration shines through. Day by day, she recorded the ups and downs of her spiritual life. On 19 November, she wrote that the union between her individual self and the Divine was constant, adding: 'I know that this state of union is poor and precarious compared with that which it will become possible for me to realise tomorrow.' Two weeks later, she noted:

> So long as one element of the being, one movement of the thought is still subjected to outside influences, not solely under Thine, it cannot be said that the true Union is realised; there is still the horrible mixture without order and light,—for that element, that movement is a world, a world of disorder and darkness.

And nine days later:

> I await, without haste, without inquietude, the tearing of another veil, the Union made more complete. I know that the veil is formed of a whole mass of small imperfections, of attachments without number. . . . How shall all these disappear?[46]

Mirra wrote regularly in her diary for fifteen years. Later, she made a selection of entries and published them under the title *Prières et Méditations* (Prayers and Meditations). This book gives us an idea of her spiritual life as she viewed it herself. But how did others view her? We get a few glimpses from the diary of a woman whom Mirra met at this time. Towards the beginning of 1912, her mother, Mathilde, began living on the first floor of a house in Montmorency, a northern suburb of Paris. One day, Mathilde told Marie Potel, the wife of the owner of the building, that she ought to meet her daughter. Mirra, she said, was around Marie's age. She had a thirteen-year-old son but 'on account of her philosophical ideas' she had divorced her first husband and married again. This put Marie off, but when the two women met, she found she liked Mirra because of her gentle nature. During the spring, they had a few casual conversations. Then, one day in mid-July, Mirra came downstairs just to visit Marie. They spoke about various things, then Mirra remarked: 'Often we don't know what we have come here to do. Ultimately it hardly matters whether we know it or not.' Marie replied: 'Yes, provided we do it.' Mirra saw that Marie understood her. For Marie, it was a transformative moment. She later wrote in her diary: 'I felt a living soul *for the first time in my life*.'[47] She thanked Mirra for her visit and said she would be happy to meet her again.

A few days later, Mirra came down while Marie was in the garden. Seeing that her new friend was feeling sad, she asked if she could read her some passages from the manuscript of *Les Dieux*. Marie agreed. Mirra's voice had a remarkably calming effect on her. After the reading, she went up to Mirra, kissed her and told her she liked her very much. Mirra said nothing but Marie read in her eyes that she returned her affection. In August, Marie was away on vacation. During this period, she fell into a deep depression. When she returned to Montmorency and saw Mirra again, she asked her if the two of them had something to do together. Mirra dodged the question but told Marie that she was her friend 'in the deepest sense of the word'. Marie blurted out that she looked on Mirra as her spiritual master. Mirra told her: 'You have only one master, who dwells within you.'[48]

'Thus began my period of spiritual initiation,' Marie wrote in her diary. In the months that followed, she recorded what she learnt from the one she now regarded as her initiator, her master, her spiritual mother. Mirra never gave her direct spiritual instruction and never played the guru, but she realized that she now had a spiritual responsibility towards Marie. She took this seriously. Once, in a tender voice she told Marie: 'You have put your trust in me. But it sometimes happens that we put our trust in someone who does not deserve it—' Marie divined that Mirra had once put her trust in someone who was unworthy of it and who had led her astray. She loved her all the more for revealing this to her.[49]

During the months that followed, Mirra, Paul and André visited Montmorency almost every weekend. Sometimes, Matteo and his wife, Éva, came too. Marie was welcome to join these family gatherings. To her, Paul seemed like an 'epitome of benignancy'. She noticed however that her husband and Matteo found him intimidating. She considered Matteo 'gentle and intelligent', but felt that his government work 'was causing him to lose his higher intellectual qualities'. Éva struck her as the sort of woman 'who loves only her husband and children'. The one member of the family who stood out was Mirra, who invariably was kind but had unspoken depths she did not show to everyone. From the end of September, Marie began to visit the Richards in Paris. At first, she found the décor at 9 Rue du Val-de-Grâce too luxurious for her taste: 'These oriental carpets and antiques, what cause do they benefit?' (In other words: Why does a spiritual master have to surround herself with beautiful things?) But when Mirra read from the manuscript of *Les Dieux*, Marie 'could see in her a higher, more accomplished self'.[50]

Mirra invited Marie to attend the meetings of her discussion group. One evening in November, Paul brought a special guest, the Indian Sufi master and musician Inayat Khan. For the last two months, Khan and his Royal Musicians of Hindustan had been performing in Paris concert halls. A few discerning listeners could appreciate the sounds of the tabla, dilruba, sitar and especially the veena, which produced 'as if by magic, all the inflections and colour of the human voice'. But most members of the audience were bewildered by the 'strange and hallucinating flavour' of the music. They liked it better when the musicians backed up the Dutch exotic dancer Margaretha MacLeod, better known as Mata Hari. Despite her claims of Indian ancestry, MacLeod knew nothing about Indian dance and, after her performances, the musicians could hardly contain their laughter. One of them later recalled: 'First she swayed to the right, then to the left, and then she stood still for a bit' and all the men in the audience exclaimed: '*Ah, c'est charmant.*'[51]

Inayat Khan, who two years later would found the Sufi Order of the West, had little opportunity to speak about Sufism while in Paris. He must have been happy to find a receptive audience at 9 Rue du Val-de-

Grâce. He described the stages of the Sufi path and the different degrees of union with the Divine. Years later, Mirra recalled he said that 'for the Sufis there was a state higher than that of adoration and surrender to the Divine . . . the last stage of progress is when there is no longer any distinction; there is no longer any sort of adoration or surrender or consecration; it is an utterly simple state in which one makes no distinction between the Divine and oneself'.[52]

A few months later, another Eastern spiritual teacher came to Paris: 'Abdu'l-Bahá, the leader of the Baha'i Faith. One of Paul's colleagues, Hippolyte Dreyfus, was a prominent Baha'i, and, in January 1913, he invited Paul and Mirra to his townhouse on Rue Greuze to meet his master. They both were favourably impressed. Over the next six months, they met 'Abdu'l-Bahá more than twenty times. From February, Mirra was sometimes asked to speak to the master's followers in French. Since she knew little about Bahaism, she drew on her 1912 talks, *L'Éther Vivant* and *Les Dieux*. The results were well received. After a presentation on 14 February, 'Abdu'l-Bahá's secretary, Ahmad Sohrab, called her 'a brilliant and inspired orator, filled with fire and enthusiasm'.[53] A month or so later, before a scheduled talk, 'Abdu'l-Bahá told Mirra he was not feeling well and asked her to take his place. She said she could hardly do that. She was not even a member of the faith. How could she address his followers? He told her it did not matter. She just should concentrate and say what came to her. Mirra did as he suggested. When the moment arrived she rose, stood quietly and then spoke for a good half-hour. Afterwards, people told her, 'You spoke admirably.' She replied: 'It wasn't me.'[54]

That April, 'Adbu'l-Bahá toured Germany and Austria–Hungary. The Richards stayed in touch with his French followers. They were among a dozen people who met the master at the station when he returned to Paris on 1 May. They attended Baha'i meetings throughout the month. Mirra often gave talks in French. On 12 May and again on 25 May, she and Paul received the master and his entourage at 9 Rue du Val-de-Grâce. They also had several private meetings with him. On 14 May, for example, they stayed up late with him talking 'on the existence of God, divine philosophy, sufism, and pantheism'.[55] On 9 June, two days before the master departed for Egypt, Mirra gave a brief talk to his followers. They might feel sad now, she said, but if they held the thought of him clearly in their minds 'separation no longer exists, it is an illusory appearance'. When he arrived in Egypt, 'Adbu'l-Bahá sent a 'Tablet' or inspired message to the Richards, urging them to continue to spread his message. Eight months later, he sent another.[56] By this time, most of his followers in Paris thought of Mirra and Paul as fellow converts but in fact they never became members of the Baha'i faith. They did, however, greatly admire 'Adbu'l-Bahá. 'His sincerity and his aspirations for the Divine were simple and very spontaneous,' Mirra later recalled.[57]

9

The year 1913 was a busy one for Mirra. Besides attending Baha'i events, she had weekly sessions with her discussion group, Sunday lunches with André, visits from and to her mother and brother, one visit with her father, occasional meetings with other members of her extended family, and numerous meetings with friends and acquaintances, including Marie Potel. The Richards' circle of friends now included the prominent artist Georges Picard, the up-and-coming painter Johannes Hohlenberg, and the young artist and poet Charles de Fontenay. Somehow, Mirra also found time to go to galleries and theatres, and to play an occasional game of tennis.

References and allusions in Mirra's talks show the range of her current reading: Psychological monographs, self-help works, the writings of Swami Vivekananda, the *Dhammapada.* Her tastes in contemporary French literature were eclectic: Maurice Maeterlinck's fairy-tale play *The Blue Bird*, with its facile moral uplift, Octave Mirbeau's decadent novel *The Torture Garden*, with its echoes of the Marquis de Sade.[58] She also read the serial novels published in the newspaper *Le Matin.* One she could still remember fifty years later was *L'Amant de la Momie* (The Mummy's Lover), a 'psychic novel' by Antoine Wylm. She found it rather silly but the themes it touched on—death, immortality and the redeeming power of love—gave her much to think about. She felt the writer had hit on something true but expressed it imperfectly. Death was not the way to immortality. Love did not mean letting somebody else spoil your life. She pondered over these questions, looking for a way to 'bring things to the true position'.[59]

Around this time, Paul accepted a commission to compile passages from the scriptures of various religions and publish them in a book meant to show that all religions and philosophies are one. He and de Fontenay were lead editors of this project. They were aided by specialists in Chinese, Islamic, Buddhist, Zoroastrian, Armenian and Greek texts. Mirra was also involved. Around this time, she made a series of translations of English renderings of Hindu and Buddhist texts, apparently with the idea of including them in the book. De Fontenay stopped by almost every evening, and he and the Richards sat up late and discussed their project and the general state of the world.

The period just before the First World War was a great time for international organizations. Mirra and her friends were part of this mostly ineffectual trend. On 1 July 1913, she had a meeting with the Duchess of Uzès, a well-known philanthropist and author, who was a member of the committee of honour of the International Union of Fine Arts and Letters. Two weeks later, she and Paul attended a session of the Sixth International Congress of Progress in Religion. Established on the model of the more famous World Parliament of Religions, the Congress brought together members of different Protestant sects, representatives of 'other religions', and a handful of spiritualists and Freemasons. Unsurprisingly, few Catholics attended. The organizers had invited 'Abdu'l-Bahá, but he could not make it. Instead, he sent a letter expressing the hope that the Congress would 'unite the hearts of the inhabitants of the world' and would be 'a means of fostering peace between religions'. Hippolyte Dreyfus was the Baha'i representative on a panel that discussed the question 'Is a universal religion desirable or possible?' Other panellists included the German theologian Rudolph Otto, the French polymath Théodore Reinach, the Scottish liberal pastor Walter Walsh, and, representing Buddhism, the Ceylonese diplomat Don Baron Jayatilaka. (Rabindranath Tagore was slated to represent Hinduism but was unable to attend.) Mirra and Paul were among those who supported the universalist position but most of those present, Otto included, spoke against it.[60]

The Richards spent all of August and part of September in southern France and Switzerland, and the next few weeks in a place near Fontainebleau, where they finished work on *Les Dieux*. For Paul, the book was a way of freeing himself from the all-powerful God of Calvinism, who never thought twice about punishing His creatures. The true God, he and Mirra insisted, was 'the Divine Presence within'—one 'who was neither the spouse nor the father but the self in its growth and progressive manifestation'. And this 'self in every being and the single universal Self were one'.[61]

Paul later wrote that this phase of his life with Mirra was 'one of harmony on every level of work, thoughts and feelings'. He was aware she was 'undergoing an intense mystic and spiritual development'. Each morning, before sunrise, she meditated. During the day, she went out or took care of household affairs. In the evening, before retiring, she wrote in her diary. Occasionally, she read passages to Paul. They seemed to him 'an uninterrupted oblation to her God'.[62]

Looking back on her inner development a half-century later, Mirra said that during this period she underwent 'a sort of reversal of consciousness'. From then on, she was aware that all she did was 'the expression of the divine will in oneself'. But, she clarified, it was 'the divine will *at the centre of oneself*' and there remained 'an activity in the physical mind'—the part of the mind that deals with tooth-brushing, meal-serving, tram-catching, meeting-attending and so forth. At first, the feeling of being moved by the Divine faded when she interacted with others but gradually it became more and more constant.[63]

On 6 October 1913, the Richards returned to 9 Rue du Val-de-Grâce. The next day, Mirra wrote in her diary:

> This return after an absence of three months to the house that is consecrated to Thee, O Lord, has been the occasion for two experiences. The first is that in my outer being, my surface consciousness, I no longer have the least feeling of being in my own

> home and the owner of anything there: I am a stranger in a strange land, much more a stranger than in the open countryside among the trees; and I smile . . . at the idea of having felt myself 'mistress of the house'.

The second experience was finding that 'the whole atmosphere of the house is charged with a religious solemnity; one goes immediately into the depths; meditations here are more ingathered and serious; dispersion vanishes to give place to concentration; and I feel this concentration literally descending from my head and entering into my heart; and the heart seems to attain a depth more profound than the head.' She concluded: 'A new door has opened in my being and an immensity has appeared before me.'[64]

In the middle of October, Mirra resumed her social life, receiving visits from de Fontenay, Marie Potel and others, having lunch with André at Rue du Val-de-Grâce, and with her mother and Matteo at their places, and once attending a conference at the Sorbonne. On New Year's Eve, she and Paul invited a dozen people for dinner. At midnight, she and her guests sat in silence, consecrating the first minute of the year to the Divine. The next day, she wrote in her diary that she hoped the new year would be glorified by this consecration, that those who sought the Divine would find him and that those who suffered would feel him gradually pierce 'the hard crust of their obscure consciousness'. She herself took a vow that she would turn all her thoughts to the Divine Presence in her heart.[65] It was hard to sustain this pitch of concentration for long. On 5 January 1914, she sat before her notebook, unable to write, overcome with the feeling that everything within her was 'mediocre, worthless, insipid, hopelessly commonplace'. Despondent, she wrote and underlined: '*I am an utter zero in the world.*' Then she realized that none of this was important: 'Provided Thy work is accomplished, Thy manifestation takes place and the earth becomes more and more Thy harmonious and fruitful kingdom, it matters little whether I accomplish this Work or not.'[66] All that mattered was that God's Will was done.

10

Paul Richard had stayed in touch with Aurobindo Ghose since the two of them met in Pondicherry in 1910. Aurobindo told him about the pressure the British government was putting on the French to have him expelled from their territory. The problem became acute in 1911 after some Pondicherry-based revolutionaries engineered the assassination of an official in British India. The government of French India sent a report to the Colonial Office in Paris. There, it came to the attention of Matteo Alfassa, who knew about his brother-in-law's connection with Aurobindo. Matteo asked to see the report and buried it in a drawer. Officials in Pondicherry wondered why they never heard back from Paris.[67]

In a letter of July 1911, Aurobindo told Richard that he planned to remain in Pondicherry until he achieved siddhi or perfection in yoga. Once that happened (he thought it might take a few years), he would return to British India to carry out the work he intended to accomplish in the world. In August 1912, he explained to another correspondent that this work would have four parts: 'To reexplain the Sanatana Dharma [eternal religion] to the human intellect in all its parts, from a new standpoint; to establish a Yogic sadhana which will not only liberate the soul, but prepare a perfect humanity'; 'to work for her [India's] restoration to her proper place in the world'; and to remodel human society 'so as to be fit to contain that perfection'.[68]

Towards the beginning of 1914, Paul decided to go to Pondicherry. His main aim was to stand as an independent candidate for the French India seat in the Chamber, but he also wanted to resume his contact with Aurobindo. Mirra would accompany him. To raise funds for the journey, she liquidated a quarter of her assets.[69] She and Paul spent the beginning of the year making preparations. On 3 March, she sat in her studio and wrote:

> As the day of departure draws near, I enter into a sort of contemplation; I turn with tender solemnity towards those thousand little nothings around us which have silently, for so many years, played

> their role of faithful friends; I thank them gratefully for all the charm they were able to give to the outer side of our life.

Then, looking towards the future, she reflected:

> What it holds in store for us I do not know nor care to know; outer circumstances have no importance at all; my only wish is that this may be for us the beginning of a new inner period in which, more detached from material things, we may be more conscious of Thy law and more one-pointedly consecrated to its manifestation.

Two or three days later, she and Paul left for Geneva. There—thinking of André, her mother, brother and friends—she wrote of 'the sentimental and physical attachment that causes a painful wrench when bodies part'.[70]

Mirra and Paul boarded their ship, the Japanese steamer *Kaga Maru,* in Marseille on 7 March. It departed the next morning and reached Port Said on 13 March. The following day, as the ship passed through the Suez Canal, with 'the immutable solitude of the desert' on either side; Mirra wrote in her diary that she understood why hermits used 'to withdraw into these immense stretches of sand' to find the Divine. But, she added, 'for one who knows Thee, Thou art everywhere'.[71] By 15 March, the ship was in the Red Sea. As it was Sunday, a Christian service was held. Mirra did not attend. Later, the clergyman asked why she had not joined them. She replied: 'Sir, I'm sorry but I don't believe in religion.' 'Oh, you are a materialist?' 'No, not at all.' 'Then why?' Mirra tried to avoid answering but when the man insisted, she said: 'I don't feel that you are sincere, neither you nor your flock. You went there to fulfil a social duty and social custom but not at all because you really wanted to enter into relationship with God.' 'Enter into relationship with God! But we can't do that! All that we can do is to say some good words.' 'That's precisely why I didn't go,' Mirra said.[72]

She could not shake the gentleman, who went on to tell her that he was going to China 'to convert the heathens'. This was more than she could handle. 'Listen,' she said, 'even before your religion was born—not even two thousand years ago—the Chinese had a very high philosophy and a path leading them to the Divine, and when they think of Westerners, they think of them as barbarians. And you are going there to convert people who know more about it than you? What are you going to teach them? To be insincere, to perform hollow ceremonies instead of following a profound philosophy and detachment from life that will lead them to a more spiritual consciousness? . . . I don't think it's a very good thing you are going to do.' 'Eh, I fear I can't be convinced by your words!' the clergyman said. 'Oh!' Mirra replied. 'I'm not trying to convince you, I just described the situation to you. I don't see why barbarians should decide to teach civilised people what they knew long before you.'[73] It is interesting to contrast her rejection of organized religion with the elevated tone of her diary, which uses what many would call religious language to express her personal relation with the Divine.

On 18 March, the *Kaga Maru* rounded Perim Island and began the longest leg of its journey: East and south to Colombo. That evening, Mirra wrote in her diary that when one opens oneself to the Divine, 'one no longer can worry about future circumstances or the turn events take; it is with perfect serenity that one does at every moment what one thinks best, convinced that the best is sure to come'.[74]

5

India and After

1

MIRRA AND PAUL DISEMBARKED IN COLOMBO ON 27 MARCH 1914. The next day, they met Anagarika Dharmapala, the founder of the Maha Bodhi Society, and later made the crossing to India. The train from Rameshwaram reached Pondicherry on the morning of 29 March. The Richards checked into the Grand Hôtel d'Europe, a rundown establishment on Rue Suffren. In the afternoon, they went to meet Aurobindo Ghose. He and his companions were living in a rented house at 41 Rue François Martin. Near the gate was a British plainclothes policeman, who kept track of all comings and goings. Inside, they crossed a courtyard and veranda, and climbed a winding staircase that led to the first floor. Aurobindo was at the top of the stairs. He led them to his room at the end of the veranda.

Mirra's meeting with Aurobindo was a crucial turning point in her life. So much has been written and spoken about it over the last 110 years that it is hard to determine how she and Aurobindo experienced it at the time. Both mentioned the meeting in their diaries but provided few details. Aurobindo wrote that he spent the morning of 29 March absorbed in his sadhana or practice of yoga. In the afternoon, he received visitors, first 'R'—that is, Richard, evidently accompanied by Mirra—then the

Tamil poet Subramania Bharati. Mirra, in her entry of 30 March, wrote that 'we'—she and Paul—saw a man the previous day—Aurobindo—whom she felt had achieved full consciousness of the Divine Presence.[1] She said nothing about the visual ambience or spiritual mood of the meeting. For that, we have to turn to a conversation of 1961: 'I climbed that staircase [in Aurobindo's house] and he was waiting for me, standing at the top of the stairs.' He looked exactly like the figure she had seen in the visions she had published in the *Revue Cosmique*: 'Dressed the same way, in the same position, in profile, his head held high. He turned his head towards me and I saw in his eyes that it was he. . . . The inner experience became one with the outer experience and there was a fusion, the decisive shock.'[2] Thinking back on the experience after forty-seven years, she was so focused on Aurobindo that Paul disappeared from the picture. She was all alone with her Lord.[3]

This account was one of several in which the Mother told others that when she first saw Sri Aurobindo she recognized him at once as the Divine. She expressed this in different ways. In her 1920 account of her early spiritual development, which I referred to in previous chapters, she said that when she saw him she 'recognized in him the well-known being whom I used to call Krishna'. In 1927 and again in 1929, she told a disciple that when she saw Sri Aurobindo she realized at once he was the Lord, the Divine. Six years later, she told another follower that the moment she saw him she 'at once recognized him for what he was', that is, 'the incarnation'. In 1961, she told a third disciple that she recognized Sri Aurobindo as the being of light she had seen in her visions of 1905–07.[4] Writing in her diary on 30 March 1914, she did not mention Krishna or the Lord or the incarnation or the being of light. She wrote of Aurobindo as a 'marvel', who had been created by the 'Divine Builder'. Seeing him, her heart overflowed with joy and gratitude; she felt a boundless hope, inexpressible adoration, wordless reverence.[5]

Aurobindo did not record his impressions of Mirra in his diary. He mentioned Paul ('Richard'), Mirra ('Madame Richard') or both fourteen times between April and December 1914. Most of these references are insignificant, giving little indication of how he felt about them.

On two occasions, he expressed reservations about Paul's ideas in *Les Dieux*. Once, he noted that the Richards were open to his ideas about dharma or spirituality but 'more in mentality & prana [life-force] than for illumination'. In a letter to an associate, he wrote that the two of them were 'rare examples of European Yogins who have not been led away by Theosophical and other aberrations'.[6] These remarks do not give the whole picture. On several occasions, Aurobindo told others that when he first met Mirra he was struck by her ability to surrender herself completely to the workings of the yoga force.[7] By 'surrender', he meant what Sanskrit writers call atma-samarpana: The offering of one's self to the Divine or to a guru, allowing a higher force to work. In 1962, the Mother explained how she experienced this. Once, when she and Paul went to see Aurobindo, she told him about her efforts to calm her mind. 'When I wanted to be silent, I could,' she said, but as soon as she ceased wanting only that, the invasion of ordinary thought resumed and everything had to be done over again. She told him this in very few words, then sat quietly as Aurobindo and Paul began to speak about 'the world, yoga, the future, all sorts of things'. Their talk did not interest her. She sat for some time, then, unexpectedly, she felt 'a great Force' enter into her—'a peace, a silence, something massive!' When the meeting was over, she got up and found that her mind was completely free from disturbing thoughts. And this time, the silence did not go away. In her heart, she thanked Aurobindo and the Lord.[8] In the days that followed, she watched as all the past results of her spiritual seeking—'a superb mental construction'—were demolished. Writing on 6 April, she said it was as if her entire 'intellectual foundation' had disappeared, as if she had 'lost the power to formulate, express, synthesize, understand her experience . . . almost as if [her] consciousness was gone'. Yet, she felt no fear. Surrendering herself to the movement, she took refuge with the Lord. Once the process of emptying was complete, 'slowly, slowly, as though falling drop by drop, something was built up again'.[9]

Mirra's surrender to the Lord, whom she identified with Aurobindo, was an inner movement, noticed by no one but him. Later, she discovered how to give it outward form. She observed it was the custom in India for people to do pranam (bending and touching another's feet) as a sign of respect to parents, elders and teachers. One day, a young follower of Aurobindo's did this to her and she felt 'a current of Power' flowing down through her body. Later, she did pranam to Aurobindo and felt a similar current of power descending through his body into hers. She realized that the true meaning of pranam was to open oneself by an outward act of surrender to the action of an inner force.[10]

2

The French East India Company set up a trading post in Pondicherry in 1674. For the next 140 years—a time of worldwide conflict between the French, British and Dutch regimes—the town passed back and forth between these imperial powers. In the middle of the eighteenth century, French Pondicherry enjoyed a period of influence and prosperity. Using the town as a base, Governor Joseph François Dupleix extended France's influence in south India. French merchants and their Indian agents amassed huge fortunes exporting textiles to France. All this came to an end when the British occupied Pondicherry during the European wars of 1792–1815. After the defeat of Napoleon, the British returned five territories in southern and eastern India to the French. Pondicherry, now a shadow of its former self, was the largest. It became the capital of the French Settlements in India, a coaling station for ships en route to Indochina, an exporter of peanuts, a centre for smuggling and a thorn in the side of British Indian officials.

The oval-shaped town was laid out on a grid, with parallel avenues running north and south, intersected by parallel streets. A drainage canal bisecting the oval split the town into two unequal halves: To the east, near the seafront, was the European quarter, called by the French the *ville blanche* ('white town'), to the west the Indian quarter or *ville noire* ('black town'). A park in the centre occupied the site of the destroyed French fort. Around it were the governor's palace, administrative buildings, a hospital, a post office and a club reserved for Europeans. The houses of French officials lay behind white-painted walls, topped sometimes by clusters of pink bougainvillea. Indian merchants built their mansions in the better parts of the Indian town. The mud-and-thatch huts of the working class merged gradually with the surrounding villages.

Under the Third Republic, a limited number of residents of French India were given the right to elect a representative to the Chamber of Deputies. The results were derisory. 'Of all the [French] colonial elections,' one writer observed, 'those of India represent the greatest travesty of democratic principles.' Everything was controlled by political bosses who presided over 'one of the best organized systems of corruption and violence existing anywhere in the world'.[11] This is what Paul Richard was up against in April 1914. There were two main parties, the 'European' and the 'Indian'—although all the candidates were European. The incumbent was a Frenchman with family links to Pondicherry, named Paul Bluysen. His Indian-party rival was Philema Lemaire, who had been unseated by Bluysen in 1910. This time around, there was a third-party candidate named J. Laporte. Richard became the fourth contestant. After trying to win over the bosses of Pondicherry, he made a trip to Karaikal, a French town 130 kilometres to the south, to drum up some support. Mirra went along. The room they stayed in was totally dilapidated and infested by white ants. This must have been a shock for a woman who had passed almost all of her life in the better parts of Paris, but she took it in her stride. She wrote in her diary on 13 April:

> In the midst of these circumstances, so complex and shifting, I have never before so completely lived Thy immutable peace or rather the 'I' has never before disappeared so completely that Thy divine peace alone is living. All is beautiful, harmonious and calm, all is full of Thee.

She and Paul were back in Pondicherry by 17 April. Here too she was focused on her inner life rather than the events around her: 'O my sweet Master, my divine Lord,' she wrote, 'tear out from my heart this illusion [of selfhood] so that this servant may become pure and may faithfully and integrally bring back to Thee all that is Thy due.'[12]

The election was held on 26 April. The results were announced two days later. Richard was trounced, getting only 231 votes against 33,154 for Bluysen, 5,624 for Lemaire and 368 for Laporte.[13] If the election had been held in today's United Kingdom or India, he would have lost his deposit. The same day, Mirra wrote: 'Thy law unfolds before us with precision, and . . . it is the best, that which will best serve Thy work in the world, that has happened.'[14] But what was the work in the world for which she and Paul had come to India? For a while, this remained unclear. Then one evening, early in May, when Mirra and Paul had gone to Aurobindo's house for a visit, Paul turned to him and said: 'Shall we start a magazine?' Aurobindo nodded in assent. Soon, they were busy doing everything necessary to launch a monthly review, with simultaneous editions in English and French. It would be called *The New Idea/L'Idée Nouvelle.* The same name would be used for a society or discussion group for people interested in their work. (The name obviously is an echo of Idéa, the group Mirra was involved with in Paris in 1905–07.) Aurobindo, who, since his arrival in Pondicherry, had been writing essays and commentaries on the Vedas, the Upanishads and yoga, sketched the proposed contents of the English edition. Paul said he would contribute a work of speculative theology, *Le Pourquoi des Mondes/The Wherefore of the Worlds,* and also work up his and de Fontenay's collection of extracts from religious and philosophical literature, to be called *Les Paroles Éternelles/The Eternal Wisdom.* He got the necessary permissions from the Government of French India and located a printing establishment. Mirra took charge of the office. The three of them would be listed as the journal's editors. Sometime in June, they decided to change its name. It would be called *Arya,* a Vedic word meaning 'noble'. The Aryan, Aurobindo later explained in the pages of the journal, 'is he who strives and overcomes all outside him and within him that stands opposed to the human advance'.[15]

In the beginning of June, Paul and Mirra moved into a spacious first-floor flat in a house on Rue Dupleix, next to the governor's mansion. From their terrace, they could see Aurobindo's place. When he wasn't writing or meditating, he used to walk on his veranda, sometimes logging several kilometres a day. The Richards visited almost every evening. On Sundays, Aurobindo and his companions—young men, some of them former revolutionaries, who had taken refuge with him in Pondicherry—went to the Richards' place for dinner. Mirra prepared some of the dishes herself. 'After dinner,' Paul later recalled, 'we would sit until late on the terrace under the beautiful southern constellations', speaking about *Arya* and the state of the world.[16] On 17 June, Paul's fortieth birthday, the editors announced the upcoming launch of the journal. Aurobindo wrote, with incredible speed, the first instalments of *The Life Divine, The Synthesis of Yoga, The Secret of the Veda,* renderings of Vedic hymns and the Isha Upanishad and some independent essays. Mirra translated all of this into French. Paul added his contributions, which Aurobindo translated into English. They planned to bring out the first issue on 15 August, Aurobindo's forty-second birthday. Towards the end of June, it looked like they would make the deadline.

One factor they hadn't taken into account was the political situation in Europe. After the assassination of Archduke Franz-Ferdinand in Sarajevo on 28 June, the Great Powers began the diplomatic dance that would lead to war a month later. Judging by their diaries, Mirra and Aurobindo were, at first, not terribly concerned about what was going on in Europe. It was not until 30 July, two days after Austria–Hungary declared war on Serbia, that Aurobindo realized the crisis could not be averted. Four days later, Mirra wrote in her diary: 'Men, impelled by the conflict of forces, are performing a sublime sacrifice, they are offering their lives in a bloodstained holocaust.'[17]

Despite the changed circumstances, the editors went ahead. On 15 August, the first issue of *Arya* appeared. It had gone to press too late for the editors to comment on the war, but, in September, Aurobindo wrote that 'the "Arya", a review of pure Philosophy', had 'no direct concern with political passions and interests'. On the other hand, it 'could not ignore the enormous convulsion that is at present in progress'. Some issues raised by the war would find a place in the philosophical synthesis that the journal proposed, but this could not be done 'in this moment of supreme tension and wide-spread agony'. The editors therefore excused themselves from discussing current events. Aurobindo continued to write about metaphysics, yoga and the Indian tradition. Paul continued to write about the meaning of existence. Mirra laboured at her editorial and translation work, and ran the office as efficiently as she had run the office of the *Revue Cosmique*. Physically, the two journals were similar. Each issue had sixty-four pages. The paper was good, the typesetting neat and clear, with few typographical errors. (In the case of *Arya,* this was something of a miracle given that the printers had so far specialized in handbills and wedding invitations.) In terms of content, the journals were worlds apart. Aurobindo's contributions show an intimate knowledge of the Upanishads and Vedas. Based firmly on this tradition, his own philosophy is logical and clear. The writings in the *Revue Cosmique,* based ostensibly on the world's original wisdom tradition, were mostly products of the Theons' imaginations. *Arya* was like an Indian fortress built of granite blocks, the *Revue* like a Celtic fairy castle made of butterfly wings.

Despite being born at an inauspicious hour, *Arya* proved a success. On the other hand, the New Idea/L'Idée Nouvelle society scarcely got off the ground. Mirra held a few meetings with some young men of the town, speaking to them about the power of thought and encouraging them to meditate. It was a far cry from the animated meetings of her groups in Paris.

3

Mirra cherished the occasions when she could speak alone with Aurobindo. One of the first things she asked him was 'Why am I so mediocre?' As a student, she had been above average, but no prodigy. She had painted: The results were not bad but not a great deal better than what others could do. She played the piano well, but no one ever said, 'Oh, what a musical genius!' The same was true of her writing: Her thoughts 'were somewhat superior to those of my friends, but nothing exceptional'. Even her physical qualities were mediocre: 'My body had its skills, but nothing fantastic; I wasn't ugly, I wasn't beautiful—' Aurobindo told her it had to be like that, the implication being that if she had been a virtuoso in any field, it might have been difficult for her to turn herself fully to the inner life. Before coming to Pondicherry, she had had 'innumerable experiences and innumerable realizations'. All that now belonged to the past. It seemed to her as if she was 'being born to a new life and that all the methods, the habits of the past can no longer be of use'. She felt 'as though

I have done nothing yet, not lived the spiritual life but only entered the path that leads to it . . . that all experience has yet to begin'.[18]

In Pondicherry, her practice took a distinctly Indian turn. Once, she had a vision 'in which four beings appeared at the four corners of an immense plateau'. She asked Aurobindo about this and he said they were the four solar gods of the Vedas: Mitra, Varuna, Bhaga and Aryaman.[19] Towards the end of July, she had the experience of the rising and descent of the kundalini power:

> There was no longer a body, no longer any sensation; all that existed was a column of light, rising from where the base of the body usually is to where the head usually is, forming there a disk of light like that of the moon; from there the column continued to rise far above the head, blossoming out into an immense sun.

Then:

> . . . slowly the column of light came down again, forming an oval of living light, awakening . . . the centres above the head, in the head, the throat, the heart, in the middle of the stomach, at the base of the spine and still further down.[20]

On a more imaginative level, she once had a vision of the Himalayas while practising meditation as she walked in her house on Rue Dupleix. Catching sight of a bit of blue-coloured glass, she saw the mountains in all their grandeur and actually felt their coolness.[21] If nothing else, it was a good way to beat the oppressive heat of the Indian summer.

4

When Britain and France, traditional rivals, found themselves on the same side against the Germans, they began to cooperate throughout the colonial world. This meant trouble for Pondicherry's political refugees and also for Paul Richard. French officials advised him to end his association with Aurobindo. In October, he went to see the British consul.

Richard told him he 'was an admirer of the British government and that Aurobindo Ghose wished to dissociate himself entirely from politics'. He asked if Bijoy Nag, one of the ex-revolutionaries who was staying with Aurobindo, could go to Bengal as an agent for *Arya* without being detained. The consul gave no promises. Bijoy went anyway. When he crossed over into British India, he was clapped in jail, where he remained until the end of the war.

Revolutionaries in Bengal and other parts of British India took advantage of the war to intensify their activities. The British were happy their old nemesis Aurobindo was cooped up in Pondicherry, where he could do no harm. Still, rumours circulated that the government of British India was pressuring the French to deport him to a distant French possession, such as Algeria or Djibouti. It was apparently this threat Mirra was thinking of when she wrote in her diary on 17 January 1915: 'The time of rest and preparation is over.' Instead of being a 'passive and contemplative servitor', she had to engage 'in a constant and heroic struggle against everything in the world that opposes the accomplishment of Thy law'.[22] She concentrated inwardly to prevent the rumoured deportation from happening. But the person actually in danger of expulsion was not Aurobindo but her husband.

Paul had completed his military duties as a youth but, at forty, he was still liable for service as a reservist in the Territorial Army. Situated as he was in a far-off colony, there was no immediate push for him to be sent back to France. Then, in February, he received a mobilization order. He appealed to the government and the order was held in abeyance. The local authorities, who considered him a troublemaker, gave him no support. Soon, the final word came from Paris. He had to return to France.

Paul took it for granted that Mirra would be going with him. She secretly hoped Aurobindo would suggest that she stay back in Pondicherry. Aurobindo said nothing. She was disappointed and confused. 'He even appeared to wish that I should go away,' she recalled later. As for Paul, it seemed to her that Aurobindo was relieved he would be going.[23] He was always engrossed in his high-flown intellectual projects and had no real call for the spiritual life.

On 22 February, a day after Mirra's thirty-seventh birthday, the Richards left Pondicherry. Four days later, they boarded the Japanese steamer *Kamo Maru* in Colombo. Before departing, Mirra said 'with great feeling and assurance, 'We shall come back!' As far as Paul could see, 'From that point on all our thoughts turned to Europe.'[24] He clearly was out of touch with his wife. In the first surviving diary entry written after her departure, Mirra cried: 'Bitter solitude! And always the strong impression of having been flung headlong into a hell of darkness! Never at any moment of my life, in any circumstances, have I felt myself living in surroundings so entirely opposed to all that I am conscious of as true, to all that is the essence of my life.' The sense of solitude and abandonment continued as the ship crossed the Arabian Sea: 'Each turn of the propeller on the deep ocean seems to be dragging me farther away from my true destiny . . . each passing hour seems to plunge me deeper into that past with which I had broken . . . everything seems to draw me back to a state of things totally contrary to the life of my soul which reigns uncontested over outer activities.' And a few days later: 'I am exiled from every spiritual happiness.' Of all the ordeals the Lord could impose, 'this surely is the most painful'. It took 'all the ardour of an untiring faith to prevent the external consciousness thus abandoned to itself from being invaded by an irremediable sorrow'.[25] The farther she got from Pondicherry, the more she felt 'emptied of something'. By the time the ship reached the Mediterranean, she couldn't hold up any longer: 'Suddenly I felt sick, sick, sick.'[26]

The *Kamo Maru* reached Marseille on 16 March. The Richards passed a day in Montpellier, then took the train to Paris. After two weeks in the capital, they returned to the south. On 30 March, they reached Lunel, a town near Paul's childhood home, where his regiment was stationed. It was a year and a day since Mirra had met Aurobindo in Pondicherry. The circumstances now were vastly different.

6

Exile

1

IN LUNEL, PAUL WAS GIVEN THE WORK OF TRAINING HORSES FOR transporting supplies to the front. Mirra stayed near the camp. Her health, already precarious, became worse. On 19 April, she wrote in her diary that her body was 'so profoundly shaken that it is unable to regain its usual balance of health'. Commenting on this passage later, she said she was suffering from an inflammation of the nerves that produced intense pain all over the body. The occult cause, she said, was the separation of her soul, which she had left behind in Pondicherry, from her body. Without its usual psychic support, the body collapsed. For some time, she felt she was close to death. She wrote what she believed would be her last letter to Aurobindo. She recovered and the letter remained unsent.[1]

On 20 May, she felt well enough to visit trains bringing wounded soldiers from the front. 'It is a moving sight,' she wrote, 'not so much because of all that these unfortunate men are suffering but, above all because of the noble manner in which most of them bear their sufferings. Their soul shines through their eyes, the slightest contact with the deeper forces awakens it.' Her remarks on the war displayed nothing of the chauvinism and hatred that possessed most hearts in Europe at that time. She viewed what was happening in terms of global evolution and the effect it had on her inner life: 'The simultaneous vision of that which is and that which is becoming takes hold of this consciousness and does not leave it for hours.'[2]

Her physical condition remained tenuous. She was shifted from Lunel to Paul's family home in Marsillargues, where she was looked after by a nun from the local convent. After a while, feeling somewhat better, she began to make twice-daily trips on her bicycle to visit Paul. One day, she learnt that his unit had been ordered to the front. On the morning of his planned deployment, she sent him a letter that, he later revealed, was so inspirational he carried it with him for the rest of his life. Barely an hour before his train was to depart, his unit was informed their orders had changed and they would remain in Lunel. A few weeks later, Paul was diagnosed with a minor heart ailment and given a conditional discharge. A second examination confirmed the findings of the first, and Paul was relieved of all military duties.[3] He joined Mirra in Marsillargues. André came down from Paris on his holidays. Mirra spoke to him about India and Aurobindo Ghose. Paul taught him how to play chess.[4] It was a welcome change from the dislocation and strain of the last six months.

Mirra and Paul remained in touch with Aurobindo. They were glad to learn that the English edition of *Arya* was coming out regularly. (The French edition ceased to appear after they left India.) In a letter dated 6 May 1915, which would have reached the Richards a month or more later, Aurobindo wrote: 'All is always for [the] best, but it is sometimes from the external point of view an awkward best'—a statement that must have cheered up the ailing Mirra. Apparently in reply to a suggestion by the Richards that they find a quiet place to sit out the war, Aurobindo wrote: 'The whole earth is now under one law and answers to the same vibrations and I am sceptical of finding any place where the clash of the struggle will not pursue us.' He concluded: 'One needs to have a calm heart, a settled will, entire self-abnegation and the eyes constantly fixed on the beyond to live undiscouraged in times like these which are truly a period of universal decomposition.' Hoping the war might open a way for a more just international order, Aurobindo began to write a series of articles entitled 'The Idea of Human Unity'. In a letter of September

1915, he told the Richards: 'I intend to proceed very cautiously and not go very deep at first, but as if I were leading the intelligence of the reader gradually towards the deeper meaning of unity, especially to discourage the idea that mistakes uniformity and mechanical association for unity.' Long before most other writers, Aurobindo saw that a push for political, economic and cultural uniformity would make true human unity impossible.[5]

On 22 October, Mirra and Paul relocated to Paris. Here, she got her first real taste of life in a world consumed by war. It seemed to her as if 'the entire nervous plane' had 'swept down upon the earth'. Its effects were felt most acutely on the battlefield but even behind the lines and in neutral countries there was a general feeling of 'weakness, nervous tension, feverishness, impatience, unbridled imagination' that sapped people of their energy. Non-combatants had a vague sense of 'the tremendous power that is driving—sometimes to the point of actual madness—the men who are fighting and killing each other'. The terminology is that of European occultism ('nervous plane' comes straight from the Cosmic Philosophy), but Mirra based her remarks on acute psychological observation:

> All those who enter the war zone . . . are seized, carried away, impersonalised in a formidable current, as impetuous as a raging ocean. They are disindividualised, as it were, reduced to an elemental state, to the state of natural forces which, like the wind, the storm, or the waters, accomplish their earthly work, moved by a Will of which they are unconscious.[6]

The potential human costs of the fighting were brought home to her at the end of October when André, now eighteen, volunteered for the army and was assigned to an artillery regiment.

On 2 November, Mirra and Paul returned to their old place on Rue du Val-de-Grâce. After spending a few minutes 'arranging familiar objects', she sat as a multitude of memories rose in her mind. Then, her heart was 'lifted up in a great surge of adoration' and she offered her being to the Lord. Over the next few months, she recorded the landmarks of her inner life in her diary. The most dramatic experience took place on 26 November. First, her consciousness became completely identified with the earth. This global body 'was absorbed in the body of the universe and one with it; the consciousness became the consciousness of the universe'. This universal consciousness then 'sprang towards the Divine in an ardent aspiration, a perfect surrender'. The experience then took a characteristically Indian turn. Her consciousness perceived the Divine as a 'radiant Being standing on a many-headed serpent whose body coiled infinitely around the universe'. Then it 'became this Being' and 'was absorbed into something which was no longer a form and yet contained all forms, something which, immutable, sees—the Eye, the Witness'. When Mirra sent a transcript of this experience to Aurobindo, he wrote back (in a letter dated 31 December) that it was 'Vedic in the real sense': the union of the Vedic and Puranic Earth with the Divine Principle above.[7]

The blossoming of Mirra's inner life went along with the ordinary and not-so-ordinary events of life in a country at war. After early successes by the invading German army, which came to within 40 kilometres of Paris, the lines between the German and Anglo-French forces stabilized in northern and eastern France. A prolonged period of trench warfare began, punctuated by horrific battles. On 21 February 1916, the Germans attacked French positions near Verdun. When the campaign ended eleven months later, more than 3,00,000 French and German soldiers had been killed and more than 4,00,000 wounded. The defence of Verdun overlapped with the even more sanguinary Somme Offensive, which resulted in the death or injury of more than 10,00,000 soldiers. Neither campaign did much to change the overall military situation.

In Paris, people got used to rationing, 'national bread' and German bombardments. When the Richards visited their friends Georges and Marie Picard, they had to walk around an enormous crater produced by a German howitzer shell. As always in extreme situations, people got on with their lives as best they could. Around this time, Paul had a brief relationship with a woman who later gave birth to a daughter. He never provided for the girl. (In a note to Paul's memoirs, his son Michel wrote that Paul believed it was a father's duty to bring children into the world but 'it was not necessarily his duty to look after them once they had entered the world'.[8]) Mirra was absorbed in her inner life but also kept up with her reading. When she went through Anatole France's *La Révolte des Anges* (The Revolt of the Angels) she was struck by similarities between its background story and the Gnostic mythology of the Cosmic tradition. A while later, she met the author and asked if he had read any Cosmic publications. No, he replied, adding politely that he would do so if he got the chance.[9] Mirra stayed in touch with Matteo, who was serving in the commissary department, and with André, who was still in training. She and Paul looked forward to letters from their friend de Fontenay, who was serving as an officer on the Western Front. One day in January, as Mirra entered her room, a framed photograph of de Fontenay she kept on a sideboard fell to the ground, shattering the glass. She had a premonition that something had happened to him. A few days later, as she opened the door of the house, a big grey cat threw itself on her and started meowing uncontrollably. She looked in its eyes and saw the eyes of de Fontenay. The next day, she read in the papers that her friend had been killed in battle a few days earlier.[10]

Around this time, Paul told Mirra he had heard the Suez Canal had been closed on account of the German submarine campaign. Mirra said at once: 'That is the sign that we must go to Japan.'[11] Why Japan? Mirra was interested in Japanese culture. She enjoyed reading Lafcadio Hearn's *Kokoro: Hints and Echoes of Japanese Inner Life,* and had been touched by the turn-of-the-century craze for Japanese woodblock prints and objets d'art. She was also interested in Buddhism and seems to have believed that Japan, like India, was a land of spirituality. Since India was closed to Paul and her, she may have thought that Japan could serve as a substitute. Whatever her reasons, Paul agreed that going to Japan was a good idea. He certainly had no desire to remain in France or to help in the war effort in any way. On 28 February, he wangled a letter of introduction from the Foreign Ministry's Department of Political and Commercial Affairs certifying that he was a representative of the National Union for the Export of French Products.[12] Meanwhile, Mirra was packing all they needed for a prolonged stay abroad. The only ships travelling to the Far East were Japanese steamers that departed from England and took the long route around the Cape of Good Hope. The first step for the Richards was to get from Paris to London. This meant crossing the English Chanel, where German U-boats prowled. Around 4 March, they boarded the passenger ferry *Sussex* in Boulogne and made the crossing to Folkestone. Three weeks later, when the *Sussex* was sailing from Folkestone to Dieppe, it was hit by a German torpedo and split in half. Around a hundred passengers and crew lost their lives.[13]

In London, the Richards had to cut through a tangle of red tape to get tickets and permission to travel. At this time, they reconnected with Dorothy Hodgson, an English Baha'i whom they had met in Paris in 1913. When Dorothy heard they were going to Japan, she decided to come along. For some time, she had been in correspondence with Agnes Baldwin Alexander, the first Baha'i missionary to Japan. She now informed Alexander that she soon would arrive in Yokohama with two French friends 'who feel the call for Japan'.[14] The three of them boarded the *Kamo Maru* (the same ship the Richards had travelled on the previous year) on 14 March. In the Channel, they were accompanied by a squad of minesweepers. For the first week, they sailed under total blackout conditions. At night, all passengers sat together in the salon, fully clothed and ready to abandon ship at short notice. Not until the *Kamo Maru* passed Cape Verde could they relax a little.

The ship called at Cape Town (where Mirra sent a postcard to André), Durban (where the passengers were entertained by Zulu dancers), Singapore, Hong Kong and Shanghai (where the Richards visited a Buddhist temple). On 14 May, two months after leaving London, the *Kamo Maru* reached the Japanese port of Kobe. Agnes Alexander was waiting at the pier. A friend of hers had told her that the annual festival at the Taima-dera Temple was being held that very day and suggested that the newcomers might like to see it. The Richards and Dorothy disembarked.[15] Once their luggage was unloaded, they proceeded by train and rickshaw to the seventh-century temple. There, they saw the procession of twenty-four priests who, each year, cross a bridge linking the Pure Land of the Buddha to the human world. Mirra doubtless was impressed by this colourful initiation into the cultural life of Japan. The next day, they travelled overland to Mount Koya, where they visited the mother-temple of the Koyasan sect of Shingon Buddhism. Then, after a stop in Kyoto, they proceeded to Tokyo, where they took lodgings with Miss Alexander.[16]

2

On 7 June 1916, Mirra wrote in her diary for the first time in several months. While travelling, her consciousness had been absorbed in the immediate experience and 'did not have the necessary perspective to see it as a whole'. Then, a 'veil was torn', light flooded her consciousness and she again communed with the Lord. The return to activity after reaching Tokyo 'meant a completely new adaptation of the vital instrument'—that is, her life energy—which generally had the tendency of acting according to its old habits and methods. Now, 'in the midst of action' it 'again found the perception of Infinity and Eternity'.[17] In the months to come, Mirra would strive to maintain a balance between the demands of her inner and outer lives.

The Richards and Dorothy Hodgson stayed with Agnes Alexander for only a few weeks. The missionary was disappointed that the new arrivals 'did not strengthen the Cause of God', that is, help her spread the Baha'i gospel.[18] Dorothy Hodgson was happy to speak with people in Tokyo about the times she had seen 'Abdu'l-Bahá in England and France. Mirra and Paul seem to have said little or nothing about their relations with the master three years earlier. Around this time, they began to make contact with local people, members of the expatriate community and foreign visitors. On 31 May, Alexander introduced them to her friend Ujaku Akita, a well-known playwright.[19] A few days later, the Bengali poet Rabindranath Tagore—famous as the first person from Asia to be awarded the Nobel Prize in literature—arrived in Tokyo. The Richards sent him a letter asking if they could meet him. Tagore agreed and they spent some time together on the morning of 11 June. Mirra did a pencil sketch of the poet. Paul talked with him about politics, philosophy and their mutual friend Aurobindo Ghose. That evening, the Richards went to the Imperial University to hear Tagore give a speech entitled 'The Message of India to Japan'. He praised Japan for being the first country in Asia to successfully take on the West. This 'child of the Ancient East' had 'fearlessly claimed all the gifts of the modern age for herself'. But he warned the Japanese people to steer clear of unthinking imitation: 'We cannot imitate life, we cannot simulate strength' for 'mere imitation is a source of weakness'. Two days later, at a reception attended by the Prime Minister and other dignitaries, the poet was more blunt. Speaking in Bengali (with simultaneous translation into Japanese), he said that since his arrival in Kobe he had been repelled by the ugliness and agitation of modern Japanese life: 'The new Japan is only an imitation of the West. This will ruin Japan.' His frankness won him few friends.[20]

On 14 June, Tagore went to Yokohama, where he passed most of the next two months at a seaside villa. The Richards were frequent visitors. One day, while Paul and Tagore were admiring the view, Paul turned to the poet and said: 'Isn't it terrible that we are enjoying all this while Europe is a hell?' (The war was entering its third year.) Tagore did not answer but apparently was deeply affected. A week later, he told Paul: 'I have thought much about what you said. Now you'll see what I'm going to do,' and he outlined his plan to transform his school in rural Bengal into a world university.[21] At some point during their acquaintance, Tagore asked Mirra if she would like to help him run the planned institution. Mirra told him her work was elsewhere.[22]

Neither Mirra nor Paul were knocked off their feet by the celebrated poet. Paul admired his intellect but found him precious, 'one of those rarefied creatures whose entire lives have to be protected'. Tagore 'would never walk in the streets for fear of seeing some ugly sight, and he travelled in a private Pullman car in order to avoid having to sit with disagreeable people'. Mirra thought the poet elegant and intelligent but without any true spiritual turn. Once, at his request, she meditated with him. Using techniques she had learnt from Theon, she followed him within and saw that he entered 'a sort of emptiness' just beyond the ordinary mind. She waited to see if he would go further but he was satisfied with that state. This, he said, was nirvana. He asked Mirra what she thought. She said her idea of nirvana was different.[23]

Towards the middle of June, Mirra and Paul took a lease on a house about to be vacated by a Christian missionary. As soon as they and Dorothy Hodgson moved in, they found themselves surrounded by dozens of Japanese who wanted to learn English and French. Dorothy took a teaching job at a local school. Mirra accepted some private students. Around this time, the editor of *Fujoshimbun*, a women's magazine, asked to interview her. She declined but sent an article she had written in English entitled 'Women and the War', which was published in Japanese translation on 7 July. The response of women to the demands of the war, she began, showed that they were the equals of men not only in traditional 'feminine' roles, such as tending the sick and wounded, but also organization and administration. The conflict demonstrated—on a massive scale—that 'purely masculine politics have given proof of incapacity'. Men had 'foundered too often in their search of strictly personal interest, and in their arbitrary and violent action'. It was time to break down the barrier between 'masculine' and 'feminine' occupations, since men and women had equal competence in all fields. It was only by recognizing 'this fundamental spiritual equality' that a 'serious and lasting solution for this problem of the relation of the sexes' could be found.[24] Two months later, *Fujoshimbun* published a two-page article on Mirra under the title 'A Truly Dedicated Woman'.

Soon after his arrival in Tokyo, Paul made contact with B.W. Fleisher, the publisher of *The Japan Advertiser*, the most prominent English-language newspaper in the Far East. Fleisher asked him to contribute some articles on the war. Paul wrote a dozen pieces, had them translated into English (apparently by Mirra), and passed them on to Fleisher. The publisher said he could not print them as they might offend the Japanese officials upon whose good graces he depended. Disappointed, Paul set them aside. Towards the end of August, he asked Tagore, who was about to leave for America, if he could take the articles with him and see that they were posted to a friend of his in Europe. (Paul feared that Japanese censors might confiscate the manuscript.) Tagore agreed and Paul put the matter out of his mind.

In October, the Richards attended a lecture by a recently arrived Indian professor named Hari Prasad Shastri at Tokyo's Waseda University. Another member of the audience was Shumei Okawa, a thirty-year-old scholar who had studied Indian philosophy at the Imperial University. Okawa and Mirra met after the lecture and decided to stay in touch.[25] Okawa also spoke with Shastri. Soon, the two men became great friends. They often dined together, talking, among other things, about relations between Japan and India. Okawa told Shastri what he knew about his new friends, the Richards, about Aurobindo Ghose, whom he greatly admired, and even, when he was sure that Shastri was reliable, about Rash Behari Bose, a Bengali revolutionary who had taken refuge in Japan after masterminding an assassination attempt against the Viceroy of India in 1912. Shastri, who was in fact a paid informant of the Government of India's Department of Criminal Intelligence, took careful note of all he heard and included it in reports he sent to his British spymasters in Delhi.[26] At the same time, Paul was being investigated by the Japanese intelligence service, which filed a report on his activities in December 1916. A key passage was this:

> Recently, the suspect [Richard] said to someone as follows: 'In India, revolutionary thoughts are spreading everywhere. There is no way Britain will be able to suppress them, no matter what means they will resort to. It is thus a matter of humaneness to release these Indians from the British yoke. And there is absolutely no other way but to rely on Japanese help in order to realize this. . . . Right now, in the middle of the Great War in Europe, is the best opportunity for this. This is why I came to Japan to persuade the Japanese people and office-holders and to ask for their help.'[27]

The last sentence was bunkum but it doubtless made Paul feel good about himself and impressed the person he was speaking with. Unfortunately for him, and even more so for Mirra, his timing was bad. They were trying to convince the British ambassador to let them travel to French

India. (British approval was needed because all ships travelling west from Japan called at British ports, such as Hong Kong, Singapore and Colombo.) Knowing what he did about Paul's activities and associates, the ambassador denied them safe passage. Learning of this decision, Mirra wrote in her diary on 10 December that formerly she had been spoilt by the Lord, who made her live constantly in his presence. Now, she realized, he wished to teach her 'how to know the unchanging bliss even in darkness'.[28] At least until the war was over, she and Paul were stuck in Japan.

Her diary of this period is filled with prayers to the Lord and accounts of inner experiences. The entry of 20 December begins: 'The days have passed, stormy and troubled in appearance but calm and strong in reality, reflecting Thy divine will.' After her meditation, she received a 'communication' from Shakyamuni Buddha: 'Learn to radiate and do not fear the storm: the wind carries us far from the shore but shows us the world. Would you be thrifty of tenderness? But the source of love is infinite. . . . If the eternal truth finds in you a means of manifesting itself, what does the rest matter?' A voice she heard in her heart—'Turn towards the earth and human beings'—showed her the path she must take.[29]

3

In February 1917, Tagore returned to Japan from the United States. This time around, he gave no public speeches and attended no sparkling receptions. After his departure the previous September, his Japanese admirers had turned against him. 'JAPANESE HOWLING FOR HIS SCALP', reported *The Japan Gazette*, noting that a section of the public was agitating against him 'on the ground that before leaving Japan he criticized the organization of the Japanese Empire'.[30] After reaching Yokohama on 3 February, Tagore and his party proceeded quietly to Kyoto in a private Pullman carriage. With them were Paul and Mirra. Tagore had a surprise for Paul. While in New York, he had shown Paul's essays to his literary agent, who thought the Frenchman's pacifism might go down well in America, where anti-war feeling was strong.[31] The essays were published early in 1917 under the title *To the Nations*, with a brilliant introduction by Tagore: 'When this idea of the Nation, which has achieved universal acceptance in the present day, tries to pass off the cult of selfishness as a moral duty simply because that selfishness is gigantic in stature, then it not only commits depredations but attacks the very vitals of humanity,' he wrote. 'What is worse, this moral aberration of peoples, decked with the showy title of patriotism, proudly walks abroad, passing itself off as a highly moral influence.' The solution of the world's problems lay not in the creation of new systems or institutions, 'but in the drainage of those stagnant moral pollutions which give rise to poisonous vapour'. He went on to say that Paul Richard's idealistic essays gave him more hope for the future of humanity than 'the big schemes which the politicians are formulating for ushering the age of peace into the world'.[32]

Paul's essays nowhere rise to the level of Tagore's introduction. He was at his best when shaping epigrams, such as: 'The big nations called themselves peaceful when, not wishing to wage war with the strongest, they contented themselves with making war—without too many risks—on the weakest.' What resonated with his readers, especially in the colonial world, was his denunciation of the Western powers and his call for 'the deliverance of the great enslaved peoples of Africa and Asia'.[33]

Tagore and his party reached Kyoto on 4 February. The next day, the poet, his secretary William Winstanley Pearson, the Japanese artist Tetsuo Hirasawa, and Paul and Mirra paused to have a now-famous photograph taken in the courtyard of their hotel.[34] Behind them looms a giant seated Buddha, which, illustrating the transience of all created things, disappeared during the Second World War, possibly melted down to make artillery shells. Later the same day, or perhaps the next, the party visited the clinic of Sanzaburo Kobayashi, a Western-trained physician who, after returning to Japan, became a proponent of the quiet-sitting (*seiza*) method of Torajiro Okada.[35] One of several 'belly-cultivation' systems that became popular in early-twentieth-century Japan, Okada's way of *seiza* used postural and breathing techniques to promote physical and spiritual well-being. Practitioners of Okada's method were instructed to sit on their heels, body upright, hands on the lap, head erect, eyes turned downward and closed. They were asked to observe their breathing, which became slow and unforced. During exhalation, practitioners concentrated on the *tanden* or lower abdomen, placing their mental energy there rather than in the head. This was said to correct the mental and physical imbalance created by Western habits of posture, breathing and thinking.[36]

Paul had heard about Kobayashi's clinic and arranged a visit for the five of them.[37] Mirra was delighted to meet the doctor and his wife, Nobuko. The two women decided to stay in touch. On 7 or 8 February, Tagore went on to Nara and Kobe, where he boarded a ship for India.[38] He left behind Willie Pearson, who had become attached to Japan and to Paul. The Englishman, observed the Tagore biographer Prabhatkumar Mukherjee, had 'a highly emotional nature' and quickly became enthralled by Paul's 'spiritual ideas'.[39] Pearson remained in Japan for about a year, staying with the Richards in Kyoto, Tokyo and various hill resorts.

4

Apart from translating Paul's writings into English, Mirra did not take part in his political activities, but these activities determined the circumstances of her life between 1917 and 1920. During the second year of their stay, Paul became a prophet of Pan-Asianism, the idea that the different countries of Asia formed a cultural and geopolitical unit that should compete on equal terms with Europe and America. India, China and Japan were the homes of ancient philosophies and religions that were inherently superior to the materialism and missionary faiths of the West. If Asian countries stood together, they could stop the incursions of the European imperial powers. Japan's defeat of Russia in 1905 had thrilled people throughout Asia and strengthened the position of the militant faction in the Japanese government. When the First World War broke out, Japan sided with Britain and France, and occupied German territories in China and the Pacific. This was the situation when the Richards arrived in Japan. Intellectuals with Pan-Asianist leanings gravitated towards the Frenchman. Among them were Mitsuru Toyama, the founder of the Black Dragon Society, an influential pressure group, and the scholar Okawa.

Aware that Richard had written some essays on European nationalism, Okawa asked if he could write something similar with a focus on Japan. Richard rose to the bait, writing a tract called *Au Japon* (To Japan) that was published in a quadrilingual edition—French, English (translated by Mirra), Japanese (translated by Okawa) and Chinese—towards the middle of 1917. 'Nation of Asia who alone hast remained free, nation of the earth who alone hast always been so, understand then that thou art born to be a liberator of nations,' Richard declared. 'Liberate and unify Asia; for Asia is thy domain. Asia is thy field of action and, if needed, thy field of war.' Japan was destined to stand 'at the head of a free federation of Asia', a pillar of 'the next and splendid equilibrium of the world'. This is what the Japanese wanted to hear, not the lectures of European statesmen or the equivocations of Tagore. Richard also wrote that Japan should grant independence to Korea and return Qingdao to China. His Japanese friends remained silent on these issues but gave him full attention when he denounced European imperialism. The book was widely distributed in schools and colleges, and a copy was presented to Crown Prince Hirohito. Another copy found its way to the British government's Department of Intelligence, which reported on it and its author in July 1917.[40] The next month, Okawa's Asiatic Association published a collection of essays on India written by Pearson. In an injudicious introduction to the book, Richard wrote that India's 'future place is not in an English Empire—will indeed a place remain in the future for such Empire?—Her place is in a free federation of Asia. For it is to create this that now works the Lord of the Nations, the Master of their Destinies.' This book too came to the attention of agents of India's Department of Criminal Intelligence. They could not touch Richard but when Pearson visited China early in 1918, British consular authorities had him arrested and deported back to England.[41]

5

In the summer of 1917, Pearson arranged for himself, the Richards and some others to stay at the country villa of Kazuo Okakura, son of the art critic and cultural Pan-Asianist Kakuzo Okakura, who had died four years earlier. (The elder Okakura was a friend of Tagore's, and his family had stayed in touch with the poet and his friends.) The house was located near Lake Nojiri, not far from the hill resort of Akakura.[42] Here, Mirra had the time to apply herself to art and writing. She began a painting of Shumei Okawa's wife seated on a veranda with fields, lake and mountains in the background. The finished work is one of the best things she had ever done, showing she had not lost her touch during her twelve-year hiatus from painting. On 9 July, she wrote, apparently at Pearson's request, a short essay in English called 'Impressions of Japan' that was published by *The Modern Review* of Calcutta.[43] 'In most cases,' she began, 'foreigners come in touch with that part of the Japanese people which has been spoiled by foreigners,—a Japan of money-makers and imitators of the West,' who had picked up 'many of those things which make the West hateful'. But, she went on, if you have 'the privilege of coming in contact with the true Japanese, those who kept untouched the righteousness and bravery of the ancient Samurai, then you can understand what in truth is Japan, you can seize the secret of her force. They know how to remain silent; and though they are possessed of the most acute sensitiveness, they are, among the people I have met, those who express it the least.' She was especially impressed by their 'perfect love for nature and beauty', though, she added, there was nothing in Japan to compare with 'the pure divine atmosphere which pervades India and makes of her such a unique and precious country'.[44] A few days after finishing the essay, Mirra wrote in her diary about the inner peace she had found after the disturbances of the previous years: 'In place of something very intensely concentrated which for a long while was intermittently tumultuous, has come an immensity so vast and calm and untroubled, filling my being; or rather my being has melted into that; for how could that which is limitless be contained in a form?' Looking out of her window, she found that the mountain ranges 'with their serene contours' were in 'perfect harmony with the rhythm of this being, filled with an infinite peace'.[45]

By September, the Richards were back in Tokyo. Mirra found it hard to maintain the concentration and peace she had felt in Akakura. She asked the Lord: 'How is it possible that having seen all that I have seen, experienced all that I have experienced', He had made of her 'so utterly common an instrument in such ordinary circumstances?' Why, when He had placed in her heart 'the pure diamond of perfect Felicity', did He allow 'its surface to reflect the shadows which come from outside'.[46] Such fluctuations of her inner life would persist in the months that followed.

6

Mirra had been exchanging letters with Nobuko Kobayashi ever since they met in February 1917. On 18 April, she invited Nobuko and her husband to come to Tokyo to see the cherry blossoms. Mirra's experience of the Cherry Blossom Festival the previous spring had been a 'magical' revelation. One day, while walking under the trees, she was seized by a 'deep concentration'. She found she was identified with a single cherry blossom, then with all of them. She heard a voice telling her that since she had become one with the cherry trees, she could understand 'that it is the Divine who makes the offering of this flower-prayer to heaven'. She felt infused with peace and force. Then, a cherry tree whispered mischievously to her: 'It is in the cherry-blossom that lies the remedy for the disorders of the spring.'[47] Now, she asked the Kobayashis to experience the festival with her. She was disappointed when they said they could not come.

A few months later, the Kobayashis found time to pay a visit to her and Paul. During their stay, Mirra began a portrait of Nobuko. Sometime later, she used this painting as an excuse to ask her friend to come again: 'The picture had such a good beginning, it is a pity to leave it unfinished. . . . Will you not be touched by such good reasons?' She got no immediate response. Two weeks later, Mirra again wrote to Nobuko saying that a friend of theirs, an American chemist named Alcan Hirsch, was coming to Kyoto to look for a house for himself, and another for Paul and her, as the two of them were thinking of spending a few weeks in the city.[48] Before the end of 1917, the Richards and Dorothy Hodgson moved into a one-storey house in the Shichijo district of Kyoto, not far from the Kobayashis' home and clinic. They ended up staying almost a year.

During these months, Mirra spent a good amount of time with the Kobayashis. Nobuko later recalled sitting with Mirra 'in her lovely attic. We sat together and explored our inner depths, each in her own way. She made me realize that we thought the same thoughts and beheld the same vision.' Mirra spoke to her about India and Aurobindo. Her 'eyes glistened with a new delight and wonder', Nobuko recalled, when she spoke of this 'master from the ancient land of Buddha'.[49] From Dr Kobayashi, Mirra learnt about the Okada quiet-sitting method. The theory behind it was 'that one can think in any part of one's being if one concentrates there'. For example, 'instead of thinking in your head, you can think in your chest'. You could even think in your stomach. Those who did this gained formidable 'power, strength and calmness'. In support of this theory, Kobayashi observed that powerful people always had big bellies and held their bodies upright. Napoleon was a prime example. Once he said to Mirra: 'Have you noticed how Tagore stands quite upright, like this, with his head erect?' Mirra pointed out that Tagore did not have a big belly. 'It will come,' Kobayashi replied. Mirra tried the quiet-sitting method and found that she could place her mental energy in any part of her body. It was, she said, a good way of getting rid of headaches and nervous strain.[50]

During the winter of 1917–18, Paul worked on another book, a mixture of Calvinistic sermonizing and pseudo-Nietzschean posturing entitled *The Lord of the Nations.* He set the scene in the introduction: 'When I wrote this book . . . I was looking to the world of men and nations from the upper room of a small wood-and-paper house, frozen under the snow, listening in the silence of this retreat to the secret words of my Lord—The Lord of Nations.' This mighty form of God was the creator of the nations. The war was his manifestation. He was punishing the nations of Europe for their evil deeds: Belgium for its tyranny in the Congo, Britain for its oppression of India, Germany and France for their colonial excesses. Imperialism was 'the sin, the mortal sin, of the nations of Europe. From that sin has come their Gehenna [place of misery or Hell], and this Gehenna will come to an end only with the end of this sin.' A new age was coming in which Asia would take its place at the forefront of the nations. India and China—'the unshakable pillars of Asia'—would become 'the Centre of the World's unity'.[51] Paul could not find anyone to publish this screed in French or English but his Pan-Asian friends brought out a small edition in Japanese. Around the same time, Okawa published a laudatory article on Aurobindo Ghose in a Tokyo newspaper. Contrasting Aurobindo with Tagore, the scholar wrote that while the latter doubtless was a great poet, 'he is far from being a great thinker, much less is he equal to Ghose in the depth and extent of thought'. The article was innocuous but the Department of Criminal Intelligence thought it important enough to mention in a report. The agent noted that Okawa, 'the leading spirit of the Pan-Asiatic movement', was 'deeply interested in Indian affairs and is bitterly opposed to British rule in India'.[52]

The Richards passed the summer of 1918 in the mountains. In mid-September, they paid a visit to the Daiunji Buddhist temple in Nagano Prefecture. On 15 September, they put their seals and signatures on a commemorative scroll featuring drawings and Japanese verses written in beautiful calligraphy:

> Like the seeds of millet sown in a ploughed field
> People in the whole world are all celestial people.[53]

While at Daiunji, Mirra made some pencil and oil sketches of the temple and its surroundings. In the visitors' book, she made an ink sketch of Paul sitting in meditation. Opposite the drawing she inscribed a motto he had composed: '*Tous sont Un, car Tout est l'Unique*' (All are One, because Everything is the One).[54]

Mirra's inner life seems to have been fairly placid at this time. On 10 October, she wrote in her diary: 'O my beloved Lord, how sweet it is to think that it is for Thee and Thee alone that I act! . . . What peace, what tranquillity, what supreme delight are bestowed by this perception and this feeling!' For the Lord to act freely all she had to do was stay 'docile, flexible, surrendered, attentive'. Then there was no room for 'errors or faults, lack or insufficiency', for what the Lord willed was accomplished, and accomplished exactly as it was willed.[55]

7

Sometime before December, the Richards returned to Tokyo, reoccupying the house in Myogadani district where they had stayed in 1916 and 1917. In January 1919, the proprietor suddenly told them he wanted them to vacate by 15 February. It was, as Mirra wrote to Nobuko Kobayashi, a bad time for them to have to look for a new place to stay. She and Dorothy Hodgson were in the middle of their English courses. And it was the dead of winter. Did Nobuko know of a temple where they could stay for a while? (It had to be a big temple, because they had a lot of baggage.) Or perhaps it would be better if they left Tokyo and found a place in the country?[56] Before the situation got desperate, their friend Okawa stepped in. He offered them a villa in the Sendagaya neighbourhood on the understanding that Paul would help him with his political projects.[57] Okawa and his wife spent most of the next year with Paul and Mirra in the Sendagaya house. The Japanese couple felt privileged to stay with these visitors from France who 'dreamed of a new Asia, a new world'.[58]

The First World War ended in November 1918 with the defeat of Germany, Austria-Hungary and the Ottoman Empire. The victorious nations—Britain, France, Italy, the United States and Japan—looked for ways to profit from the situation. At the Paris Peace Conference, which began in January 1919, the European victors were interested primarily in punishing Germany, snatching its colonies, and redrawing the maps of Central and Southeast Europe and the Middle East to their advantage. The United States made no territorial claims but wanted President Wilson's Fourteen Points to set the agenda of the conference. Japan was offered few spoils of war but was determined to keep the German possessions in China and the Pacific it had seized during the conflict. It also insisted that the conference accept the principle of racial equality. This issue was discussed in Tokyo on 11 February at the first meeting of the newly formed League for Racial Equality. The participants, self-described as members of 'thirty-seven great Japanese associations', sent a telegram to Paris demanding 'the final abolition of all racial discrimination and disqualification'.[59] Two days later, the Japanese delegation put this demand before the conference. Paul may have had a hand in drafting the racial equality proposal, and he certainly was involved in the discussions and agitation that followed.[60]

For a few months, the Richards' place was the chief resort of Japanese intellectuals wishing to exchange ideas about Pan-Asianism and racial equality. They also took advantage of the Richards' hospitality. Their 'table became famous' among Tokyo thinkers, to the extent that Okawa had to warn Paul that 'this style of life might become habit-forming'.[61] Another visitor at the Richards' place was the French philosopher Félicien Challaye, who had been sent to Tokyo on a propaganda mission after being wounded at the front. Years later, he could remember passing pleasant evenings with his new friends and going with Mirra to the Mitsukoshi department store, where she helped him buy a suitcase.[62]

Racial equality was a burning issue in Japan at this time. Okawa and his colleagues meant by it the acknowledgement that Japan was the equal of the Great Powers of Europe, and that Japanese people in the United States and elsewhere should be protected from discrimination and mistreatment. (They left out of the picture Japan's mistreatment of Koreans, Manchurians and Taiwanese.) They were glad to have a European intellectual like Paul on board. At the second meeting of the League for Racial Equality, Paul gave a speech condemning the proposed League of Nations, which he characterized as 'a League of wolves clothed in the skins of sheep'. He called for the formation of a 'League of the Nations of Asia—the United States of Asia'. When the racial equality amendment was defeated in Paris, Paul told the members of the League for Racial Equality that the League of Nations was a farce and Japan should take the lead in founding 'a true Society of Nations, of all the nations, small or great, white, yellow or black, and red also', and as a first step towards that, establish a 'Congress of the free nations of Asia'.[63]

We have no idea of what Mirra thought about these political issues. We have, in fact, almost no record of what she was thinking or doing in 1919. In May, she wrote to her friend Nobuko about her flower garden ('it looks so nice with the new leaves') and vegetable garden ('the best you can find in Tokio!'). She mentioned a 'disaster', apparently a house-fire, that had befallen their artist friend Tetsuo Hirasawa. He had found a new place not far from the Richards and was taking his loss philosophically.[64] Mirra sometimes meditated with Hirasawa and silently guided him. One day, she succeeded in opening him to the direct experience of his soul. The next day, he disappeared. When she met him again, she asked what had happened. He replied to this effect: 'You see, I discovered my soul and saw that my soul was more powerful than my faith in the Japanese nation and the Mikado; I would have had to obey my soul and I would no longer have been a faithful subject of my emperor. I had to go away.'[65]

In June, the Irish writer and Theosophist James Henry Cousins came to Tokyo as a visiting professor of English at Keio University. The Richards learnt about his arrival and invited him to their place for lunch. Mirra went to pick him up at Shimbashi station. 'There were several Europeans at the station when I reached it,' Cousins later recalled, 'but I knew Madame Richard immediately though I had never seen her before. She was different.' (He didn't specify how.) Paul too was 'different'; he had about him 'an atmosphere of masterfulness', but also an off-putting 'inquisitorial aloofness'. The two men engaged in intellectual duelling while Mirra sat quietly, sometimes helping Paul express himself in English. (Cousins found his accent hilarious.)[66] In July, Mirra and Paul invited their new friend to come with them to Oiwake, a village in Nagano Prefecture on the flank of the ever-active volcano Asamayama. The three of them stayed in a one-storey house, which opened onto a garden with rolling farmland beyond. Above them rose the volcano, with its perpetual plume of smoke. It was a wet summer but when the skies were clear Cousins and Paul went for walks around the mountain or up its slopes. During these excursions, Paul noted down some aphorisms that came to him as he walked. Eventually, he turned them into a book called *The Scourge of Christ,* which Cousins translated into English. On 18 August, the Irishman left Oiwake to visit another friend named Speight. As they parted, Paul remarked: 'You have managed to live with me for a month. You will be able to live with Mr Speight for three weeks.' Cousins mused: 'I had felt the power of his masterful personality, and realised that not everyone could live with him unless they were prepared to forego a good deal of their own desire, and take a spectacular interest in a great mind that was almost too exclusively mental.'[67]

One person who was finding it difficult to live with Paul was Mirra. So far, she had managed to put up with his smugness, vanity and occasional violent temper, but, as time went on, she began to wonder if it was worth the trouble. Even Paul, who was rather obtuse about such matters, realized his relationship with Mirra was under strain: 'There had been a long series of deep inner shocks and disturbances but now there were also visible signs of conflict.' Things came to a head early in September. One evening, Mirra prepared a special dinner. Paul was in one of his 'silent and destructive moods', and refused to sit and eat.[68] Mirra turned this episode of passive aggression into an occasion for spiritual progress: 'Since the man refused the meal I had prepared with so much love and care, I invoked the God to take it,' she wrote in her diary. God accepted her invitation, sat at her table and 'in exchange for my poor and humble offering' he granted her 'the last liberation'. The effect on Mirra was immediate: 'My heart, even this morning so heavy with anguish and care, my head surcharged with responsibility, are delivered of their burden. Now are they light and joyful as my inner being has been for a long time past.'[69]

Superficially, Paul had always been the dominant partner in their relationship. Mirra, by nature retiring, let him call the shots. For twelve years, she had gone where he had gone and helped him do what he did. Now she saw that all along her role was to be his guru and her task to convert him. She had tried her best but failed. She realized 'with an absolute, inner certitude that nothing could be done—it was not possible, not possible to do it this way'. She turned to the Lord and prayed for guidance. The Lord told her it was time to go to Pondicherry.[70]

8

Paul and Mirra returned to Tokyo in September or October. Mirra and Dorothy began to make plans for going to India. Paul was drawn into more Pan-Asian projects. Okawa and some of his colleagues had decided to bring out an English-language monthly 'managed and edited by

Japanese' called the *Asian Review*. Okawa asked Paul to serve as an editorial advisor. He agreed and asked Cousins to join him. Mirra and Dorothy also helped out.[71] On 4 November, the proprietors and editorial staff attended a ceremonial dinner at a high-end restaurant. The visitors spread themselves 'along three sides of the room, each on a cushion with a small lacquered table in front and a hibachi at each hand', Cousins later recalled. 'A group of *geisha* danced and sang in a row across the unoccupied end of the room.' After several courses had been served, the editor told the others about the inception of the magazine and expressed his hope that it would offer 'a true understanding of the national aims and methods of Japan'. Cousins closed the proceedings with an invocation, 'praying that the ancient ever-living Soul of Japan may use it as an instrument through which She may again incarnate fully in Her people, for the uplifting of the world'. A quarter-century later, he wondered whether he and Paul had been helping the cause of Pan-Asian unity or 'subtly paving the way for the subsequent attempt to civilize Asia, in Japan's own way, which ended in tragedy'.[72]

During the last weeks of 1919, Paul and Mirra worked on contributions that appeared in the first issues of the *Asian Review*. Paul offered his usual Japan-flavoured Pan-Asianism: 'Fulfil thy mission,' he urged the people of the country. 'Redeem Asia. Make her peoples happy. For such is thy work.'[73] Mirra polished up an essay—presented earlier as a speech—entitled 'To the Women of Japan'. She began by addressing her audience directly: 'To speak of children to the women of Japan is, I think, to speak to them of their dearest, their most sacred subject.' Moving from biological facts to spiritual development, she observed: 'True maternity begins with the conscious creation of a being, with the willed shaping of a soul coming to develop and utilise a new body.' Further enlarging her frame of reference, she noted that people of the present generation were 'living in an exceptional time at an exceptional turning point of the world's history. Never before, perhaps, did mankind pass through such a dark period of hatred, bloodshed and confusion. And, at the same time, never had such a strong, such an ardent hope awakened in the hearts of the people'. For this hope to be fulfilled, there had to be a change of consciousness that prepared the way for the birth of a new species. Alluding to the evolutionary philosophy of Aurobindo, she said that 'the appearance of a new species always announces the manifestation on earth of a new principle, a new plane of consciousness'. The new principle announced by Aurobindo was what he called the 'supermind'. One who embodied the supermind consciousness would be a 'superman' or supramental being. It would be the task of the women of the future to give birth to this new being.[74]

By the time the first issue of the *Asian Review* reached the printers, Tokyo was in the grip of the second wave of the 1918–20 influenza pandemic. The Spanish flu, as it was called, arrived in Japan at the end of 1918. Within a month, it killed more than 1,00,000 people. The first wave subsided by January 1919 and there was a lull until late December. Then things got bad very quickly. Among the people who caught the flu at this time was James Cousins. He recovered after a day or two in bed and left Tokyo for a place by the sea. The Richards remained in the city.[75]

Around the start of the new year, a 'three-week terror' began in Tokyo. Corpses brought to the municipal crematorium surpassed its daily capacity.[76] The newspapers urged people to stay home and wear face masks if they went out. Influenza was the only topic of conversation. Paul sat in the house in Sendagaya, and said again and again: 'But what is this disease? What's behind this disease?' It began to get on Mirra's nerves. She herself was not worried—her approach, she later said, 'was simply to envelop myself with my [occult] force, my protection so as not to catch it and not think any more about it but continue to do my work'. One day, an acquaintance invited her to come to her home, which was on the other side of town. Mirra took the tram. On the way, seeing people with masks on their faces and feeling the atmosphere of fear, she too began to ask herself: 'Really, what is this disease? What's behind this disease?' She passed about an hour with her friend and took the tram home. By the time she arrived, she had a terrible fever. A doctor was called. He offered her some medicine. She said she would not take it. She just lay in bed, too weak to get up, burning with fever. During the second day, she saw an apparition: A half-decapitated soldier sitting on her chest trying to suck the life out of her. She fought against this vampire and succeeded in driving it away. After a few days, she began to get better.[77] The influenza outbreak continued for another three months. By the time it was over, almost 5,00,000 people in Japan, and at least 50 million worldwide, had lost their lives.[78]

Paul caught the flu at the same time as Mirra. The two of them 'were sick together, but like two strangers: distant and almost unaware of one another', he later recalled. 'It was a painful sign to both of us of our growing separation.'[79] For Mirra, the crisis marked a separation not only from Paul but from her whole previous life. After her recovery, she wrote a declaration that she published years later under the title 'Myself and My Creed':

> I belong to no nation, no civilisation, no society, no race, but to the Divine.
>
> I obey no master, no ruler, no law, no social convention, but the Divine.
>
> To Him I have surrendered all, will, life and self; for Him I am ready to give all my blood, drop by drop, if such is His Will, with complete joy; and nothing in His service can be sacrifice, for all is perfect delight.[80]

9

Early in March, the Richards finished their travel preparations. With the war a year in the past, Paul had few fears he would be detained when their steamship touched British ports. He himself was not inclined to leave. Still in demand among members of Okawa's circle, he recently had become friends with the French ambassador, who offered him some attractive opportunities. Paul was tempted but Mirra was adamant. This time, nothing would keep her from going to Pondicherry.[81]

Looking back on her stay in Japan three decades later, she remembered especially the country's physical beauty: 'For four years, from the artistic point of view, I lived from wonder to wonder'. Not only were there beauty spots all over the country—some of them famous for blossoming trees, others for autumn foliage—but even in the cities there were places of unexpected charm. She loved to roam the streets of Tokyo: '. . . you go wandering and turn the corner and suddenly find yourself in a sort of paradise: magnificent trees, a temple that is beautiful as can be . . .' On the other hand, she found there was 'a dearth of spirituality as complete as could be'. Life in Japan was interesting and enjoyable but she never had the feeling of being 'in contact with something other than a marvellously organized mental–physical domain'.[82] For spirituality, there was no place like India.

On 20 March 1920, the Richards and Dorothy Hodgson departed from Kobe on the *Ganges Maru.*[83] Nine days later, the ship called at Hong Kong. British agents at the port reported Paul's arrival to their superiors, who chose not to take any action. On 30 March, the *Ganges Maru* began the long journey to Colombo, which it reached on 16 April. Again, Paul's arrival was reported but no action was taken. In the Ceylonese capital, the Richards met Margaret Cousins, who had come to meet her husband, James, whose ship was due to arrive on 18 March. That morning Paul and Mirra took her to the port, where she and James had a warm reunion.[84] Four days later, the Richards and Dorothy Hodgson boarded a Messageries Maritimes steamer bound for Pondicherry. As the ship approached the city on the morning of 24 April, it seemed to Mirra that the very substance of the air was transformed. She took this to mean they were entering the aura of Aurobindo Ghose.[85]

7

Return

1

ON 24 APRIL 1920, THE RICHARDS AND DOROTHY HODGSON TOOK rooms at the Grand Hôtel d'Europe, the misleadingly named establishment where Paul and Mirra had stayed for a few days in 1914. Their arrival was noted by British and French intelligence agents, who reported it to their governments. The two imperial powers agreed to exchange information about Paul, who was thought to be 'bearing correspondence from extremists who have taken refuge in Japan addressed to the refugees in Pondicherry, in particular Aurobindo Ghose'.[1] A few days later, the three of them moved to the Hôtel de Paris et Londres, an equally rundown establishment not far from Aurobindo's house. After a brief stay here, they rented rooms at 4 Rue Saint Martin, an old building with a terrace overlooking the sea. Once they had settled in, Aurobindo and his companions got in the habit of going over for Sunday dinner. Mirra oversaw the cooking and made some of the dishes. After dinner, they went up to the terrace to enjoy the sea breeze and talk. On the other days of the week, Mirra and Paul often went to Aurobindo's place to visit. All this socializing was unusual for him and his *Arya* work fell into arrears.[2]

For Mirra, the reunion with Aurobindo was indescribably joyful and spiritually productive. Years later, she spoke of it as a continuation of the experience she had had when she first saw him in 1914. On one occasion, the two of them were standing together, she later recalled, 'and then *together*, precisely, we felt, "Now the Realization will take place."'[3] Aurobindo's retrospective impressions were somewhat similar: 'When I came to Pondicherry, I got from within a programme for my sadhana. I did it myself, but could not figure out how to help others,' he once said. 'Then [in 1920] Mirra came and I found out [the method] with her help.'[4]

For more than ten years, Aurobindo had lived in seclusion, writing and practising yoga. Now, as he explained in a letter to Motilal Roy, a young follower from Chandernagore (a French settlement in Bengal), there was 'the beginning of a pressure from many sides inviting my spiritual attention to the future karma [work] and this means the need of a greater outflowing of energy'. Soon, he would be in a position to 'see what and how much can actually be done under the new circumstances'.[5] These circumstances included the arrival of the Richards, the release of his brother Barin from the prison colony in the Andaman Islands, and Motilal's activities in Chandernagore. In a letter written to Barin in April 1920, Aurobindo spoke of establishing a sangha or community: 'Not a fixed and rigid form like that of the old Aryan society, not a stagnant backwater, but a free form that can spread itself out like the sea with its multitudinous waves.' In practice, this would mean a loosely connected group of centres operating under one inspiration. He did not want 'tens of thousands of disciples', he said; it would 'be enough if I can get as instruments of God one hundred complete men free of petty egoism'.[6]

Barin and Motilal were intrigued, and also somewhat puzzled, by the Frenchwoman who, along with her husband, was now part of Aurobindo's circle. (Up to this time, few foreign women had studied under spiritual teachers in India.) A month or two after Mirra's arrival, Motilal asked her to write an article for *Prabartak*, a Bengali journal he edited, explaining how she had met 'AG' (that is, Aurobindo Ghose) and how she conceived her 'mission'. In response, she wrote a few paragraphs in English that Motilal published along with her photograph and a brief Bengali article about her. I have quoted from Mirra's piece when discussing her early spiritual development and her recognition of Aurobindo as the spiritual master she had seen in her inner visions. This recognition was enough, she concluded, 'to explain why I am fully convinced that my place and my work are near him, in India'.[7]

After his release from the Andamans, Barin began to write for *Narayan*, a Bengali monthly published by the well-known nationalist politician Chittaranjan Das. In the June–July issue, *Narayan* printed a photograph of Mirra along with a brief note on her. (She now was known to Bengali readers through her 1918 article in *The Modern Review*, her 1920 essay in *Prabartak*, and the photographs and notes in *Prabartak* and *Narayan*.) Sometime before August 1920, Barin came to Pondicherry. His first impressions of the Richards was positive: Paul, with his long beard and shining eyes, seemed to have 'stepped out of the pages of the Rig Veda into this world of ours'. Mirra was 'an exceptionally beautiful woman of medium height, with a face lit up with power and intelligence and [a] very graceful and active body. Her movements were quick, yet rhythmic and in full control. Her smile was of rare sweetness, which broke out as she looked at you.' Yet, Barin got the impression that she was holding something back: 'Her depth of culture, rare intuitive intellect and yogic powers were seldom manifest to a casual observer.'[8]

2

In June 1920, Mirra noted in her diary:

> After granting me the joy which surpasses all expression, Thou hast sent me, O my beloved Lord, the struggle, the ordeal and on this too I have smiled as on one of Thy precious messengers. . . . It is Thou whom I see unravelling the entanglement of events and jarring tendencies and winning in the end the victory over all that strives to veil Thy light and Thy power.[9]

At this point, the main entanglement she had to deal with was her relationship with Paul. Before leaving Japan, she had come to the conclusion that the two of them had reached a dead end. He could make no further spiritual progress and now was just holding her back. After they settled in Pondicherry, Paul kept himself busy with various publication projects. He put together a collection of his speeches, persuaded Aurobindo to translate them into English, and issued them under the title *The Dawn over Asia.* With the help of James Cousins, he found an Indian publisher for his older collection *To the Nations* and his new book of aphorisms, *The Scourge of Christ.* He tried to launch an Indian branch of the League for Racial Equality but found few people were interested. Since the end of the war, the Indian national movement had become increasingly dynamic. In September 1920, the Indian National Congress endorsed Mahatma Gandhi's Non-Cooperation Movement. Mass action against the British government began. No one in India had time for a French intellectual with no real knowledge of the country. For Paul, it was quite a comedown from the days when flattering Pan-Asianists filled his home in Tokyo.

The last years in Japan had drained Mirra physically and psychologically. In Pondicherry, she spent most of her time in her room, going out only for visits to Aurobindo's house, and receiving him and his companions on Sundays. After dinner, she and Aurobindo sometimes stood apart and spoke quietly together. Despite her undemonstrative nature, she could not keep herself from showing her feelings for the one she looked upon as her spiritual master. Once, while sitting at a table with him, she took his hand in hers. On another occasion, she knelt at his feet with her arms outstretched before her. It did not take long for Paul to catch on to what was happening. When they were alone, he asked Mirra to explain. She said she had nothing to tell him. He asked Aurobindo what form his relationship with Mirra would take. He said it would take any form she wished. Realizing he was losing his hold over the one who had been the source of his intellectual and spiritual accomplishments, he became insistent, then violent. Mirra endured it as well as she could.[10]

Paul had made plans to attend the December 1920 session of the Indian National Congress in Nagpur. He left Pondicherry towards the end of November. That year, the monsoon was unusually heavy. Rain lashed the building where Mirra and Dorothy were staying, flooding the rooms. Hearing of their predicament, Aurobindo invited them to stay at his place until the rains abated and their house could be repaired. His companions shifted the ladies' things to the first floor of 41 Rue François Martin.[11] Mirra and Dorothy were comfortable there. Eventually, the idea of their going back to Rue Saint Martin was dropped.

In Nagpur, Paul had little luck in getting people to listen to his ideas. Afterwards, he went to Chandernagore at the invitation of Motilal Roy. He stayed there for a week or so, pondering his next move. He told Motilal he wanted to visit 'Indian centres of culture' such as Tagore's Santiniketan, Swami Shraddhanand's Gurukul near Haridwar and Gandhi's ashram in Ahmedabad, after which he would go on a world tour 'to prepare an international cradle of the new race of gods'.[12] In the event, he went to a village in the Himalayas to engage in meditation. After a couple of months, he wrote a tract called *To India: The Message of the Himalayas*, and sent some letters to the Nobel Prize–winning author Romain Rolland. In overwrought prose, he told Rolland he had fought 'a dreadful inner battle, which cast me, alone, face to face with death—the inner Death—and the divine possibility ahead'. Now he was ready to descend to the world again.[13] In December 1921, he attended the Ahmedabad session of the National Congress. Afterwards, he spent some time with Gandhi at his ashram and then moved around Gujarat, meeting people and giving speeches. When summer came, he went back to his Himalayan village, where he wrote some essays and poems that later were published in Theosophical journals. Towards the end of 1922, he returned to France. Six years later, he met an American woman named Ethel Linda Todd, who took him to New York. In 1929, his lawyers obtained a long-distance divorce from Mirra—French law now allowed couples who had been living apart for more than three years to divorce without much trouble—and he and Ethel were married. For a while, he appeared as an expert on international affairs at conclaves in New York and Palm Beach, Florida. In 1930 or 1931, he and Ethel parted ways. After a while, he found another woman to support him. He died in New York in 1967.

3

For more than six years, Aurobindo had been writing sixty pages of philosophy every month and publishing it in *Arya.* In November 1920, for the first time, he did not have enough matter to fill an issue. He may have been distracted by the tension between Mirra and Paul or he may just have felt he had said all he had to say. The next month, he published a combined November–December issue, followed by an issue in January. Then *Arya* ceased publication. For the next seven years, Aurobindo wrote practically nothing and published nothing new. What was he doing during this period? In occasional conversations, he said he was absorbed in his yoga but offered few details. More than a decade later, in answer to a question posed by a disciple, he said that while he was working on *Arya* 'the sadhana [practice of yoga] and work were waiting for the Mother's [Mirra's] coming'. In an 'alpha' biography like this one, 'omega' statements like that have to be turned around: When Mirra came back to Pondicherry, his real sadhana and work began.

What sort of sadhana was Aurobindo doing and what sort of work did he have in mind? Like all mystics, he regarded his main task as achieving union with the Divine, the Absolute, the Brahman. Unlike many mystics, he did not regard this union as the final goal. Once he had completed his 'subjective sadhana', he would apply what he realized to 'life, practical knowledge & shakti [power]' and direct it to his 'work in life'. He sketched the scope of this work in a letter of August 1912 that I cited in Chapter 4: To explain the Indian tradition to the human intellect from a new standpoint, to establish a new method of yoga, to work for the restoration of India to its right place and the world; and to remodel society to make it fit to contain 'a perfect humanity'.[14] This is similar in some respects to what Mirra said in May 1912 about 'the most useful work to be done at the present time'. The last part of the fourfold work she proposed was 'to establish an ideal society in a propitious spot for the flowering of the new race'.[15] In Pondicherry, she found a propitious spot and the seed stock for this new society—the eight or ten people who had gathered around Aurobindo.

When Mirra and Dorothy moved in to 41 Rue François Martin, the character of that previously all-male domain began to change. There was a new sense of tidiness and order, and some unspoken constraints on the carefree life the young men who stayed there were used to. Aurobindo had never imposed a 'yogic' style of life on his household. Concentrated on his sadhana, he 'acted very much on a principle of laissez faire with the few sadhaks [practitioners] who were there'. The young men helped out with household chores, read, wrote, did a bit of meditation and, in the evening, went out to play football. Now, reported Barin Ghose, 'the light gossip and desultory bohemian life was quite perceptibly changing'. A 'hushed and deeper tone' took hold.[16] This change was not the result of any direct intervention by Aurobindo or Mirra, who were absorbed in their own practice. What exactly this practice was is hard to pin down, since both of them stopped keeping their diaries, wrote few letters and rarely spoke about themselves. We get a brief glimpse of Mirra's inner life in 1922 from a letter she wrote to Nobuko Kobayashi that October: 'I am still exclusively busy with my "yoga" (I think you know the meaning of that Indian word), seeing nobody and never going out. But what is the use of moving about when you are constantly aware of the presence of the Infinite!'[17]

4

The fact that life at 41 Rue François Martin was quieting down did not mean it had become a cloister. The young men continued their usual activities. Friends from town dropped by. All members of the household, Aurobindo and Mirra included, had their meals together. In the afternoon, there was informal talk covering a wide range of topics or else 'a natural silence verging on meditation'.[18] Afterwards, Mirra served cocoa to everyone. When the others departed, she and Aurobindo meditated together until it was time for dinner.

During the years of the war, practically no one from outside French India came to see Aurobindo. When things opened up, there was a slow but steady stream of visitors—some of them obscure, some well known. Many were connected in one way or another with the Indian freedom movement. Some of Barin Ghose's former revolutionary comrades—Upendranath Bannerjee, Hrishikesh Kanjilal, Abinash Chandra Bhattacharya and others—showed up between 1920 and 1922. They were disappointed to learn that Aurobindo was uninterested in resuming his political work. So were Devadas Gandhi, a son of the Mahatma, and B.S. Moonje, a Congress leader who was also active in the Hindu Mahasabha. It is unlikely that Mirra interacted with these political visitors. She probably took more interest when Sarala Devi Chaudhurani, a niece of Rabindranath Tagore, who was active in the sphere of women's empowerment, came for a few days. Another well-connected visitor was Mrinalini Chattopadhyaya, sister of the political activist Virendranath Chattopadhyaya and the poet and politician Sarojini Naidu. Mrinalini discussed literary projects with Aurobindo and showed Mirra how to wear the sari. The writer James Cousins, who had known Mirra in Japan and had literary relations with Aurobindo, came with his wife, Margaret, in August 1921. James spoke with Aurobindo on two successive days. He retained from his interviews 'a flavour of gentleness and wisdom, breadth of thought, and extent of experience that marked him out as one among millions'.[19] Neither he nor Margaret mentioned Mirra in their joint autobiography. In all likelihood, Mirra kept herself in the background during their visit.

Few of the people who came to Pondicherry during the 1920s were interested in practising Aurobindo's path of yoga. An exception was Ambalal Purani, a former revolutionary who had turned from activism to yoga after Aurobindo assured him that India's liberation was certain. During his second visit to Pondicherry in 1921, Purani met Mirra and was struck by her appearance: 'Such unearthly beauty I had never seen—she appeared to be about twenty years of age when she was more than forty.'[20] A year later, a friend of Mirra's from her days in Paris, a Russian Theosophist named Irma de Manziarly, came for a day or two. Mirra arranged a meeting between her and Aurobindo, and later reported to Nobuko Kobayashi that 'like all those that approach him she felt a great peaceful and luminous happiness at that time'.[21]

5

The number of sadhaks slowly increased and the house on Rue François Martin became too small to accommodate them all. In 1922, Barin learnt that a house at 9 Rue de la Marine, a block north and a block west from the place on Rue François Martin, was available. He told Aurobindo, who spoke about it with Mirra. A day or two later, Aurobindo called Barin and said that Mirra had told him that the Rue de la Marine house would be very important for their work, and he should take it on lease. The negotiations were completed by October 1922, and Aurobindo, Mirra, Dorothy, Barin and two or three others moved in. Mirra occupied a room on the first floor with windows facing north. It communicated with Dorothy's rooms to the west and a sort of salon in front. This led to Aurobindo's room, which had windows facing south and east. They also kept the old place at 41 Rue François Martin, which became known as the Guest House. The little colony now consisted of ten or fifteen people in two houses in the French quarter of Pondicherry.

Two visitors of 1923 left accounts of their meetings with Aurobindo and Mirra. The first was Willie Pearson, who had stayed with Mirra and Paul in Japan for several months. When he saw her again he could hardly recognize her. 'What has happened to you?' he exclaimed. Mirra took this to mean he had noticed that she now looked like an eighteen-year-old girl. This was the result, she later remarked, of her sadhana on the 'vital plane' (the plane of the life-force). When Pearson left the house, a French gendarme followed him to his ship and then to Colombo, where he handed him over to the British authorities. A year later, Pearson visited Romain Rolland in Switzerland and spoke to him about Aurobindo. He was, Pearson told the novelist, 'accompanied by Martha and Mary'—that is, Dorothy and Mirra reminded the former pastor of the active and silent disciples of Jesus in the Bible story.[22]

In October, Aurobindo gave an interview to a journalist named G.V. Subbarao. Aurobindo told him he had 'long been absorbed in a sadhana for yoga siddhi [perfection in yoga]' because he was convinced that a higher spiritual power was 'necessary to solve the moral, material, social, and even political problems of the world'. His isolation did not prevent him from taking an interest in the lives of people who wrote to him about their spiritual and personal problems. Subbarao noted that he sometimes spoke with Mirra before replying. He learnt she was considered 'the best of his disciples' and that Aurobindo consulted her 'on many affairs, including Yoga'.[23]

The evening talks and meditations that were part of the routine at Rue François Martin continued in the new house. People asked Aurobindo about all sorts of things: Local happenings, national and international politics, cultural and literary affairs, philosophy and yoga. Mirra sometimes attended, wearing a sari and veil. If she spoke, her voice was barely audible. In January 1924, she had a bout of illness. Soon after this, Aurobindo stopped the talks and meditations. They obliged him, he said, 'to descend lower in the consciousness'. He would rather give all of his attention to his joint yoga practice with Mirra. When they had succeeded in overcoming certain inner obstacles, all the disciples would benefit. This was no consolation to the disciples, who felt he was becoming more and more remote. After a couple of weeks, he resumed the evening sessions.[24]

The celebration of Aurobindo's birthday on 15 August had become a major event. The usual evening meeting was transformed into a darshan (viewing). Purani left a description of the ceremony of 1924: The veranda of the house was decorated with jasmine garlands and lotus flowers. As the moment approached, everyone gathered in hushed anticipation. At 4.15, there was the usual creak of the door as it swung open. Aurobindo stepped out, clad in an immaculate white dhoti. Mirra followed, wearing a cream-coloured sari with a broad red border. Aurobindo sat on his usual Japanese chair, Mirra to his right on a stool: 'For a short time there is complete silence! Then he glances at each one separately. The minutes are melting into the silence. There is again a wave of emotion in all; all bathe again into an ocean of some divine emotion.'[25] All this was in contrast with Aurobindo's earlier routine, when he received visitors seated at a small table, his cigar burning in an ashtray. The new mise en scène was

Mirra's work, an expression of her aesthetic sensibilities and her feeling that Aurobindo ought to be placed on a pedestal.

In January 1925, Mirra went through another period of ill health. Her knee swelled up alarmingly. Aurobindo was anxious and consulted several doctors, eventually summoning a specialist from north India, who said it was a bad case of rheumatism. Her sedentary habits may have been a predisposing factor. She took little exercise apart from an occasional stint in the garden.

The number of people practising Aurobindo's yoga continued to increase. In 1925 and 1926, a few seekers from France joined the community. The first was Philippe Barbier Saint-Hilaire. An engineering graduate of the École Polytechnique, he had served as an artillery officer in the war. During his spare time, he developed an interest in the occult and Asian religions. After the armistice, he went to Japan, where he helped found the Tokyo lodge of the Theosophical Society. Leaving the country in 1924, he spent a year in a Buddhist monastery in Mongolia before going to India. His first stop was Pondicherry, where he met Aurobindo and Mirra. Accepted as a disciple, he eventually became Mirra's secretary. In March 1926, her old friend and admirer Marie Potel came with her husband, Léon. They imported a 1925 Lorraine-Dietrich automobile, which they presented to Mirra. Now in the evenings, she could go for drives in the countryside, with Saint-Hilaire at the wheel.

Only a few of the people who asked to become disciples of Aurobindo were admitted to the Pondicherry centre. Others stayed where they were and tried to follow the guidelines he laid down in his published writings and letters. Many made some progress. Others remained unchanged. A few went off the deep end. One danger in yoga is for practitioners to assume that the increased power they feel is a sign of special divine favour. This can cause them to lose their balance. When such problems emerged, Aurobindo often turned to Mirra for advice and assistance. In one case, he wrote to his brother Barin, who had opened a yoga centre in Calcutta, to say that the visions a sadhak was having were common to 'people whose Yoga runs strongly on psychic lines and . . . similar ones of still stronger character have been experienced by Mirra at least a thousand times during her sadhana'. The person in question had to face them without fear because 'fearlessness is the first necessary condition for going through this yoga'.[26] Unfortunately, the person was unable to do this and he lapsed into insanity. Eventually, Aurobindo asked Barin to close the Calcutta centre.

6

During 1926, Mirra began more and more to guide the disciples' sadhana while Aurobindo moved to the background.[27] Up to that point, he wrote in a letter of March 1926, she was 'not mixing with the sadhaks . . . partly because they themselves were not ready to take the right relation and receive her influence, partly because the difficulties of the physical plane made it necessary for her to retire from all direct contact with anyone'. Still, she had acted 'on the psychic and vital levels to do whatever might be possible at the time'. Now, as she came forward, there was a division of labour between him and her that he explained using Indian philosophical concepts: Purusha (soul, spirit) and shakti (force, power). He 'represented the Purusha element', acting 'directly on the mental and on the vital being [of the sadhak] through the illumined mind'. Mirra's force, 'representing the Shakti element', acted 'directly on the psychic being and on the emotional, vital and physical nature through the illumined psychic consciousness'. Her spiritual knowledge was 'predominantly practical in its nature . . . a large and detailed knowledge and experience of the mental, vital and physical forces at play and with the knowledge[,] the power to handle them for the purposes of life and of Yoga'.[28]

The idea that shakti or force is the feminine complement of the masculine purusha is important not only in Indian philosophy but also in the spiritual discipline known as tantra. Most tantric scriptures are structured as dialogues between a god such as Shiva, who represents the supreme spirit, and a goddess such as Parvati, who represents the divine creative power. According to these scriptures, the universe is the issue of the mystical union of Shiva and Shakti. In some tantric paths, this union is enacted ritually by a man and a woman. This has led to the belief that one way of engaging in yoga is for a male practitioner to find a female partner, who will give him the energy he needs to reach enlightenment. Some of Aurobindo's disciples wondered if a partnership of this sort was possible for those who practised his yoga. He did not deny the possibility: If a 'man seeking the higher divine life . . . meets the woman of the right type—the woman who is his Shakti—then his spiritual life, the life which he is to manifest, is enriched and becomes full'. But, he went on, such a relationship was not a necessity for those practising his yoga and most men who wanted a Shakti were just looking for a way to indulge their sexual desires. He and Mirra discouraged close relations between men and women. When married couples came to Pondicherry to practise yoga, he expected them to live apart and look on each other as friends.[29]

What about Aurobindo and Mirra? As we have seen, Mirra told Paul Richard before they got married that she had gone beyond sex and wanted nothing more to do with it. In later life, she described the 'physical act of procreation' as 'wholly animal, most often even bestial'.[30] Aurobindo was married in 1901 to a woman who, in accordance with the customs of the period, was a great deal younger than him. They spent little time together and he showed no interest in pursuing the usual aims of married life. (She died of the Spanish flu in Calcutta in 1918.) When Mirra and Aurobindo began practising yoga together, their relationship was free from sexual intimacy but it was, in a different way, a union of masculine and feminine elements. Mirra may have viewed this as the fulfilment of the Cosmic idea of *dualité d'être* (duality of being).[31] Aurobindo viewed it in terms of 'the relation between the Purusha and Prakriti', that is, 'the male and female divine principles in the universe'.[32] This duality became the model of his joint action with Mirra: He withdrawn behind, she active in front.

Aurobindo's disciples sometimes tried to draw him out about his relationship with Mirra. Only once did they succeed in getting him to speak:

> In my own case it was a necessary condition for the work that I had to do. If I had to do my own transformation, or give a new Yoga, or a new ideal to a select few people who came in my personal contact, I

> could have done that without having any Shakti. But for the work that I had to do it was necessary that the two sides must come together.

When he and Mirra joined forces, conditions were created that made it possible for others to achieve 'transformation'. It was up to the disciples 'to take advantage of those conditions'.[33]

7

To understand what Aurobindo meant by transformation we have to look briefly at the nature of his path of yoga. In Indian systems such as Theravada Buddhism, Jainism and Advaita Vedanta, the goal is release from the painful, delusory world and the attainment of extinction (nirvana), isolation (kaivalya) or liberation (moksha). Once the goal is achieved, the practitioner takes no further interest in the world. For Aurobindo, the experience of nirvana or moksha was a first step towards the realization of the Divine both within and above the universe. There is, he said, a series of 'planes of consciousness' between the 'lower hemisphere' of matter, life and mind, and the 'higher hemisphere' of divine existence, divine consciousness and divine bliss. The highest of these planes is 'supermind' or truth-consciousness, which has the power to transform the lower hemisphere into the image of the higher. Aurobindo's diary entries between 1912 and 1920 chronicle his ascent through the planes of consciousness between mind and supermind, and his attempt to bring the power of those levels into the lower world. When Mirra joined him in 1920, they 'helped each other in perfecting the sadhana' as they moved towards supermind.[34]

In a talk given on 15 August 1926, his fifty-fourth birthday, Aurobindo reminded his disciples about the goal of his yoga: 'It is the bringing down of a Consciousness, a Power, a Light, a Reality that is other than the consciousness which satisfies the ordinary man upon earth—a Consciousness, a Power and Light of Truth, a Divine Reality.' This supramental consciousness was 'destined to raise the earth-consciousness and transform everything here'.[35] That year, Mirra played a special role in the celebrations. In the morning, after the disciples had a darshan of Aurobindo on the veranda, they went to his room, where Mirra was sitting, and did pranam to her. In the evening, she and Aurobindo presided together over a group meditation.

Mirra's new role was a sign of her increased responsibility for the spiritual life of the community. In September, a few sadhikas (women disciples) began to have regular meditations with her. Soon, some men joined the group. The Indian disciples related to Mirra in the traditional pattern of disciple and guru, with formal expressions of devotion such as pranam. She knew Western disciples might find this disconcerting. When Saint-Hilaire asked to join the group, Mirra told him: 'I must ask you not to feel surprised in your outer consciousness if you see certain things that might make you wonder.' The Indians considered the room where they meditated a temple 'and behave[d] as they would in a temple only replacing the idol with a human figure'—that is, herself. 'That gives them the plenitude they need. You were brought up differently—' Saint-Hilaire told her not to worry. It was true he 'had less need for outer manifestations' but he wasn't put off by the others' behaviour.[36] Mirra seems to have had little trouble accepting Hindu expressions of guru worship. From now on—until the end of her life—it was part of her normal routine.

During the autumn of 1926, many people in the community felt as if something extraordinary was about to happen. From the beginning of November, Purani recalled, the pressure 'became almost unbearable'. Another disciple, a young woman named Jaya Devi, told Aurobindo one evening that she and many of the others could feel a 'great wave of peace and delight. We are dancing with an inner joy'. He told her there would be more joy to come.[37]

On the evening of 24 November, Mirra asked everyone to assemble on the veranda of the house. When all of them were there, she, then Aurobindo, came out of his room. He sat in his usual chair, she on a stool at his side. For forty-five minutes, there was a powerful group meditation. Then the disciples, one by one, bowed before them and received their blessings. This was followed by another meditation, after which Aurobindo and Mirra went into his room. In the silence that followed,

Dorothy Hodgson exclaimed: 'The Lord has descended into the physical today'—or something to that effect.[38] Everybody felt that Aurobindo and Mirra had taken a big step towards the final transformation.

The next morning, a disciple asked Mirra what had happened the previous day. She said that the god Krishna 'had descended and conquered everything in the physical except a few obstacles that will be done by 15th August'. The disciples spent the day going about their usual activities. In the evening, there was a group meditation. Aurobindo did not come out. The next afternoon, he called Barin and gave him a message to deliver to the members of the community. The main points, as recorded by a sadhak in his diary, were these: 'The power has descended into the unconscious' and he and Mirra 'will have to work things out . . . by the help of that power'. Secondly, 'Mirra is my Shakti. She has taken charge of the new creation. You will get everything from her. Give consent to whatever she wants to do.'[39] Another point, not mentioned in the sadhak's diary but soon understood by all, was that Aurobindo would not be coming out of his room for an indefinite period.

8

In later years, 24 November would be commemorated annually as the Day of Victory or Day of Siddhi. At the time, no one but Aurobindo and Mirra had any idea what this victory or siddhi (perfection) was all about. Many assumed that what happened was the long-awaited descent of the supermind. Aurobindo said nothing to support this. In fact, he made no explicit statement about the 1926 experience for almost a decade. In August 1935, a disciple asked him directly whether he had 'achieved the Supermind' on 24 November 1926. He replied: 'What was said [in 1926] was that the Divine (Krishna or the Divine Presence or whatever you like) had come down into the material.' This statement caused some puzzlement among those who read it. One of them asked for details. Aurobindo explained: 'The descent of Krishna would mean the descent of the Overmind Godhead preparing, though not itself actually bringing, the descent of Supermind and Ananda.' At the time of the experience, he did not speak of 'overmind' because he had not yet coined the term.[40]

In later works, he described overmind as the highest of the intermediate planes between mind and supermind.

Besides being observed as the day of Sri Aurobindo's siddhi, 24 November 1926 is also remembered as the birthday of Sri Aurobindo Ashram. At the time, however, nobody felt a dramatic change had taken place in the organization of the community. On 26 November, the sadhaks learnt that Mirra was now in charge but this came as no surprise since she had been assuming more and more responsibility since August. Sri Aurobindo's announcement just formalized the existing arrangement. Up to this time, the community that had taken shape around him had no special name. He began to refer to it as an 'ashram' sometime during 1927. He did not like the term on account of its monastic connotations but eventually accepted it 'for want of a better word'. What he wanted to establish was not a hermitage but a dynamic collective in which all human activities—literature, art, music, education, agriculture, commerce—would flourish along with yoga. This community would serve 'as a means for bringing down a higher consciousness and making it a power not merely for "salvation" but for a divine life upon earth'.[41]

During the last months of 1926, most people in the community began to refer to Aurobindo as 'Sri Aurobindo' and to Mirra as 'the Mother'. In ordinary usage, 'Sri' or 'Shri' is an honorific, more or less the equivalent of the English 'Mr'. When applied to a male spiritual figure, it is a mark of special respect. Female spiritual figures in India are often addressed as 'Mother' (in various languages). The term evokes the Mother Goddess, the nurturing form of the divine Shakti. By mid-1927, the appellations 'Sri Aurobindo' and 'the Mother' were the normal forms, and from this point on I will use them in this biography.

PART TWO

1927–1973

8

The Mother's Creation

1

On 21 February 1927, the Mother's birthday was marked by special celebrations. Sri Aurobindo wrote a five-page message for the occasion. He stressed the need of surrendering to the supramental force, which alone could 'victoriously handle the physical Nature and annihilate its difficulties'. During the next months, he wrote four letters on different aspects of his yoga as well as a long essay on the divine Shakti: The individual, universal and transcendent Mother. In lush poetic prose, he described her four 'powers and personalities': Maheshwari, the mother of wisdom; Mahakali, the mother of strength; Mahalakshmi, the mother of harmony; and Mahasaraswati, the mother of perfection. He did not mention Mirra, the mother of the ashram, but most members of the community understood that he identified her with the individual Divine Mother who mediated 'between the human personality and the divine Nature'.[1] Early the next year, Sri Aurobindo published the message, the letters and the essay in a short book entitled *The Mother.* It was a brief introduction to the practice of his path of yoga. It also served as an announcement—not for the public but for those in the know—that Mirra Alfassa was the Mother, an incarnation of the divine Shakti.

How is a biographer of Mirra Alfassa to deal with this? One way would be to treat the rest of her earthly existence as a progressive manifestation of divinity. Another would be to continue to record the contingencies of a complex life. I explained in the Prologue that I had neither the competence nor the inclination to write a chronicle of divine manifestation. My task as an 'alpha' writer has been to collect, organize and arrange contingent facts in a continuous narrative. Other biographers of the Mother have treated her 'outward life' (as they called it) as an expression of inner divinity. There are problems with this approach. Virtually everything written in every biography of the Mother has to do with her outward life: Birth, family, education, journeys, meetings, writings and so forth. In presenting these events, her biographers relied on the usual biographical materials: Official documents, memoirs, letters, etc. (Most biographers actually relied on summaries of this material in secondary sources and not the primary sources themselves.) They also wrote about events in her inner life, relying on things she wrote or said about herself and statements that Sri Aurobindo, her partner in yoga, made about her. To use such accounts is legitimate as long as those who do so make it clear they are simply reporting what the Mother or Sri Aurobindo said. Many biographers went further, speaking of her inner experiences as though they had privileged access to the states she described and first-hand knowledge of her divinity. The results were not biography but theology.

The Mother lived for forty-seven years—half of her long life—after 1926. During this period, she underwent great inner development but, at the same time, was constantly at work in the world. The accomplishments for which she is known—the organization of Sri Aurobindo Ashram, the creation of Sri Aurobindo International Centre of Education, the foundation of Auroville—date from these forty-seven years. During the first half of her life, she was active in many ways—as a student, artist, spouse, mother, writer, speaker, spiritual guide—but she kept herself in the background and had little perceptible effect on the world around her. This changed after Sri Aurobindo put her in charge of the ashram. From now on, she was constantly in motion, constantly interacting with others, constantly in touch with the wider world.

While writing about the second half of the Mother's life, I often will mention world events that framed her endeavours and influenced her actions. It was a period when European imperialism was undermined by anticolonial uprisings, and the international order was shaken by the Second World War and its aftermath. All this had its effect on the little world of the ashram. A different sort of biography would give more space to local events: Happenings in the ashram community, and accounts of the interactions of disciples with the Mother and with other disciples. There are dozens of books and hundreds of articles that go into such things in minute detail. I leave it to interested readers to explore this literature on their own.

2

'The Asram is the Mother's creation and would not have existed but for her,' wrote Sri Aurobindo in 1935.[2] Taken literally, the statement means simply that if the Mother had not been there to organize it, the group of men and women that had grown around Sri Aurobindo would have remained a loose aggregation of individuals practising yoga on their own. But the statement can also be understood metaphorically. One meaning of creation is 'work of art'. The Mother never ceased to be an artist, and, zafter 1926, her canvas consisted of the people and activities, the buildings and grounds that made up the ashram.

In 1925 and 1926, Sri Aurobindo and the Mother had taken three houses on rent: 7 Rue de la Marine, 8 Rue Saint Gilles and 28 Rue François Martin. These properties, along with 9 Rue de la Marine, which they had occupied since 1922, formed a complete town block. In January 1927, the Mother wrote to her son, André:

> Our community is growing more and more; we are nearing thirty (not counting those who are scattered all over India); and I have become responsible for all this; I am at the centre of the organisation, material as well as spiritual, and you can easily imagine what this represents. . . . New recruits are coming from all parts of the world. With this expansion, new activities are being created, new needs are arising that require new skills.[3]

On 7 February 1927, the Mother and Sri Aurobindo moved from 9 Rue de la Marine to 28 Rue François Martin, the house occupying the northeast corner of the block, which they had purchased the previous month. Everyone was asked to leave the buildings so that the two of them could walk across without being seen. The only witness was a cat named Bushy, who ran ahead and showed them the rooms of their new abode. Sri Aurobindo occupied a suite on the first floor, with windows looking north and east. The Mother took no room as her own. She was trying to cut down the time she spent sleeping, so at night she just relaxed in a room on the first floor. On 16 February, she brought André up to date: 'We have just bought, repaired and comfortably furnished one of these [four] houses and just the other day Sri Aurobindo and I moved in, along with five of the closest disciples.' The linking together of the buildings created a little private realm, where she could walk freely without having to go out into the street. She found this 'rather pleasant'.[4]

Somewhat earlier, the Mother introduced some practices and ceremonies that helped her stay in touch with the disciples. In November 1926, she started giving bowls of soup from which she had sipped to individual disciples. To one she said as she gave it: 'Take this cup and you will be fully conscious.' Towards the end of December, she organized a collective soup ceremony during which she concentrated over a tureen of vegetable broth and then distributed it to the dozen or so disciples who were present. The purpose, Sri Aurobindo later explained, was 'to establish a means by which the sadhak might receive something from the Mother in the material consciousness'.[5] The atmosphere during the ceremony was, by all accounts, intense. The collective meditations that had been a feature of the community's life since the early 1920s continued. During 1927, there were three group meditations per day. Later, the morning meditation was replaced by the ceremony of pranam, during which the sadhaks prostrated themselves before the Mother and received her blessings. Often, she gave flowers, using them as a way to send messages or transmit power. She assigned a special significance to each variety—jasmine was 'purity', shefali was 'aspiration' and so forth. When the sadhaks received a certain flower, they understood the Mother was giving them that power or pointing out something they needed to work on. Flowers were also distributed at a regular meeting in the ashram stores before the soup ceremony. The atmosphere at this get-together was more relaxed. Sometimes, they all played games. The Mother proved to be particularly adept at balancing fruits on her head. In addition to these collective gatherings, she had occasional one-on-one meetings with disciples during which she spoke with them about their sadhana and the work they did for the community.

Members of the ashram later looked back on the months that followed the realization of 24 November 1926 as the brightest period in the spiritual life of the ashram. 'Suddenly,' the Mother explained thirty years later, 'things took a certain shape: a very brilliant creation was worked out in extraordinary detail, with marvellous experiences, contacts with divine beings, all kinds of manifestations that are considered miraculous.' One day, she went to Sri Aurobindo and told him what was taking place. 'Perhaps,' she recalled, 'I showed a little enthusiasm when I told him what was happening.' Sri Aurobindo replied in words like these: 'All this is very interesting, very well done. You will perform miracles that will make you famous throughout the world.' But, he added, this 'is not the success we want.... One must know how to renounce immediate success in order to create the new world, the supramental world in all its completeness.' The Mother understood and 'a few hours later the creation was gone. From that moment we began again on other bases'.[6] Instead of establishing a new creation inhabited by gods and saints, the Mother laid the foundation for an ashram peopled by fallible human beings who aspired for something greater.

Almost as soon as the ashram was founded, people began to spread rumours about it. Most traditional ashrams are all-male institutions. If women are allowed, they are segregated from the men. There was no such rule in Sri Aurobindo's ashram, and some people began whispering that Sri Aurobindo and his disciples were practicing tantric sadhana and indulging in meat, drink and sex. In May 1927, a Bengali writer named Jatindranath Sen Gupta published a newspaper article refuting such rumours, which were, he said, being spread 'by interested persons'.

The members of the ashram, he continued, 'led a rigorously simple and unostentatious life', eating simple vegetarian food. When not absorbed in meditation or sadhana, they engaged in cultural activities such as writing and painting. All forms of 'sensual indulgence' were 'absolutely forbidden'. The precincts were filled with 'a spiritual atmosphere of calmness and purity' that 'cannot adequately be described'. Its 'central figure' was 'Mira Devi, who is the mother of the ashram people' and 'the very embodiment of grace and purity, of love and compassion'. At the end of his piece, Sen Gupta added a paragraph drafted by Sri Aurobindo on the need for funds to help the ashram grow. Sri Aurobindo's sadhana was not just 'for himself and a few disciples'; it was meant to be 'the foundation for a great spiritual work for India and for all the world'.[7] This was the first and last time Sri Aurobindo made a public appeal for funds.

3

By the middle of 1927, the Mother was getting used to being the Mother of the ashram, but she remained Mirra to her mother, Mathilde, and brother, Matteo, and *maman* (mum) to André.[8] She wrote regularly to Matteo, keeping him informed about developments in Pondicherry. He kept her up to date on family affairs and his official postings. After the war, he had been appointed lieutenant-governor of Middle Congo, the southeastern part of French Equatorial Africa (Afrique-Équatoriale Française or AEF). In July 1924, he was named acting governor-general of AEF until the arrival of the new governor-general, Raphaël Antonetti. Over the next ten years, Matteo would act as governor-general six times for a total of around thirty-six months—whenever Antonetti was in Paris and he was in Africa.

The governor-general of French Equatorial Africa was responsible for a colony with a population of around 3 million and an area four times larger than France, comprising the present Gabon, Republic of the Congo, Central African Republic and Chad. This enormous territory was poor and undeveloped, the 'Cinderella' of the French Empire. The French companies that dominated its economy found it hard to exploit its resources—copper, timber, ivory, rubber, pistachios, manioc—because they did not have an efficient way of moving the material to the coast. For decades, there had been plans to construct a railway linking Brazzaville, the capital, to a port on the Atlantic. Work on the proposed Congo-Océan railway began in 1921 but nothing much was done before the arrival of Antonetti, a brash career bureaucrat who was determined to finish the job, whatever the cost. The project took ten years to complete, cost France around a billion francs (more than 2 billion dollars in today's money), and resulted in the deaths of between 15,000 and 23,000 Africans (with unofficial estimates up to four times higher). It was, writes historian J.P. Daughton, 'one of the deadliest construction projects in history'.[9]

In a recent book, Daughton depicts in horrifying detail the violence inflicted on African workers by their French overlords, and describes the many ways they succumbed to illness and death. Forced recruitment, inhumane modes of transport, substandard housing, insufficient food and drinking water, dangerous working conditions, inadequate medical care—all contributed to the toll. By 1925, these problems were being discussed in the Paris press and the Chamber of Deputies. This prompted André Gide, one of France's most celebrated writers (and later a Nobel laureate in literature), to go to the Congo to see what was going on. In August, he was the guest of Matteo, then acting as governor-general in Antonetti's absence. Later, as Gide toured the districts, he learnt how mid-level French officials tortured and killed African workers with impunity. In November, he sent a report on one atrocity to the acting governor-general, commenting dryly: 'This unfortunate affair risks having the most unfortunate repercussions.' Matteo immediately launched an enquiry, which did little to improve the situation.[10]

Matteo's responsibilities involved a great deal more than the railway construction project. Writing to his sister about his work in general, he said his position gave him a chance to do 'much good for many people'. Responding in the same letter to a remark she made comparing her work as head of the ashram to his as a government official, he said that 'at least in regard to intensity of work' their lives were similar.[11]

4

The Mother wrote little about her inner life during the 1920s. She preserved only two extracts from her diary for the entire decade. The second is dated 6 May 1927:

> One must know how to give one's life and also one's death, give one's happiness and also one's suffering, to depend for everything and in all things upon the Divine Dispenser of all our possibilities of realisation, who alone can and will decide whether we shall be happy or not, whether we shall live or not, whether we shall participate or not in the realisation.[12]

Nothing is known about the context of this passage but it is clear from other sources that she was going through some intense and difficult experiences. In January, she and Sri Aurobindo began to experiment with ways to achieve 'self-maintenance independently of food'. The Mother took up the challenge with her usual enthusiasm but soon ran into trouble. Sri Aurobindo saw that her body was passing through a crisis. Finally, he called off the experiment. The problem, he wrote, was that they had begun 'on a mistaken or merely theoretic knowledge about absorption from outside'. He realized now that the 'giving up of food' was 'not the condition for finding the secret' but 'the result of finding the secret'. The Mother had to 'take food again and build up the body again as a necessary support'.[13] Along with her fasting, the Mother was trying to reduce her sleep to an absolute minimum. For a while, she was able to continue her daily routine—'receiving the sadhaks for meditation or otherwise working and concentrating all night and day without sleep and very irregular food'—but eventually she had a breakdown.[14]

It is possible that the prayer of 6 May marked her recovery from this crisis. She increased her intake of food but continued the experiment of going without sleep. News of this reached André in France and caused him some concern. She wrote to him on 3 July that it was true she did not sleep 'in the ordinary sense of the word', that is, did not 'fall into the unconsciousness that characterizes ordinary sleep'. She did, however, lie down for two or three hours in a state of 'absolute immobility' in which her entire being—mental, psychic, vital and physical—entered a state of rest 'composed of perfect peace, complete silence and total immobility, while the consciousness remain[ed] perfectly awake'. Sometimes in this state of *repos* (to use the Cosmic term), she carried on various occult activities, of which she was fully conscious. As a result, she explained to her worried son, she was 'giving my body the rest that it needs'.[15]

During his youth, Matteo had read some Cosmic publications and still was interested in unconventional ideas. In September 1927, he wrote to his sister about the work of the French inventor Gëorgia Knap, who, among other things, had developed a process for prolonging life by means of 'regeneration of the cells'. 'To live 140 years instead of 70 and keep one's youth is not as good as being physically immortal as in the *corps glorieux* [body of glory] of the Cosmic teaching,' Matteo joked, adding that as far as he could see life extension would just 'allow the production of more good and evil things'. Later, the Mother read Knap's book and took it more seriously than her brother.[16] She had never forgotten the Cosmic ideal of 'integral immortality'. In some of her letters to Matteo, she gave him a glimpse of her spiritual progress. In one, she wrote: 'What I have succeeded in establishing permanently in my being is a calm, a peace, a perfect equanimity that neither success nor failure can alter in any way.'[17]

5

When Sri Aurobindo retired at the end of 1926, word went round that he would re-emerge on 15 August and begin a new phase of his yoga. Nothing like this happened. He did, however, give darshan that day. One by one, his disciples approached, prostrated themselves at his feet and remained for a minute or two. He blessed them by placing his hand on their heads. No words were exchanged. Afterwards, he went back into his room. On 24 November, the realization of 1926 was commemorated by a joint darshan of Sri Aurobindo and the Mother. A third darshan was held on 21 February 1928, as part of the celebrations of the Mother's fiftieth birthday. The procedure was now formalized. The sadhaks passed before Sri Aurobindo and the Mother in the order given on a typewritten list, which Sri Aurobindo consulted if he saw a new face. (That February, sixty-five disciples and visitors were on the list.) Each person offered flowers and did pranam before them both.[18] From this point on, darshans were held every year on 21 February, 15 August and 26 November. For the sadhaks, they were eagerly awaited red-letter days. For Sri Aurobindo and the Mother, who had to sit for several hours at a stretch, they must have been rather tiring.

By the beginning of 1928 the Mother's daily schedule was packed: Pranam, the soup ceremony, group meditations, consultations for work, meetings with individuals—and almost no time for herself. The transformation of the self-effacing Mirra Alfassa into the dynamic Mother of the ashram was a marvel to Dorothy Hodgson, now known as Vasavadutta or Dutta, who had lived with her since 1916: 'She organizes everything under Sri Aurobindo's leadership, working practically day and night,' Dutta wrote to a friend. 'I always knew she was wonderful—but how wonderful I did not at all realize.'[19] In May, after a year of incessant activity, the Mother suffered a collapse. The problem, Sri Aurobindo explained in a notice posted in the ashram, was that the sadhaks were drawing away all her energy without giving anything in return: 'The whole burden of the progress has fallen physically on the body of the Mother'; the more her 'physical consciousness' advanced, the more it was 'pulled back towards the unchanged obscurity of [the sadhaks'] unprogressive external nature'. This could not go on, he said, and immediately reduced the number of meditations and pranam ceremonies, and temporarily stopped personal interviews with the Mother.[20] Before long, however, pressure from the sadhaks obliged her to resume the old routine with only slight modifications.

Apart from darshan days, Sri Aurobindo saw no one but the Mother and one or two attendants. In 1928, he twice relaxed this rule to meet distinguished visitors. The first was Rabindranath Tagore. The poet, who had known and admired Sri Aurobindo for decades, was on his way to America and his ship was scheduled to stop in Pondicherry on 28 May. His secretary, Charles Freer Andrews, telegraphed ahead from Madras and Sri Aurobindo agreed to a meeting. Led to his room by Nolini Kanta

Mirra Alfassa around the age of seven

Source: Sambit/Wikimedia/4.0 International license

Mirra around the age of eighteen

Source: Alamy

Square du Roule, Paris, where Mirra lived with her family between 1887 and 1897

Source: Branor/Wikimedia/3.0 Unported license

PETITE SALLE PLEYEL
22, Rue Rochechouart, 22

VENDREDI 11 JUIN 1897, à 8 heures 1/2 du Soir

CONCERT

DONNÉ PAR

Mlle Eva Rolland

VIOLONISTE

1re Audition des Œuvres de M. ENESCO

AVEC LE CONCOURS DE

Mlle MURER, Mlle Mirra ALFASSA
M. D'EINBRODT, M. BERNARD, M. MALKINE, M. HAAS

1. *Sonate en* ré majeur (Violon, Piano).
   Allegro vivo, Adagio, Allegro.
   Mlle Eva ROLLAND, M. BERNARD.
2. *Suite dans le Style ancien* (Piano seul).
   Grave, Adagio, Presto.
   Mlle MURER.
3. a) *Le Saphir* . . . . Porto-Riche.
   b) *Les deux différentes manières d'aimer.* . Victor Hugo.
   Mlle Mirra ALFASSA.
4. a) *Nocturne.*
   b) *Saltarello* pour Violoncelle.
   M. d'EINBRODT.
5. *Quintette* pour Piano et cordes.
   Allegro Moderato, Scherzo, Andante, Final.
   Mlles MURER & Eva ROLLAND, MM. MALKINE, D'EINBRODT & HAAS.

PRIX DES BILLETS :

Places Réservées : 20 fr. — Premières : 10 fr. — Secondes : 5 fr.

Poster for an 1897 concert listing Mirra Alfassa as a participant

Source: George Enescu: A Tragic Life in Pictures *by Viorel Cosma, 2000*

Poster promoting the 'Antisemitic Candidate' in the French legislative election of 1889

Source: Willette, Adolphe/ Gallicia Digital Library

William-Adolphe Bouguereau with his students at the Académie Julian, 1896 (Mirra is standing at the far right)

Source: Del Debbio Collection

Account of Mirra Alfassa at the Académie Julian, 1896–97

Source: Bibliothèque nationale de France

Henri Morisset

Source: Filidauro/ Wikimedia/3.0 Unported license

Henri Morisset, *Terrasse du Café Wepler (Place Clichy)*, 1903, as reproduced in the German magazine *Jugend*, December 1905

Source: Jugend, *1905*

Max Theon

Source: Sandivas/Wikimedia/ United States public domain tag

Mirra Alfassa, *Villa Zarif, Tlemcen*, 1906

Source: Tal Gilad collection provided to Boaz Huss on courtesy for his publication listed on ResearchGate

Taima-dera temple complex, which Mirra visited on 14 May 1916

Photo credit: Author

Rabindranath Tagore with Tetsuo Hirasawa, William Winstanley Pearson, Mirra and Paul Richard (Kyoto, 5 February 1917)

Source: Old Indian Photos

Sri Aurobindo in Pondicherry, circa 1915–18

Source: Alamy

41 [now 33] rue François Martin, Pondicherry, the house occupied by Sri Aurobindo and some of his followers between 1913 and 1922, and where the Mother lived between 1920 and 1922

Photo credit: Author

Main entrance to the Sri Aurobindo Ashram

Source: Pinakpani/Wikimedia/4.0 International license

The Matrimandir

Source: Canta/Wikimedia/3.0 Unported license

Gupta, Tagore went to throw his arms around his old friend. Aurobindo caught his hands and held them. The two talked animatedly for several minutes. The Mother sat on a chair nearby. When the time came for Tagore to leave, Nolini led him down the stairs. The Mother came after them, stopping near the bottom of the staircase. As Tagore and Nolini walked away, the poet asked him who that lady sitting next to Aurobindo was. Nolini said she was Mirra Alfassa, now known as the Mother. The poet, who had spent several weeks with her in Japan, said he had not recognized her. (It was just a day or two after her physical collapse.) The next day, Tagore wrote an essay about the meeting, later published in *The Modern Review*. 'At the very first sight I could see that he had been seeking for the soul and had gained it,' the poet said. 'His face was radiant with an inner light.' He did not mention the Mother.[21] In the beginning of August, Sylvain Lévi, the French Indologist, who was on his way back to Europe from the Far East, disembarked in Pondicherry, spoke with the Mother and had a meeting with Sri Aurobindo. The two are said to have conversed in Sanskrit.[22] Eleven days later, the sadhu, scholar and poet Ganapati Muni saw Sri Aurobindo at the August darshan. Afterwards, he had two meetings with the Mother. During the first, they meditated together. Ganapati Muni, a worshipper of Shakti, felt a 'spiritual current passing into him from all directions'. The Mother was impressed by his capacity, telling a disciple that he 'immediately entered into my spiritual Consciousness and stuck to it to the end'.[23]

Given the precariousness of the ashram's situation in French India, the Mother was interested in making a good impression on officials and writers from France. Early in 1928, Matteo told her he had given a letter of introduction to a functionary and film-maker named Alfred Chaumel, who was planning a visit to Pondicherry. In August, Chaumel published an article in *Le Monde Colonial Illustré* that was filled with travellers' clichés (elephants, rickshaws, temples, beggars) and did not mention the ashram. He concluded: 'Since India is the cradle of religion, since so many gods preside over her destiny, which one will accomplish the miracle of resuscitating this city?' The Mother was not amused. After reading the article, she wrote in a private note: 'Blinded by false appearances, deceived by slander, held back by fear and prejudice, he passed by the side of the god whose intervention he implores'—this would be a reference to Sri Aurobindo—'and did not see him; he approached, without wanting to admit it, the forces that will accomplish the miracle he asks for'.[24]

Slowly, public opinion in France began to turn in the ashram's favour. In December 1928, Nobel laureate Romain Rolland wrote of Sri Aurobindo as 'the greatest thinker of contemporary India', who had realized 'the greatest synthesis yet achieved of the genius of Asia and the genius of Europe'.[25] Rolland's essay aroused considerable interest among French intellectuals. In 1934, the writer Louise Morin visited the ashram and later told a newspaper that it was 'one of the most significant experiences of my voyage to India'. She added she had heard that 'a good deal of gossip was going on about the Asram' but as far as she could see the members were 'following their "quest" in absolute sincerity'.[26] The next year, the poet and novelist Maurice Magre passed a few days in the ashram and later published an account in his book *À la Poursuite de la Sagesse* (In Search of Wisdom). In this early example of the Westerner-finds-spiritual-truth-in-Asia genre, Magre wrote admiringly about Sri Aurobindo, whom he did not meet, about his disciples, whom he considered 'the wisest people in the world', and about the Mother, who stood 'between the master and the disciples'. She was 'at once a woman, made of flesh and bones, and the metaphysical symbol of the soul of the world'.[27] Other French visitors during the mid-1930s were Jean Herbert, an interpreter at the League of Nations, the physicist Gabriel Monod-Herzen and the surrealist poet Valentine Penrose (the wife of the English artist Roland Penrose and a friend of Paul Éluard, Man Ray and Pablo Picasso), who wrote some poems during her stay that she dedicated to the Mother.[28]

Most people in India had a positive view of Sri Aurobindo, but some deplored his retirement and looked askance at the ashram. One such was Subhas Chandra Bose, a rising star of the Indian nationalist movement. On 25 December 1928, Bose told a meeting of Indian National Congress workers that they should reject the philosophy of the 'Sabarmati school' of Mahatma Gandhi because it was hostile to modern life, and the

'Pondicherry school' of Sri Aurobindo because it overemphasized 'peaceful contemplation', making people forget that 'spiritual progress under the present-day conditions is possible only by ceaseless and unselfish action'.[29] Anilbaran Roy, who had been active in Congress politics before becoming a member of the ashram, volunteered to write a refutation. The Mother told him not to bother. 'So many stupid things are said about our sadhana,' she said. 'Those who have no faith [in us] will not be convinced by what you write.' Her aim was not to win debates but transform human life. Later that day, she heard a voice that told her that beyond the highest human attainments were 'the Power, the Happiness, the Light, the Knowledge, the Bliss, the Love, the Peace that are the result of the Divine Grace'. She gave a typed copy of this message to Anilbaran and later included it among her published *Prayers and Meditations*.[30]

In April 1929, the Mother began to hold regular Sunday meetings with a group of disciples who spoke English well: Dilip Kumar Roy (a Cambridge graduate and Indian classical musician), Nolini Kanta Gupta, the French engineer Saint-Hilaire, now known as Pavitra, an American couple named Vaun and Jeanette McPheeters, a visiting Englishwoman named Olive Maitland, and two or three others. The Mother arranged the meetings along the lines of the *réunions* she had held in Paris sixteen years earlier. Most sessions began with a meditation on a given subject. The Mother then asked everyone to recount what they had experienced. Later, the participants asked questions about various subjects: The nature of yoga, occult powers, meditation, divine and hostile beings, death, the spiritual life. The Mother replied in simple, straightforward language, avoiding the obscurity of the Cosmic teachings and the technical yogic idiom of some of Sri Aurobindo's works. Asked 'What is the way to establish unity and homogeneity in our being?', she replied: 'Keep the will firm. Treat the recalcitrant parts as disobedient children. Act upon them constantly and patiently. Convince them of their error.' The way to unify 'all these divergent parts, all these contradictory movements' was to bring them in contact with the soul: 'Once you have got the consciousness of the psychic being and its aspiration, these doubts and difficulties can be destroyed.'[31]

On 9 June, while speaking about religion and yoga, the Mother brought up the idea of the avatar. 'Each time that something of the Divine Truth and the Divine Force comes down to manifest upon earth, some change is effected in the earth's atmosphere.' A few people are 'awakened to some inspiration' from the descending power. If they are capable of holding it, they tell others: 'A great force has come down; I am in contact with it and what I understand of it, I will tell you.' But most lose their balance and proclaim: 'I have the Divine Truth, I possess it whole and entire.' There were now, she continued ironically, 'at least two dozen Christs, if not as many Buddhas; India alone can supply any number of Avatars, not to speak of minor manifestations. But in this way, the whole thing begins to look grotesque'. Still, she said, there was something to such claims: 'The truth is that the human personality has come in contact with some Being, some Power, and under the influence of education and tradition calls it Buddha or Christ or by any other familiar name.'[32] The Mother did not relate this observation to the situation in the ashram. At no time did she or Sri Aurobindo make any public declarations about their spiritual status. On the other hand, they did not object when people treated them as avatars.

The Sunday meetings continued until August. Jeanette McPheeters noted down the questions and the Mother's answers in shorthand. Later, Nolini expanded her transcripts. His versions were typed and circulated in the ashram, and, in 1931, printed in a limited edition as *Conversations with the Mother*. The Mother sent copies to André and Matteo, neither of whom could make much of the talks. A year or two later, the Mother translated the book into French under the title *Entretiens avec la Mère*. An early reader was Romain Rolland, to whom she sent a copy through Dilip Kumar Roy. Rolland noted in his diary that the Mother expressed 'the intuitionist or mystical ideas of Aurobindo' with 'a remarkable mastery of expression'. He also wrote that he imagined the Mother was trying to catch hold of him. Nevertheless, he sent her a complimentary note in which he said that Western people like him could not 'retire into the bosom of God in order to radiate from there, at a later time, the new life. We have to hasten to the aid of oppressed men and nations'.

Sometime later, the Mother remarked that Rolland possessed the same sort of stupidity as Paul Richard: Both were incapable of distinguishing the intellectual from the spiritual.[33]

During 1930 and 1931, the Mother held another series of talks with disciples. Her remarks, noted down by a disciple, and later worked up and translated, display what might be called her spiritual common sense. Asked about the uses of imagination, she replied: 'The imagination is like a knife which may be used for good or evil purposes. If you always dwell in the idea and feeling that you are going to be transformed, then you will help the process of the Yoga. If, on the contrary, you give in to dejection and bewail that you are not fit or that you are incapable of realisation, you poison your own being.'[34]

In August 1930, the Mother wrote to André, not without a hint of pride, that the ashram was 'becoming a more and more interesting establishment'. There were now between eighty-five and 100 members, lodged in twenty-one houses. Her informal inventory of moveable property and workplaces included: 'Five cars, twelve bicycles, four sewing machines, a dozen typewriters, many garages, an automobile repair workshop, an electrical service, a building service, sewing departments . . . a library and reading-room containing several thousand volumes, a photographic service, general stores containing a wide variety of goods . . . large gardens for flowers, vegetables and fruits, a dairy, a bakery, etc.' She was looking after all of this, so, she concluded, 'I can truly say that I am busy.'[35]

She still permitted herself very little sleep. By October 1931, the strain was beginning to tell. On 19 October, she fell ill with a high fever. For a month, she remained in her room, receiving almost no one. To a sadhak who clamoured to see her, Sri Aurobindo wrote that she 'must absolutely husband her forces in view of the strain the [darshan of] 24th November will mean for her. It is quite out of the question for her to begin seeing everybody and receiving them meanwhile—a single morning of that kind of thing would exhaust her altogether'.[36] To the sadhaks' great relief, she came down for pranam on 17 November and took part in the darshan of 24 November. That evening, she wrote an entry in her diary, explaining her illness in occult terms: 'O my Lord, my sweet Master, for the accomplishment of Thy work I have sunk down into the unfathomable depths of Matter, I have touched with my finger the horror of the falsehood and the unconsciousness, I have reached the seat of oblivion and a supreme obscurity.' From the depths, a prayer arose from her heart: 'Lord, give the command to conquer and victory will be there. I know we are unworthy, I know the world is not yet ready. But I cry to Thee with an absolute faith in Thy Grace and I know that Thy Grace will save.'[37]

After the darshan, she began to resume her activities, but the soup ceremony was stopped. It had become, Sri Aurobindo wrote, 'a sort of semi-ecclesiastical routine', which, 'because of the mistaken attitude of the sadhaks', was a drain on her energies. In order to get some exercise and a bit of fresh air, she began to walk on the terrace of one of the ashram houses in the evening. This soon became an occasion for 'terrace darshan' as sadhaks stood in the courtyard below to see her. Before long, she began to stand and concentrate on those who had gathered in the courtyard before going inside. This too became part of the daily routine. Finally, Sri Aurobindo had to ask the sadhaks to let her take her evening exercise without being watched because this was 'the only time she could concentrate a little on herself'.[38] In 1934, she began to give darshans and meditations in the evening inside the ashram building, standing on her staircase while the sadhaks sat below. Still later, she started receiving people on the first-floor landing of the staircase. These meetings were intended for a limited number, but 'as it always happened with the Mother', a sadhak later recalled, 'more and more people were permitted and soon there was a big queue'.[39]

During the early 1930s, the Mother began to write letters to people inside and outside the ashram. This correspondence soon became substantial: Her collected letters and messages fill more than seven volumes. Written mostly in English, rather than French, the letters deal with a vast range of subjects: Yoga, spirituality, occultism, work, practical affairs and her relationship with the disciples, some of whom were very demanding. Unlike Sri Aurobindo, who sometimes wrote long letters on philosophical and literary topics, the Mother kept it short and sweet. A few letters from the first half of 1932 give an idea of her approach. When someone asked her how to start out in yoga, she replied:

> Three things indispensable to begin with:
>
> Absolute sincerity in the whole being and all its activities.
>
> Complete self-surrender without any reservation.
>
> Patient work on oneself and at the same time a steady conquering of perfect unshakable peace and equanimity.

Members of the ashram who looked on her as their mother did not hesitate to pour out their feelings to her, and she replied as a loving but clear-eyed parent. To someone who recited a tale of woe, she replied: 'Do not cherish suffering and suffering will leave you altogether. Suffering is far from being indispensable to progress. The greatest progress is made through a steady and cheerful equanimity.' Earlier, she had set up departments to facilitate the running of the ashram—kitchen, carpentry workshop, garage, gardens, accounting office and so forth. Those in charge sent her regular reports and barraged her with questions. She replied in meticulous detail. When a cook asked her how to mix wheat flour with vegetables, she replied: 'It is better to mix it first in a separate sauce-pan with a small quantity of water or, better, of vegetable soup. . . . After it has reached the boiling point you can safely add it to the vegetables.' When, on an inspection tour, she saw a worker absent-mindedly sanding a table, she wrote to the man's supervisor: 'He was rubbing violently and in any direction with one or the other hand, while he was looking at anything and everything *except at what he was doing*; poor table, what a treatment!' At the same time, she was responsive to the well-being of workers. When she heard that a manager had abused a subordinate, she offered this advice: 'You should be very polite with those who depend upon you for their living. . . . There may be some dignity in being rough with your superiors, but with those who depend on you, the true dignity is to be very courteous.'[40]

6

An increasing number of people wanted to study the teachings of Sri Aurobindo and the Mother but there was little for them to read. The Mother's *Conversations* and its French translation were available in typescript and in limited editions that were *hors commerce.* Only a few of the works Sri Aurobindo had published in *Arya* between 1914 and 1920 had been reprinted. Typed and handwritten copies of his letters passed from hand to hand. He did not allow them to circulate outside the ashram but, from 1933, he began to prepare small collections of letters for publication. The first to appear was called *The Riddle of This World.* I will examine this book and the Mother's *Conversations* in parallel to show how the two authors, drawing from different traditions and influencing one another, arrived at a common set of teachings and practices.

The central theme of both books is yoga, in particular 'integral yoga', that is, yoga on all levels of the being: Body, life, mind and spirit. For Sri Aurobindo, the key to the integral path was the descent of the supermind. Some ancient yogis had known about this power of consciousness but had missed 'the way to make it integral for the life and to bring it down for transformation'. To do so was the aim of his yoga. The Mother took a more down-to-earth approach. 'In the integral Yoga, the integral life down even to the smallest detail has to be transformed, to be divinised.' For both, the idea of transformation was of central importance but they explained it in different ways. Writing with reference to the Indian systems of Vedanta and tantra, Sri Aurobindo said that the final transformation would be a 'transition beyond the human into the divine'. For this to be possible, two things were necessary:

> First, there must be a conversion inwards, a going within to find the inmost psychic being and bring it out to the front, disclosing at the same time the inner mind, inner vital, inner physical parts of the nature. Next, there must be an ascension, a series of conversions upwards and a turning down to convert the lower parts.

The Mother spoke about transformation and the role of the psychic being in psychological rather than philosophical terms. It was the influence of the psychic being 'gradually spreading from within towards the most outward and material boundaries of your consciousness that will bring about the transformation of your entire nature'. The effort of yoga was to become conscious of the psychic being 'so that the process of your transformation, instead of a slow labour extending through centuries, can be pressed into one life or even a few years'.[41]

The concept of the psychic being was the Mother's main contribution to the theory and practice of integral yoga. She first came across the term *être psychique* in the *Revue Cosmique* and *Tradition Cosmique.* (She perhaps did not know that like other Cosmic ideas it derived from earlier sources such as Pythagoreanism, Orphism, Gnosticism and Hermeticism, which speak of a soul-spark or portion of the divine in the human being.) In the Cosmic Philosophy, the *être psychique* inhabits the psychic *degré* or level, which is the source of all expressions of the soul.[42] A passage in the *Tradition Cosmique* explains that if the psychic *degré* of a human being can 'retain its individuality' after death, it can 'reassume the nervous–physical degree [that is, the body] from which it has been stripped for a time' and continue its evolution on earth.[43] The Mother and Sri Aurobindo took up this idea, which is not fully developed in Cosmic literature, and made it a central element of their philosophy. 'The psychic being is that which persists after death, because it is your eternal self; it is this that carries the consciousness forward from life to life,' said the Mother in one of her *Conversations.* 'The psychic being is the real individuality of the true and divine individual within you.'[44] Sri Aurobindo incorporated the concept of the psychic being, which has no exact equivalent in Indian philosophy, into his evolutionary Vedantism: 'The psychic being is especially the soul of the individual evolving in the manifestation the individual Prakriti [nature] and taking part in the evolution,' he wrote. 'It is that spark of the Divine Fire that grows behind the mind, vital and physical as the psychic being until it is able to transform the Prakriti of Ignorance into a Prakriti of Knowledge.'[45] In the system of yogic practice he worked out for his disciples during the 1930s, he gave a central place to the psychic being because he found that without it 'no true transformation is possible'.[46] The Mother hinted at the indirect influence of the Cosmic philosophy on Sri Aurobindo's thought when she put a modified form of the Cosmic symbol—two interlocking triangles enclosing a square with a lotus in its centre—on the cover of the first edition of *The Riddle of This World.*

7

By 1934, the ashram had around 150 permanent residents. It was a struggle to find places for all of them to stay. There were only so many houses on the Pondicherry real estate market, and Sri Aurobindo and the Mother had bought or rented forty. This caused a good deal of resentment among French locals, most of whom were not well-disposed towards the yogis from British India and their reclusive leaders. An article published in a colonial journal gives some idea of what people in the French community were saying: 'A religious society of Hindus named "Ashram" has been founded, of which several French people are members.' Notable among them were the ex-engineer Saint-Hilaire and a certain Madame Richard, 'who has converted to this religion and remains constantly shut up in her house, not going out but once a year'.[47] The Mother had in fact registered an association named 'Sri Aurobindo Ashram' with the government of French India in 1929.[48] It is not clear why she did this—perhaps to improve the standing of the ashram vis-à-vis the government. In any event, it proved to be a mistake, for it gave the government a means to apply pressure in regard to the housing problem. On 16 February 1934, she sent an urgent telegram to Matteo in Brazzaville telling him that the Pondicherry administration was threatening to declare the ashram an illegal association. He immediately wrote to the Colonial Office in Paris and spoke with a colleague in the AEF administration whose brother was the presiding judge of the court of French India.[49] Meanwhile, Sri Aurobindo published a statement saying that the ashram was not an 'association' but simply 'the house or houses of a Teacher or Master of spiritual philosophy in which he receives and lodges those who come to him for the teaching and practice'. After a month, things quieted down. The government did not press its inquiry and the Mother promised not to buy or rent more houses.[50]

Matteo did what he could to help his sister even though he was overwhelmed with work. The Congo-Océan railway was inaugurated in July 1934. In his dedicatory address, Governor-General Antonetti paused to remember the workers, French and also African, who gave their lives for the cause. His voice trembled with emotion when he spoke of his second-in-command, Governor Alfassa, 'whose name will always be attached to this Congo-Océan project, which is also very much his'.[51] Matteo's contributions have largely been forgotten and the responsibility for the railway, and the death and dislocation it caused, have rightly been laid at Antonetti's door. As a loyal bureaucrat, Matteo sometimes had to put his signature to cringeworthy reports and orders, but he does not seem to have been directly involved in the project's more disreputable aspects.[52]

The Mother had great respect for her brother but did not endorse everything he did. In 1969, she remarked that after his graduation from the École Polytechnique, Matteo 'had a choice among various posts, and he deliberately chose that post in the colonies, because he wanted to "help the backward races progress"—all that nonsense'. All forms of colonialism were unjustifiable, she said: 'Ambitions, territorial expansions—of course, all colonies and all that—have to be swept off the board.'[53]

8

After the Mother agreed not to buy or rent more houses in Pondicherry, new admissions were put on hold. Now, the only way for the ashram to expand was to construct its own housing. Around 1934, the Mother was given a plot of land near the main ashram buildings. Sir Akbar Hydari, the prime minister of Hyderabad State, who was an admirer of Sri Aurobindo, arranged for a donation of 1,00,000 rupees for constructing a dormitory on the site. Wishing to create something aesthetically distinctive, the Mother got in touch with the Czech–American architect Antonín Raymond, a former associate of Frank Lloyd Wright, through her secretary, Pavitra, who had known Raymond in Japan. In October 1935, Raymond sent plans for a building that combined International Style modernism with traditional Japanese design. The Mother was pleased and gave Raymond the commission. He entrusted the on-site work to two of his associates, the Japanese–American George Nakashima and František Sammer, a Czech, who had studied with Le Corbusier in Paris. Construction began in 1938. Work was carried out largely by members of the ashram. Intimately involved in the project herself, the Mother received almost daily reports from the architects, the engineer and the heads of the various work teams. Golconde—as the dormitory was called after the Golconda diamond mines of Hyderabad—was a pioneering structure, the first in India to be built using high-strength reinforced concrete. The brass fittings were forged in the ashram's foundry. The furniture, designed by Nakashima, was produced in ashram workshops. (These were Nakashima's first furniture designs. Later, resettled in America, he became world-famous as a furniture designer and woodworker.) On account of wartime delays, the main work on Golconde was not completed until 1945. Eighty years later, the building is still in excellent shape, housing members of the ashram and the occasional visitor. Historians and critics consider it one of the masterpieces of Modernist architecture in India.[54]

Between 1934 and 1937, the membership of the ashram remained stable at around 150. The Mother found this a good number. Looking back thirty years later, she said: 'We began with thirty-five, thirty-six; but even up to a hundred and fifty' the disciples 'were as though held in an egg in my consciousness, so close, you know, that I could direct all their movements, inner and outer, all the time, everything was under complete control, at every moment, night and day'.[55] Gone was the time when the sadhaks struggled on their own to conquer their lower natures. The sadhana now consisted of surrender to the Mother, at work, in meditation and at pranam, when the surrender was given physical form. The procedure of pranam was straightforward: The sadhaks went up to the Mother one by one and placed their foreheads on her feet. She looked at each one, placed her hand on their heads in blessing, and gave them a handful of flowers. The purpose, Sri Aurobindo wrote, was 'not that sadhaks should offer a formal or ritual daily homage to the Mother, but that the sadhaks may receive along with the Mother's blessings whatever spiritual help or influence they are in a condition to receive or assimilate'.[56] Many felt the Mother's spiritual energy coursing through them as they prostrated before her. Others worried about the way she looked at them, the length of time she held her hand on their heads and the sort of flowers she gave. They looked on anxiously as others passed before her. Did she give them more time? Warmer smiles? Longer blessings? Nicer flowers? Sri Aurobindo had to write dozens of letters to set people's minds at rest:

> All this idea about the Mother's looks and her hand in the blessing which is current in the Asram is perfectly irrational, false, even imbecile. . . . She does not, as certain people annoyingly believe, dose out her smiles or blessings in such a way as to assign a number of marks for each sadhak according to his good behaviour or bad behaviour.[57]

The reactions may have been 'imbecile' but they were almost inevitable in a small community focused on one person.

Narratives of ashram life during the 1930s are filled to overflowing with personal impressions of the Mother and accounts of her activities. Each disciple saw her from his or her own viewpoint. This makes it impossible to paint a comprehensive picture of how she looked and moved. She dressed in the Indian manner but kept some European habits of personal care, such as wearing make-up and perfume. When a visitor criticized her for this, she remarked: 'Caring for one's skin and scalp is no more a contrivance than caring for one's teeth.' Speaking of female disciples (and by extension of herself), she said there was no harm in wearing make-up, provided it was not done 'out of vanity or excessive preening'.[58] Knowing her fondness for fine perfumes, people offered her fragrances imported from France. (She favoured *Je Reviens* by Worth.) Knowing her love of beautiful fabrics, people gave her gorgeous saris. Indians with traditional ideas of how holy women should look found this a bit hard to take. 'Why does the Mother wear rich and beautiful clothes?' a teenager once asked Sri Aurobindo. When he showed this to the Mother she wrote back somewhat sharply: 'Is it your idea that the Divine should be represented on earth by poverty and ugliness?'[59]

People remembered the Mother as beautiful, gracious, patient, smiling, but also, on occasion, fierce and inexorable. Monod-Herzen, who used to see her when she came to speak with Pavitra, recalled that she 'had the look of a kind, gentle, affectionate grandmother. She would come in her dressing gown, with her grey hair pulled back: it was extraordinarily comforting'.[60] Another disciple remembered that Pavitra sometimes had to deal with a different side of her personality:

> I heard her coming out of her bathroom at about 6 a.m. shouting, actually shouting, 'Pavitra, Pavitra!' I got a bit alarmed. God knows what he was doing, shaving or taking coffee. He cried back, 'Oui, Mère!' and came almost running. She scolded him about some School matter and he quietly and submissively listened.[61]

In February 1937, the Mother developed an eye problem and the morning pranam was replaced by a group meditation. The sadhaks complained and pranam was restored on alternate days. Then, in 1938, it was stopped completely. The same year, she began to give darshan each morning from the rear balcony of the ashram. Sadhaks assembled on the street below to receive her blessings from a distance. It wasn't the same as the touch of her hand or a specially chosen flower but was still something worth waiting for.

9

Integral yoga does not demand a retreat from the world. Its aim, the Mother said, was 'the divine conquest of this world, the conquest of all its movements and the realisation of the Divine here'. A change of consciousness was essential but 'the true change of consciousness is one that will change the physical conditions of the world and make it an entirely new creation'. She conceived of the ashram as a microcosm of the world and encouraged sadhaks to engage in activities of every sort, from concreting and carpentry to poetry and music, using them all as a means of transformation. At the same time, she and Sri Aurobindo felt that the young sapling that the ashram was had to be protected from storms from outside. 'It is necessary,' he wrote, 'to stand apart from the rest of the world so as to separate ourselves from the ordinary consciousness in order to bring down a new one.'[62] The Mother discouraged sadhaks from mixing with outsiders except when necessary. Participation in political activities was forbidden. There were practical as well as spiritual reasons for this. The British still considered Sri Aurobindo and his earliest disciples to be dangerous ex-revolutionaries, and kept the ashram under surveillance. The French government tolerated their presence in Pondicherry as long as they did not cause trouble. During the 1930s, however, it became impossible for people in the ashram to ignore political developments in India and abroad.

After a lull during the mid-1920s, the Indian national movement picked up steam towards the end of the decade. At its 1929 session, the Indian National Congress resolved that its aim was complete independence from Britain. (This came twenty-three years after Sri Aurobindo first called for independence in his Calcutta newspaper.) In March 1930, Mahatma Gandhi launched a civil disobedience movement that galvanized the country. At the same time, the internal contradictions of Indian nationalism were becoming acute. Various groups, including Muslims and members of the 'depressed classes' (formerly known as untouchables), demanded an increased say in assemblies and negotiations with the British. Gandhi managed to patch up an agreement with depressed-class leader B.R. Ambedkar, but he had no luck in bridging the gap between the Congress and the Muslim League, led by Muhammad Ali Jinnah. After the League lost out in provincial elections in 1937, Jinnah went to the people with a new message: India's Muslims were not an endangered minority community but a completely separate 'nation'.

While Indians were struggling to throw off British imperialism, militaristic countries in Europe and East Asia were extending their territorial holdings. In 1934, Italy, under the Fascist dictator Benito Mussolini, consolidated its colonies in North Africa. The next year, it invaded Abyssinia (Ethiopia) and subdued it after a seven-month resistance. Meanwhile, Germany, under the Nazi dictator Adolf Hitler, reclaimed lands that had been occupied by France, supported anti-

Republican forces in Spain and formed an alliance with Mussolini. These events filled newspapers and dominated conversations throughout the world. Many members of the ashram gave them a 'spiritual' interpretation. In a letter of February 1937, Sri Aurobindo poured cold water over their speculations:

> You write as if what is going on in Europe were a war between the powers of Light and the powers of Darkness—but this is no more so than during the Great War. It is a fight between two kinds of Ignorance.

He went on to say:

> Our aim is to bring down a higher Truth, but that Truth must be able to live by its own strength and not depend upon the victory of one or other of the forces of the Ignorance. That is the reason why we are not to mix in political or social controversies and struggles; it would simply keep down our endeavour to a lower level and prevent the Truth from descending.[63]

In March 1938, Hitler annexed Austria and then demanded that Czechoslovakia hand over territories inhabited by ethnic Germans. On 30 September 1938, Britain and France endorsed this demand, thinking that their betrayal of the Czechs would preserve peace in Europe. André wrote to the Mother asking if Hitler had been bluffing or if the world had narrowly escaped disaster. She replied on 22 October: 'It would be nearer the truth to say "both at the same time."' She went on to give an occult explanation of the situation:

> The play of these [non-human] forces is very complex and generally eludes the human consciousness; but for ease of explanation and understanding, they may be divided into two main opposing tendencies: those that work for the fulfilment of the Divine work upon earth, and those that are opposed to this fulfilment.

Hitler was, she wrote, a chosen instrument of the 'anti-divine forces which want violence, upheaval and war, for they know that these things retard and impede the action of the divine forces'. His threats had brought Europe very close to war even though 'no human government consciously wanted it'. At the moment, all that could be said was that 'war has been avoided—for the moment'.[64]

Life in the ashram continued in its usual manner. On the night of 23–24 November, the Mother completed the preparations for the next day's darshan and lay down to rest. Around 2.20 a.m., she got up with a feeling that something was wrong. Going into Sri Aurobindo's room, she found him stretched out on the floor, unable to get up. She rang the emergency bell. Purani, who was preparing hot water for her bath, rushed upstairs. 'Sri Aurobindo has fallen down,' she told him. 'Go and fetch Dr Manilal.' Within minutes, Manilal Parekh, a disciple who had come for the darshan, arrived. He examined the patient. The Mother sat by his side, a fan in her hand and a look of deep sorrow on her face. Whenever Manilal turned his leg, Sri Aurobindo let out an involuntary 'Ah!' 'Is it hurting you?' the Mother murmured. After a few minutes, Manilal concluded that his right thigh was broken. He and the ashram's doctors put the leg in a temporary cast and moved the patient to his bed. That evening, a specialist came from Madras. He examined Sri Aurobindo's leg but said that before going ahead he had to wait for a radiologist he had summoned. In the interval, the Mother asked him many probing questions about Sri Aurobindo's condition, the prognosis, possible treatments and so forth. In the evening, she gave darshan to the disciples and visitors, who were stunned that something like this could have happened. Her confident smile set their minds at rest.[65]

The radiologist arrived around 11 p.m. He took a set of X-rays and developed them on the spot. When the doctors examined them they saw the injury was serious: An impacted fracture of the thigh above the knee, with two fragments locked together. The specialist decided the best he could do was put the leg in a cast and support it with splints. He told the doctors that the cast should stay on for ten weeks.[66]

9

The Ashram and the World

1

THE DAY AFTER THE ACCIDENT, THE MOTHER ASKED DR MANILAL what he thought about Sri Aurobindo's condition. He gave an evasive reply. She screamed, 'Don't hide it! We know the truth', then prostrated herself on the floor before Sri Aurobindo. Shaken, Manilal and the others realized she took the matter very seriously indeed.[1] She chose a team of attendants, who remained on duty around the clock. At her suggestion, a wheeled table was made for serving Sri Aurobindo his meals. She arranged the dishes, pushed the table in, and stood by his side as he ate. She also took charge of combing his hair and applying lotion to his upper body. For the next year and a half, she was focused almost exclusively on his health and comfort. She gave no interviews to members of the ashram but continued to meet department heads and other trusted assistants. The activities of the ashram went on, more or less as usual.

Sometime in January 1939, the Madras specialist returned and removed the splints on Sri Aurobindo's leg. It immediately swelled up to twice its normal size. The Mother interrogated the doctor about the cause of the swelling, steps to be taken, possible complications and so forth. He was not used to being questioned by a woman in this way, and later remarked that she seemed to be a rather intelligent person. Sri Aurobindo smiled when this was reported to him.[2] Soon he was walking, at first with the help of his attendants, and eventually on his own. The twenty-first February, the Mother's birthday, passed without the usual darshan. By April, Sri Aurobindo had recovered sufficiently that she decided to hold a special darshan on 24 April, the anniversary of her final arrival in Pondicherry in 1920. The evening before, she and the attendants washed Sri Aurobindo's hair in his room—a complicated affair with basins of hot and cold water, soap, powder and so forth. The next morning, she came in, offered Sri Aurobindo a flower, and did pranam at his feet. Then she rushed off to look after the preparations for the big event. In the afternoon, the two of them sat in their usual places in the darshan room. But the format was changed. The disciples and visitors passed silently before them, halting briefly before moving on. The whole thing was over in an hour. From this point on, 24 April became a regular darshan day.

Around this time, Sri Aurobindo's publishers asked him if he would revise *The Life Divine*, a philosophical work that had appeared in *Arya* twenty years earlier, so they could bring it out as a book. The Mother encouraged him to go ahead. The revision kept him busy for more than a year, after which he took up other *Arya* writings and his epic poem *Savitri*. Seeing that he was getting along well, the Mother spent more time with members of the ashram. Early in the morning, she gave darshan from her balcony. On the way, she checked in with Sri Aurobindo, returning afterwards to see to his grooming, and sometimes to talk privately with him. When he had his meals she hovered nearby, asking him if he liked the dishes. He always replied in the affirmative. (As far as his attendants could see, he took little interest in what he ate.) In the evening, after collective meditation with the disciples, the Mother came in to wash his eyes, apply cream to his body, and talk about the day's developments.

2

A week or two after the accident, Sri Aurobindo began to hold informal discussions with his attendants. The talks covered a wide variety of topics: Sri Aurobindo's early life, ashram news, yoga, occultism, philosophy, religion, literature, current affairs. On 14 December, for example, they began with Theosophy and freemasonry, moved on to Cagliostro and Nostradamus, then, returning to the present, Prime Minister Neville Chamberlain. At this point, the Mother entered and the discussion turned to Buddhism. She remarked that in her experience there was no real Buddhism left in Japan and China: 'Only ceremonies remain.' She added: 'In Ceylon they say there is still some authentic Buddhism.' After a while, she began to meditate and the others tried to follow her example. When she left, Sri Aurobindo asked two of the attendants about their meditations. One said he thought that Sri Aurobindo had no need to ask, since he was omniscient. Sri Aurobindo laughed this off, adding: 'I am not occupied with this sort of thing [details of occult workings]. I leave it to the Mother. . . . She saw exactly what was going to happen in the recent European trouble. We know what we have to know for our work.' The talk passed on to medical diagnosis, intuition and the power of the 'hostile forces'. Sri Aurobindo remarked, in response to an unspoken question, that the accident happened because he was 'occupied with guarding the Mother' and forgot about himself. In regard to the application of spiritual force, he said he usually was successful when he used it in the ashram but had mixed results when applying it to world events. During the Siege of Madrid in 1936, he found that Republican general José Miaja responded well to his force. He was generally successful in regard to Ireland. In the Sino-Japanese War, he avoided taking sides. Asked about the state of the Indian freedom movement, he said it looked like some of the leaders were pushing it in the direction of European socialism, which was not a good thing.[3]

This conversation was not typical of Sri Aurobindo's talks. He generally avoided speaking about himself and almost never referred directly to his use of occult force. (If he did so this time, it was because he assumed his words would never leave the room. The talks were published after his death and the transcripts never approved by him.) I summarized this particular talk because it sets the tone for his and the Mother's approach to the events that preoccupied them during the late 1930s and early 1940s. They viewed the Second World War as a clash of occult forces, and only superficially as a series of military and diplomatic events. I do not consider it part of my job as a historian to endorse or refute such ideas but I have to take them into account when I examine the Mother's and Sri Aurobindo's lives during the war years and after.

During the early part of 1939, Sri Aurobindo, along with the rest of the world, watched as the Great Powers jostled for position in Europe and Africa. With help from German forces, Francisco Franco's Nationalist army occupied Madrid in March. (A month earlier, Sri Aurobindo observed that Miaja, the Republican general he favoured, could do nothing without arms and food.) Also in March, Hitler gobbled up what was left of the Czech lands and made Slovakia a client state. Two weeks later, Britain and France agreed to defend Poland if Germany should attack it. In May, Germany and Italy signed a political and military agreement. Three months later, Germany signed a non-aggression pact with Soviet Russia. The stage now was set for a pan-European war.

At first, Sri Aurobindo thought there was little to choose between Britain and France, the established imperial powers, and Germany and Italy, which were eager to expand their territorial holdings. They represented, as he had written in 1937, 'two kinds of Ignorance'. Within a year or two, however, he and the Mother concluded that Hitler was, in occult terms, possessed by a 'vital power'. Following his 'inner voice', he was able to outmanoeuvre the Western democracies, whose primary interest was defending themselves and their empires. In September 1939, Germany invaded Poland. Britain and France declared war on Germany, and the Soviet Union attacked Poland from the east. After Poland succumbed, there was little military action for six months. Then, in April 1940, Hitler invaded Denmark and Norway, followed in May by Blitzkrieg attacks against the Low Countries and France. From this moment, Sri Aurobindo 'put his spiritual force' behind France and Britain.[4]

The Mother and Sri Aurobindo were stunned when German troops entered Paris on 14 June. They were disgusted when Marshal Philippe Pétain agreed to negotiate an armistice with Hitler. Pétain became the head of a puppet government set up in the spa town of Vichy, while the Germans occupied Paris and the northern and eastern parts of the country. Before France fell, Sri Aurobindo and the Mother made a donation to the French National Defence Fund, followed by donations to the Viceroy's War Fund and Madras War Fund in India. Along with the third donation, they issued a statement:

> We feel that not only is this a battle waged in just self-defence and in defence of the nations threatened with the world-domination of Germany and the Nazi system of life, but that it is a defence of civilisation and its highest attained social, cultural and spiritual values and of the whole future of humanity.

This occasioned a good deal of negative comment in India, where many, out of hatred for the British, were sympathetic towards Hitler. Even some ashram members were disturbed. Why, one of them asked, were the Mother and Sri Aurobindo supporting a country that had exploited India for 200 years and acted against the interests of the ashram since it was founded? The Mother explained that in the present conflict, Britain and its allies were 'blindly the instruments of the divine forces', while Hitler's Germany was 'an instrument for the Asuric forces'. To defeat Nazism, it was necessary for people to put themselves on the side of the 'divine force' through an effort of inner purification.[5] The grumblings in the ashram persisted. In a letter to a disciple that later was released to the public, Sri Aurobindo explained his and the Mother's position at greater length:

> You should not think of it as a fight for certain nations against others or even for India; it is a struggle for an ideal that has to establish itself on earth in the life of humanity, for a Truth that has yet to realise itself fully and against a darkness and falsehood that are trying to overwhelm the earth and mankind in the immediate future.

In intellectual terms, the war was 'a struggle for the liberty of mankind to develop, for conditions in which men have freedom and room to think and act according to the light in them and grow in the Truth'. If Germany and its allies won—and, at the time, many thought they would—'there will be a reign of falsehood and darkness, a cruel oppression and degradation for most of the human race such as people in this country do not dream of and cannot yet at all realise'.[6]

If to the occult eye the war was a fight between divine and anti-divine forces, and to intellectuals and moralists a clash between democracies and dictatorships, on the ground, it was a struggle between ordinary men who, following the orders of their superiors, killed and were killed in vast numbers. This side of the conflict came home to the Mother when she learnt about the Nazi persecution of the Jews. She never spoke openly about fears she may have had for family and friends in France. According to laws promulgated by the Vichy regime in 1940 and 1941, people who had three or four Jewish grandparents were regarded as members of the 'Jewish race', whether or not they practised the Jewish religion. The Mother's mother, Mathilde, and her brother, Matteo, were among 3,00,000 people living in France who fell in this category. They were forbidden to work in government service or practise certain professions and were liable to be interned in camps. From mid-1942, internment camps became staging grounds for deportation to extermination camps in Poland.

Since 1938, Matteo Alfassa had been living in retirement in a village near Blois, just north of the Demarcation Line. His mother lived nearby. Neither of them attracted the attention of the Germans or the Vichy government.[7] Other Alfassas were not so lucky. Five people with that surname, all originally from Adrianople or Constantinople and possibly related to Maurice Alfassa, were deported from France to Auschwitz. Only one survived.[8] One of the most prominent French Holocaust victims was Béatrice Reinach (née Camondo), first cousin once removed of Clarisse Alfassa, the wife of Mirra Alfassa's uncle Léon. Born in Paris in 1894, when Mirra was sixteen, Béatrice grew up in the opulent mansion of her father, Moïse de Camondo. In 1918, she married Léon Reinach, the scion of another Jewish banking family. Her father bequeathed her an enormous fortune but gave the mansion and its artistic treasures to the French state as a memorial to his son, Nissim, who was killed in action during the First World War. (Today it is the Musée Nissim-de-Camondo.) Béatrice was well known in Parisian society as a hostess and horsewoman. She did not consider herself Jewish and because of her connections felt secure from the Nazi menace. To be on the safe side, she converted to Catholicism in the beginning of 1942. A year later she, Léon and their two children were arrested and sent to an internment camp. From there, they were deported to Auschwitz, where all of them were murdered or died of disease.

Matteo Alfassa died in 1942, worn out by his labours but still a firm believer in France's imperial mission. (His last article, published shortly before the German invasion, was entitled 'Why We Want to Keep Our Colonies.') Mathilde Alfassa died in 1944 and, after the war, was laid to rest in the family crypt in Paris.

3

Sri Aurobindo was one of the few important public figures in India who condemned the Nazis unequivocally and came out strongly in favour of the Allies. The leaders of the Indian National Congress expressed disapproval of Fascism and Nazism but, at the same time, refused to cooperate with the British. Towards the end of 1939, Congress governments in the provinces resigned. Provincial governments led by Muslim parties remained in power and worked closely with the British. This gave Muslim separatists the opening they had been waiting for. In March 1940, the All-India Muslim League passed a resolution calling for Muslim-majority areas in western and eastern India to become independent states. From this point onward, the threat of Pakistan overshadowed the Indian freedom movement.

After the fall of France, Louis Bonvin, the Governor of French India, recognized the puppet government of Pétain. He reversed himself when the British consul in Pondicherry told him bluntly that British forces would occupy the French settlements if he did not declare his support for Charles de Gaulle's government-in-exile. Bonvin did so in September 1940. Despite the ashram's support for the Allies, as shown by Sri Aurobindo and the Mother's donations to the French National Defence Fund and Viceroy's War Fund, some people in the French Indian government considered it 'a dangerous and subversive body'. In

July 1940, Bonvin's private secretary, Pierre Brutinel, told the British consul he thought the ashram should be 'liquidated'.[9] Bonvin himself was well-disposed towards the ashram but, as Sri Aurobindo remarked to his attendants, 'even he—if he hears that people in the Ashram are pro-Hitler—will be compelled to take steps'. It was within his powers 'to dissolve the Ashram at any moment'. Those in the ashram who expressed support for Hitler had 'no idea about the world and talk like children. Hitlerism is the greatest menace that the world has ever met. If Hitler wins, do they think India has any chance of being free?' If they wanted the ashram to be dissolved, 'they can come and tell me and I will dissolve it instead of the police doing it'.[10]

Sri Aurobindo followed the war news closely—at first, through transcripts of BBC broadcasts made by a disciple, later by listening to the broadcasts himself on a radio receiver installed in his room. The Mother got up every morning at four to tune in to 'Front Line Family', a BBC radio drama about the wartime travails of ordinary English people. In the evening, she presided over a curious ritual. Every day, each flower collected from the ashram's gardens was brought to her. Then she, with the help of ashram women, counted every flower of every variety. When Dr Manilal asked Sri Aurobindo why the flowers were being counted, he replied, 'Why shouldn't they be? The stars are counted in astronomy.' When the laughter subsided, Manilal said that when he asked one of the people who was collecting the flowers what was going on, the man replied: 'All I know is that it has an occult reason. I don't know any more and can't tell you any more.' To which Sri Aurobindo added: 'Nor can I. Even that much I do not know.'[11]

To people in the ashram, the war in Europe was far away, and Sri Aurobindo and the Mother were close. Most them felt they were under the Mother's protection and nothing bad could happen to them. In May 1941, the Mother set them straight. 'The world situation is critical today,' she wrote. 'India's fate too is hanging in the balance.' If India was in danger, 'Pondicherry cannot be expected to remain outside the danger zone. It will share the fate of the rest of the country.' Those who relied on her spiritual protection should realize it was not unconditional:

'It goes without saying that any sympathy or support for the Nazis (or for any ally of theirs) automatically cuts across the circle of protection. Apart from this obvious and external factor, there are more fundamental psychological conditions which demand fulfilment. The Divine can give protection only to those who are whole-heartedly faithful to the Divine.' If people insisted on their own preferences, they put a barrier between themselves and the Divine protection: 'If you seek to impose your will upon the Divine, it is as if you were calling on a bomb to fall upon you.'[12]

When the war finally came to India, the aggressor was not Germany but Japan. On 7 December 1941, the Japanese air force bombed the American naval base at Pearl Harbor. Almost simultaneously, Japanese armed forces attacked the Philippines, Hong Kong, British Malaya, Singapore and, a little later, the Dutch East Indies (Indonesia). Within four months, American, British and Dutch forces in all these places surrendered. In January 1942, the Japanese invaded Burma and, by April, had pushed to within a few hundred miles of the Indian border. Panic seized hold of the country. Thousands of people fled from coastal cities and took refuge in the interior. On 5 April, Japanese planes bombed the south Indian port of Visakhapatnam. The next day, Sri Aurobindo issued a message saying, 'The Mother does not wish that anyone should leave his post because of the danger. Those who are very eager to remove their children may do so, but no one should be under the illusion that there is any safe place anywhere.' The Mother followed this up with a withering message for 'those who quake for their skin and run away': 'Why should you be in safety when the whole world is in danger? What is your special virtue and special merit for which you are to be specially protected?' The only safety lay in the Divine: 'Take refuge in Him and cast away all fear.'[13] On 20 December, the Japanese bombed Calcutta, Sri Aurobindo's birthplace and the home of many of his followers. Hundreds of thousands of people fled the city. Meanwhile, British and Indian troops were engaging Japanese forces in Burma. A full-scale invasion of India seemed imminent.

4

Life in the ashram went on. Once Sri Aurobindo had recovered from his accident, the Mother resumed her daily interactions with sadhaks and visitors. From ten in the morning until one in the afternoon, she stood at the top of the staircase leading to her room and met people who came to speak with her or receive her blessings. Besides her routine work, she was involved in two large projects—Golconde, which was nearing completion, and the creation of a printing establishment for Sri Aurobindo's books. In the evening, she led a group meditation, standing on the staircase while the disciples sat below. Later, apparently to accommodate greater numbers, she had the disciples sit in the courtyard of the ashram while she stood on a terrace above. When the evening meditation was over, she paid a visit to Sri Aurobindo, returning later with his supper.[14]

As the war approached India, there was an influx of new disciples. Some of them brought their children. The Mother didn't want them to just 'knock about in the streets', so she decided to start a school.[15] On 2 December 1943, thirty-eight students aged four to sixteen began to take regular classes in a building not far from the ashram's main buildings. The youngest children played and sang together. The older ones studied French, English, mathematics and science. When disciples outside the ashram learnt that the Mother had opened a school, many requested admission for their children. To accommodate new arrivals, the Mother acquired a property next to the school that was converted into a boarding house. The courtyard of this building became the children's playground.[16]

From the beginning, the Mother gave special importance to physical education. At first, some young men of the ashram played games like king of the castle and croquet with the children. In 1945, the Mother asked Pranab Kumar Bhattacharya, a boxer and physical-culture enthusiast recently arrived from Bengal, to take charge of the older boys. They cleaned up and levelled the courtyard, turning it into a ground for marching, drills and games. Later, some girls asked the Mother if they could participate. She said they could use the playground on alternate days. To begin with, they wore saris or salwar suits, but these were too cumbersome for active sports. The Mother designed a uniform consisting of loose-fitting pyjamas and Magyar blouses. These too proved impractical, so she asked the girls to wear shorts, blouses and a sort of turban (called a 'kitty-cap') for their hair. At that time, asking girls to wear shorts was revolutionary and many in the ashram were shocked. When people tried to tell the Mother that this was not the done thing in India, she replied, rather sharply: 'Why should we follow the others? . . . I have come to break down old conventions and superstitions.'[17]

The Mother once remarked that when children are there, 'everything revolves around them'. When children became part of the ashram community, 'the entire organization of the Ashram changed completely'. Up to this point, she had been able to handle the problems that accompanied the growth of the ashram one by one. Now, she had to deal with multiple problems in a hurry. 'One learns a lot of things that way,' she said. 'But it becomes more complicated.'[18] Many of the difficulties were financial. By 1944, there were 350 adults and children in the ashram. That meant buying more of everything just when the war was making prices soar sky-high. One evening, the Mother went to Sri Aurobindo and handed him a paper on which was written: 'Rs 2,000 for milk per month. Rs 8,000 for grains', etc. Quietly, she added: 'You see, how much is our expense!' Sri Aurobindo replied: 'Oh, oh!' This meant, in practical terms, that she would have to figure out how to deal with the situation herself. She always found a way. Six months later, Sri Aurobindo wrote to a disciple who complained about the way the ashram was run:

> It has been an arduous and trying work for the Mother and myself to keep up this Asram, with its ever-increasing numbers, to make both ends meet and at times to prevent deficit budgets and their results, especially in this war time, when the expenses have climbed to a dizzy and fantastic height.

They depended on donors but what they got was 'nothing compared to what is needed'.[19] Despite the challenges, the Mother keep things going and the ashram and school prospered in adversity.

5

From the beginning of 1943, the tide of war began to turn against the Axis powers. In Russia, the Red Army, now on the Allied side, defeated the German army at Stalingrad. Allied victories over Italian and German forces in North Africa opened the way to the invasion of Italy. After defeating the Japanese navy in the Battle of Midway, American forces moved island by island across the Pacific. Japanese attempts to invade India from Burma were stopped by British and Indian forces at Kohima and Imphal—considered by many the decisive campaign of the Second World War in Asia. In these battles, the Japan-allied Indian National Army (INA) played a minor role. Composed of Indian soldiers who had surrendered in Malaya and Singapore, the INA was led by Subhas Chandra Bose, a former president of the Indian National Congress who was, in his youth, an admirer of Aurobindo Ghose and later a critic of his ashram. In 1941, Bose escaped from house arrest in Calcutta and went to Germany, where he met Hitler and other German leaders, who arranged for him to go to East Asia. In June 1943, he conferred with Japanese dictator Hideki Tojo, who sent him to Singapore to take charge of the INA. There, he declared himself the leader of the Provisional Government of Free India. The Japanese humoured him, although it is clear they intended to use him as a puppet.

After the defeats at Kohima and Imphal, Bose withdrew to Saigon and then to Taipei, where he died in an airplane crash. In India, he remained an enormously popular figure. In the ashram, he created an uproar. Some, including his old friend Dilip Kumar Roy, defended him. Others considered him a traitor. Sri Aurobindo and the Mother believed that Bose had made himself an instrument of the anti-divine forces. If the Japanese had managed to enter India, 'it would have been almost impossible to get them out'. Once they occupied the country, 'they would have joined the Germans in Mesopotamia and the Caucasus and nothing could have saved Europe and Asia from being overrun. This would have meant the destruction of our work and a horrible fate for this country and for the world'. Later, the Mother met Bose's secretary, Abid Hasan, who convinced her that Bose's motives were good even if his actions were, at best, quixotic. She therefore 'modified her attitude toward him', particularly because by then Japan had been defeated.[20]

The Mother greeted the victory of the Allies with a prayer of thanksgiving and a reminder to the victors that it was by the force of the Lord that they had conquered. Now they had to keep the promises they made during the conflict. She also wrote a message on the atomic bomb, which had helped end the war. The harnessing of atomic power was a 'most wonderful achievement and the sign of a growing power of man over material nature'. Unfortunately, 'this material progress and mastery' was not 'in keeping with a spiritual progress and mastery which alone has the power to contradict and counteract the terrible danger coming from these discoveries. We cannot and must not stop progress, but we must achieve it in an equilibrium between the inside and the outside.'[21]

6

The ashram school continued to grow and diversify. At first, its classes were more or less the same as in schools throughout the world. The teachers instructed, gave classwork and homework, corrected student papers and so forth. On the other hand, the school's physical-education programme was far in advance of anything available in all but a few schools in India. In December 1945, the Mother organized a physical-culture demonstration to celebrate the school's second anniversary. The following May, she set up a series of athletic competitions and games tournaments. A year later, some of the boys asked if they could play table tennis. She agreed and asked them to set up the table in a place where she could join them. This proved such a success that the next year the ashram leased a piece of land for building tennis courts and other sports facilities. It was an uninviting place, used by townspeople as a dumping ground and overrun by feral pigs. Under the Mother's guidance, ashramites and older children constructed a sea wall, cleaned the place up and laid out two courts. The Mother inaugurated them in May 1948. For a lady of seventy, she played remarkably well, with solid forehand returns.[22] By this time, the school's sporting activities included athletics, football, cricket, volleyball and other Western games, along with traditional Indian disciplines such as mallakhamb and asanas. Not just the children but even ashram members took part. To begin with, the Mother was not a fan of football, calling it a 'brutal' sport when some ashram boys got injured. She became a convert during a visit by the famous Mohun Bagan club of Calcutta. Seeing the 'beautifully coordinated' play, with each player doing his bit, she cried out, 'What an artistic game!'[23]

The Mother was now spending much of her time outside the main ashram buildings. She went by car to the various departments, including farms located some distance away. She oversaw games and drills at the playground, watched the ashram boys play football, and went regularly to the courts to play tennis. Members of the ashram found themselves sucked up in the tornado she created. Not everyone was happy about this. Dilip Kumar Roy, a stay-at-home poet and musician, wrote anguished letters to Sri Aurobindo complaining that the ashram was turning into a gymnasium and that the Mother now favoured sportsmen over everyone else. Sri Aurobindo assured him that participation in sports was voluntary but went on to consider the larger question of the place of physical activities in yoga. The ashram, he said, was not 'concerned only with meditation and inner experiences and the escape from life into the Brahman'. His path of yoga included all of life, 'and once we admit life, we can include anything that we find useful for life's ultimate and immediate purpose and not inconsistent with the works of the Spirit'.[24]

In February 1949, the Mother launched a quarterly journal, the *Bulletin of Physical Education.* The first issue contained an article by Sri Aurobindo. Sports and physical activities, he wrote, were not just healthy and entertaining expressions of physical energy. Properly carried out, they could help individuals and groups 'in most . . . of the provinces of a combined human endeavour'.[25] The Mother added a message on youth and old age. 'Youth does not depend on the number of years one has lived, but on the capacity to grow and progress,' she began. 'To grow is to increase one's potentialities, one's capacities; to progress is to make constantly more perfect the capacities that one already possesses.' It followed that old age 'does not come from a great number of years but from the incapacity or the refusal to continue to grow and progress'. By these standards, she was one of the youngest people in the ashram, having begun a whole new chapter of her life when she was in her late sixties. Physically, she was more active than she had been since 1913, when she was rushing around Paris attending meetings. Intellectually, she was developing a new approach to education, one based on the assumption that 'human possibilities exceed all imagination'.[26]

In the November 1950 issue of the *Bulletin,* the Mother published an essay entitled 'The Science of Living'. 'Whatever ideal you put before yourself', she wrote, 'you cannot realise it perfectly until you have realised perfection in yourself.' The first step towards attaining perfection was 'to become conscious of yourself, of the different parts of your being and their respective activities'. The principal parts of the being were four: Psychic, mental, vital and physical. This taxonomy owed something to the fourfold being of the Cosmic philosophy—mental, psychic, nervous and nervo-physical—but the Mother gave supreme importance to the psychic, making it the key to transformation. The psychic is 'the psychological centre of our being, the seat within us of the highest truth of our existence', she wrote. It therefore is 'of capital importance to become conscious of its presence in us, to concentrate on this presence until it becomes a living fact for us and we can identify ourselves with it'. There are many methods of finding and opening the psychic being, some psychological, some religious, some mechanical. Each one has to find the way that suits him or her best. 'To complement this movement of inner discovery,' the Mother continued, 'it would be good not to neglect the development of the mind. For the mental instrument can be either a great help or a great hindrance.' In its natural state, the human mind 'is always limited in its vision, narrow in its understanding, rigid in its conceptions'. One has to make a constant effort 'to widen it, to make it more supple and profound'. Learning scholastic subjects is necessary but more important are disciplines for silencing the ordinary mind and opening it to 'the realm of pure ideas'. None of this is possible if one's vital energy is out of control. The centre of our vitality 'is the seat of impulses and desires, of enthusiasm and violence, of dynamic energy and desperate depressions, of passions and revolts. It can set everything in motion, build and realise; but it can also destroy and spoil everything'. When it acts up, one has to deal with it 'as one deals with a rebellious child . . . showing it the truth and light, trying to convince it and awaken in it the goodwill which has been veiled for a time'. Finally, one has to make one's body 'strong and supple enough to become a fit instrument in the material world for the force of truth that wants to express itself through us'. When we have achieved a balanced development of these four parts of our being, 'The psychic will be the vehicle of true and pure love, the mind will be the vehicle of infallible knowledge, the vital being will manifest an invincible power and strength and the body will be the expression of a perfect beauty and harmony'.[27]

7

During the 1940s, the British government tried to find a way to keep a united India in its geopolitical sphere while granting it self-government. These efforts foundered on the rock of Pakistan. On 3 June 1947, the Viceroy of India, Louis Mountbatten, broadcast a plan by which political power would be 'transferred to Indian hands' but provinces would be able to choose whether they wanted to remain in India or join the 'new entity'. This made the partition of the country a virtual certainty. In a message issued later the same day, the Mother wrote that the Mountbatten Plan was 'not a solution' but 'a test, an ordeal which, if we live it out in all sincerity, will prove to us that it is not by cutting a country into small bits that we shall bring about its unity and its greatness'.[28] India and Pakistan became independent nations on 14–15 August 1947. It was a time of celebration but also of violence and bloodshed, as people in the partitioned provinces of Punjab and Bengal turned on their neighbours if they happened to belong to a different religion.

Pondicherry remained under French rule. From the beginning of 1947, when the British first announced they would be leaving the country, the French government and political parties in Pondicherry put forward their competing visions of the colony's future. The French wanted it to become an autonomous member of the Union Française (French

Union), a short-lived attempt to turn the tottering French Empire into something like the British Commonwealth. Indian nationalists wanted the five French settlements to merge with independent India as quickly as possible. A few wished to keep some of the benefits of French rule when the territories became part of India. The wrangling went on for seven years, until France finally ceded the colony. During this period, the ashram was pulled in different directions, and ended up antagonizing the Government of India and most of the local political parties.

The Mother made no public statements on the issue, both because she disliked politics and because anything she said was likely to be misconstrued. She was, after all, French. During the quarter-century she had lived in Pondicherry, she had adopted many Indian habits, but, at the same time, she retained a strong attachment to her homeland. Despite her dislike of colonialism in general, she seems to have thought that Pondicherry would benefit by joining the French Union. Certainly, she believed this would benefit the ashram, at least in the short term. For three decades, she had cultivated friendly relations with the Government of French India so that the community she founded could thrive. If Pondicherry suddenly became part of India, there was no telling how the new government would deal with the ashram, its members and her.

In March 1946, a new governor, François Baron, took office. His task was to convince the people of French India that they had much to gain by joining the French Union. There would be no more empire, no more colonies, only 'a great nation of 100 million people all perfectly equal . . . a free association of original communities with the French Union.'[29] Before the war, Baron had visited the ashram, and developed a high regard for Sri Aurobindo and the Mother. After his appointment as governor, he often spoke with the Mother and her secretary Saint-Hilaire (Pavitra), and in May 1947 he wrote to his superiors that they were in favour of the French plan.[30] A month later, Sri Aurobindo drafted a manifesto for a Pondicherry political party in which he backed autonomy within the French Union but insisted that this arrangement could only last if there was 'some kind of close connection and even union with the rest of India—industrial, economic and other'. The best outcome would be a sort of 'dual citizenship' by which people in French India 'could be in the French Union and participate without artificial barriers in the life of India as a whole'. When Pavitra sent a copy of the manifesto to his father in France, he told him it represented what 'we want to see realized in French India'. He added that 'our friend Baron' was then in Paris trying 'to convince the ministers of the urgent need to grant this country the autonomy it asks for'.[31]

The idea that the 'country' of French India could become an autonomous member of the French Union never had a snowball's chance in hell. Before going to Paris, Baron had a meeting with Jawaharlal Nehru, the head of the provisional government of India (and Prime Minister-in-waiting). Baron did not push the autonomy idea, which he knew Nehru would never accept. Instead, he suggested that France should establish an 'international university based on French culture' in Pondicherry. In this way, France would keep 'a "cultural" foothold in Pondicherry' after it left the country. Nehru was open to this idea. 'Despite our political struggle' with Britain, he told Baron, people in India 'still looked at the world with British glasses'. The English language was here to stay, 'but we wish to know other languages and we are interested by other cultures'. India had 'a strong intellectual sympathy' for France. Therefore, he would be happy if Pondicherry became 'an open window on France'.[32]

Baron's meeting with Nehru was private and had no immediate effect on the political situation in Pondicherry. In the weeks leading up to Indian independence, all parties in Pondicherry stepped up their agitation. The communists and the local unit of the Congress Party demanded immediate merger with India. A few diehard French Indians hoped to join the French Union, while others supported a hybrid French Union–Indian Union proposal. The belief that the Mother endorsed the third option created much ill feeling in the town. Some alleged that Sri Aurobindo did not support merging with India because he was under the Mother's thumb. The fifteenth of August 1947, the day chosen by Mountbatten to grant independence to British India (and, coincidentally, Sri Aurobindo's seventy-fifth birthday), was the occasion for day-long celebrations by ashram members. In the morning, the Mother issued an 'invocation', calling on India to show its 'true visage, as a leader in the ways of the spirit, and a friend and helper of all the peoples'. She had a banner she called 'the flag of India's spiritual mission' hoisted above the main ashram building.[33] Afterwards, the usual August darshan was held with thousands in attendance. In the afternoon, she stood on her terrace as members of the ashram sang the national song 'Vande Mataram' and cried out 'Victory to the Mother'. She replied by crying 'Jai Hind' (Victory to India)!' In the evening, there was a cultural programme, which went ahead despite rumours of trouble brewing in the town. While the programme was underway, rioters stoned the ashram and attacked members who happened to be outside. One of them, Mulshankar Jani, was stabbed in the neck. He was rushed to the hospital where he died.

Five days later, the secretary of the ashram issued a statement saying that the attackers 'were mostly professional goondas of the town hired and organized for the purpose' by a political party hostile to the ashram. Rumours insinuating that people in the ashram were for 'the continuance of French rule' were false. It was, however, true that Sri Aurobindo was in favour of 'autonomy within the French Union accompanied by a dual citizenship and a close association with the Indian Union'.[34] That idea was now a dead letter.

In September, French Prime Minister Paul Ramadier sent the Resistance hero and politician Maurice Schumann to India to persuade Nehru not to take precipitous action against the colony. (Ramadier feared this would set a bad example for nationalists in Algeria and Indochina.) Before going to Delhi, Schumann stopped off in Pondicherry, where he and Baron had a meeting with Sri Aurobindo, the first he had granted anyone since 1928. The Mother presented the two French officials, then sat as they and Sri Aurobindo conversed for about an hour. The political question was kept on the sidelines. According to an official press release, Sri Aurobindo said: 'France, after India, is the country for which I have the most affection and respect. Your idea of making Pondicherry a permanent meeting place between France and India has my full support.' Later, the Mother spoke at length with Schumann, asking him about the current situation in France. After dinner, she suddenly said: 'Wouldn't you like to play a game of ping-pong?' He agreed and was amazed to see how she flew around the table. Schumann's meeting with Nehru a few days later was less entertaining. The Prime Minister received him coldly and said nothing to bolster his hopes.[35]

Hoping to prolong its influence, the Government of France took the position that the people of French India had to be given the chance to decide their political future. In June 1948, the National Assembly passed a declaration calling for referendums to be held in the five settlements. In retaliation, the Government of India cancelled its customs agreement with French India. Isolated, the colony suffered from shortages and high prices. This, along with rising political tensions, made life in the ashram difficult for the next few years. In June 1949, Chandernagore held its referendum. Ninety-eight per cent of the voters opted for merging with India. As always in French–Indian elections, party leaders hired bands of rowdies to influence the outcome and there was scattered violence. As a result, the referendums in Pondicherry and the other southern settlements were postponed. The political stalemate and economic hardships continued.

8

In November 1949, André Morisset came to Pondicherry and met his mother for the first time since 1915. After serving in the First World War, he studied at the École Polytechnique, married, had two daughters and became a successful businessman. As we have seen, he and the Mother exchanged letters during the 1920s and 1930s. When communications were restored after the Second World War, they resumed their correspondence, and, in the summer of 1949, André wrote saying he would be coming to India. On the way, he stopped off in Calcutta where, at a gathering of devotees, he shared some reminiscences of his childhood. Even in those far-off days, he said, his mother told him that she had come to earth to fulfil a special mission. On the day of his arrival in Pondicherry, the Mother told Sri Aurobindo: 'It is many years since we last met. Perhaps if we met on the road without being introduced to each other I would not know him, and he too would not recognise me.

For many years have passed—' She arranged for someone to meet him at the airport and take him directly to Golconde, where she would wait for him. Due at five in the evening, he was held up by police formalities and it was dark when he finally reached the guesthouse. He climbed the stairs and, as he later related, 'in the dim light of the corridor, I saw a white shape with her back against the door in a very familiar attitude'. They met as mother and son: 'We were at once in full understanding and I had the strong impression of being still a small boy seeking safety in his mother's lap.' On 24 November, André witnessed the darshan. Seeing Sri Aurobindo and the Mother sitting together, he had an 'overwhelming impression of benevolence, knowledge and strength'.[36]

André was present in December for the ashram school's anniversary celebrations, which now stretched over two days. The main feature of the cultural programme was a play written by the Mother entitled *Vers l'Avenir* (Towards the Future). The plot is clearly based on her early life. The characters are 'She', her childhood Friend, her husband the Poet, his friend the Painter, and a Clairvoyant. 'She' is modelled on Mirra Morisset, the Poet on Henri Morisset (with touches of Theon and Paul Richard), the Painter owes much to Morisset's artist friends, and the Clairvoyant is a passive sensitive of the Cosmic type.

As the play opens, She and her Friend are talking about the old days. The Friend expresses amazement that She, who formerly mocked social conventions, is married. She reminds her Friend that she never said anything against true love, a 'great shared love that was free from all animal activity'. She then confides: 'I have loved deeply, with great sincerity and intensity, but my love has not met the response it hoped for.' The two women agree to meet later. The Poet enters. He tells his wife about a poem he is working on in which he tries to express his high ideal of life. She listens sympathetically, then says she plans to visit her Friend to speak to her about the teaching that guides her. She departs. The Poet tells himself that he admires and respects his wife, but that this, alas, is not love. When will his dream of love become a reality? Just then, he hears a woman with a beautiful voice singing a melody. Immediately afterwards there is a knock on the door. It is his friend, the Painter, who tells him he has met a wonderful singer, who, as it happens, lives nearby. He wants to introduce her to the Poet, who agrees. The Painter goes out and returns with the Clairvoyant, whom he leaves with the Poet. The two talk about the coincidences that have brought them together. The Clairvoyant explains that she is 'a helpless and unprotected orphan who is forced to earn her living by herself'. While they speak, she is overcome by an imperious need to sleep and also complains about a headache. The Poet places his hand on her forehead. The pain vanishes and she slips into deep sleep. The Poet is attracted by her beauty and feels an urge to protect her but reminds himself of his responsibilities towards his wife. The Clairvoyant wakes and tells the Poet of the lands she has visited while she slept. The Poet, drawing on his knowledge of occultism, explains her experiences. The Clairvoyant tells him she feels that 'from now on your protection will always enfold me'. He admits he loves her but—Just then, She, who has been waiting behind a screen, comes forward. She tells the two of them not to be upset. She reminds the Poet: 'We promised we would give each other freedom if love for another awoke. That is why I listened, and now I have come to tell you: you are free; be happy.' The Poet is overcome by her generosity. He asks her whether she won't feel lonely. She replies: 'Oh, I shall not be alone, for I shall go and join those through whom we have found the path, those who possess the eternal wisdom and who have, from a distance, guided our steps up till now.' To the Clairvoyant, she says: 'Now I know for sure that only one love can satisfy my being: it is the love for the Divine, the divine love, for that alone never disappoints.'[37]

André later wrote, somewhat indulgently, that there was 'nothing amateurish' about the first performance of *Vers l'Avenir*.[38] If he had any thoughts about the biographical elements in the plot, he kept them to himself.

9

During the late 1940s, the life of the ashram was a whirlwind of activity, all of it revolving around the Mother. She spent more and more of her time with the younger generation, overseeing the development of the school and its sports programme. The *Bulletin* for these years is full of articles on these activities and photographs of drills, games, *tableaux vivants*, sporting competitions and theatrical presentations. Throughout the year, she gave balcony darshan in the morning, followed by pranam. During the day, she went out in a car to inspect the ashram's departments. In the evening, she was driven to the tennis ground, where she played a game or two. Afterwards, she visited the playground to see the marching and to give a French class to some of the children. Then, there was a group concentration. She stayed up late almost every night, taking care of administrative matters and writing letters. Sri Aurobindo's attendant Nirodbaran wondered how this septuagenarian managed to do it all. 'Her body was frail,' he mused, her 'food and sleep were medically quite inadequate to cope with her super-abundant vitality'. To doubts like this, she replied: 'Do you think I live on these frugal meals alone? One can draw any amount of energy from universal Nature.'[39]

The four darshan days remained the high points of the ashram's yearly calendar. Hundreds of visitors came on these occasions. Sri Aurobindo was the chief attraction but people were told that the Mother was his spiritual equal. Most were favourably impressed. 'The savant sits in a chair,' wrote one visitor from Bengal, 'while the only other chair in the room is occupied by a venerable-looking French lady—known to everyone interested in the Ashram as the "Mother".' The Ceylonese writer Jinadasa Vijayatunga described her as 'a woman of great dignity and beauty in her youth, as well as of great intellect' who 'embodies in her frail frame to-day an amazing vitality, through her eyes pours a radiance that is not earthly. The "darshan" of her and the receiving of her blessing in the form of a flower is no mere idolatry.' Others had mixed feelings. One magazine writer accepted that the Mother had become, 'through lengthy austerities and meditation, a true yogini', but felt that beneath her excessive make-up, she was just 'a little old woman with big teeth and hypnotic eyes, gorgeously dressed and supreme in the power she exercises over the smallest details of the lives of her six hundred subjects'. The American journalist Vincent Sheean likewise was disturbed by her clothing and make-up, which made him think of the celebrated

French actress Sarah Bernhardt: 'Madame Bernhardt had the same physical scrawniness and extremely heavy stage make-up, and there was something very similar in the expression of mouth and eyes.' In addition, both the Divine Mother and La Divine Sarah 'were acting at all moments, internally and externally'. But Sheean had to admit that the Mother was sincere and had extraordinary power. 'The Divine Mother, when she said *"Bonjour, chéri,"* to me' was 'off in some kind of state or condition which had hardly anything to do with this physical existence' yet her presence 'hit me with an impact that almost caused fear'.[40]

In April 1950, the photojournalist Henri Cartier-Bresson, who was on a tour of India, wrote to Pavitra asking for permission to take photographs of the 24 April darshan and to make 'a photographic record of the life of the ashram'. After consulting with the Mother, Pavitra sent his approval. Cartier-Bresson arrived on 23 April. Governor Baron presented him to the Mother, who told him he was free to take pictures of ashram activities but not of her. Later, she relaxed this prohibition and he took some pictures of her interacting with disciples. He wrote in his notebook of her 'sweet smiles coming from some other world'. He added: 'She has a tremendous personality and the Ashramites say that she is "the manifested aspect of divinity". She seems to be a very kind person with a tremendous energy which has absorbed the will of all the disciples.' On the morning of 24 April Cartier-Bresson took some shots of the disciples looking up at the Mother during balcony darshan. When she appeared, 'all hands joined with ecstatic smiles on their faces. Mother was turning her head at the slowest motion from the extreme right of the street to the other end with an enigmatic smile. This very slow motion gave her time to see exactly who was there, and at the end she disappeared inside as an apparition'. After breakfast, everyone stood in line for the joint darshan of Sri Aurobindo and the Mother. At the last minute, the Mother gave Cartier-Bresson permission to take photographs provided he kept the atmosphere of 'artistic darkness' she had imparted to the room where they sat. On account of the low light, the pictures were not very successful. The next day, Cartier-Bresson asked for permission to take photographs of Sri Aurobindo in his room. After some hesitation, the Mother concurred. 'Sri Aurobindo did not wink an eye during the entire ten minutes I was watching him,' Cartier-Bresson later reported, 'he did not seem to belong to that impersonal setting.'[41] This time, the pictures turned out all right because he used a tripod. They were the first photographs of Sri Aurobindo taken since 1920—and the last to be taken during his lifetime.

10

Towards the middle of 1949, Sri Aurobindo began to experience urinary problems. His doctors suspected enlargement of the prostate. Dr Prabhat Sanyal, a surgeon from Calcutta, confirmed this diagnosis and explained the situation to the Mother. For the moment, the condition was not serious, he said, but it had to be carefully watched. When Sanyal returned in November, he was glad to report that the symptoms were much reduced. The Mother continued her daily routine, which, this year, included rehearsals for *Vers l'Avenir.* An essay by her appeared in each issue of the *Bulletin.* In February 1950, the topic was 'Foresight'. 'By yogic discipline one can not only foresee destiny but can alter it, change it almost completely,' she wrote. In critical situations, one can call on one's 'higher destiny', which, if one is perfectly sincere, can change the course of events.[42]

The normal life of the ashram went on as usual. Between January and April, the students and many adults took part in sporting tournaments. The Mother oversaw the proceedings and handed out the prize cards. In a message for the occasion, she wrote: 'Do not aim at success. Our aim is perfection.'[43] During these months, Sri Aurobindo's symptoms reappeared. Albumin showed up in his urine, then acetone—both bad signs. The doctors informed Sri Aurobindo, who told them to tell the Mother. She listened in silence. That November, Dr Satyabrata Sen came for the darshan. Asked to examine Sri Aurobindo, he reported that the prostate was much enlarged. Ordinarily, he would have recommended surgery but he knew the Mother and Sri Aurobindo would never approve of this. Nirodbaran monitored Sri Aurobindo's condition closely. Once, the flow of urine stopped completely. Alarmed, he ran to tell Dr Sen. By the time he returned, the flow had resumed. When the Mother heard about his panicked response, she said: 'Having passed so many years with Sri Aurobindo, you still get frightened?' Nirodbaran said defensively: 'We are dealing with no other person than Sri Aurobindo.' She replied, 'That is exactly why you should never be afraid. Don't you know that his mighty Force is always with you and helping you? No, fear has no place at all, especially among you who are serving him.'[44]

Sri Aurobindo's symptoms worsened. On the evening of 29 November, the Mother sent a telegram to Dr Sanyal: 'Fly—urgent—Mother.' He caught the next plane to Madras and, from there, took a taxi to Pondicherry, an unusual step at the time. When he arrived, the Mother was at the playground, where preparations for the school's anniversary programme were in full swing. She gave him a 'heavenly smile' and sent him to Sri Aurobindo's room. After a brief examination and consultation with his colleagues, he concluded that Sri Aurobindo was suffering from a mild kidney infection. He recommended a round of antibiotics. The Mother said this would not be necessary. Over the next four days, Sri Aurobindo's condition fluctuated between relatively normal and quite serious. The Mother, who was busy with the upcoming anniversary programmes, stopped in when she had time. Whenever she was there, she succeeded in getting Sri Aurobindo to drink a little juice but felt he was 'losing interest in himself'. On the morning of 4 December, there was a brief remission. Sri Aurobindo sat up and spoke with those around him. A few hours later, the symptoms returned in force. 'He is withdrawing,' the Mother told Dr Sanyal. In the evening, there was a momentary improvement. When the Mother came, the doctors asked again if they could begin antibiotics. 'I told you this is not necessary,' she replied, 'he has no interest in himself.' Around 1 a.m. on 5 December, she came and stood silently by Sri Aurobindo's bed. She asked Dr Sanyal: 'What do you think? Can I retire for one hour?' He did not know what to say. 'Call me when the time comes,' she said and went out. After twenty minutes, Sri Aurobindo stopped breathing. Sanyal sent Nirodbaran to fetch the Mother. She entered and stood by Sri Aurobindo's feet. 'Her hair had been undressed and was flowing about Her shoulders,' Sanyal later recalled.

'Her look was so fierce that I could not face those eyes.' She calmed the weeping attendants and told Sanyal to handle the legal formalities.[45]

Sri Aurobindo's body remained intact for almost four days. During that period, thousands of people came to pay their last respects. On 9 December, his remains were placed in a vault of a samadhi or tomb that had been built in the courtyard of the ashram. The Mother wrote a prayer that later was inscribed on a plaque that was affixed to the samadhi: 'To Thee who hast been the material envelope of our Master, to Thee our infinite gratitude. Before Thee who hast done so much for us . . . we bow down and implore that we may never forget, even for a moment, all we owe to Thee.'[46]

10

Alone

1

FOR TWELVE DAYS AFTER SRI AUROBINDO'S DEATH, ALL NON-essential activities in the ashram ceased. People in the community were overcome with despair. There had been murmurs that Sri Aurobindo was indisposed but few imagined the problem was serious. The idea that it might lead to his death had never occurred to anyone. Now, he was gone.

In the days following the event, the Mother issued several messages of consolation and encouragement. 'What has happened on the physical plane affects in no way the truth of [Sri Aurobindo's] teaching,' she wrote on 8 December. 'All that he has said is perfectly true and remains so. Time and the course of events will prove it abundantly.' Six days later, she scolded the disciples: 'To grieve is an insult to Sri Aurobindo who is here with us, conscious and alive.' And on 15 December: 'Sri Aurobindo is here, as living and as present as ever and it is left to us to realise his work with all the sincerity, eagerness and concentration necessary.'[1] The next day, she distributed a photograph of Sri Aurobindo taken the morning of his death. This marked the end of the twelve-day period of reflection. The ashram's activities resumed.

What was the Mother thinking and feeling when she wrote these confident messages? She left no contemporary account but scattered comments from later years show she was deeply shaken by Sri Aurobindo's death. As she once graphically put it, it was like 'getting hit over the head with a club'. During the thirty years she had lived with him, she was wrapped in 'a feeling of perfect security'. This feeling was so strong that even during his last illness it never occurred to her that his life was in danger. Only on the last night did she sense that he wanted to depart and she was holding him back. At this point, she told his doctors she was going to her room to rest. Within minutes, Sri Aurobindo died. The doctors called her back and even then she 'didn't want to believe it'. During their thirty years together, she had never felt any sense of responsibility. True, she was doing all the work, all the organizing and so forth: 'He supposedly had passed the responsibility on to me but it was he who was doing everything.' As long as he was there, 'nothing unfortunate could happen'. When he died, it was like 'falling into a hole'.[2]

In these statements, the Mother framed her aloneness in spiritual terms. It had a mundane side as well. Like most women of her generation, she had never been alone in the ordinary sense of the word. From her birth until the age of eighteen, she lived in her parents' home. From there, she went straight to her husband's. When the marriage fell apart, she found support from Paul Richard. She lived with him for twelve unhappy years, then stayed with Sri Aurobindo when Richard went away. From that point on, she always lived in the same house as Sri Aurobindo. This was the physical basis of her sense of security. Now, she was on her own. To be sure, she was surrounded by adoring disciples, some of whom were competent managers and workers. Then there were the children, who thought of her simply as their mother and gave her unstinting love. But now, there was no one for her to confide in, no one she could turn to in a tangible sense.

She could, and did, turn to the Divine. Two days after Sri Aurobindo's death, she wrote in a prayer that was distributed to the sadhaks: 'Lord, this morning Thou hast given me the assurance that Thou wouldst stay with us until Thy work is achieved, not only as a consciousness which guides and illumines but also as a dynamic Presence in action.'[3] This was a transcription of one of several experiences she had in the aftermath of the event. Years later, she told a disciple that after Sri Aurobindo's death, when she was alone in his room with his still-warm body, 'all that supramental force that was in him passed from his body into mine'. The sensation was so concrete that she could 'feel the friction of the passage'. Experiences like these were so vivid that she could write that Sri Aurobindo was 'still with me, day and night, thinking through my brain, writing through my pen, speaking through my mouth and acting through my organizing power'.[4]

Virtually no one in the ashram doubted that the Mother was Sri Aurobindo's spiritual successor. The few who did went away of their own accord. There also was no doubt who was the active head of the community. The Mother had held that charge since November 1926. The question of legal proprietorship was more complex. In 1934, Sri Aurobindo had written that the ashram was not a registered association but just 'the house or houses of a spiritual Teacher or Master of spiritual philosophy' where people could come to practise yoga. Most of the ashram's buildings were registered in the Mother's name because she could, as a French citizen, hold title to property in French India without difficulty. Despite this, some legally minded sadhaks thought it was necessary to affirm that 'the Mother had been all along in charge of the Ashram and that she still had the executive power'. A document to this effect was drawn up and signed before a French *notaire* by some senior members of the ashram.[5]

2

Before the events of early December, the Mother had been giving French classes to a group of young children. When the ashram's activities resumed on 17 December, she continued those classes and also began to give lessons to older students she hoped would become teachers in the school. These quickly became a great deal more than exercises in French conversation. Commenting on passages from her own works or translations from Sri Aurobindo's, she took up a variety of topics, personal, intellectual and spiritual. From 21 December, someone began to keep a shorthand record of what she said. This was the start of her recorded conversations, which, by the time she stopped in 1958, numbered more than 400. Published in French as *Entretiens* and in English as *Questions and Answers,* they are among her most accessible works.

On 21 December, the text under discussion was an extract from one of the Mother's *Prayers and Meditations.* After explaining the literal meaning of the passage, she made some general observations: 'To choose without preference and effectuate without desire is the great difficulty at the root of the development of the true consciousness and self-control. . . . One must be able to act without any preference, free from all attractions and likings, basing oneself solely on the Truth that guides.' This is a tenet of many religious writings, for example the Bhagavad Gita, but the Mother presented it as a matter of psychological observation and practice rather than a doctrine. She preferred to say 'the Truth which guides' instead of 'the Voice of God' or 'the Will of God' because the meaning of those terms had become distorted. Religious people gave the name God 'to an all-powerful being who is different than his creation and stands outside it'. This was a false idea. Questioned further about the 'divine will', she returned to yogic psychology: 'One does not know it, one feels it. And to feel it one must want it with such intensity, such sincerity, that every obstacle disappears.'[6]

The texts that provided the basis of the discussions dealt mostly with spiritual things, but her treatment was never pious. She spoke in straightforward conversational French, and spiced her remarks with wit, humour and sometimes gentle teasing. In February 1951, after reading a passage from one of her books, she paused, looked at her audience and said: 'The main problem is that you think with words, but these words are empty of meaning; most of the time they are just words. You talk of the Divine, you talk of the Supreme, you talk of yoga, you say many things, but does all that correspond in your head to something concrete, to a thought, a feeling, a clear idea, an experience? Or are they simply words?' It was necessary to 'see the thing, the experience behind the words'. In the ashram, people talked about yoga, others might say 'I am seeking my *raison d'être*', and so forth. 'There are fifty ways of saying the thing but it is *the thing* that is important; you must feel it in your head, in your heart, everywhere. It must be concrete, living, otherwise you can't make any progress.[7]

Those present at the Mother's talks always were happiest when she drew on her personal life to illustrate a point. When talking about physical charm and beauty, she recalled her wanderings around Tokyo. To explain how cultivated people sometimes acted like morons when out enjoying themselves, she recalled some of her artist friends in Paris. When somebody asked about unexpected disasters, she told the story of the Paris Charity Bazaar fire, when more than 125 people, some from the highest ranks of society, perished in the flames. When the imperilled aristocrats started running for the door, 'it was a real free-for-all! All these elegant, refined people, who usually were so well-mannered, began to fight like street rowdies'![8] Sometimes, she referred to the teachings of the Theons, usually without mentioning them by name. In January 1951, she cited the central Cosmic doctrine: 'There is no evil, there is only disequilibrium.' Five months later, she mentioned the 'twelve senses', another Cosmic belief of which she retained only a vague memory.[9] One evening, she spoke of the idea, based on Cosmic teachings, that there are four evil beings who are responsible for the lamentable state of the world: The Lord of Darkness, the Lord of Suffering, the Lord of Falsehood and the Lord of Death. She mentioned such things in passing and never tried to develop an esoteric system like the Cosmic movement or Theosophy.

Only rarely did the Mother go into the details of Sri Aurobindo's philosophy. Once, she made a stab at explaining to the children what the supramental consciousness was like. In that state, she said, 'you are able to see at the same time all the theories, all the beliefs, all the ideas that human beings have expressed in their highest consciousness . . . and in that state, not only do you put each thing in its place, but everything appears to you marvellously true and completely necessary for understanding anything at all about anything whatsoever'. Then, realizing she had gone beyond her audience, she said: 'One must be able to see all the aspects of the truth perceived by the human intelligence and—something more'.[10] Her remarks on self-awareness are among the most valuable things in the talks. 'If you observe yourself,' she said on 15 January, 'you will see that as soon as you do something that disturbs you a little, the mind immediately gives you a good reason to justify your action.' This self-deception comes in the way of self-knowledge. To avoid it, 'you have to be absolutely sincere', to 'see clearly through all the little falsehoods of the mental being'.[11]

One subject she never spoke about with the children, or anyone else, was Sri Aurobindo's death. If the pain of the 'clubbing over the head' still throbbed, she never let anyone know. In a public message of 18 January 1951, she wrote reassuringly that Sri Aurobindo had 'sacrificed his physical life in order to help more fully his work of transformation'. He was, she continued, 'always with us, aware of what we are doing, of all our thoughts, of all our feelings and all our actions'.[12]

3

Most of the students in the ashram school were children of disciples who had settled in Pondicherry during or after the war. Most of the teachers were ashram members who taught the children the same way they were taught when they were young. The Mother, who led some classes herself, considered the possibility of a different sort of education—one that aimed primarily at helping young people become alert and conscious human beings. Preparing future yogis was not her idea: 'What we want is for humanity to progress. It matters little whether it claims to be leading a yogic life or not, so long as it makes the necessary effort to progress.'[13]

When the Mother set her mind on something, she pulled out all the stops. Early in January 1951, she announced that she would open an 'International University Centre' for 'students from all over the world'. This would constitute 'the most fitting memorial' to Sri Aurobindo. A press release issued at the time added: 'To give effect to this proposal, it is necessary to collect a substantial amount of money.' Since tuition would be free, the funds would have to come through donations. By March 1951, enough money had been collected for the Mother to purchase the first buildings meant to house the university-to-be.[14]

An international university, the Mother said, was 'one of the most recent forms under which Sri Aurobindo conceived of the development of his work'.[15] She was thinking of the French–Indian cultural institution that Sri Aurobindo spoke about with the diplomat Schumann in 1947. As the project took shape, France was rarely mentioned, and the committee formed to expedite the project had no French or French–Indian members. Its chairman was the Bengali politician Syama Prasad Mukherjee, until recently a minister in the Union cabinet. (He resigned over the Nehru–Liaquat Pact in 1950 and, in October 1951, would found the Bharatiya Jana Sangh, a Hindu nationalist party.) Other committee members included the chief ministers of Uttar Pradesh and Orissa, some leading academics and assorted dignitaries. On 24–25 April, a Sri Aurobindo Memorial Convention was held in Pondicherry to discuss ways to bring the project to fruition. Present were most of the committee members along with scores of delegates from around the world. The Mother opened the proceedings. Standing before a microphone in a silk salwar kameez, flanked by a row of serious-looking gentlemen in starched kurtas, she said in a firm voice:

> Sri Aurobindo is present in our midst, and with all the power of his creative genius he presides over the formation of the University Centre which for years he considered as one of the best means of preparing the future humanity to receive the supramental light that will transform the élite of today into a new race manifesting upon earth the new light and force and life.[16]

In his presidential address, Syama Prasad, echoing Sri Aurobindo's *Renaissance in India,* said the 'master idea that has governed the life, literature, and culture' of India has always been 'the seeking of man for his true spiritual self and the use of life'. He added that this seeking could not ignore 'the evolution of man's lower, physical, vital, and mental nature'.[17] Indra Sen, a Freiberg-trained philosopher, who was a member of the ashram, reversed these priorities: Instructors in the new university, he wrote, had to develop the usual instruments of sense and mind but must do so 'in the knowledge that there are higher and yet higher instruments of cognition'. He added: People should not expect the university to spring into being with 'a full-fledged formal structure and organisation'.

A living institution had 'to be allowed to grow as the inspiration and the idea grows'.[18]

In his address, Syama Prasad made it clear that the university would 'function without reference to the nature of Government of Pondicherry' and would continue to exist when the colony joined India. At that time, three years after Indian independence, the French were not making any plans to leave. The government of Pondicherry functioned as before, and bureaucrats ground out reports on the ashram, the proposed university and the Mother. Would the ashram survive the death of Sri Aurobindo? Would the university project get off the ground? What exactly was the Mother's position? Where did she get her money? The governor-general, André Ménard, thought it would be best for the Government of French India to maintain a cordial relationship with the ashram but stopped short at supporting the proposal of ex-Premier Ramadier, now a simple member of the Assembly, to actively assist the university project. The ashram was quite capable of finding its own funds, Ménard wrote, and he worried about 'the exclusive powers that Madame Alfassa held over finances'. There was also the problem of what sort of degree the new university would offer. The ashram school offered none.[19] This lack of interest in certification was in accordance with the Mother's ideas. She believed that education should be given 'not for passing examinations or obtaining certificates and posts but to enrich existing faculties and bring forth new ones'.[20]

After the university project was launched, it took almost a year for it to settle into orbit. Sri Aurobindo International University Centre finally opened its doors on 6 January 1952. The student body consisted primarily of young men and women who had entered the ashram school as children. Most of the teachers were ashram members, but a few came from other parts of India and abroad. One of the newcomers was Suzanne Karpelès, a leading scholar of Southeast Asian Buddhism. Forced to resign her post in Phnom Penh in 1940 by the pro-Vichy government of French Indochina, she resumed her work in 1944 and settled in the ashram after she retired. The Mother asked her to be the head of the university's department of comparative religions. For the moment, she taught French to the older students.

At this point, the university centre was little more than the upper classes of the ashram school. When K.M. Munshi, a politician who was a member of the University Fund committee, asked the Mother how the project was going, she replied: 'I do not believe in starting in an ostentatious way. I am building up slowly, step by step, but firmly, and in ten years you will see what this university will be like.'[21] An important figure in the Congress party, Munshi had served as a central cabinet minister from 1950 until 1952, when he was appointed governor of Uttar Pradesh. While on a tour of south India, he paid a visit to the ashram and later wrote an article about it. This gives an unusually frank and balanced picture of the ashram and the Mother at that time. Munshi said he had come to the ashram once before, while Sri Aurobindo was alive. Now, he 'wanted to understand the Mother'. Before his visit, he and his friends had raised a number of questions about her: 'What is she? What is her spiritual stature? What is the source of her inspiration? And also the vexed question—where does she get her money?' At the time, his own ideas were somewhat critical: After all, 'a tennis-playing lady of seventy-five, carrying a tenuous veil and saluting the Ashramites at the march-past day after day was not exactly a symbol of spirituality to the normal Indian mind.' (Munshi was a conservative Hindu who had founded the Bharatiya Vidya Bhavan, an educational trust, and in 1964 would be among the founders of the Vishva Hindu Parishad or Universal Hindu Council.) After his arrival in Pondicherry, he was taken to see the Mother. 'Imagine a fragile woman a little bent with age, but agile, her eyes clear and compassionate, her smile an affectionate caress,' he wrote. She was on her way to the tennis courts and arranged to meet him later. In the meantime, he toured the ashram, admiring its organization and learning about its finances. ('The Mother receives [money] from disciples, friends, and sympathizers,' he was told, and gives departments and individuals what they needed for their projects and maintenance.) When he met the Mother, he asked her some questions regarding his personal life. 'She replied in a quiet, firm tone, in a simple straightforward way. There was no attempt on her part to play the teacher or mystic or as someone of superior power.' Later, he accompanied her when she went to the playground and watched as she distributed sweets to the children. The next morning, he left the ashram 'with infinite regret'. Suppose, he mused, that this foreign lady, instead of wearing a silk salwar suit 'was dressed in the saffron coloured robes of a sannyasin'? What if, instead of playing tennis, 'she stood on her head in shirshasan and spun the charkha'? If she had played that role, 'India would have gone down on her knees before her in ardent devotion'. On his way back to Madras, he reflected: 'If the spirit has to permeate and transform life, it must be through life as we live it.'[22]

4

Now more than ever, the life of the ashram revolved around the Mother. All the sadhaks longed to see her and speak with her, but with the membership approaching 800 it was impossible for her to give time to everyone. She arranged her schedule so that as many people as possible had a chance for some personal contact. In the morning, she gave darshan from the back balcony of the ashram and, later, pranam from the staircase. She had regular meetings with close disciples and heads of departments. Other disciples came for personal pranam on their birthdays. During the afternoons and evenings, she went to the tennis ground for exercise, then to the playground to watch the march-past and interact with the children. At this time, she did not have a room of her own. She met people in her salon and in the 'green room' she had used since the Rue Saint Gilles house was remodelled in 1932. People who had access to her came and went incessantly. In 1953, a disciple suggested that a new room for her be built above Sri Aurobindo's old room. She agreed on the condition that funds from the ashram's account would not be touched. The disciple found someone to give the needed sum and construction work began. In December 1953, the Mother moved into the new room. Here, she passed her nights. In the mornings, she went down and continued her relentless routine.

During 1952, the Mother used her classes with older students for translating works by Sri Aurobindo into French. In March 1953, she resumed the conversation classes. They were open not only to older children but also adults who knew French. (Others who did not know the language found ways to gatecrash.) As in 1951, the classes began with a brief reading from one of her works, followed by questions from the children. In answering, she moved freely from reminiscences and stories to artistic and occult subjects to spiritual guidance. Speaking about people who claimed to remember past lives, she explained that in most cases this was just imagination. To have genuine memories of previous existences, one had to be 'completely identified with the psychic'.[23] This, as we have seen, was an extension of an idea she learnt while associated with the Cosmic movement. Asked whether a person who followed a religion could eventually go beyond it and achieve union with the Divine, she replied, tersely: 'That is impossible.' 'Religion,' she went on, 'is always a limitation of the spirit.' If a religious person had a spiritual life independent of religious forms, he or she might be able to pass beyond, but this was the exception. People with developed minds 'absolutely have to leave their religions if they don't want to be halted in their progress'. On the other hand, people 'who have practically no mental activity, who do not ask themselves any questions, who just have an intense devotion in their heart and an urge to give themselves to something that is infinitely greater than them'—for such people, it did not matter whether they had a religion or not. But they 'could never go beyond', that is, beyond the limitations of their beliefs.[24]

During the 1950s, it became customary for the Mother to give special pranams on days devoted to puja or worship of the mother goddesses of Hinduism. The disciples bowed before her as to a deity in a temple. This concession to popular religion gave them an outlet for their devotion but presumably put them at risk of being hemmed in by the limitations of their beliefs. In messages issued on puja days, she tried to bring out the spiritual side of the occasions. On Durga Puja in 1954, she wrote: 'It is victory day; let it be a true victory of the Spirit over ignorance and falsehood.' The same year, in a note to herself about the disciples' attitude, she wrote: 'It is their mental and vital formation of me that they love; it is not myself. . . . All of them have made for themselves an image of me in conformity with their needs and desires, and it is with this image that they are in relation.'[25]

5

The funding drive for the international university ran out of steam after a year or so. In 1952, the Mother offered her jewellery for sale to help finance the project. She asked her secretary to write to the Government of India asking for an exemption on taxes and duties arising from sales to Indians. Munshi brought the request to the attention of Prime Minister Nehru, who refused to grant it. 'Sri Aurobindo was undoubtedly a great man,' he wrote in a memorandum of 13 December 1952, 'and we should welcome any proper memorial to him, more especially a new educational centre.' But to grant an exemption to a private individual would be unprecedented. It would allow Indian currency to flow into foreign territory—something a country with a struggling economy could hardly encourage. In addition, relations between India and France were at a low point, and Nehru believed that the Mother and others in the ashram were not completely on India's side. He went on to note that some reports he had received were 'not favourable and we have even heard that there are internal conflicts there'. One source of such reports was Dilip Kumar Roy, who had decided to leave the ashram after living there for twenty-four years. As a parting shot, he went to Delhi and had a talk with Nehru. The Mother was pro-French, he told the Prime Minister. She 'controlled everything autocratically' and 'gave no account' of funds collected for the ashram or the university. He advised Nehru 'to bring some pressure on the Mother or on the French government in regard to the ashram and in regard to the so-called university'. Nehru, who was familiar with Roy's volatile personality, told his finance secretary that none of this was the government's business except the request for a tax exemption, which he already had refused.[26]

The uneasiness over the ashram's finances expressed by Ménard, Munshi and Nehru showed that they viewed it as a public institution that ought to have publicly audited books. The Mother did not see it in those terms. She had looked after the community's finances from the time it consisted of a single house and had a cash balance of a few hundred rupees. She did not believe in investment, and, when money came in, she spent it immediately on the maintenance and development of the community. Her personal needs were few. At the same time, she was inundated with costly gifts from disciples, many of which she gave away or, in the case of jewellery, sold when the need arose. Still, the impression that she lived in luxury and drove a hard bargain persisted. In 1954, Pierre Landy, a special envoy of the French government, wrote to Stanislas Ostroróg, the French ambassador in New Delhi, that 'in the case of Madame Alfassa, the internationally renowned spiritual guide is coupled with a formidable businesswoman'.[27] The Mother would not have considered this an insult.

The political deadlock between France and India over the future of the French settlements continued. The sticking point in the negotiations was the referendums that were supposed to be held to determine whether people in the four southern settlements wanted to merge with India. The Chandernagore referendum of 1949 showed that virtually all voters of that Bengali town were in favour of a merger. The situation in Pondicherry and the other southern settlements was less clear cut. This left the door open to political manoeuvring, bribery and street violence. Tensions eased after June 1954, when a new French Premier, Pierre Mendès France, took office. The next month, the Council of Ministers agreed to allow the cession of French India without popular referendums. A body of elected representatives of the four southern settlements would vote on whether they wanted to remain part of the French Union or join the Republic of India.

It was at this point that the Mother made her declaration (discussed in the Prologue) that she wished to become an Indian citizen, but, at the same time, retain her French citizenship. Landy thought the Mother's equal attachment to India and France might 'orient local political opinion in a conciliatory direction' but wondered whether dual nationality was possible under international law.[28] The Government of India thought the same way and never gave her proposal serious consideration. More significant in the long run was an essay the Mother published in the *Bulletin* in August 1954. It was called 'A Dream'. 'There should be somewhere on earth,' she began, 'which no nation could claim as its own, where all human beings of goodwill who have a sincere aspiration could live freely as citizens of the world and obey one single authority, that of the supreme truth.' In this place, 'the needs of the spirit and the concern for progress would take precedence over the satisfaction of desires and passions'. Each person's physical needs 'would be equally provided for'. All would be able to develop themselves intellectually, artistically and spiritually. 'Human relationships, which are normally based almost exclusively on competition and strife, would be replaced by relationships of emulation in doing well, of collaboration and real brotherhood.' She admitted that such a community was not ready for realization. This was why she called it a dream. Yet, she added, 'this dream is in the course of becoming a reality; that is what we are striving for in Sri Aurobindo's Ashram, on a very small scale, in proportion to our limited means'. As well as publishing her 'Dream' in the *Bulletin*, the Mother asked a French disciple, Bernard Enginger, to discuss the topic in an essay meant for publication in France. His piece appeared in *Le Monde* on 2 October. At this moment, when French India was about to disappear, he began, Pondicherry should remain a 'Franco-Indian cultural centre'. The sleepy French colony, now a relic of the past, could become a 'sort of laboratory, a place of experimentation, where humanity could try to elaborate a new formula in its ascent towards the indispensable, inevitable Unity'.[29] This was a big scaling-up of the Mother's dream. There is no indication it attracted any attention at the time.

In the middle of October, representatives from Pondicherry and the other French settlements voted overwhelmingly for a merger with India, effective 1 November. The day before the transfer, the Mother gave an interview to a press representative, her first in more than thirty years. The reporter began by asking about Goa, still held by the Portuguese. The Mother replied: 'It is quite evident that Indians are right when they are seeking to have Goa integrated with their land.' If the people of India went forward 'with faith and confidence in divine Grace' without resorting to violence, 'it may be that reason will come to the Portuguese'.

India's mission was to show other countries how to live 'according to the truth in all sincerity and straightforwardness with a feeling of friendship and mutual help to all'. This was the spiritual way of solving political and economic problems. 'How can spiritualism deal with these mundane and material problems?' the reporter pressed. The Mother replied: 'Spirituality means putting oneself entirely under the law of truth and bringing down that law of truth upon earth. That is bound to bring a solution to all problems.'[30]

At seven in the morning of 1 November, Indian and French diplomats met in Pondicherry to formalize the transfer of power. The Indian foreign minister raised the flag of the Republic of India above the customs house. In a separate ceremony, the Mother hoisted the 'spiritual flag of India' above the main building of the ashram. An ashram choir sang the national anthem. Later, ashram students and other members took part in public ceremonies, giving musical and dance performances, and a physical-culture demonstration. In the evening, there was a fireworks display. Pondicherry was now in fact (de facto), if not yet in law (de jure), part of the Indian Union.

6

Once the border check-posts were closed, a stream of visitors from other parts of India poured into Pondicherry. Among them were the governor of Bihar, the governor of Madras and other Indian officials, many of whom visited the ashram and spoke with the Mother. On 16 January 1955, Prime Minister Nehru made his first official visit to the city. In the course of a public address, he said he hoped Pondicherry would remain a seat of French language and culture. Before giving his speech, he stopped off at the ashram, paid his respects at Sri Aurobindo's samadhi and spoke privately with the Mother. In the evening, he witnessed a physical-culture demonstration in the ashram playground. Later, he conveyed his impressions to his daughter, Indira Gandhi. About the Mother, he wrote: 'The lady has grown quite old and looks fragile', adding, 'She produced no great impression of spirituality on me.' He appreciated the physical demonstration but was flabbergasted that 'girls of all ages were clad in the most diminutive of attire' (shorts and short-sleeved shirts).[31]

On 4 October, Nehru visited Pondicherry again, this time in the company of Madras Chief Minister K. Kamaraj, Union Railways Minister Lal Bahadur Shastri and Indira. During a speech to the public, Nehru expressed his frustration over the time it was taking for the de jure transfer to be finalized. Later, he visited the ashram. The Mother received him and his party in the playground. A picture taken on the occasion shows her speaking with the Prime Minister, who stares off into the distance. With him are Kamaraj, Lal Bahadur and Indira, who spent much of her day in the ashram, visiting the samadhi and Golconde. Afterwards, she had a private interview with the Mother.

Faithful to the vision of Sri Aurobindo, who had never resigned himself to the 1947 Partition, the Mother considered India an indissoluble unity. Previously, she had asked ashram artists to model a 'spiritual map of India' on the wall of the playground. In terms of political geography, the map depicts the British Indian Empire before 1937, inclusive of the present Myanmar, Bangladesh, Bhutan and Pakistan, along with Sri Lanka. One does not know how Nehru and his party reacted to this map, which formed the backdrop of their meeting with the Mother. Perhaps they smiled at her political naïveté. Perhaps she smiled back.

Sometime earlier, Munshi had recommended that the ashram be reorganized as a trust. Now that Pondicherry was part of India, it was possible to do this. A trust deed was drawn up and, on 7 October 1955, was signed in the headquarters of the Madras State subdivision where the ashram owned a piece of land. By the terms of the deed, all properties of the ashram, held hitherto in the name of Sri Aurobindo or the Mother, were transferred to the trust. The Mother and four others were named trustees. This arrangement satisfied bureaucrats who worried about the ashram's status but did not change much in the way the ashram was run. The other four trustees just gave administrative and legal advice to the Mother, and saw to it that her decisions were carried out.

The Treaty of Cession of the French Settlements to India was not signed until May 1956. Several of its articles aimed at preserving the

French character of the former colony. Most importantly, the four southern settlements would keep their 'special administrative status'. This meant they would not be absorbed by the states surrounding them but would become a single, centrally administered 'union territory'. French Indians born in the settlements could opt to keep their French citizenship. French would, for the moment, remain the official language. French cultural and educational institutions would be protected, and institutes of higher learning promoting French culture could be created in the future. All this was in accord with Nehru's idea of making Pondicherry 'an open window to France'. It also reflected the hopes of Sri Aurobindo and the Mother that Pondicherry would keep something of its cultural autonomy. Sri Aurobindo had written in 1946 that if the settlements were incorporated into the surrounding states, they would become 'unimportant mofussil [provincial] towns'.[32] This is what happened to Chandernagore after it merged with the state of West Bengal. Pondicherry, in contrast, has become a city of some importance, economically as well as culturally. The 1956 treaty was approved almost immediately by the Government of India. The Government of France, distracted by the war in Algeria and the domestic turmoil it was causing, found no time to take it up.

7

In February 1954, the Mother published an essay called 'The Fear of Death and the Four Methods of Conquering It'. It was, on the surface, an objective treatment of a philosophical problem, but she clearly had a personal interest in the subject. She was now seventy-six and her health was in decline. Although her vitality was undiminished, she looked, as Munshi and Nehru both noticed, increasingly fragile. (It is interesting, but not surprising, that her disciples never mentioned this in their writings about her.) She began the essay with a general statement: 'Of all fears the most subtle and most tenacious is the fear of death.' How to overcome it? First, one must realize 'that life is one and immortal'. Forms may dissolve, but not life itself. Keeping this in mind, everyone had to find an appropriate way to conquer the fear of death. There were four main methods. The first relies on rational argument: 'In the present state of the world, death is inevitable,' 'Reason teaches us that it is absurd to fear something that cannot be avoided.' Ergo it is absurd to fear death. This method is suitable for intellectual people but not for those who are ruled by their emotions. For them, the right way is to plunge into the depths of their souls. When they reach the innermost psychic consciousness, they will 'awaken to the sense of immortality' and know that death is only a transition. The third way is for those who believe in God: When they surrender themselves completely, there is 'no longer any room in their consciousness for fear, anxiety or torment'. Finally, there is the path of born warriors, who 'feel pulsating within them their right to immortality, a complete and earthly immortality'. This way takes the form of a battle against the collective suggestion of death, attachment to life, over-sensitiveness and physical weaknesses. The Mother also mentioned a fifth method, suitable only for experts in occultism: 'To enter into the domain of death deliberately and consciously while one is still alive, and then return from this region and re-enter the physical body, resuming the course of material existence with full knowledge of the process'.[33] This essay may be viewed as a blueprint of the Mother's sadhana between 1954 and 1973, which was, in brief, an attempt to transform her body and attain 'integral immortality'.

However outrageous this attempt might seem, it was not without precedent. The attainment of spiritual or physical immortality has been a dream of human beings for millennia. Most religions and many philosophies assumed that the essence of the human being—atman, psyche, anima, soul, spirit—survives the death of the body. A few proposed that the body itself could be made immortal by magical or alchemical means. In the royal tombs of Egypt and China, corpses were preserved using physical and magical techniques, and souls were provided with written or painted guidebooks that showed the way to the heavenly worlds. In medieval and modern times, alchemists, Kabbalists, spiritualists, Theosophists and others sought the secrets of immortality in ancient scriptures of Egypt, Mesopotamia, Israel, China and India. This age-long effort of conquering death continues today. Silicon Valley billionaires (our modern royalty) are investing heavily in biotech start-ups that promise radical life extension leading eventually to physical immortality.

The Mother first encountered the phrase 'integral immortality' in the *Revue Cosmique.* The motto of the movement, printed on the cover of each issue, was '*La mortalité est temporaire et accidentelle. L'Homme a droit à l'Immortalité intégrale* (Mortality is temporary and accidental. Human beings have the right to integral Immortality).'[34] By integral immortality, the Theons meant immortality on all four levels of the being: Physical, vital, psychic and mental. It would find its fullest expression on the physical plane: 'It is on earth, as an integral human being, in our physical body, that we rightly shall recover the integral immortality that has been stripped away from us.' The Theons wrote countless pages on the subject, some of them philosophical, some of them mythical—and none of them terribly clear. In one comparatively lucid passage, they said the 'natural and eternal way' to recover immortality was a 'perpetual evolution of the formations [components of the human being] toward perfection'. On this evolution depended the 'auric efficacy' of the individual and on the auric efficacy depended 'the progressive longevity which is essential to continual progress toward perfection'. This would lead to 'the restitution of the glorious body' and the achievement of immortality.[35] This passage demonstrates the Theons' eclecticism. Spiritual evolution was a central theme of dozens of late-nineteenth- and early-twentieth-century teachings.[36] Many ancient traditions spoke of 'subtle bodies' but the modern idea of the 'aura' was developed by mid-nineteenth-century magnetic healers and popularized by the Theosophists. Restitution (*tikkun*) is an important idea in Lurianic Kabbalah. In many religions, gods and saints have light-emitting bodies, but the *corps glorieux* or glorious body is primarily a Christian concept, based on a verse in Saint Paul's *Epistle to the Philippians.* The Mother learnt about such ideas from the Theons and they influenced her thinking when she gave her attention to immortality fifty years later.

Like the Theons, the Mother wanted immortality on all the planes of her being. Also like her former teachers, she wanted it on earth, in her physical body. In this, she differed from Sri Aurobindo. When he wrote about immortality, he generally took it in its psychic and spiritual senses: The survival and rebirth of the psychic being and the union of the individual self with the immortal cosmic Self. In a few letters written after he met the Mother, he spoke of physical transformation, sometimes mentioning the Theons' idea of the *corps glorieux*. But his focus was always on 'the consciousness of immortality *in* the body', not 'immortality *of* the body'.[37] His death was a wake-up call for the Mother. She concluded she could not fulfil his yoga without solving the problem of physical immortality.

Her first writings dealing with the subject appeared in the April and August 1954 issues of the *Bulletin* under the heading 'Experiences of the Body Consciousness'. In the first instalment, she stated the problem: 'Every time a god has taken on a body, it has always been with the intention of transforming the earth and creating a new world.' But so far, each incarnating being 'had been obliged to give up his body without completing his work. And it always was said that the earth was not ready and that human beings had not fulfilled the conditions necessary for the work to be achieved'. The reference here evidently is to Sri Aurobindo. She had written in December 1950 that it was 'the lack of receptivity of the earth and men' that made him decide 'to give up his body'. Now, he was gone and she was faced with the same dilemma. The progress of the incarnating being and the progress of the environment were 'simultaneous and complete each other'. What she seems to be saying is that her environment—the world and its people, including the people of the ashram—was holding her back but she could not achieve complete perfection if she cut herself off from her environment.[38]

In the second instalment, she went more deeply into the meaning of physical transformation. The method she proposed was not biological, not magical, not religious, but supramental. The supramental light, which to her was a concrete reality, would act first on the 'body consciousness' and then take control 'of all the movements and the functioning of all the organs of the body'. This would lead to a change 'of the constitution of the organs themselves'. In the end, the organs would be replaced 'by centres of concentration of forces'.[39] The idea that the physical organs would eventually be transformed was one that Sri Aurobindo had speculated about in an article of 1949: 'There would have to be a change in the operative processes of the material organs themselves and, it may well be, in their very constitution and their importance; they could not be allowed to impose their limitations imperatively on the new physical life.'[40] It is worth noting that he wrote this while suffering from the prostatic enlargement that caused the kidney infection that brought about his death.

Sri Aurobindo and the Mother did not think the supramental transformation was meant only for them and a handful of disciples. It was a step on the way to a general transformation of life on earth. After the 'overmind descent' of 1926, Sri Aurobindo set his sights on the supermind, which alone had the power to bring about the full transformation. In letters of the 1930s, he told his disciples that he was getting closer to the supermind but, as late as 1947, he wrote that he still was focused on the 'supramentalisation of the Overmind'.[41] In an article published just weeks before his death, he spoke of another plane he called the 'Mind of Light' that served as a 'transitional passage' between 'supermind and superhumanity' on the one hand and a partly divinized 'illumined humanity' on the other.[42] But this transitional plane was far from the supermind itself.

In writings and talks during the early 1950s, the Mother sometimes mentioned the supramental descent and encouraged her disciples to prepare themselves for it. 'The Supramental Force is ready for manifestation,' she wrote in a message of July 1954, 'let us get ready also and it will manifest.'[43] In a note written to herself the previous month, she said that the higher force was descending into her 'and penetrating more and more completely all the atoms of my body'. She added that this was making her feel cut off from her surroundings. She felt as if she was floating 'in an atmosphere of radiant consciousness' that was utterly beyond the understanding of those around her.[44]

Throughout these years, the Mother continued her normal routine, including her talks and meditations in the playground. During one of these meditations, on 29 February 1956, she had a landmark experience.

'This evening,' she wrote later, 'the Divine Presence, concrete and material, was there present amongst you.' Like most of her spiritual experiences, this one had a strong visual component:

> I had a form of living gold, bigger than the universe, and I was facing a huge and massive golden door which separated the world from the Divine. As I looked at the door, I knew and willed, in a single movement of consciousness, that 'the time has come', and lifting with both hands a mighty golden hammer I struck one blow, one single blow on the door and the door was shattered to pieces.

Then, she concluded, 'the supramental Light and Force and Consciousness rushed down upon earth in an uninterrupted flow'.[45] The force she felt was so powerful that she expected to find everyone lying flat on their backs when she opened her eyes. In fact, they were just sitting there waiting for her to end the meditation. She did so and they all went home.[46]

A month later, she announced in the *Bulletin*:

> The manifestation of the Supramental upon earth is no more a promise but a living fact, a reality.
>
> It is at work here, and one day will come when the most blind, the most unconscious, even the most unwilling shall be obliged to recognise it.

She also said, recalling a prophesy she had made years earlier in her *Prayers and Meditations*: 'The things that were promised are fulfilled.'[47] This caused some puzzlement in the ashram. People were more than willing to recognize that the long-awaited event had happened but none of them felt any different than they had before 29 February. It was left to a child to put the question everyone wanted to ask: 'You said: "The Supramental has descended upon earth." What does that mean exactly? You also said: "The things that were promised are fulfilled." What are these things?' The Mother replied, somewhat gruffly: 'Well, that's real ignorance! This was promised a very long time ago, this was said very long ago—not only here: since the beginning of the earth.' Dozens of prophets had announced that there would be 'a new heaven and a new earth, a new race will be born, the world will be transformed—' But, the child persisted, 'You have said, "They are fulfilled."' 'Yes. And so?' 'Where is the new race?' 'The new race? Wait for something like—a few thousand years, and you will see it!' She went on to explain that many centuries had passed between the first manifestation of mind in the 'earth atmosphere' and the appearance of thinking human beings. Why should less time elapse between the manifestation of supermind and the appearance of the supramental race?[48] This caused still more confusion, which she tried to clear up a few months later: 'It seems that some people thought that I was announcing that the *surhomme* [the 'overman', precursor of the supramental being] would not come for another million years. I want to correct this impression.' According to Sri Aurobindo, 'as the development rises in the scale of consciousness, the movement becomes more and more rapid, and that when the Spirit or the Supermind intervenes, it can go still faster. Therefore we may hope that in a few centuries, the first supramental race will appear.'[49] A few centuries rather than a few thousand or million years! This cannot have offered much reassurance to those who wanted to be supramentalized in a hurry.

Since 1960, the anniversary of the supramental manifestation on 29 February 1956 has been celebrated every leap year. The Mother wrote uplifting messages for these occasions but she had some reservations that she expressed in private conversations. In 1961, she told a disciple that the 1956 manifestation had not been 'a complete descent'. The light and consciousness, but only part of the power, came down and had immediately been 'absorbed in the world of the Inconscience'.[50] Four years later, she remarked that she hesitated to give labels to spiritual events because people 'make a dogma out of it. That's what happened when what was called "the first supramental manifestation" took place in 1956. I tried my best to keep it from being turned into a dogma', but it was no use. Now, anyone who questioned the dogma would be told: 'You are a heretic.' Nevertheless, she continued, it was 'undeniable that the atmosphere has changed, that there is something new in the atmosphere'. You could call it 'the descent of the supramental Truth' if you liked, but that shouldn't be considered '*the* classic or "true" way to describe the event'.[51]

One can sense in the Mother's playground talks of the late 1950s an increasing frustration with the unresponsiveness of people of the ashram. During a conversation on 30 May 1956, she recalled her youthful dream of creating 'a small world where people would be able to live without having to be preoccupied with food and lodging and clothing and the imperative needs of life, to see whether all the energies freed by this certainty of a secure material living would turn spontaneously towards the divine life and the inner realisation'. Now, as she looked around her, she saw that the people who lived in the small world she had created were not making good use of the opportunity. She had provided them with a place where they did not have to struggle to stay alive. This freed up a whole mass of energies but, rather than applying them to spiritual effort, people wasted them 'in idle stupidities', in particular, gossip: 'To keep the tongue wagging: chatter, chatter, chatter. I have not known a place where people chatter more than here, saying everything they should not say, busying themselves with things they should not be concerned with'.[52]

The Mother never gave any sign that she wanted to leave the disciples on their own, but the problem of balancing her individual progress with the needs of those around her remained acute. 'It is very hard to pursue both at the same time: the transformation of the body and taking care of people,' she remarked to a disciple in 1958. 'But what can I do? I told Sri Aurobindo I would do the work and I'm doing it—I can't just leave it all behind.'[53]

8

The Mother continued to have experiences connected with the supramental manifestation, most dramatically on 3 February 1958. For an hour that afternoon, she found herself moving in the higher worlds as concretely as she used to walk the streets of Paris. The setting was an enormous boat, as big as a city, which she understood to be a symbolic representation of an intermediary zone between the physical and supramental worlds. There were other people on board, some of them from the ashram, some from elsewhere. The boat reached a wharf where the passengers were received by two tall, beautiful beings who had been sent to supervise the landing. The Mother watched the disembarkation process closely: She wanted to see who were ready to get off and who had to continue their training. After a while, she felt she was being drawn back. She resisted the pull as long as she could. Finally, she heard a clock strike three and found herself back in her room. At once, she dictated an account of the experience to one of her attendants. She was struck at the time by the enormous difference between the human and supramental worlds, as great as the difference between the animal world and ours. She could see that everything in ordinary life is artificial while everything in the supramental world is true, spontaneous and significant: 'A surging out of things by an act of conscious will'.[54]

Three months later, the Mother told a disciple that she was having 'all the experiences it is possible to have in the body'. This led to a state of inner bliss, but again brought to the fore the problem of balancing inner experience with action in the world. If she was to accomplish Sri Aurobindo's work, to realize the supermind on earth, she had to remain physically active. For that, she needed a healthy body. So she told her body: 'Now you will set right everything that has been demolished and, little by little, realize this intermediate superhumanity between the human being and the supramental being'.[55] In this work of transformation, she found that repeating a mantra was a useful aid. She knew quite a few but finally settled on one she first heard in a Hindi film screened at the ashram playground: '*Om namo bhagavate*'. She found that when she repeated this formula, or it repeated itself inwardly, the life of her cells became 'a solid, compact mass' pulsating with 'a single vibration'.[56]

The Mother's problems with the 'environment' continued. On 5 November, frustrated that the children in her class had no questions to ask her, she had the experience of 'going down into the mental atmosphere of the people around me, in order to find there the small light, the thing that responds'. She felt she 'was literally dragged down to the bottom, as if into a hole'. Down and down she plunged, until she asked herself, 'But what is there at the bottom of this hole?' Hardly had she formulated the question when 'it was as if I had touched a spring that was there at the very bottom of the hole . . . which acted at once with a tremendous force and at one bound shot me up straight into the air'. Later, she transcribed this as a message for the New Year: 'At the very bottom of the inconscience [that is, the plane of the Unconscious] most hard and rigid and narrow and stifling I struck upon an almighty spring that cast me up forthwith into a formless limitless Vast vibrating with the seeds of a new world.'[57]

Towards the middle of November 1958, the Mother became unwell and drew back from her regular activities. On 26 November, she held her last Wednesday class. Soon afterwards, she stopped all other classes. On 1 December, she played her last game of tennis and visited the playground for the last time. Eight days later, after presiding over a meditation on the anniversary of the day Sri Aurobindo's body was entombed, she was confined to bed. She explained the breakdown in occult terms: It was an attack on her body by hostile forces in the environment. It took her more than a month to recover.

11

New Directions

1

IN JANUARY 1959, THE MOTHER BEGAN SLOWLY TO RESUME HER contacts with people in the ashram. She gave daily darshans from the balcony and, on 21 February, a birthday darshan inside the building. Soon, she was making occasional trips outside. She went to the playground for prize distributions and to the sports ground for the annual demonstration. She cut ribbons and laid foundation stones for new industrial units, and visited workplaces, farms and gardens. She met department heads on a regular basis, and ashram members, students and visitors on their birthdays. These events and meetings were of the greatest importance to disciples and devotees. For her, they were a strain.[1] She soldiered on without complaint for three years.

The ashram now consisted of around 1,200 adults and children. The Mother kept tabs on the work of all departments, reading reports, making decisions, and offering advice and encouragement. In 1959, she was involved in the reorganization of the University Centre, which, in January, was renamed Sri Aurobindo International Centre of Education. The international university, launched eight years earlier, had never really taken shape. What had emerged was a school with classes from kindergarten to the college level. A report published in the February issue of the renamed *Bulletin of Sri Aurobindo International Centre of Education* set forth the centre's principles and methods. Viewing the child 'as a soul with a body, life-energy, and mind to be harmoniously developed', it fostered the training of the body, the growth of character and creative expression, the acquisition of knowledge and the development of understanding. All the students—there were now around 360—took part in physical activities every afternoon. Divided into six groups by age and gender, they engaged over the course of the year in athletics, gymnastics, games, combative sports and swimming. Lessons in drawing and painting, vocal and instrumental music, and dance were available to all. Older students could gain practical experience in the ashram's workshops, embroidery section, cottage-industry departments and farms. Mental education comprised languages (French, English and the student's mother tongue), mathematics and science (taught in French), and history and geography (taught in English). Tests were given throughout the year but there was no final examination and no leaving certificate or diploma. Behind the centre's activities, the *Bulletin* concluded, was the 'spiritual atmosphere' of the ashram, which helped 'the soul come forward and gradually begin to govern the rest of the being'.[2]

This was the theory and current set-up. The Mother was aware that the actual situation fell far short of the ideal. A few years earlier, she had explained to a teacher: 'From the worldly standpoint, from the point of view of result achieved certainly things can be done better.' There were many schools in India and abroad that did a better job of preparing students for examinations. She was not trying to compete with them: 'We move in a different sphere, on a different level.' In a letter to a teacher, she wrote that her goal was to draw a few students 'out of the general human routine of thought, feeling and action', help them break free 'from the slavery to the human way of thinking and doing', and learn 'how to live and become a *true being*'. 'It is not a number that we want,' she concluded, 'it is a selection; it is not brilliant students that we want, it is living souls.'[3]

From the start of the ashram school sixteen years earlier, the Mother and the teachers had experimented with different approaches, trying to find the right balance between structure and freedom, fixed curricula and unfettered exploration. One innovation was to allow each student to advance in the various subjects 'according to the progress he [or she] makes in them,' rather than being stuck the whole day in the same age-based class.[4] Over time, this developed into a 'free progress' system, described by the Mother as 'a progress guided by the soul and not subjected to habits, conventions, or preconceived ideas'. She strongly favoured this approach; many teachers felt it did not work for everyone. When some of them asked if they could revert to a more structured system, she accepted, reluctantly: 'Classes as a whole may be reorganised so as to fulfil the needs of the majority,' she wrote, but the free progress system 'should be maintained in order to allow outstanding individuals to show themselves and develop freely'. This was the true aim of the centre: 'It should be known—we should not hesitate to proclaim it—that the whole purpose of our school is to discover and encourage those in whom the need for progress has become conscious enough to direct their lives.'[5]

Another thorny problem was the issuance of certificates or degrees. The Mother was dead set against this. In a letter of 1960, she wrote that for the past hundred years—since the Second Empire in France and the Victorian period in England—the world had been infected by the disease of utilitarianism. Even young children were not immune: 'At an age when they should be dreaming of beauty, greatness and perfection . . . children now dream of money and worry about how to earn it.' The true aim of education was 'to learn for the sake of knowledge, to study in order to know the secrets of Nature and life, to educate oneself in order to grow in consciousness, to discipline oneself in order to become master of oneself, to overcome one's weaknesses, incapacities and ignorance, to prepare oneself to advance in life towards a goal that is nobler and vaster, more generous and more true'.[6] The fact remained that some of the older students wanted to go to university and later find employment outside the ashram. The Mother never stood in their way. In fact, she helped a few of them go abroad for higher studies. Firm in her convictions, she was flexible when applying them in real-life situations.

In 1961, the Ministry of Education of the Government of India sent a three-person committee to evaluate the Centre of Education. They were favourably impressed. One result was that the following year the Union Public Service Commission agreed to treat completion of the Centre's Higher Course as the equivalent of a BA or BSc degree when applying for jobs in government service.[7] Later, some Indian universities followed the government's lead, allowing Higher Course students to sit for entrance examinations. Many did well and went on to have successful careers in science, business and academia.

2

In 1960, two organizations inspired by Sri Aurobindo's teachings—World Union and Sri Aurobindo Society (SAS)—were registered with the government. The founders of both groups asked for and received the Mother's blessings. Up to this point, the ashram had never encouraged outreach organizations. 'I don't believe in advertisement except for books, etc., and in propaganda except for politics or patent medicines,' Sri Aurobindo once wrote. That sort of thing led invariably to stunts or booms or movements, where 'hundreds or thousands of useless people join in and corrupt the work or reduce it to a pompous farce from which the Truth that was coming down recedes into secrecy and silence'.[8] In allowing the formation of the two new groups, the Mother seems to have accepted that different people needed different outlets for their energies. One of the officers of World Union caught hold of an idea in Sri Aurobindo's *Human Cycle*—that a free world union was better than a repressive world state—and decided that everyone everywhere should know about it. He was sincere and energetic, and the idea was good in itself so the Mother 'let him go, as one lets a horse gallop'. But she advised him and his associates, 'World Union is an outward movement for those who need an outward activity and organisation to give a more concrete reality to their faith.'[9] She viewed the SAS as 'a completely external thing, organized by businessmen to bring in money—*exclusively*'. She added that this 'has nothing to do with realizing an ideal, it's *completely* practical'. The organizers wanted to collect money for the ashram, the ashram needed money for maintenance and development, so she let them go ahead. They asked her to be their president and she accepted in order to reassure donors that funds would not be misused. When officers of the SAS began posing 'almost as instructors' she told them 'Nothing doing!' but allowed them to continue their fundraising work. For the SAS's first annual meeting in February 1962 she sent the message: 'The true fortune is to spend in the right way. You become truly rich when you dispose of your wealth in the best possible way.'[10]

3

Since 1957, the Mother had been having regular conversations with Bernard Enginger, mentioned in the last chapter as the author of the 1954 article in *Le Monde*. A nephew of François Baron, the governor of French India between 1946 and 1949, Enginger passed the years of the war in the French Resistance and then in a concentration camp. Afterwards, he came to Pondicherry, worked in his uncle's office, and learnt about Sri Aurobindo and the Mother. When Baron was ousted from his post, Enginger voyaged to South America and Africa, returning to Pondicherry in 1953, where he became a disciple and later a confidant of the Mother. She often spoke with him about her personal sadhana—something she rarely did with others. She gave him the name Satprem.

From 1958, Satprem began to tape-record his conversations with the Mother. Many of them touched on her current sadhana. Together, they constitute a running record of her progress. She called them collectively the 'Agenda of the supramental manifestation'.[11] (The published English version is called *Mother's Agenda.* A better translation of the French word *agenda* here would be 'diary' or 'logbook', since this *agenda* was not a list of forthcoming events but a record of current developments.) Eventually transcribed and published in thirteen volumes, the *Agenda* is an enormous collection of spiritual and occult experiences, reminiscences, reflections, commentaries on current affairs, along with bits of chit-chat. It presents the biographer with an unusual problem. There are comparatively few accounts of the Mother's inner experiences before 1958. From that year onward, there is an *embarras de richesses.* An adequate summary would take a book much longer than this one. With only a few pages at my disposal, the best I can do is provide a glimpse of some of the major landmarks, turning points and vistas.

Looking over the years 1959–1962, a pattern emerges: Periods when the Mother had powerful spiritual experiences, followed by periods of physical exhaustion and suffering. Recovering quickly from the crisis of December 1958, she made significant progress during the first half of 1959. At the end of July, she had an experience she identified as the 'first penetration of the supramental force into the body'. By March of the next year, such experiences were 'coming at a rapid pace'. In July, she told Satprem she was living in a state 'in which one is completely outside time'. At night, she often had symbolic dreams that she recounted to him. Sometimes, she had visions of gods and goddesses. But the problem of the 'environment' remained. What made the work difficult, she said on 22 October 1960, were the 'vibrations of agitation' that people who came to see her brought with them. From November, she began to have physical problems, notably in her legs. Then, in January 1961, she had a minor collapse. Towards the end of the month, she realized 'the almost complete lack of importance of the material, external expression that reflects the state of the body'. Still, her legs bothered her. Her doctors told her she was suffering from filariasis, a parasitic infection transmitted by mosquitoes. A Tantric guru Satprem was in touch with said that the problem was due to an attack of black magic. Whatever the cause, the Mother resolved to cure herself—without immediate success. There were, however, many good moments. In November 1961, while walking and repeating her mantra, she found herself 'entirely surrounded by white light, in total silence'. But her physical problems continued. In January 1962, she was too ill to see anyone for several days. Then, at the end of February, the problem in her legs was swept away. She 'literally almost danced'.[12]

The relief did not last long. Towards the end of March, she had the worst breakdown she ever experienced. Exhausted, she took to her bed. Then, during the night of 2–3 April, she suffered a cardiac arrest.[13] For some time, she hovered close to death. By the morning of 3 April, she had regained sufficient strength to dictate a statement, in the course of which she said: 'Now is the last fight. If the purpose for which this body is alive is to be fulfilled, that is to say, the first steps towards the Supramental transformation, then it will continue today. It is the Lord's decision.'[14]

In her 1954 essay on death, the Mother wrote that the way of the warrior becomes in the end 'a wild race between two opposite tendencies, a race to see which will reach the goal first: transformation or death'.[15] Applying this metaphor to the Mother's current condition, we may say she entered the last lap of the race in March 1962. On the night of 2–3 April, Death took a big lead. The Mother, wearing the colours of Transformation, surged back. The race—or 'fight' as she called it in 1962—continued. What was the reality behind these figures of speech? The Mother's doctors viewed her condition in medical terms: She had a malfunctioning heart. In all likelihood, she suffered already from chronic heart failure, the disease that would eventually bring about her death. On 2–3 April, she had a cardiac arrest. She recovered, doubtless with her doctors' help, and continued the battle.[16]

The Mother would certainly have rejected this reconstruction. She had a general distrust of doctors: 'They are very useful, they have a great social utility', she said, ironically, in February 1961. As for herself, she did not believe in their so-called science.[17] What she did believe in was the play of spiritual and occult forces. In her statement of 3 April, she explained that her illness was caused by people hostile to her who were pawns of 'adverse forces'. She took refuge with Sri Aurobindo and overcame them. From that moment, her recovery began.

Ten days after the crisis, on the night of 12–13 April, the Mother woke to an awareness of what she called the Yoga of the World. She felt 'formidable pulsations of Love' passing through her. The false appearances of ordinary life were swept aside: 'Death was an illusion. Sickness was an illusion. Ignorance was an illusion.' There was nothing but 'Love and Love and Love'. After several hours, her individual consciousness returned and with it the pain that accompanies all manifestation. She emerged from this experience convinced that 'Truth alone exists' and that 'it alone will be manifested'. After relating what she had felt and seen, she told the people around her that what she said was 'nothing but words': The experience itself was ineffable.[18] In this and other respects, her account is similar to reports of what now are called near-death experiences. In her case, the 'death' phase lasted ten full days.

In the beginning of May, the Mother received a letter from her old friend Alexandra David-Neel, who complained of physical infirmities and isolation. The Buddhist scholar wrote that she sometimes wondered whether the solution to her problems was suicide. Without mentioning her own trials, the Mother replied that one should not be in a hurry to leave the physical life even if it was 'to enter eternal repose or the beatitude of the Void'. Whatever one's age, whatever one's difficulties, if one had a body, one had something to learn or something to accomplish on earth. 'This conviction,' she concluded, 'gives one the force needed to deal with all vicissitudes.'[19] This was the conviction that kept the Mother going despite her physical problems. On 13 May, she told Satprem that in the middle of her experience of 12–13 April, she heard a 'sort of Voice [that] reminded me of my promise, that I had promised to do the work on earth and it would be done. I promised to do the work and it will be done'.[20]

4

After the crisis of April 1962, the Mother did not leave her room for almost a year. She did not resume the morning balcony darshans, and, for the first time, did not appear on the special darshan days in April, August and November. Her weak legs did not allow her to go downstairs. Towards the end of 1962, ashram engineers built a new room next to the one she occupied. They also, without consulting her, added a covered terrace in the hopes she would resume her morning darshan. She did not go along with this but, on 21 February 1963, she gave her first public darshan from the new terrace. She later remarked that it seemed to her then that the earlier darshans had happened centuries before.[21]

Satprem was one of the few disciples the Mother saw on a regular basis. She kept him informed about the status of her sadhana and also commented on current affairs. For the first time in her life, she began to take an active interest in politics, becoming a fierce supporter of India. When the Sino-Indian War broke out in October 1962, she followed the situation closely. She blamed the war on Chinese aggression: A push to capture the Assam oil fields and to impose communism on India. This had to be resisted, she said. She sent her blessings to Prime Minister Nehru and gave 940 grams of gold to the National Defence Fund. When the Chinese drew back to their claimed line of control, she was content. Seven months later, Nehru paid his third visit to Pondicherry. Looking haggard, he toured the Centre of Education and spent fifteen minutes with the Mother. She said little but gave him what she called a 'bath of the Lord'. After he departed, twenty members of his entourage trooped up the stairs to have a darshan of the holy woman. The Mother was aghast but her secretary, Nolini Kanta Gupta, told her there was nothing he could do. When he tried to stop yet another dignitary from joining the queue, the man shoved him aside, saying, 'I'm a minister too.'[22]

Something similar, if less violent, happened almost daily when the Mother began to receive people again. There were 2,000–3,000 ashramites, students and regular visitors who wanted to see her as often as they could. Many felt they had a claim on her time because of past association or recent services. She could hardly see them all. Still, her appointment book filled up. 'They tire me, they really tire me out,' she complained.[23] All ashramites and students, as well as some visitors were allowed to go to her on their birthdays. She signed their cards herself, sometimes adding personal wishes. She resumed her correspondence and soon was inundated with letters. When not otherwise occupied, she worked on her French translation of Sri Aurobindo's *Synthesis of Yoga.* When she finished that, she began to work on his epic poem *Savitri.*

5

In July 1962, the French National Assembly finally ratified the 1956 Treaty of Cession of its Indian settlements. It went into force on 16 August and the four remaining French enclaves officially became a Union Territory of India. The Ashram Trust now had to be re-registered in Pondicherry. This took place in March 1964. Three years later, when the Mother came to know that the word 'religious' had been used in the original trust deed, she issued a 'clarification and rectification' removing that word from the text. She noted at the time that 'Sri Aurobindo had made it clear that it was never his intention "to propagate any religion, new or old".'[24]

Since the de facto transfer of 1954, the ashram had established good relations with the central Government of India. Relations with the territorial government of Pondicherry and the people of the town were not so warm. Ashram members kept mostly to themselves and made few efforts to associate with locals. A silent pressure of mutual misunderstanding built up. In February 1965, it exploded. The previous month, protests had been held in many parts of Madras State against the imposition of Hindi as the sole national language. In some places, the protests became violent. In Madurai, around seventy people were killed. During the second week of February, the unrest spilled over into Pondicherry. Protesters announced there would be a hartal (general strike with forced closure of businesses) on 12 February. On the evening of 11 February, sensing that the police were unprepared, a thousand protesters pillaged the railway station (a symbol of the central government) and made off with its strongbox.[25] Their numbers swollen by rioters and looters, they moved towards the ashram. Its members were caught off guard. They had no reason to think they would be targeted. Few of them spoke Hindi as their mother tongue, but more than half were originally from north India and this made it easy for the rioters to brand them pro-Hindi 'outsiders'. The mob attacked and plundered the ashram's fair-price shop, set fire to its post office and clinic, and stoned other buildings, including the one where the Mother lived. Young ashramites and some of the older boys did what they could to prevent further depredations. After a few hours, they and the police brought the situation under control. A number of ashram members were injured but no one was killed.[26]

The Mother had just sat down for dinner when the rioters reached the ashram. She directed Pranab Kumar Bhattacharya, the head of the physical education department, to coordinate the defence. Then she observed the situation: 'Many fires were being lit, then hundreds of brickbats—not stones, brickbats—were bombarding all the windows and doors.' It was 'a mob of several hundred people, all drunk, screaming, shouting'. In the midst of this chaos, she later explained, she had a remarkable experience: 'I wasn't this body anymore, I was the earth—the physical truth-consciousness of the earth.' She felt 'a peace, an *immobility*, unknown to the physical being'. She now knew the state the body must be in 'to be able to respond to the Truth, to *be* the Truth'. This was the lesson she had learnt. 'Everyone has learned something,' she concluded, 'I hope it won't be forgotten.'[27]

People throughout the country were aghast by the attack on the ashram. Members of Parliament demanded an inquiry and a one-man commission was appointed to investigate. The commissioner submitted his report in June. It stated the trouble began with protests by students but soon 'anti-social elements took over and they were largely responsible for the ugly happenings, particularly incidents of arson and assault'. The rioters decided to target the ashram out of resentment over the ashramites' 'exclusive attitude'. Along with this was 'an element of jealousy' over the properties owned by the ashram and the success of its commercial enterprises. The report also noted that after the event 'a wave of horror spread' through the town over the attack on what was 'essentially a spiritual institution' that did not have 'the remotest connection with the language policy of the government'.[28]

Shortly after the riot, the Mother issued a statement concerning the relationship between the ashram and the town. She acknowledged that some Pondicherry residents did not like the ashram but pointed out there were many in the town who 'not only have welcomed the Ashram but have expressed their sympathy, admiration and good-feeling'. She then stated the ashram's position:

> We do not fight against any creed, any religion.
>
> We do not fight against any form of government.
>
> We do not fight against any social class.
>
> We do not fight against any nation or civilisation.
>
> We are fighting division, unconsciousness, ignorance, inertia and falsehood.

> We are endeavouring to establish upon earth union, knowledge, consciousness, Truth, and we fight whatever opposes the advent of this new creation of Light, Peace, Truth and Love.[29]

The ashram quickly rebuilt the destroyed properties. The post office was back in service, in an improved building, by 21 February. On that day, the Mother gave darshan from the terrace. Photographs show her standing erect at the parapet, looking down on the hundreds of people who filled the streets below.[30]

The Mother was deeply concerned in August 1965 when thousands of Pakistani soldiers crossed into Jammu and Kashmir in an effort to seize territory and foment an uprising against the Indian government. The Indian army counterattacked and soon the two countries were at war. On 16 September, the Mother sent a message to Prime Minister Shastri and the army chief of staff in which she said: 'It is for the sake and triumph of Truth that India is fighting and must fight until India and Pakistan have once more become One because that is the truth of their being.' When, after two months of fierce but inconclusive fighting, the countries agreed to a ceasefire, the Mother told a correspondent that this unsatisfactory conclusion was inevitable given the circumstances. A few months later, she proposed that India and its northern neighbours form a federation 'with India as their protective centre, against the possible aggression' of Pakistan and China.[31]

6

From time to time, since the early 1930s, there had been talk of expanding the ashram outside Pondicherry or even relocating it to another place entirely. Around 1938, the Mother imagined an 'ideal city' set somewhere in the country, with a house on a hill for Sri Aurobindo and everything arranged on the model of the Mother's symbol (three concentric circles, the second and third divided into four and twelve 'petals'). Akbar Hydari, the Prime Minister of Hyderabad State, offered her a place but died before the project could come to fruition.[32] A dozen years later, when the Mother was making plans for the International University Centre, she imagined it would include a 'permanent world-exhibition' where 'every nation with a well-defined culture' would have a pavilion where its arts and sciences would be displayed. (She evidently was thinking back to the national pavilions she had visited at the 1900 Exposition Universelle in Paris). This idea too never took form but the Mother continued to look for ways to realize her 'Dream', as she called it in her 1954 article. Around 1956, she oversaw plans to develop some land around a lake a few kilometres west of Pondicherry. The place would have a film and television school, and even a small airfield. This project went through many permutations but nothing much happened for several years.

In August 1964, the first world conference of Sri Aurobindo Society was held in Pondicherry. The Mother sent a message stating that the 'future of the earth depends on a change of consciousness', and it was left to men and women 'to decide if they will collaborate for this change or if it will have to be enforced upon them by the power of crashing circumstances'. (She was writing at the height of the Cold War.) One of the questions proposed for discussion at the conference was 'What is the way of making the consciousness of human unity grow?' The Mother's answer: 'Spiritual education, that is to say an education which gives more importance to the growth of the spirit than to any religious or moral teaching or to the material so-called knowledge.'[33] On the last day, the delegates approved six proposals. One was to establish a film studio. Another was to develop a township near Pondicherry for people who wanted to prepare themselves for a more conscious life. The film studio, a holdover from the Lake Estate scheme, never took shape. The idea of a spiritual township got some traction. At first comparatively uninterested, the Mother soon became deeply involved in the project. She gave it the name Auroville, which evoked both Sri Aurobindo and *aurore,* the French word for dawn.

The Auroville project was unveiled to the world in the April 1965 issue of the ashram's *Bulletin.*[34] The City of Dawn would have houses, schools, an artist colony, industrial units, farms and gardens, an air strip and national pavilions. The same issue reproduced photographs of the site. They show a featureless stretch of arid land. In June, the Mother had a long conversation with Satprem about Auroville. She told him about her old idea of establishing an 'ideal town' on a hill and her childhood vision of a park, 'perhaps the most beautiful thing in the world', with a pavilion of Divine Love in the centre. Auroville would be all this and more. It would have four zones: Residential, cultural, industrial and international. At its centre, would be 'a pavilion of the Mother' (dedicated not to her but to 'the principle of the Mother'). There also would be areas for public services, shops, restaurants and transportation hubs. All this would take a lot of money. For this, she turned to Keshav Dev Poddar, the chairman of Sri Aurobindo Society, to whom she had given the name Navajata. A man with a proven record as a fundraiser (he had played a major role in launching the University Centre project and provided the money for the Mother's new room in the ashram), he had already arranged to purchase the first parcel of Auroville land and was trying to get a loan from the government of Madras. ('Nava has a knack for this,' the Mother remarked, 'he's already got results.') She did not imagine Auroville quickly would become the 'ideal city' of her dreams. It was only a 'small intermediate attempt' but it was worth giving it a try.[35]

7

After her 'near-death' crisis of April 1962, the primary locus of the Mother's sadhana shifted to her body. This meant, from the medical point of view, that she had a lot of physical problems to deal with. From the inner point of view, it meant she was involved on a daily basis with the transformation of her body by the supramental light and force. This comes out clearly in the *Agenda*. I give here, with minimal comment, some extracts from her conversations of the 1960s. On 9 June 1962, she offered what she called a scientific explanation of how the transformation would happen. 'There's nothing to change!' she began. 'Only the relations [between things] change.' Every body, every object 'is composed of atoms; and these atoms are composed of something that is *identical*'. The differences we see—different bodies, different forms—are due to the interrelations of this multiple 'something'. The power of the supermind could change the interrelations and, in this way, transform the whole universe. Once this was understood, she said, 'it becomes *evident* that one can achieve immortality!' Easy to say. Not so easy to carry out. In September, after a bad patch (she was having fainting spells), she commented: 'For three days it's been battle, battle, battle.'[36]

The fluctuations continued. 'I feel the work is going on rather fast inside,' she said in January 1963, 'there are some interesting things . . . like promises. But the sensitivity [of the body] and possibilities of imbalance have become worse', so that even a small mishap could upset the body's equilibrium. She came to see that 'illnesses are a necessary way of looking at things, so as to be able to resist properly'. Once the body was fully resistant, once it had achieved 'complete purification . . . from the cellular point of view', the transformation would be complete 'and once it was complete, the body *itself* . . . would decide whether it wanted to go on or to dissolve itself'. In March 1964, she had an experience that represented a step in this direction: It was as if 'everything was filled with a power of transformation'—not yet the 'final transformation that will change the appearance [of the body]', but rather the ananda or bliss of progress, something like 'ananda of progress of the animal becoming man'. The force that was acting on her 'was *completely separate* from any spiritual notion, from any religious notion, from any psychological notion'. It was simply the action of what she called 'the vibration of truth'. By the end of September, she was having problems again: 'It's a terribly dark toil without clearly visible effects,' she said.[37]

Towards the end of 1964, Satprem and the Mother began collecting passages from their *Agenda* conversations for publication in the *Bulletin* under the title 'Notes on the Way'.[38] The first published extract, dated 7 October 1964, begins on a positive note: 'Things clearly have taken a turn for the better, not from the ordinary point of view but from the higher.' But 'the material consequences' on her body were still apparent, indeed the difficulties seemed to be getting worse. If the effect on the body was to be lasting, not just 'a miraculous effect that comes, dazzles and goes away', it had to be part of an overall process of transformation. The going was not always easy. One day in January 1965, she felt she was being bombarded by 'adverse forces'. The only way to endure, she realized, was to remain calm. In August, she noted that the greatest difficulty was 'in the nerves, because they are so accustomed to the ordinary conscious will that when that stops, to allow the direct action from the highest, they go mad, as it were'. The difficulties continued but from time to time she had glimpses of what complete transformation might be like: 'I experienced this morning,' she said on 22 January 1966, 'a kind of blissful state in which there was such a clear consciousness that all the forms of life, in all the worlds and at each moment, are the expression of a choice—one chooses to be like that.' Once the being realized this, 'all illnesses, all incidents, all dramas, all that: disappeared'.[39] One thing that held the Mother back was 'contagion'—what she earlier had called the problem of the environment. Her 'material consciousness' responded to the supramental contact but it lacked 'the power to assert itself spontaneously against what comes from outside, this perpetual contagion'. Still, there were moments 'when the contact is conscious' and all the cells of her body cried out 'Oh, yes, it's true!'[40]

So it went, the ups and downs, through 1967 and 1968. Finally, there was a crash. Early in August 1968, she went through 'an ordeal that threatened her physical body', as the editor of the *Bulletin* put it. On 22 August, when she was somewhat back in form, she remarked: 'The doctor advises me not to get tired. What is tiring? Only what is useless. To see sincere people who benefit from it is not tiring.' But to see judgmental people 'who in their intelligence believe they are very superior . . . people like that indeed are tiring and to see them useless, to say the least'.[41]

8

Between 1965 and 1968, while absorbed in her sadhana of transformation, the Mother continued to devote much of her time to other projects. In March 1965, she asked Roger Anger, an established French architect who was the husband of her granddaughter Françoise, if he would like to be the lead architect of Auroville. He accepted and began to make plans.[42] The same month, she asked a member of the ashram to make contact with the United Nations Educational, Scientific and Cultural Organization (UNESCO), requesting sponsorship and support. In 1966, the General

Conference of UNESCO passed a resolution commending Auroville to member states and non-governmental organizations, and inviting them to participate in its development.[43] The Mother was glad to have this support but she wanted to keep her distance from official organizations. When someone proposed linking Auroville to an existing UNESCO project she replied emphatically: 'To hand over the management of Auroville to any country or any group however big it may be is an *absolute impossibility*.' If any such step had been taken it was, she said, '*without* my knowledge—because I say to it an emphatic *NO*'.[44]

In September 1966, after reading a report Anger had submitted, the Mother wrote a message for the public saying that Auroville would be 'a universal town where men and women of all nations are able to live in peace and progressive harmony, above all creeds, all politics, and all nationalities'. Its aim was 'to realize human unity'.[45] By now, the centre of the proposed city had been shifted to an area northeast of the original site. More land was bought and a few small communities established. Life for the pioneers was hard. Most lived in huts consisting of bamboo frames covered by woven palm fronds. The soil was poor and water scarce. There were hardly any trees. For nine months of the year, the sun beat down mercilessly.

In 1967, the Mother decided that Auroville would be inaugurated on 28 February the next year. There was a rush to get things ready. A small amphitheatre was built. At its centre was a marble urn in which soil from all the nations of the world would be deposited. When the day arrived, around 5,000 people assembled at the site. At ten in the morning the Mother, sitting in her room in Pondicherry, read aloud a message that was broadcast simultaneously at the amphitheatre 12 kilometres away: 'Greetings from Auroville to all men of good will,' she began. Those 'who thirst for progress and aspire to a higher life' were invited to participate. She then read the Auroville Charter in French. It has four clauses: 'Auroville belongs to nobody in particular' but 'to humanity as a whole'. Auroville will be 'a place of unending education, of constant progress, and a youth that never ages'. 'Taking advantage of all discoveries from within and from without', Auroville will 'boldly spring toward future realisations'. Finally: 'Auroville will be a site of material and spiritual researches' to embody 'actual human unity'. When she finished, delegates at the site recited the Charter in sixteen other languages, and young people representing 124 countries and twenty-four Indian states and territories deposited soil in the urn. Auroville now existed symbolically and verbally, but there still was little on the ground. Not much changed during the rest of 1968 but the Mother had many discussions and answered dozens of letters about the city-to-be.

Also during 1968, the administrators and teachers of the ashram's Centre of Education worked with the Mother to revamp its structure and methods. They chalked out an eighteen-year course of study, with five levels: Kindergarten, primary, lower secondary, higher secondary and college. In accordance with the Mother's wishes, the administrators and teachers made the free-progress system mandatory for older students. They were divided over how much freedom to give the younger ones. Replying to their questions, she wrote: 'Up to the age of seven, children should enjoy themselves. School should all be a game, and they learn as they play. As they play they develop a taste for learning, knowing and understanding life. . . . Above the age of seven, the new system can be applied to those who are ready, provided that there is a class where the others can work in the ordinary way.' In thrashing out the details, the teachers should avoid doctrinaire positions: 'Everyone, without exception, *without exception*, should know that he is not someone who knows and applies what he knows. Everyone is learning to be what they should be and to do what they should do.' When the teachers continued to snipe at one another, she wrote firmly: 'I take this opportunity to assure you that spiritual progress and the service of Truth are based on harmony and not on division and criticism.'[46]

9

On 28 August 1968, the Mother explained to Satprem that the attack that threatened her physical body earlier that month was 'very intense'. It reached the point where her body told her: 'It's all the same to me if I am dissolved; I'm quite ready to live, but the state I am in is impossible, it cannot continue—either live or die, but not this.' Once her body had had its say, things began to get better. During her recovery, she jotted down some notes. In one, she wrote of seeing marvellous landscapes, with everything in perfect harmony. Then the scene shifted: 'Many, many buildings, huge towns being built—' In another note, she wrote: 'The vital and the mental sent packing so that the physical is truly left to its own resources.' For some time, she suffered severe pain and could not sleep. Then, on the night of 26–27 August, there was what she called a 'powerful and prolonged penetration of supramental forces into the body, everywhere at once—'[47] From September, she began to resume her regular activities.

The next year began promisingly. On the morning of 1 January 1969, 'there was as though a golden dawn, and the atmosphere was very gentle. The body felt: "Well, this is really, really new." A golden light, gentle and—benevolent.' She later understood that this was the descent of the consciousness of the *surhomme* or overman, the intermediary between the human and the supramental being. For more than a month, her physical condition was excellent. 'Never had the body been so happy,' she said in mid-February, 'the complete Presence, absolute freedom.' By May, things were getting difficult again: 'It has been, hour after hour, a labour,' she said towards the end of the month. In November, she had a 'vision of the creation—the vision, the understanding, the why, the how, the where it's going, everything was there, all together, and clear, clear, clear—I tell you, I was in a golden glory—luminous, dazzling'. This luminous consciousness was, she understood, the supramental consciousness itself. A month later, she remarked: 'The progress is taking giant strides—it shakes the house a little, but it's taking giant strides.'[48]

As always, progress was followed by a recoil. 'The body has difficult moments, really difficult moments,' she said at the end of January 1970. They seemed to increase along with 'what one might call "conversion"', that is the conversion from the ordinary to the supramental functioning. By April, her physical health was affected in several ways: Failing eyesight, inability to eat. Still, she kept to her routine: 'A dozen letters every day, from people imploring for help. Everything is becoming difficult.' After the April darshan, she had a recurrence of her cardiac problems. For most of May, her condition was very bad and, during the months that followed, not much better. Finally, in the beginning of September, it all became too much to bear: 'For the first time, the brain was affected, in the sense that I have uncontrolled movements. I'm able to control them, but—it's very annoying. And I pass utterly sleepless nights on account of that.' After a week, she was able to resume her normal activities: Conversations, meetings, letters. But the respite was brief. Between late December and the middle of January 1971, she passed through a series of afflictions. It seemed to her that one of her legs was paralysed. A month later, she walked, with help, to the terrace to give darshan on her ninety-third birthday. The rest of the year was marked by low points and high. In June, she spoke of feeling 'a relentless attack of disagreeable things' that had a direct effect on her body: 'It reached a point where I could not swallow when eating—until everything, everything understood: I exist only through the Divine, I subsist only through the Divine—and I can only be myself by being the Divine.' The following March, she had, for the first time, the sense of inhabiting the 'supramental body' or, if not that, at least a 'body in transition'. This new body was 'truly a harmonious form': white, slim, pretty, sexless. She had the feeling that it might somehow take the place of her physical body. Eight months later, she said she had experienced 'for a moment—just a few seconds—the supramental consciousness'. It was a wonderful experience but she knew if she got more than a brief taste of it, she would not want to continue the labour of transformation. On 30 December, she remarked: 'Things have taken an extreme form.' There was 'an uplifting of the atmosphere' towards an 'almost inconceivable splendour'. At the same time, she felt that 'at any moment one may— one may die—not "die", but the body may be dissolved'.[49]

10

During the challenging years between 1969 and 1972, the Mother worked whenever she could. She had regular meetings with those responsible for the day-to-day running of the ashram and Auroville, wrote dozens of messages and letters, and gave her blessings to an unending flood of people, from VIPs to new arrivals. Outwardly, she looked more and more stooped and frail, but her memory was sharp and her command of detail remarkable. She kept herself informed on current affairs and, in 1969, took special interest in the Indian presidential election. Indira Gandhi had become Prime Minister in 1966 with the help of K. Kamaraj, Neelam Sanjiva Reddy and other Congress Party bosses, who thought they could use her as their puppet. She proved to be an agile and independent leader, and, by 1969, was in control of the party and the country. In July of that year, the Congress parliamentary board nominated Reddy as the party's presidential candidate. Gandhi, fearing he would use the position to topple her, put her weight behind V.V. Giri, the then vice president, who ran as an independent. The Mother thought Reddy a man of integrity but when he approached her for support she told him that she backed Indira, whom she respected for standing up to the big banks. From her early years in France, the Mother had considered electoral democracy 'utter nonsense'. After seeing the Indian version in action, she wondered whether it was really 'in accord with India's spirit'. The problem, she said, was that 'it's not at all the entire assembly of people that does things, it's a few scoundrels who put themselves in front, saying, "I represent this, I represent—"'[50]

Giri won the 1969 election and became India's fourth President. Less than a month later, he paid a visit to the ashram and had an audience with the Mother. After several minutes of silence, she declared: 'Let us all work for the greatness of India.'[51] Afterwards, he toured the ashram and Auroville. On 6 October, Prime Minister Gandhi took time off from political intrigues in Delhi to visit Pondicherry. She saw an exhibition on Auroville, spoke with the lead architect and the SAS chairman, met Aurovilians from different countries, and was shown around the ashram. Then, she had a twenty-minute meeting with the Mother, who had messages ready for her: 'Let India work for the future and set the example. Thus she will recover her true place in the world' . . . 'The time has come to govern through union, mutual understanding and collaboration.' . . . 'The greatness of a country does not depend on the victory of a party but on the union of all the parties.'[52]

Mrs Gandhi was enthusiastic about Auroville. Earlier that year, she had sent a message of support: 'Pondicherry was Sri Aurobindo's place of political exile and spiritual unfolding. . . . It is appropriate that seekers of enlightenment from various lands should found a new city there bearing Sri Aurobindo's name'. She hoped it would help in 'bringing about harmony among different cultures and for understanding the environmental needs for man's spiritual growth'.[53] Like most pronouncements about Auroville at this time, the Prime Minister's message was filled with vague, upbeat bromides about its ideals and potential. People who lived on Auroville land had to deal with the hardships of a bleak physical environment and conflicts between groups that differed drastically from one another: University-educated Westerners and Tamil villagers, conventional Indian businessmen and bidi-smoking hippies, Hindu devotees and social activists. All problems—from changes in the master plan to the supply of food for paid workers—were referred to the Mother. As well as giving specific answers, she laid down general guidelines. 'To establish in Auroville the harmonious atmosphere which, by definition, ought to reign there, the first step is for each one to look within himself for the cause of friction and misunderstanding,' she said in July 1969.[54]

By the beginning of 1970, it was clear that the project was not moving forward at the expected pace. Settlers were few, money insufficient, legal and administrative problems abundant. The Mother decided to concentrate on the central 'pavilion of the Mother'. It would be, she wrote, 'the soul of Auroville', and 'the sooner the soul is there, the better it will be for everybody and especially for the Aurovilians'.[55] She spoke of her ideas for the pavilion with Anger, Satprem and others, first in broad terms, then in minute detail. By the middle of the year, the pavilion had a new name: Matrimandir. Its foundation stone was laid in February 1971. Excavation work began a month later. By this time, other buildings had begun to come up: A national pavilion for India, two or three schools, all of them more impressive on the drawing board than on the ground. Meanwhile, Aurovilians were building houses, planting gardens and making babies. The Mother never intended Auroville to be a monastery; on the other hand, she did not want it to become a place for people 'to live like cats and dogs'. Earlier, she had written there would be no marriage in the community—'If a man and a woman love each other and want to live together they may do so without any ceremony'—but she found that when she 'set aside all conventions, immediately everybody thinks: "Ah! Nice place to satisfy our desires."' What she wanted instead was for people to 'realise and manifest the Divine' in their daily lives.[56]

She continued to follow the news. During the early part of 1971, the papers were filled with stories of atrocities against Bengalis in the eastern wing of Pakistan. On 25 March, the Pakistani army began a genocidal campaign against them. The next day, the Bengali leader Sheikh Mujibur Rahman declared that East Pakistan was now the independent nation of Bangladesh. The Mother viewed the ensuing war as a step towards the breakup of Pakistan and its eventual reunification with India, something Sri Aurobindo had always considered inevitable. On 4 April, she sent a letter to Prime Minister Gandhi urging her to recognize the new country. The Indian government sat on the fence for several months. On 3 December, after the Pakistani air force launched pre-emptive strikes against Indian positions, India declared war against Pakistan. In Bangladesh, Indian and Bangladeshi units overran the Pakistani army, which surrendered on 16 December. A week or two later, the Prime Minister wrote a letter to the Mother in which she said, 'Through these critical months I have thought constantly of you.' After expressing gratitude for the Mother's support, she concluded: 'If India is to be great we must improve the quality of the minds of our people. I know that this is your desire. In my humble way I am trying to do what I can.' The Mother was pleased and sent this reply: 'India must be proud of your leadership. Let the country take its true place in the world.'[57]

The year 1972 was the centenary of Sri Aurobindo's birth. A host of commemorative events were held in Pondicherry and other parts of India and the world. The Mother issued many messages to mark the occasion. Despite her indifferent health, she gave darshan on 15 August. Over the next few days, hundreds of people passed through her room to receive her blessings. Her interest in Auroville remained strong. Throughout the year, she wrote letters about many aspects of the project: The design of the Matrimandir, the cause of a fire at a workshop, the kind of films to be shown to children, and, above all, the need for harmony. When she heard that Westerners were acting superior to the local people, she wrote: 'From the spiritual point of view, India is the foremost country of the world. . . . This fact is so obvious that a simple and ignorant peasant here is, in his heart, closer to the Divine than the intellectuals of Europe.' People who wanted to live in Auroville had to understand this and behave accordingly.[58] Conflict also arose between the people who were supposed to expedite the project. Once, she summoned three of them and said: 'For centuries and centuries humanity has waited for this time. It is come. But it is difficult.' She admitted that her body 'has some difficulty, so I can't be active, alas. It is not because I am old, I am not old. I am not old, I am younger than most of you. If I am here inactive, it is because the body has given itself definitely to prepare the transformation. But the consciousness is clear and we are here to work—rest and enjoyment will come afterwards.'[59]

11

During the first months of 1973, the Mother spoke regularly with people about Auroville, the Centre of Education and the ashram. On 21 February, her ninety-fifth birthday, she gave darshan from the terrace. A week later, she remarked: 'When I am completely calm, when there is no one around, no one to disturb me', then 'a certain condition' of consciousness came and she entered 'a luminous immensity'.[60] Around the beginning of April, she became unwell and most of her meetings were cancelled. On 7 April, she told Satprem: 'I seem to be gathering all the world's resistances.' If she stopped calling the Divine, feeling his presence for a single minute, the pain in her body became unbearable. She went on: 'Sometimes I ask myself: "Does the Lord want me to leave?" I am *quite willing* . . . but does He want me to stay?' To this there was no answer, 'No answer except "Transformation".' She then made a stunning disclosure: 'I have a solution for the transformation of the body, but—it's never been done before, so it's so—unbelievable. I can't, I can't believe that that's it. Yet, it's the only solution I see—the body wants to fall asleep and awake—"sleep" in a certain sense, of course: I remain perfectly conscious in consciousness, in the movement—and awake only after it is transformed.' In other words, she would enter into a death-like state and emerge from it transformed.[61] The problem was that while she was dormant, people might think she was dead and bury her. Satprem suggested she speak about this with her attendants, in particular Pranab Kumar Bhattacharya, who, for decades, had been her 'bodyguard'. The Mother and Satprem broached the subject with him. Pranab replied angrily that this was nothing new, the Mother had told him everything long ago. From this point on, Satprem became persona non grata in the Mother's room. His conversations with her were short. Usually, the two passed their time together in meditation. On 9 May, she told him she was 'constantly uncomfortable—and so weak!' Ten days later, she explained: 'The consciousness is clearer, stronger than it ever has been, and I look like an old—' Her voice trailed off.[62]

This was Satprem's last meeting with the Mother. From then on, only her regular attendants and her son, André, who now spent much of his time in Pondicherry, were allowed to enter her room. She passed most of the day in bed, eyes closed, rarely speaking. The few words she uttered were about her physical condition: She was cold or thirsty or uncomfortable and needed to be shifted. She said nothing about the ashram or Auroville, nothing about her inner life. Her attendants had to struggle to get her to eat or drink. On 15 August, she gave darshan from her terrace. Supported by Pranab, she stood briefly at the railing and then went back inside. September and October passed without any major incident. In the beginning of November, she developed persistent hiccups. Doctor Sanyal examined her and found that her blood pressure was extremely low. She was in constant discomfort on account of bedsores. On 13 November, she asked Pranab and another attendant to lift her off her bed. This gave her some relief but, after some time, they had to put her down. The whole night passed with them lifting her up and putting her down again. On 14 November, she asked them to make her walk. They tried but she could not remain upright. Things went on like this for three more days. On 17 November, her condition worsened. In the evening, her pulse and breathing became irregular and weak. At 7.25 p.m. her heart stopped beating. Sanyal attempted manual cardiopulmonary resuscitation. She did not respond and he told the others that she had left her body.[63]

12
Epilogue

1

BEFORE LEAVING THE ROOM, DR SANYAL TOLD THE OTHERS NOT TO disturb the Mother's body for some time. Nothing was done until 11 p.m., when the attendants cleaned her and dressed her in fresh clothes. Then, Pranab and another attendant went to inform Nolini Kanta Gupta. He said he had been told by the Mother 'not to be in a hurry, but see that her body was properly kept, and then wait'. They waited around two hours. At 2 a.m., Pranab and others took her body downstairs, and placed it on a reclining chair in the meditation room. An hour later, the people of the ashram were informed. Stunned, they rushed to see her. At 4.30 a.m., the gates of the ashram were thrown open and people from town joined the queue.[1]

Later in the day, the ashram authorities issued a statement. It began: 'The Mother left her body on 17–11–73 at 7.25 p.m. The immediate cause of Her passing away was heart failure.' It went on to say that her body 'will remain in state as long as it is possible to keep it'.[2] Over the next two days, tens of thousands of people flocked to the ashram to have a last darshan of the Mother. Dr Sanyal and Dr Nirodbaran examined her body twice daily. On the morning of 19 November, they found signs of decomposition and decided that the Mother's remains should be interred the next morning.

Twenty-three years earlier, the Mother told the person who designed Sri Aurobindo's samadhi to leave room for two chambers, one above the other. On 19 November, the upper chamber was opened and preparations made for the interment. At 8 a.m. on 20 November, the Mother's body was placed in a rosewood casket that was carried to the samadhi in solemn procession and lowered into the vault. André and Nolini scattered rose petals over the casket. Then the chamber was closed.

2

News of the Mother's death and funeral was carried by most Indian newspapers. Many reproduced messages issued by government officials, including the President and Prime Minister. In a long and heartfelt statement, Mrs Gandhi expressed her grief at the Mother's passing, saying 'it was a privilege to know such a being and have her in our midst for so many years'. The Mother 'was a dynamic, radiant personality with tremendous force of character and extraordinary spiritual attainments. Yet she never lost her sound practical wisdom which concerned itself with the running of the Ashram, the welfare of society, the founding and development of Auroville and any scheme which would promote the ideals expressed by Sri Aurobindo'. A writer in the *Weekly Mail* concluded his laudatory article by saying that the Mother's consciousness had 'seemingly withdrawn from the body, but only to manifest itself more widely and more fully, the more creatively in the Ashram and the earth atmosphere'.[3]

The foreign press was less effusive but still respectful. The *New York Times* reviewed the Mother's life and devoted a paragraph to Auroville, a township 'intended to be free of skyscrapers, pollution and tension', where 'more than $13-million has already been spent on homes for fewer than 200 people'. (The source for these figures was not given.) The journalist Jean-Pierre Clerc, writing in *Le Monde,* also reviewed the Mother's life and spoke of her significance in financial terms: 'A mystic, the "Mother" was also an astute businesswoman. Under her direction the ashram has become a very prosperous community' whose houses, farms, orchards and industrial units 'are valued at several million dollars'. The most lyrical obituary was published by *Time* magazine. 'Dark-haired and beautiful, she might have grown up in that age of *fin de siècle* elegance to become one of those delicate butterflies that flutter through the paintings of Renoir,' the writer began. 'But even as a child Mira Alfassa had mystical experiences.' Later, she became a disciple of Sri Aurobindo, and still later the head of his ashram and the founder of the 'utopian international community of Auroville'. The writer noted that 'some members [of the ashram] seemed to hope that the Mother had so infused herself with the divine that she had achieved the gift that Aurobindo predicted for the spiritual beings of the future: bodily immortality', but that ultimately she joined him in his tomb.[4]

3

Shortly after the Mother's death, Nolini Kanta Gupta wrote that the Mother's body belonged to the 'old creation'. She had used it as a pedestal 'to uphold the New Body'. The old body had done its job. She would return in the New Body. A month later, he explained: 'For a new mutation, a new procedure was needed. "Death" was the first state in that process.' He reaffirmed: 'The New Body will come.'[5] Other disciples enlarged on this millennial theme. 'By passing away as she did,' wrote one, the Mother 'accomplished the task set to her by Sri Aurobindo in 1950 and repeated in his new mode his own master-stroke of conquering all while appearing to perish utterly.' When another disciple was asked if the Mother's mission could still succeed, he answered immediately, 'What do you mean? It has already succeeded.' A third declared: 'The New Body will come as a certain climax of the working of the Supramental manifestation, and as a sign of the complete victory of Spirit over Matter.'[6] Nolini Kanta Gupta, who first announced the New Body prophecy, walked it back a little: 'Obviously, the immediate programme of physical transformation is postponed—not cancelled.' The new body—the one the Mother had spoken about in talks of March 1972—existed 'in the inner world' and was 'at work within us, and around us in the world'.[7]

These speculations of 1973–74 offered consolation and hope but were not in accord with anything the Mother ever said. She never suggested she would return in a new body or that her death would be a victory.[8] Twenty years earlier, she wrote that the battle between death and transformation 'can end only with the defeat of one of the two combatants'. Her own battle with death began in April 1962 and continued for more than eleven years. It ended on 17 November 1973.

The Mother believed in the post-mortem existence of part or all of the individuality of spiritually developed beings. In talks of the 1960s and 1970s, she spoke of spending time with Sri Aurobindo on a certain subtle plane. She also said that some of her close disciples remained in touch with her after their deaths. She accepted the theory of reincarnation and, on occasion, made comments that caused others to conclude that she had been one or another famous woman of the past. She did not deny the possibility but cautioned that only those with special expertise were entitled to speak about such things: 'To say something about past lives without taking up the thread that runs through everything would be opening the door to dogmatism'.[9] All this was of minor interest to her. She was concerned not with past or future lives but the work she wanted to do in the present.

4

In the course of this book, I have spoken briefly of some of the Mother's spiritual experiences, basing myself on her own accounts. She presented them as a single continuous development, but it is possible to distinguish four overlapping movements: Psychic, occult, cosmic and physical. From her childhood, she had visions and inner experiences, culminating in what she called an identification with her psychic being. Later, she learnt how to move through the occult planes and to view the saga of the world as a clash between occult beings and forces. After meeting Sri Aurobindo she reconceived this conflict as an evolution of cosmic beings and powers, leading ultimately to the emergence of what Sri Aurobindo called the supermind. The culmination of this movement, she said, would be the descent of the supermind into her physical body and into the 'earth-consciousness'.

It has been possible for me to say something about the Mother's psychic and occult experiences, which are similar in some respects to those of other mystics. I have been less inclined to discuss her views on cosmic evolution. No one except Sri Aurobindo and she were aware of the action of what they called the supermind. As a result, there is nothing to compare it to, no framework to place it in. I therefore have confined myself to reporting what they said about it. The search for physical transformation leading to immortality is as old as human civilization. Egyptian priests, Chinese shamans, Indian tantrics and others developed magical and alchemical techniques to conquer death. Biotech researchers continue this search through physical interventions of various sorts. Sri Aurobindo's approach was different. He believed that physical immortality might be 'one of the sequelae of supramentalisation' but did not consider it a matter of pressing concern.[10] A year before his death, he said that his writings about a transformed 'divine body' were 'far-off speculations about what might become possible' in the course of evolution and 'could not be anything near or immediate'. Perhaps, he said, he 'should have insisted more on present limitations'.[11] The Mother was never one to accept limitations. For eleven years, she sought to prolong her life, in spite of great physical suffering, because she believed this was necessary for the fulfilment of Sri Aurobindo's work. During the same eleven years, she stayed the course of Sri Aurobindo Ashram, refashioned its school and founded an international community. Few nonagenarians have ever done as much.

The Mother considered the ashram, the Centre of Education and Auroville to be expressions of the workings of a higher consciousness. We have made an effort, doubtless inadequate, to grasp what she meant by this higher consciousness. Now, we can turn to the projects themselves.

5

After the Mother's death, the ashram continued to be administered by the board of trustees, which soon selected a new member and named a new managing trustee. After a pause, the life of the community resumed.

There were a few lean years during the mid-1970s, but the Mother's admirers made sure that the institution she founded had the means to survive and grow.

In 2026, the ashram will celebrate the centenary of its founding. During the first half of this period, when it was under the Mother's guidance, it grew from around two dozen to around 2,000 members. Its activities, at first confined to two houses, spread to numerous buildings, farms, industrial units and sports facilities. The Mother established the ashram as a place for the practice of yoga—Sri Aurobindo's 'integral yoga' includes not only meditation and devotion but also work. 'This is not an Asram like others,' he wrote in 1932. 'What is being done here is a preparation for a work [of world-transformation]. Meanwhile every member here is expected to do some work in the Asram as part of his spiritual preparation.' Expanding on this idea some years later, the Mother stipulated: 'Each one must devote at least one-third of his time to a useful work', adding, 'all activities are represented in the Ashram and each one chooses the work congenial to his nature'.[12] This last statement was somewhat hyperbolic, but the ashram did offer a large variety of activities. Besides essential services—farming, cooking, house maintenance, accounting and so forth—there were cultural pursuits, such as art, music and literature, along with teaching and physical training. The Mother established these spheres of activity and oversaw their development. For many years, she looked into every detail herself. Later, she deputed some responsibility to department heads but never lost touch with individual members. Visitors to the ashram invariably were impressed by her powers of organization. The ashram's orderliness was particularly striking to Indians because, as Sri Aurobindo once remarked, India is not among the countries 'in which organised work is successfully done'.[13]

The structure and procedures the Mother implemented during her lifetime have endured. Five decades after her passing, the ashram remains a model of effective institutional functioning. The members of the board of trustees never tried to take the Mother's place as spiritual guides but have done a good job in responding to the challenges of a new century.

When the Mother was alive, conflicts between members were referred to her and what she decided was accepted without question. The trustees inherited the unenviable task of having to adjudicate such matters without possessing her spiritual authority. Their low-key approach along with the goodwill of most members have ensured a generally smooth operation. The greatest challenge the ashram faces is demographic. Few young people now become members and the ashram has to deal with the problems of an ageing population. Still, it remains a dynamic, flourishing community. After the foundation of Auroville, the Mother wrote that the ashram would 'retain its true role of pioneer, inspirer and guide'.[14] As it enters its second century, it continues to fulfil this role.

The ashram's school was opened in 1943 for practical reasons: When the Mother allowed families with children to join the community, she became responsible for the children's education. The small school she set up became the basis of Sri Aurobindo International University Centre, which, in 1959, was reorganized as Sri Aurobindo International Centre of Education. From the earliest years of the school, the Mother took a personal interest in the students, and in the instruction and training they received. As well as teaching classes herself, she developed a theory of 'integral education', which aimed at a holistic development of body, life, mind and soul. She was particularly interested in physical education and saw to it that all the students participated in sports or exercises every day. She also encouraged students to take part in artistic, musical and theatrical activities, and gain practical experience in ashram workplaces. She did not expect the school to turn out ready-made yogis but did insist that its primary purpose was 'to discover and encourage those in whom the need for progress has become conscious enough to orient their life'. With this in mind, she developed a free-progress system that gave as much freedom to the students as they were able to handle. At the same time, she took away the artificial lure of certificates and diplomas. 'To learn for the sake of knowledge, to study in order to know the secrets of Nature and life, to educate oneself in order to grow in consciousness, to discipline oneself in order to become master of oneself, to overcome one's weaknesses, incapacities and ignorance, to prepare oneself to advance in life towards a goal that is nobler and vaster, more generous and more true'—this and not earning degrees was the aim she set before the students.[15] Those who chose to pursue higher studies in degree-granting institutions had the benefit of fourteen years of primary, secondary and college education without the stress of preparing for examinations, which blights the school-going years of students around the world, not least in India.

Sri Aurobindo International Centre of Education is still going strong after more than sixty-five years. Many more parents wish to have their children admitted than there are openings for them. The student body comes from all parts of India and a sprinkling of foreign countries. Boys and girls are equally represented. Dozens of 'integral schools' in different parts of India, especially Odisha, Punjab and the south, are modelled on the ashram's Centre of Education and try to put the Mother's educational ideas into practice.

Auroville is the youngest of the Mother's institutional offsprings and the one that has suffered the most severe growing pains. For a year or two after the Mother's death, work continued along the lines she had established. People in Auroville had to scale back their ventures and tighten their belts, but they went ahead with projects deemed crucial to the city-to-be: Developing sustainable agriculture, planting trees, building the Matrimandir. At the same time, disputes between administrators and Aurovilians, which had germinated while the Mother was still alive, began to spread like weeds. The main points of contention were money and power. The assets of Auroville were held in the name of Sri Aurobindo Society, and officers of the SAS claimed the right to direct the project and allocate its funds as they saw fit. In November 1975, a group of disaffected residents, advised by a breakaway member of the SAS, registered a new society called 'Auroville' that challenged the right of the SAS to control the life of the community. The SAS chairman filed for an injunction against the new society. Soon things got nasty. On the land, there were demonstrations, confrontations and occasional violence; in New Delhi, attempts by different factions to get the support of politicians; in the courts, a seemingly endless succession of cases. This story has been told by many different authors from different points of view and is far too tangled for me to go into here. In 1980, after five years of confusion, the Government of India passed an ordinance placing Auroville under government control for a limited period. The SAS challenged the ordinance. The case eventually went to the Supreme Court. One of the arguments of the SAS was that it was a 'religious denomination' and that the Constitution of India prohibits the government from interfering in religious matters. The court rejected this contention on the grounds that the writings of Sri Aurobindo and the Mother 'unmistakably show that the Ashram or [Sri Aurobindo] Society or Auroville is not a religious institution'. The court also found no merit in the other arguments of the SAS and dismissed its petition in November 1982.[16]

In the years that followed, Auroville residents made progress in many of their endeavours—agricultural, environmental, architectural, educational—but the life of the community was marked by a lack of direction, internal discord and magical thinking.[17] The SAS, which technically still held Auroville's assets, framed the situation as a conflict between Indians and foreigners, and this played well in the Indian press. Auroville residents, Indian as well as foreign, relied on the goodwill of well-placed friends, such as the industrialist J.R.D. Tata. Most of them were happy when the government extended the 1980 ordinance. In 1988, the Indian Parliament passed the Auroville Foundation Act, which transferred all of Auroville's assets to the Government of India and established a foundation to look after its functioning. The Mother would not have approved. As we have seen, she made it clear that handing over 'the management of Auroville to any country or any group however big it may be' was 'an *absolute impossibility*'.

The Auroville Foundation consists of a Governing Board of seven persons nominated by the Government of India, an International Advisory Council (IAC) of five persons nominated by a government ministry, and a Residents' Assembly consisting of all residents of Auroville aged eighteen and above.[18] The functions of the IAC are strictly advisory. The Residents' Assembly has the responsibility of overseeing the admission of new members and constituting committees to expedite the running of the community. It may submit recommendations to the

Governing Board, which is expected to 'coordinate activities and services of Auroville in consultation with the Residents' Assembly'. In practice, all power rests with the Governing Board, which leaves day-to-day decisions to a government-appointed secretary. So far, successive government administrations have declared their intention to help Auroville develop along the lines laid down by the Mother. All governments have agendas, however, and it remains to be seen whether future administrations will be able to resist the temptation to take full control of Auroville and run it without the advice and consent of its residents.[19]

As of October 2024, Auroville had 3,307 residents. Fifty-one per cent were from India, the rest from sixty countries of Europe, North and South America, Africa, Asia and Australasia. Many projects undertaken in the infancy of the community have reached successful conclusions. Work on Matrimandir, the 'soul of Auroville', was completed in 2008. To the distress of many residents, it has become a major tourist attraction. A decades-long tree-planting programme has created well-established forests that have had a beneficial impact on the local climate. This has made neighbouring lands attractive to developers, who are eager to use Auroville's infrastructure but indifferent to its ideals. Aurovilians have received many national and international awards for sustainable building and architecture, renewable energy projects, rural health services and other initiatives. Products manufactured by Auroville's handicraft units, which provide employment for thousands of local people, are distributed throughout the country. The community has a vibrant cultural life, with many artists, musicians, dancers, dramatists, film-makers and photographers.[20] Along with its successes, Auroville has had more than its share of conflicts, many of which elude easy resolution.

6

In February 1972, the Mother predicted that 'in fifty years the world, the entire receptive side of humanity . . . will be as if enveloped—not "enveloped"—*absorbed* by the power of Sri Aurobindo's thought'.[21] This manifestly has not come to pass. People around the world read Sri Aurobindo's works but his thought remains a minor current in contemporary cultural life. There are a number of reasons for this: The esoteric nature of some of his and the Mother's writings, the unwillingness of their advocates to develop critical thinking, the Eurocentric bias of modern philosophy. In recent years, this bias has been challenged by distinguished scholars and Sri Aurobindo's thought has begun to find a place in studies of global philosophy.[22]

The Mother's writings are rarely mentioned in studies of global thought and literature. They deserve more attention. Pragmatic rather than metaphysical in her approach, she showed how Sri Aurobindo's ideas could be applied to real-life situations. She believed that French was 'the most precise and clearest language' and these qualities are present in her own French prose.[23] Her pre-1920 writings and talks combine intellectual lucidity with psychic sensitivity. *Prayers and Meditations* is a classic of devotional literature as well as a chronicle of her sometimes difficult passage to spiritual attainment. Her published conversations deal with a vast array of subjects—yoga, psychology, art, philosophy, occultism—in a relaxed, informal way. Her letters and messages often reveal unexpected depths.

The Mother's achievements as an artist and musician are attested by her paintings and drawings, and recordings of her organ music, but the projects into which she put most of her creative energy are the ashram and Auroville. She conceived of them as oases of harmony in a world of dissonance, with well-designed, well-appointed buildings, surrounded, when possible, by gardens and trees. To facilitate productive interactions between residents, she organized units—work departments, schools, sports clubs and so forth—in both communities. Clear about her ultimate aim, she avoided rigid plans. Her watchword was a 1939 statement by Sri Aurobindo: 'There has never been, at any time, a mental plan, a fixed programme or an organisation decided beforehand.' Rather, things had taken shape 'as a living being by a movement of consciousness'. This approach, the Mother explained, 'is just that which permits miracles, reversals, etc.; it permits everything'. She was aware it often upset 'the ordinary human mentality which believes it can decide everything in advance. But,' she added, 'from the spiritual point of view it is inevitable.'[24]

Underlying the activities of the ashram and Auroville is the aim the Mother set before the residents of both communities: Spiritual growth leading in the end to the establishment of an 'ideal society' in which a 'new race' could evolve.[25] The path of yoga that she and Sri Aurobindo developed was meant to encourage this growth. It differs in many respects from traditional paths of yoga. There are no fixed practices or observances. Individuals may, or may not, engage in formal meditation, worship, study, mantra repetition, asanas and so forth. Nothing is obligatory. The only things asked of every sadhak are regular work performed in the spirit of karmayoga, and an inner attitude of openness and surrender. Most sadhaks give expression to this attitude in devotional acts and words. Following the advice of Sri Aurobindo, they treat the Mother as an incarnation of the Divine Mother. As we have seen, during her lifetime, she accepted this devotion but at the same time was aware that the disciples tended to create an 'image' of her 'in conformity with their needs and desires', and it was with this image, and not her, that they were in relation.[26]

It is ironic that a Paris-born woman who rejected religion should have been proclaimed a divine incarnation in India. When she was young, Mirra Alfassa had 'a horror of religions'. It was only after she learnt that 'the Divine is within' that she could begin her spiritual quest.[27] This led her from France to Algeria and finally to India, where she met Sri Aurobindo. From 1927, her spiritual identity, whether 'image' or spiritual reality, overshadowed all other aspects of her personality. Her followers viewed her artistic, intellectual and active life before that time as an interesting but ultimately insignificant preparation for her predestined spiritual role. To me, this sells her short. Even those who accept her spiritual identity as primary should appreciate her life as a whole.

In one of her last messages, dictated on 19 March 1973, the Mother said: 'Here we do not have religion. We replace religion by the spiritual life, which is truer, deeper and higher at the same time, that is to say, closer to the Divine.'[28] Many spiritual teachings of the past have succumbed to the allure of religion. Time will tell whether the spiritual path of the Mother and Sri Aurobindo will escape this fate.

Abbreviations

A&R	*Sri Aurobindo: Archives and Research*
AA	*Annuaire-almanach du commerce, de l'industrie, de la magistrature et de l'administration*
AM	*L'Agenda de Mère*
AN	Archives Nationales
ANOM	Archives Nationales d'Outre-mer
AVP	Archives de la Ville de Paris
BN	Bibliothèque Nationale, Paris
CWM	Collected Works of the Mother
CWSA	Collected Works of Sri Aurobindo
FAPI	Familles Alfassa–Pinto–Ismalun
GA	Jean Benilan, *Le Gouverneur Alfassa*
MA	*Mother's Agenda*
MADN	Maison Alexandra David-Neel
MAP	Matteo Alfassa Papers
MFP	Morisset Family Papers
MM	Mirra Ismalun, 'Mes Mémoires'
OM	Œuvres de la Mère
PTP	Pascal Thémanlys Papers
RC	*Revue Cosmique*
TMAC	Correspondence between the Theons and Mirra Alfassa

Notes

Prologue: Becoming the Mother

1. CWM 13:43.
2. CWSA 35:229.

1: A Banker's Daughter

1. When the Mother said in 1954 that she was French 'by birth and early education' (see the Prologue) she was simplifying matters. Under laws of 1849 and 1851, amended in 1867 and 1874–75, a person born in France of alien parents was considered a French citizen only if one or both parents were born in France (Plender, *French Nationality Law,* 711). Mirra became a French citizen in 1890 when her father and his family were naturalized.
2. FAPI, under Alfassa, Nissim; Alfassa, Samuel; and Alfassa, Maurice. Maurice's name at birth apparently was Moshe, which was the name of his father's father. The literal French equivalent is Moïse (Moses in English). Maurice was a common French substitute for Moshe/Moïse. In official French documents, his name is given as Moïse Maurice or simply Maurice.
3. Shaw, *Jews of the Ottoman Empire,* 163; Rodrigue, *French Jews, Turkish Jews,* 44–45.
4. AM 2:342. M. [Maurice] and L. [Léon] Alfassa are listed among arrivals in Vienna guesthouses in May 1862 (*Fremden-Blatt,* Vienna, 24 May 1862). Maurice's stepmother (Léon's mother) Rachel is listed as an arrival in June 1859 (*Weiner Zeitung,* Vienna, 8 June 1859).

5. Kohen, 'Kal de los Francos'. Cf. Rodrigue, *French Jews, Turkish Jews,* 39 and note 67; Shaw, *Jews of the Ottoman Empire,* 170.
6. Transcription of 'Acte de Naissance' of Maurice Alfassa (Italian original and official French translation) forming part of his *Dossier de naturalisation* (see note 47 below).
7. *Bulletin de l'Alliance Israélite Universelle,* January 1865.
8. *Bulletin de l'Alliance Israélite Universelle,* July 1864:34; Rossi, *La Banque Camondo,* 5.
9. Gary, *Camondo Legacy,* 31.
10. Many biographers of Mirra Alfassa write that her grandmother Mirra Ismalun, née Pinto, spelt her forename with one R, while Mirra Alfassa spelt hers with two. This is incorrect. Mirra Ismalun used two Rs when she signed her name. All documents relating to her, from her birth certificate to her death certificate, spell her name with two Rs.
11. MM.
12. *Archives Israélites* 35, 20 (15 October 1874):629.
13. MM.
14. GA13.
15. *Neue Freie Presse,* Vienna, 11 September 1875: 8–9; *Das Vaterland,* Vienna, 14 September 1875: 3.
16. Matteo is the Italian form. In France, he sometimes used the French equivalents Mattéo or Mathieu.
17. D31U3/393 (Statuts. Acte du 24.10.1877) (AVP), cited in FAPI under Alfassa, Maurice.
18. V4E/3550 (Acte de Naissance, number 390) (AVP).
19. For Printemps see AA 1878: 105, 699, 1916. In 1878, the address of Printemps was 123–125 rue de Provence, which is one block from 41 boulevard Haussmann. At present, the store, greatly expanded, occupies a building on boulevard Haussmann opposite number 41, as well as other buildings. For synagogues, see Matteo Alfassa diary for 1889 (MAP).
20. Ferry and Clemenceau, Débat des 28–31 Juillet 1885, quoted in BN exhibition, 'Exploration du monde: Races supérieures, races inférieures', available online at http://expositions.bnf.fr/socgeo/pedago/t21.htm.
21. AM 3:297 (trans. cf. MA 3:280). This is one of several versions of this anecdote.
22. Pournapréma, *Petite fille,* 9–10.
23. AM 3:204.

24. Letter Léon Alfassa to Jacques Alfassa, 4 April 1885 (Archives du Musée Nissim-de-Camondo PF4), quoted in FAPI, under Alfassa, Jacques.
25. *Figaro*, 16 April 1885.
26. GA 14.
27. FAPI under Alfassa, Maurice, and Pinto, Mirra. The information given in these entries does not align perfectly with dates in Matteo Alfassa's diary for 1887. It is clear from the diary that the Alfassas moved, apparently to 3 Square du Roule, in January 1887. They definitely were living there in June of that year (MAP). It is not certain when Mirra Ismalun occupied 1 Square du Roule or whether the Alfassas lived with her there for some time before moving to number 3.
28. GA 14.
29. Pournapréma, *Petite fille* 10–11.
30. Matteo Alfassa diary for 1886 (MAP).
31. Matteo Alfassa diary for 1886–89 (MAP).
32. Matteo Alfassa diary for 1887 (MAP).
33. OM 4:49.
34. Matteo Alfassa diary for 1888 (MAP).
35. Matteo Alfassa diary for 1889 (MAP).
36. AM 3:181.
37. GA 14–15.
38. AM 2:343 (trans. cf. MA 2:343).
39. OM 10:168.
40. AM 5:56.
41. Matteo Alfassa diary for 1889 (MAP).
42. If the Mother mentioned 'Jews' or 'Israelites' in her published writings or recorded talks she spoke of them as a group to which she had no special connection. On the other hand, if people mentioned to her in private conversations that they were Jewish, she sometimes said, with a smile, '*Moi aussi.*'
43. Schnapper and Johnstone, 'Israélites and Juifs'.
44. In 1961, the Mother told a disciple: 'My mother despised all religious feelings as weakness and superstition and absolutely denied the invisible' (AM 2:341). It is hard to reconcile this with what Matteo wrote about Mathilde in his diary: Her observance of Jewish holidays, including fasting on Yom Kippur, reading Jewish prayers to the children before bed and so forth. Doubtless, many parents participate in rituals they do not believe in for the sake of their children, but at least during the period of

the diary (1886–89) Mathilde seems to have been sincere in her religious observances.

45. Doizy, 'Willette', 115.

46. Drumont, *France juive,* 2 vols. The quoted passages are *'Camondo, ce gros Juif qui ressemble à un chef d'eunuques abyssins'* and *'ce Turcaret levantin'* (vol. 2:150).

47. Décret de naturalisations du 28 août 1890 (AN BB/34/399, document 48 *or* sous-série BB/11, dossier 9808 X 88).

48. We do not know when Mirra entered her *cours pour jeunes filles.* The only evidence we have is negative. Matteo, who wrote very often about his sister in his diary (1886–89), never mentioned a *cours* or any other sort of instruction outside the house for her.

49. AM 8:251. The description the Mother gave of her *cours* closely matches the descriptions in advertisements Madame Evelart-Deleury placed in the Paris Directory, *Tout Paris,* and provincial publications. The Mother said the *cours* she went to had a high reputation at the time. Judging from Madame Evelart-Deleury's advertisements, hers was perhaps the most prominent *cours* in Paris. It was located just a twenty-minute walk from Square du Roule.

50. AA 1887: 1234; *Le Ménestrel,* 22 January 1888: 31; *La Démocratie de l'Ariège,* 12 July 1885:3.

51. OM 2:3–6; AM 8:251.

52. Pournapréma, *Petite fille,* 15–16. Pournapréma says this happened when Mirra was thirteen. I have placed it after she left her *cours,* apparently in 1893, when she was fifteen. About Mirra's difficulties in remembering her age when certain events happened, see note 66 below.

53. Pournapréma, *Petite fille,* 17; cf. AM 2:218.

54. AN: Fonds de l'Académie Julian: cotes 63AS/10 ('Livre des Nationalités – Dames / Rue de Berri') and 63AS/16 ('Dames Berri/Atelier de M.Mrs Bouguereau et G. Ferrier. Années 1896– / 1897–1899–1900–1901'). The entry on the page devoted to Mirra ('Melle Alfassa' of 3 Square du Roule) in the 'Dames Berri' register begins 'Recom^{ce} [Recommence] | Un Abo^{nt} [Abonnement (subscription)] de Six Mois le 6 Octobre 1896'. The word 'Recommence' indicates she had studied at the school before October 1896. A portrait study she painted in 1895 (*The Mother: Paintings and Drawings,* Plate 17) has the look of exercises done by Académie Julian students (compare Figures 27–32 in Weisberg and Becker, *Overcoming All Obstacles*). It is likely that Mirra began her studies at the Académie Julian in 1895 or

even 1894, but I was unable to locate any registers confirming this in AN. Such registers, if they existed, may not have survived.

55. Denis, 'L'Influence de Paul Gauguin', *Occident*, July 1903, 160.
56. OM 7:207.
57. Possibly the most realistic and certainly the most entertaining account of classes at Julian's around this time is found in Jules Lemaître's 1905 comedy *La Massière*.
58. Pournapréma, *Petite fille*, 17.
59. Concert poster reproduced in Cosma, *George Enescu*, 59; Grandival, 'Courrier des théâtres', 3.
60. GA 22. John de Medicis (aka Giovanni Hakim) was a son of Mirra Pinto's sister Allegra, hence a cousin of Mathilde Alfassa.
61. MM; letter H. Morisset to G. Moreau, 4 August 1897, Archives Musée Gustave Moreau, reproduced in FAPI under Morisset, Henri.
62. Acte de mariage, Morisset–Alfassa , 13 October 1897. AVP V4E 8732.
63. Undated note by Wanda Morisset (André Morisset's wife) in MFP; FAPI under Morisset, Henri Georges.
64. Pandit, ed., *Champaklal Speaks*, 128–29.
65. AM 7:99 (trans. cf. MA 7:95).
66. AM 5:61. See also AM 1:467, 501; AM 3:309; OM 6:327. In 1958, the Mother said she began her conscious sadhana when she was around twenty-two or twenty-three (AM 1:162); in 1962, she said she began her conscious yoga after she met Theon, when she was around twenty-one (AM 3:298). (She first met Theon in 1905, when she was twenty-seven.) In 1964, she spoke of having begun her conscious yoga when she was twenty-five, that is, in 1908 (AM 5:62). (In 1908, she turned thirty.)
67. Sethna, 'The Mother', 4; Pournapréma, *Petite fille*, 14–15; AM 4:73–74.
68. AM 4:73–74; Sethna, 'The Mother', 3; Pournapréma, *Petite fille*, 6.
69. See for example, Schlieter, *What Is It Like to Be Dead*, 107–10, 179–80, 209–10; Arstila, 'Time Slows Down'; David Eagleman interviewed by Abumrad and Krulwich, 'Why a Brush with Death Triggers the Slow-Mo Effect'; Wallis, 'Near-Death Experience'.
70. AM 4:74 (trans. cf. MA 4:73).
71. AM 11:243, AM 1:230.
72. AM 3:295–96; AM 13:268.
73. OM 5:151.
74. Medhananda, 'Queen Hatshepsut', 40.
75. AM 8:230 (trans. cf. MA 8:220); cf. AM 3:246.

76. AM 2:216; AM 3:412 (trans. cf. 3:391); OM 5:288–89.
77. OM 8:132; OM 1:89.
78. CWM 13:39. Article first published in the *Prabartak* (Chandernagore) 5 (13) (*Ashar* 30, 1327 [14 July 1920]): 291–92.
79. OM 10:386; AM 1:129.

2: An Artist's Life

1. It is not known when exactly the Morissets moved into 15 rue Lemercier. The first evidence they were living there is an entry in the catalogue of the 1898 exhibition of the Société des amis des arts de Seine-et-Oise, which opened that July. The 1897 and 1898 editions of the Paris Directory give Henri's address as 92 rue de la Victoire. He had lived with his parents in a flat in this building since 1872, and paid the rent for it between 1895 and 1898. It seems likely that he and Mirra lived in this flat immediately after their marriage before shifting to 15 rue Lemercier.
2. OM 6:118.
3. Undated note by Wanda Morisset in MFP. In his reminiscences (Morisset, 'Remembrances', 64), André speaks of his 'foster sister' Genèvieve. Here, 'foster sister' does not have the usual sense of the term in English (Mirra and Henri never became foster parents of a girl) but translates the French *sœur de lait* ('milk-sister'), that is, the daughter of a wet nurse whom she brings up along with the client's child.
4. Romanet, 'Mise en nourrice'. In 1887–88, almost a third of all babies born in Paris were placed with wet nurses outside the city. Among the higher classes, the percentage was much higher (Rollet, 'Allaitement, mise en nourrice', 1198).
5. Louis de Bonald, cited in Romanet, 'Mise en nourrice'.
6. OM 12:397.
7. *Journal officiel de la République Française. Lois et décrets.* 14 October 1898: 6350.
8. AM 2:341 (trans. cf. MA 2:310).
9. Bouyer devoted a few words to Morisset in his review of the 1897 Salon des Artistes Français (*L'Image* 6 [May 1897]:189). In his ninety-five-page review of the Salons of 1898, he wrote four lines on Morisset, calling him an artist of great promise (*L'Artist* 68, no. 2 [April–June]: 131).
10. Morse, 'Dreyfus and Zola Trials', 589.
11. AM 6:201.

12. AM 3:299. In an earlier talk, the Mother said: 'All the artists I knew at that time truly were artists, they were serious and did admirable things that have remained admirable. It was the period of the Impressionists, it was the period of Manet' (OM 4: 332). Several writers have concluded from this that the Mother knew Manet and the other Impressionist painters (see for example Jayawardena, *White Woman's Other Burden,* 208). She did not. Manet died in 1883, when Mirra was five. Renoir, Degas and Monet lived past 1916, when she left France, but there is no evidence she met any of them. She, of course, was familiar with their works.
13. More than 500 artists exhibited in the salons of the Exposition Universelle of 1900. Only a dozen of them are mentioned even in detailed histories of modern art and none of them are regarded, retrospectively, as among the leading artists of the era.
14. OM 6:79–81.
15. AM 2:219.
16. Société des amis des arts de Seine-et-Oise, 'Description des œuvres', 15, 18, 54.
17. OM 10:167.
18. Nirodbaran, ed., *Talks,* vol. 1: 203.
19. Undated note by Wanda Morisset in MFP; Fort, 'Infant nursing', 124.
20. Romanet, 'Mise en nourrice'.
21. Morisset, 'Remembrances', 64.
22. *Fémina,* 15 June 1903.
23. Hoffmann, 'Comptes rendus des expositions', 757.
24. Bouyer, 'Henri Morisset', 155, 152, 145.
25. Vauxcelles, 'Notes d'art', 1; Méré, 'Questions d'art'; 'Causerie.'
26. Mirra signed the manuscript of her October 1906 story *Conte saphirin* (OM 2:10–15) 'M. Almyre'. In Mirra's artistic and esoteric milieu, people often formed pseudonyms by transforming or rearranging elements of their actual names, for example 'Éliphas Lévi' for Alphonse Louis (Constant) and 'F.Ch. Barlet' for Albert Faucheux (see Chapter 3 for both). The two syllables of 'Almyre' are the first syllables of Mirra and Alfassa in reverse order. Almyre is normally a forename. No one with the surname Almyre appears in the Paris Directories of 1905 or 1907. Apart from the 'M. Almyre' who wrote for *Les Tendances nouvelles,* no one with that surname appears in any online database of French books, journals or newspapers.
27. Almyre, 'Les Expositions', 66–68.

28. Hue, 'Le Groupe Idéa', 59–63.
29. Proceedings of the Groupe Idéa, 25 February–1 May 1905 (MAP).
30. Raimbault, 'Le Salon du Congrès d'Angers', 158.
31. *Les Tendances nouvelles,* nos 12–14 (September–November 1905).
32. *Gil Blas,* 1 July 1905: 1.
33. Vauxcelles, 'Le Salon des Indépendants', 1.
34. Almyre, 'Quelques réflexions', 78.
35. Forty-five years later, the Mother recounted this story as fact to a group of children (OM 4:328–30). She, of course, had no first-hand knowledge of the alleged incident. Presumably, she heard the story from an artist who disliked Matisse's art and was jealous of his success. It should be recalled that Mirra was the 'little sister' of the artists in Morisset's circle and therefore liable to take the story at face value. The 'palette-scrapings' gibe had been around for some time. A critic covering the first Impressionist exhibition (1874) called the furrows in Pissarro's *Ploughed Field,* now in the Pushkin Museum, 'palette-scrapings placed uniformly on a dirty canvas' (Louis Leroi, *Le Charivari,* 24 April 1874).
36. Compare Henri Morisset's remark that the paintings of Georges Rouault 'were not paintings but carpets' (Janine Panier to Gilles Guigan, 14 September 2007).
37. One of her paintings, *Coin de salon,* was included in a small exhibition held in Bordeaux in February 1907 (Société des amis des arts de Bordeaux, 'Compte-rendu', 11). Mirra did not necessarily attend this exhibition in person.
38. AM 3:299.
39. AM 2:217.
40. OM 6:333.
41. Chakravarti and Besant, *Conférences,* 3–15. *Conférences* includes a French translation of Chakravarti's talk. The original English text was published more than a decade later as Chakravarti, *Spirituality and Psychism.* I take my quotations from the English text, pp. 7–9. Chakravarti was a prominent member of the Theosophical Society. His speech was the first of five delivered during the Fourth Theosophical Congress in Paris on 24–28 June 1900 (Ransom, *Short History,* 336). The other four were delivered by Annie Besant. There is no evidence to suggest that Mirra was present at Besant's speeches.
42. OM 6:332; cf. Nirodbaran, *Talks,* vol. 2, 956.
43. CWM 13:39.

3: Cosmic Interlude

1. 'Avis' published in the front of every issue of the *Revue Cosmique* from January 1904 to December 1908; AM 2:218.
2. Letter Theon to Mirra Morisset, 15 January 1905, from unpublished correspondence (letters, postcards, telegrams) of the Theons to Mirra Alfassa (Morisset). I received permission from the holders to read this correspondence in order to prepare a précis for the use of historians but not to quote from it. In the notes that follow I will refer to the collection as 'Theons–Mirra Alfassa correspondence' (TMAC).
3. 'Éliphas Lévi' was Constant's attempt at Hebraizing his given names Alphonse Louis. His best-known work is *Dogme et rituel de la haute magie*, published in 1854.
4. The most important single source of this narrative is Pacscal Thémanlys, *Max Théon et la philosophie cosmique.* Most of what the Mother said about Theon's life before she met him follows the outlines of the established narrative.
5. See especially Chanel, *L'Œuvre de Max Théon*; Godwin, Chanel, and Deveney, *Hermetic Brotherhood*; Huss, 'Madame Théon'; Chajes and Huss, *The Cosmic Movement.* Following in the footsteps of these scholars, I uncovered a few additional documents. I discuss all this material in depth in Heehs, 'The Myth of the Theons' (2024).
6. Old Bailey records, 'Maximillian Binstein [*sic*]. Royal Offences: Coining Offences. 10th December 1877. Reference Number t18771210-81', available online at https://www.oldbaileyonline.org/browse.jsp?id=def1-81-18771210&div=t18771210-81#highlight. Among the many British newspapers that reported Bimstein's arrest were *Daily Telegraph & Courier*, 16 November 1877:3; *The Morning Post*, 17 November 1877:6; and *Lloyd's Weekly London Newspaper*, 18 November 1877:3.
7. Marriage no. 121, Register Office, Westminster, 21 March 1885, reproduced Godwin, Chanel, and Deveney, *Hermetic Brotherhood*, 294.
8. *The Era*, 6 September, 1884:8.
9. Una, *Sayings*, 7.
10. Jennings, ed., *Divine Pymander*, 112–13. The advertisement listed the contact person as 'Theosi'. An erratum on the next page corrected this to 'Theon'.
11. The Mother always referred to Theon as such and to his wife Mary Ware as Madame Theon. Louis and Claire Thémanlys, not knowing Mary's name, called her 'Alma' (Chanel, *L'Œuvre de Max Théon*, 215, 267). Claire

referred to her as such in her 1931 book *Un Séjour chez les grands initiés.* No one else ever called her by this fictitious name. The construction 'Alma Theon', found in many biographies and reference works, was invented by later writers and was never used by anyone before 1978, seventy years after her death.

12. Godwin, Chanel, and Deveney, *Hermetic Brotherhood,* 92–97.
13. Godwin, Chanel, and Deveney, *Hermetic Brotherhood,* 68–77.
14. Godwin, Chanel, and Deveney, *Hermetic Brotherhood,* 293–96; Chanel, *L'Œuvre de Max Théon,* 223.
15. Theon may have learnt something about Kabbalah in Warsaw, where it was an established part of Jewish life, but there is no such thing as 'initiation' in traditional Kabbalah (Boaz Huss, personal communication). The idea that initiation was of central importance to esoteric teachings was borrowed from Freemasonry.
16. Blavatsky was in Egypt between October–November 1871 and April 1872 (TenBroeck, 'Chronological Review') but there is no evidence to support a meeting between her and Theon. In 1871, the twenty-one-year-old Max Bimstein was just starting his career in the tobacco trade in London. His supposed meeting with Blavatsky clearly was invented by him or his followers to bolster his standing among people attracted to the Theosophical Society.
17. Warlick, *Max Ernst and Alchemy,* 23–24.
18. *Journal du magnétisme et de la psychologie,* 5 February 1899: 61–62.
19. *Journal du magnétisme et de la psychologie,* February to December 1899. All of the pieces were signed 'Max Théon'. Three were literary pieces that presumably were written by Madame Theon. The rest, more philosophical, were apparently written by Theon, but it may be assumed that both of them contributed to all ten pieces.
20. *Journal du magnétisme et de la psychologie,* 20 March 1899: 132.
21. *Journal du magnétisme et de la psychologie,* November 1899: 428.
22. Chanel, *L'Œuvre de Max Théon,* 409. 'F.-Ch.' comprises the two consonantal sounds of Faucheux. 'Barlet' is an anagram of Albert.
23. *L'Écho de l'au-delà et d'ici-bas,* 15 September 1900: 145–46.
24. RC 1 (1) (January 1901): 7. In the 1898 edition of his *Traité élémentaire de science occulte,* Papus reproduced a diagram consisting of two intersecting triangles created by 'our friend and master F.-Ch. Barlet' (Papus, *Traité élémentaire,* 52).
25. For details on the split between Barlet and Theon, see Chanel, *L'Œuvre de Max Théon,* 426–29, 444.

26. Chanel speculates that Theon used a new pseudonym so that people in Europe would not connect the editor of the *Revue* with Theon of the discredited H.B. of L. Otherwise, he continued to use the name Theon.
27. RC 3 (1) (January 1904): 1.
28. TMAC.
29. RC 4 (7) (July 1905): 428, 437–38.
30. Postcard to Mirra Alfassa, reproduced photographically in Sujata Nahar, *Mirra the Occultist,* 26. In the postcard, Madame Theon wrote 'transcription' and not 'translation'.
31. L. Thémanlys, *Exposé sur le mouvement cosmique* (quoted passages pp. 7, 8, 36).
32. Vauxcelles, 'La Vie artistique', 2.
33. OM 6:208–09.
34. AM 1:457–58.
35. C. Thémanlys, *Séjour,* 5; AM 2:72.
36. Theon, 'Le Portail du palais de l'art', in *Les Tendances Nouvelles* 2 (14) (30 November 1905): 210–12.
37. AM 2:337.
38. AM 2:71.
39. OM 9:68–70.
40. C. Thémanlys, *Séjour,* 26–28.
41. AM 2:416.
42. AM 12:269.
43. AM 5:62, AM 13:53.
44. Teresa diary (PTP).
45. In 1961, the Mother said that she had these visions when she began to work with Louis Thémanlys in Paris (AM 2:445). She met Thémanlys in Paris at the end of 1904. She published her accounts of the visions in the *Revue* between November 1906 and June 1907.
46. *Bulletin,* November 1982: 50–54.
47. *Bulletin,* August 1984, 20; cf. *Principes généraux,* 27.
48. AM 2:446.
49. An undated leaflet in the collection of Boaz Huss gives the meeting place of the Idéa group as 54 Rue Nicolo. This was the address of Louis Thémanlys. According to Louis's son Pascal Thémanlys, Idéa 'was created' by Louis and Mirra, both of whom were deeply involved in the Cosmic movement (information given by Pascal Thémanlys to Francis Bertaud). Theon took

great interest in Idéa (TMAC) and seems to have wanted to use it as a centre for the diffusion of Cosmic ideas.

50. OM 2:16-22. In her account, Mirra noted that this meeting with the unnamed revolutionary leader took place in January 1907.
51. TMAC.
52. Richard, *Without Passport*, 50–51.
53. Unpublished letter Paul Richard to friends, 11 March 1907.
54. Letter Aliana (Mirra Alfassa) to Claire Thémanlys, 25 April 1907 (PTP).
55. Teresa diary (PTP).

4: Pivotal Years

1. A sketch by the Mother, dated 14 November 1907, is of a bridge that looks somewhat like the one that crosses the Loire at Beaugency (*Paintings and Drawings*, p. 143, Figure 129.)
2. TMAC.
3. Jugement de divorce Morisset/Alfassa, 11 March 1908 (AVP cote DU 1489).
4. Laé, 'Le Pouvoir des corps et des mots: l'injure grave dans le divorce', citing A. Berthellot, *Excès, sévices et injures graves en matière de divorce* (1907).
5. Jugement de divorce.
6. 'Courage!', RC 8 (2) (February 1908): 75–79. In the French original, the masculine pronoun *il* agrees with the masculine nouns *travailleur* (worker) and *ami* (friend), and does not necessarily imply that the person in question is a man. In translating, I have used the feminine pronoun 'she'. Mirra incorporated a revised version of this essay in a talk she delivered in Paris on 21 April 1912 (OM 2:49–52).
7. TMAC.
8. A letter in TMAC shows that Theon once made a suggestion that Mirra found shameful. She told him she was not in the habit of doing shameful things. Years later, Sri Aurobindo (basing himself on information received from Mirra) remarked that Theon 'was poorly developed in the control of the vital plane', in other words, had a strong libido he felt no need to repress ('Some Talks', 349). 'Sex magic' was part of the programme of the H.B. of L., which Theon helped found in 1884 (Urban, *Magia Sexualis*, 79). Asher Binyamin reports that Pascal Thémanlys, the son of Louis and Claire, 'used to say that there was certainly a sexual aspect to the Cosmic Philosophy, but that the time to speak about it openly had not yet arrived' (Binyamin, 'Fidélité et Erreurs', 390–91). Louise Duban, who was closely

associated with Theon during the 1920s, wrote of his efforts to find 'sensitives' who were open to sexual practices. One young woman with whom he formed a relationship left him because she 'did not feel any desire to play the Avishag'. (In the Bible, Avishag or Abishag was a young woman chosen to lie next to the aged King David in order to pass her vitality on to him.) (Duban, quoted in Binyamin, 'Fidélité et erreurs', 389–90).

9. TMAC.
10. RC 8 (4):199. Like all other pieces in the *Revue,* this one was unsigned.
11. Pascal Thémanlys wrote that Madame Theon 'wished to make a trip to the Island of Jersey by herself' (P. Thémanlys, *Max Théon,* 29). According to Jackie Semenoff, daughter-in-law of Marc Semenoff and Denise Semenoff (Claire Thémanlys's younger sister), Madame Theon decided to leave Courseulles because she had discovered that Theon was carrying on with yet another young woman. (Information given by Jackie Semenoff to Patrice Ghirardi in 1989 and conveyed by Ghirardi to me via email in 2021.)
12. *Jersey Evening Post,* 11 September 1908: 1; 12 September 1908:2. Death certificate reproduced in Huss, 'Madame Théon', 236.
13. RC 8 (12) (December 1908): 757–61. Some writers have ascribed this essay to Mirra. It certainly was not written by her.
14. According to information given by Janine Panier, a daughter of André Morisset, to Francis Bertaud and Gilles Guigan, the friend was Jeanne Lombard, a sister of Marie Thérèse Lombard, who, after marrying Boleslas Wilczynski, gave birth in 1905 to Wanda Wilczynski, who, in 1923, would marry Mirra's son, André.
15. Richard, *Without Passport,* 53.
16. Richard, *Without Passport,* 75–76.
17. AM 9:25–26.
18. AM 3:299.
19. AM 2:404; Richard, *Without Passport,* 54; Bosc, review, 191.
20. OM 2:23–24.
21. Richard, *Without Passport,* 55–56.
22. CWSA 35:28.
23. AM 2:446.
24. Richard, *Without Passport,* 52.
25. OM 10:107.
26. Personal communication from Janine Panier to author.

27. In all likelihood, the talk that Mirra heard was the one David-Neel delivered at the Hôtel des Sociétés Savantes on Saturday, 17 December 1910 (announced in the *Aurore* and other Paris newspapers on 16 December). This seems to be the only talk on Buddhism David-Neel gave in Paris at that time. Her first meeting with the Richards was on Monday, 19 December 1910.
28. David-Neel, 'Le Cult et les croyances', 76; David-Neel, 'Quelques écrivains', 638.
29. AM 7:267.
30. David-Neel diary, 19 December 1910 (MADN).
31. When David-Neel added her husband's name to hers, she dropped the accent over the e.
32. David-Neel, *Modernisme bouddhiste*, 91, 151.
33. MADN: Diary; Letter Marie Madeline Peyronnet to Francis Bertaud, 3 March 1986; David-Neel, *L'Inde où j'ai vécu*, 232.
34. David-Neel, *Journal de voyage*, 69.
35. David-Neel, *Journal de voyage*, 126–27, 174–75; David-Neel diary 27 September 1912 (MADN); David-Neel, *Auprès du Dalaï-Lama*, 468–76.
36. Hélène Richard, cited in Richard, *Without Passport*, 101.
37. Postcard Mirra Richard to Johannes Hohlenberg, reproduced A&R 13 (1) (April 1989): 80.
38. Postcard Mirra Richard to Alexandra David-Neel, reproduced A&R 13 (1): 82.
39. Morisset, *Remembrances*, 64–65.
40. Préfecture de la Seine, *Recueil des actes administratifs de l'année 1913*, 3 (March): 208. Lydie Martial was the pen name of Anna Carnaud (1861–1929), who founded the Union de Pensée Féminine in 1902 and the École de la Pensée at roughly the same time.
41. OM 2:92.
42. OM 2:28–29.
43. OM 2:64–67.
44. OM 2:55.
45. OM 2:79.
46. OM 1:1, 4, 9, 14 (translations by Sri Aurobindo CWM 1:1, 4, 8, 13).
47. Bertaud, 'Marie Potel', 1–3, citing Diary of Marie Potel, 166–73.
48. Bertaud, 'Marie Potel', 4–5, citing Diary of Marie Potel, 166–73.
49. Bertaud, 'Marie Potel', 5, citing Diary of Marie Potel, 173; Diary of Marie Potel, 71.

50. Bertaud, 'Marie Potel', 6–8.
51. *Gil Blas* 25 October 1912: 4; *Comœdia* 18 December 1912; Keesing 77–78.
52. OM 5:61.
53. Jasion, *'Abdu'l-Bahá en* France, 384–385.
54. AM 8:61. In all likelihood, the meeting in question was held on 17 March 1913 (Jasion, *'Abdu'l-Bahá en France,* 488).
55. Jasion, *'Abdu'l-Bahá en France,* 583–601.
56. Tablet dated 6 July 1913, in Sohrab, *'Abdul-Baha in Egypt,* 31; Bahá'i Archives: Tablet to Paul Richard, March 1914.
57. OM 2:124,115.
58. OM 7:66; AM 2:294.
59. AM 6:127-28. The Mother did not give the title of the novel she referred to, but the only one published in *Le Matin* between 1905 and 1915 that at all matches her description was *L'Amant de la momie: grand roman psychique inédite* by Antoine Wylm (pseudonym of Joseph Maxwell). It was serialized in *Le Matin* between 24 October and 6 December 1912. She was in Paris at that time and certainly would not have missed this 'psychic novel' that dealt with the 'science of the occult' (Wylm, *Amant de la momie, préface,* in *Le Matin,* 24 October 1912:2).
60. Jasion, *Quelques rencontres,* 14; *Le Temps,* 19 July 1913: 3.
61. Richard, *Without Passport,* 54; *Les Dieux,* 204.
62. Richard, *Without Passport,* 62.
63. AM 1:169. In this conversation, the Mother dated the 'reversal' to 1910. It should be recalled she often said that she could not remember dates.
64. OM 1:34–35.
65. OM 1:47; Banerji, 'Some Notes,' 577.
66. OM 1:51.
67. Richard, *Without Passport,* 60; AM 10:25–26. In her version, the Mother places the incident in 1914, which almost certainly is wrong.
68. CWSA 36:283–84,177–78.
69. CWSA 36:204.
70. OM 1:95, 97.
71. OM 1:107.
72. OM 8:167–68.
73. OM 8:168–69.
74. OM 1:111.

5: India and After

1. CWSA 10:421–22; OM 1:124. In some of her prayers to the Divine, Mirra used *nous* (we) to mean the whole of humanity, of which she felt herself to be the representative. In this passage, however, she clearly was referring to the two people who saw Aurobindo in his room.
2. AM 2:446-47 (trans. cf. MA 2:405).
3. In her account of 1961, the Mother provided an explanation for Richard's absence: '. . . there was something in me that wanted to meet Sri Aurobindo, the first time, alone. Richard went to see him in the morning and I had an appointment for the afternoon' (AM 2:446). This is not in agreement with Aurobindo's and her diary entries, which were written immediately after the event. It is clear from Aurobindo's entry of 29 March that he saw no one that morning and saw 'R', that is Richard, in the afternoon (CWSA 10:422). In an entry of 30 March, he again mentioned Richard's visit on the afternoon of 29 March. This second entry makes it clear that neither of the Richards had an appointment on 29 March: They had arranged to come on 28 March, but arrived a day later (CWSA 10:423). Aurobindo did not mention Mirra in either entry but it is obvious she went with her husband on 29 March. Her diary entry of 30 March makes it clear that she and Paul saw Aurobindo the previous day. Someone anxious to preserve the Mother's solitary first meeting with Aurobindo on 29 March might speculate that she went on the morning of 29 March, while Paul went alone in the afternoon. This would imply: (1) that Aurobindo did not think the presumed meeting with the Mother on the morning of 29 March was worth recording in his diary; (2) that Mirra, after an exhausting journey, decided to go alone to meet Aurobindo immediately after she and Paul had checked in at the hotel, without resting or freshening up, (3) that she, a European woman on her second day in India, walked or took a rickshaw across a strange town without anyone to accompany her and knocked on the door of a man she had never met, saying that Paul, whom Aurobindo was expecting, was otherwise occupied, but she would like to meet him herself.
4. CWM 13:39; Roy, 'Notes [I]', 48; Roy, 'Notes' [II], 65; Ventakataraman, 'My Diary Leaves', 367; AM 2:447.
5. OM 1:124.
6. CWSA 10:560; CWSA 36:195.
7. Gupta, *Reminiscences*, 89; Amrita in Sethna, *Our Light and Delight*, 7; Barin Ghose cited in Mrityunjoy, 'A Look Behind', 65.
8. AM 3:305–06.

9. AM 3:305–06; *Bulletin* 37 (1) (February 1985): 24 (the year 1934 on this page is a typographical error for 1914; the date is given correctly on page 25).
10. Pandit, *Mother and I*, 127–28.
11. Winnacker, 'Elections in Algeria and the French Colonies', 273.
12. OM 1:136, 139.
13. *Journal officiel des Établissements Français dans l'Inde*, 28 April 1914, reproduced in A&R 13 (1) (April 1989):100–01.
14. OM 1:144.
15. CWSA 13:442–43. This is Aurobindo's 'psychological' explanation of the term. Historically, ārya was the self-designation of speakers of the Indo-Iranian languages, a branch of the Indo-European language family.
16. Richard, *Without Passport*, 67–68.
17. CWSA 10:582; OM 1:235.
18. AM 3:355–56 (trans. cf. MA 3:335); OM 1:127.
19. Banerji, 'Some Notes' (May 1979), 269.
20. OM 1:226.
21. AM 3:183–84; cf. Ventakaraman, 'My Diary Leaves', 365–66.
22. OM 1:319.
23. Roy, 'Notes' [II], 72; AM 2:407.
24. Richard, *Without Passport*, 71.
25. OM 1:324, 326.
26. AM 6:277; AM 5:90.

6: Exile

1. OM 1:329; Banerji, 'Notes' (March 1979), 146; Roy, 'Notes [I]' (1976), 48.
2. OM 2:149–50.
3. Richard, *Without Passport*, 74. When the Mother spoke about Paul's ailment years later, she expressed some doubt about its genuineness (AM 2:407).
4. Morisset, 'Remembrances', 65.
5. CWSA 36:285–86.
6. OM 2:150.
7. OM 1:338, 342–43 (translation by Sri Aurobindo CWM 1:311–12); CWSA 36:288.
8. Richard, *Without Passport*, 75–77.

9. AM 3:55 *La Révolte des anges* was published in the beginning of 1914.
10. OM 4:355–56. De Fontenay was killed on 10 January 1916. His death was announced in *Le Gaulois* on 19 January and in other Paris papers a day or two later.
11. Richard, *Without Passport*, 79.
12. AM 2:407. A letter authorizing Richard to act as a trade representative is reproduced in A&R 18 (2) (December 1994): 238.
13. Richard, *Without Passport*, 79; *La Lanterne*, 27 March 1916.
14. *Star of the West* 7 (5) (June 1916): 40; Alexander, *History of the Bahá'í Faith*, 20.
15. Alexander, *History of the Bahá'í Faith*, 20. Richard, *Without Passport*, 80–82. It is unclear whether the Richards disembarked at Alexander's suggestion or had already decided to get off at Kobe rather than continuing on to Yokohama.
16. Alexander, *History of the Bahá'í Faith*, 20.
17. OM 1:348–49.
18. Alexander, *History of the Bahá'í Faith*, 20.
19. Krämer, 'Euro-Asian Political Activist', 330.
20. Tagore, *Message of India to Japan*, 11–12; Tagore in Hay, *Asian Ideas*, 66.
21. Rolland in *Inde: Journal*, 48-49; cf. Hay, *Asian Ideas*, 126.
22. Mitra, *Liberator*, 175.
23. Richard, *Without Passport*, 86; Purani, *Talks*, 610.
24. CWM 2:147–50.
25. Krämer, 'Euro-Asian Political Activist', 337, note 14; Okawa in Gokak, 'Three Prose Poems', 168.
26. Popplewell, *Intelligence and Imperial Defence*, 278.
27. 'Eiryō Indo No Bu Kakumeitō Kankei (Bōmeisha O Fukumu)' [British India: involving revolutionaries (including those in exile)], a contemporary document from the Diplomatic Archives of the Ministry of Foreign Affairs of Japan, cited by Krämer, 'Euro-Asian Political Activist', 320.
28. OM 1:361. In 1953, the Mother explained to a follower that this passage referred to her inability to go to India on account of 'the misguided zeal of a British ambassador' (Banerji, 'Some Notes' [May 1979], 268).
29. OM 1:365–66.
30. *Japan Gazette*, 8 September 1916.
31. *Japan Gazette*, 31 January 1917; Richard, *Without Passport*, 85.
32. Tagore, introduction to Richard, *To the Nations*, vii–xv.
33. Richard, *To the Nations*, 4, 22.

34. *Japan Chronicle* (Kobe), weekly edition, 8 February 1917. Date of photograph given in WhatsApp message Toshio Akai to Chhalamayi Reddy, 28 February 2020, cited in C. Reddy, 'Voyage Miraculous', 27. Paul Richard's account of the trip in *Without Passport* (86–87) contains several errors but I have made use of it to reconstruct the sequence of events.
35. *Seiza* means 'sitting', in particular sitting on the heels in traditional Japanese style. In English writings, the Okada technique of *seiza* is known as quiet-sitting, still-sitting or silent-sitting.
36. Wu, 'Straighten the Back to Sit'; Teo, 'Okada Torajiro'.
37. Gokak, 'Interviews in Japan', 236.
38. *Japan Chronicle* (Kobe), weekly edition, 8 February 1917.
39. Mukhopadhyaya, *Rabindrajibani*, vol. 2, 432.
40. Richard, *Au Japon/ To Japan*, passages reproduced in Satomi, *Japanese Civilization*, 204, and in Saaler and Szpilman, eds., *Pan-Asianism*: 238–39; Richard, *Without Passport*, 90–91; Cousins, *New Japan*, 152; Government of India, Political Proceedings-B, July 1917, nos 426–30, reproduced in A&R 18 (2) (December 1994): 239.
41. Richard, 'Introduction', vii; Nauriya, 'Willie Pearson', 30–34.
42. Richard, 'Introduction', vii.
43. *Modern Review* 23, 1 (January 1918): 69–70. Mirra had no direct contact with the editors of *The Modern Review*. The journal gave considerable coverage to Tagore and the members of his circle, Pearson among them.
44. CWM 2:152–54.
45. OM 1:403 (translation by Sri Aurobindo CWM 1:368).
46. OM 1:404-05 (translation by Sri Aurobindo CWM 1:369).
47. OM 1:399 (translation by Sri Aurobindo CWM 1:364).
48. Letters Mirra Richard to Nobuko Kobayashi, 1 November 1917, and 13 November 1917, copy provided by Toshio Akai.
49. Gokak, 'Three Prose Poems', 165.
50. OM 6:344–46.
51. Richard, *Lord of the Nations*, x, 48, 108.
52. Shumei Okawa, 'A Sage, Aurobindo Ghose,' *Asia Jiron*, August 1918, and Government of India Political Proceedings-B, December 1918, nos 158–59, both reproduced, the former in English translation, in A&R 18 (2): 240–42.
53. *The Mother: Paintings and Drawings*, Plate 41 (p. 48 and note on p. 171).
54. *The Mother: Paintings and Drawings*, Figure 25 (p. 60).
55. OM 1:411.

56. Paul Richard, draft letter circa January 1919, reproduced in French and English translation in A&R 18 (2): 239; letter Mirra Richard to Nobuko Kobayashi, 16 January 1919.
57. Richard, *Without Passport*, 91.
58. Gokak, 'Three Prose Poems', 168.
59. 'Appendix: League for the Equality of Races', reproduced in Richard, *Dawn over Asia*, 90–91.
60. Richard said in his memoirs: 'We put together a declaration of racial equality which was sent to Woodrow Wilson at the Peace Conference in Paris' (*Without Passport*, 90). Richard's name is not mentioned in any account I have read about the drafting of the amendment but Okawa and other members of the Black Dragon Society certainly were involved (see Shimazu, *Japan, Race, and Equality*, 177), and they may have consulted Richard. Cf. Kuzuu, 'Farewell,' 282.
61. Richard, *Without Passport*, 91.
62. Letter Challaye to the Mother, 6 June 1950.
63. Richard, *Dawn over Asia*, 18, 6, 19–20.
64. Letter Mirra Richard to Nobuko Kobayashi, 17 May 1919.
65. OM 4:342.
66. Cousins, *The New Japan*, 86–88.
67. Cousins, *The New Japan*, 151.
68. Richard, *Without Passport*, 93.
69. OM 1:412 (translation by Sri Aurobindo CWM 1:377). Many years later, the Mother gave an entirely spiritual interpretation to this prayer, with no reference to the physical circumstances (CWM 15:221). Speaking about the incident in 1961, she seems to have conflated three memories. The setting, she said, was 'a Japanese country-house where we were living, near a lake'. This would be the Okakura house near Lake Nojiri, where she and Paul stayed in the summer of 1917, and not Oiwake, where she was when the incident took place. The time (just before the departure from Japan) and Paul's refusal correspond to the experience recorded in the diary on 3 September 1919. The response of the Lord, in particular his taking her in his arms, seems to refer to an experience recorded in the diary on 10 October 1918 (OM 1:411).
70. AM 2:448.
71. Kuzuu, 'Farewell', 281–283.
72. Cousins, *New Japan*, 270–72; Cousins and Cousins, *We Two Together*, 351. In the war crimes tribunal that followed Japan's defeat in the Second

World War, twenty-eight men were indicted as Class A War Criminals. The only one who was not a government official or military officer was Shumei Okawa, who distinguished himself between 1920 and 1945 as a propagandist for the militant Japanese state (the Western press called him the Goebbels of Japan). The case against him was dismissed after he convinced the judges that he was insane.

73. Richard, 'Democracy', *Asian Review* 1.3 (April 1920): 275.
74. CWM 2:157–68. The essay was first published in the *Asian Review* in March 1920.
75. Cousins, *New Japan*, 294. In a talk of 1953, the Mother said she caught the Spanish flu in Tokyo in January 1919 (OM 5:199). The month is probably right, the year certainly is wrong. Paul Richard wrote that he and Mirra caught the flu sometime after they returned from Oiwake at the end of 1919 (*Without Passport*, 93). There is nothing in Mirra's letter to Nobuko Kobayashi dated 16 January 1919, or in her letter concerning the house situation of February 1919, or in other letters of that year, to suggest that she was or had been ill. There were comparatively few cases of influenza in Tokyo in January 1919. On the other hand, January 1920 was the month when Tokyo had the maximum number of cases and the people were most consumed by fear (Hayami, *Influenza Pandemic in Japan*, 96–97, 115, 118). Paul Richard, in an article published in April 1920, mentioned the surge of influenza in January 1920 that affected 5,00,000 people in Tokyo (*Journal des débats*, 4 April 1920).
76. Hayami, *Influenza Pandemic in Japan*, 96.
77. OM 5:199–201.
78. Hayami, *Influenza Pandemic in Japan*, 112. Akira gives the total in Japan as 4,53,152. For worldwide figures, see Center for Disease Control, '1918 Pandemic (H1N1 virus)', available online at https://www.cdc.gov/flu/pandemic-resources/1918-pandemic-h1n1.html.
79. Richard, *Without Passport*, 93.
80. CWM 2:170.
81. Richard, *Without Passport*, 95–96. In 1961, the Mother mentioned that the Japanese government intervened with the British on their behalf (AM 2:407). Richard did not mention this in his account.
82. OM 4:339–40.
83. The *Ganges Maru* was the only ship departing from Kobe that arrived in Colombo in mid-April 1920 (*Lloyds List*, via librarian, Guildhall Library, London, 10 December 1986).

84. Letter Governor of French India to Colonial Ministry, Paris, 3 June 1920 (ANOM), reproduced in A&R 18 (2) (December 1994): 242; Cousins and Cousins, *We Two Together*, 369, 380.
85. The *Dupleix*, coincidentally the same ship that brought Aurobindo from Calcutta to Pondicherry in 1910, left Colombo on 22 April and reached Pondicherry at 8.30 on 24 April; OM 4:247, 253.

7: Return

1. Letter Governor of French India to Colonial Ministry, Paris, 3 June 1920 (ANOM), reproduced in A&R 18 (2) (December 1994): 242.
2. Gupta, *Reminiscences*, 75; CWSA 36:245.
3. AM 2:447
4. Roy, ed., *Sri Aurobindo's Talks of 1926*, 160.
5. CWSA 36:245.
6. Letter Aurobindo Ghose to Barindra Kumar Ghose, circa April 1920, reproduced in Bengali and English translation in A&R 4 (1):17, 21.
7. CWM 13:39. The piece was published in the *Ashar* 30, 1327, issue of *Prabartak*. This corresponds to 14 July 1920.
8. Barindra Kumar Ghose, unpublished memoir, quoted in Heehs, *Lives*, 323.
9. OM 1:413 (translation by Sri Aurobindo CWM 1:378).
10. Heehs, *Lives*, 326–27; AM 2:409.
11. There are three accounts of the shifting: One by Mirra, in a letter of 18 December 1920 to her mother, in which she mentions the move as something that happened more than a week earlier; one by Barin Ghose, who apparently was in Pondicherry at the time but provided no dating information; and one by Nolini Kanta Gupta (*Reminiscences*, 75), who apparently was not there at the time (see Purani, *Life*, 174) and gave no dating information. In *The Life of Sri Aurobindo*, first published in 1958, A.B. Purani, who was not in Pondicherry at the time, writes that the shifting took place on 24 November. This has become the accepted date of the event but its accuracy is doubtful. There is no reason to believe that anyone noted down the date when the shifting took place. It is probable that Purani or his informant or both were influenced by a love for numerical coincidences: 24 November 1926 was the date of a spiritual experience described at the end of this chapter. Purani made much of this retrospective 'coincidence' in his book (Purani, *Life*, 174). See also, footnote 38 below.
12. *Standard Bearer* 1 (19) (January 1921): 1.

13. Rolland, *Inde*, 24.
14. CWSA 36:177–78.
15. OM 2:55.
16. Barindra Kumar Ghose, unpublished memoirs.
17. Letter Mirra Alfassa to Nobuko Kobayashi, 7 October 1922, copy provided by Toshio Akai.
18. Purani, *Life*, 174.
19. Cousins and Cousins, *We Two Together*, 394.
20. Purani, *Life*, 296–97.
21. Letter Mirra Alfassa to Nobuko Kobayashi, 15 January 1923, copy provided by Toshio Akai.
22. Purani, *Life*, 185; AM 2:417; Rolland, *Inde*, 42.
23. Purani, Life, 189–90.
24. Purani, *Life*, 191–92.
25. Purani, ed., *Talks*, 525.
26. CWSA 36:362–63.
27. Purani, *Life*, 211–12
28. CWSA 36:329–30
29. Purani, ed., *Talks*, 132–35.
30. CWM 14:125.
31. Cf. Theon, *Journal du magnétisme et de la psychologie*, 5 February 1899: 61–62.
32. CWSA 25:8.
33. Purani, ed. *Talks*, 349–50.
34. CWSA 32:81–82.
35. Purani, ed., *Talks*, 541–42.
36. Saint-Hilaire, ed., *Conversations avec Sri Aurobindo*, 141.
37. Purani, *Life*, 213–21; Jaya Devi, 'At the Feet', 624.
38. Purani, *Life*, 217. There are five or six accounts of what Dorothy said. They differ in the details but have the same overall sense. Purani states that precisely twenty-four sadhaks were present. This number is certainly wrong. The only sadhak who left a contemporary account of the event, Haradhan Bakshi, is not on Purani's list. Neither are Marie Potel and her husband, Léon, who were in Pondicherry at the time. In saying that there were precisely twenty-four sadhaks on 24 November, Purani apparently was swayed by numerological considerations.
39. Diary of Haradhan Bakshi, quoted in Heehs, *Lives*, 345.

40. CWSA 36:270–71; CWSA 11:1272. Sri Aurobindo first used 'Overmind' in his diary on 29 October 1927. At that time, he used it in a different way from how he used it in later works such as *Letters on Yoga* and *The Life Divine.*
41. CWSA 36:441. On 6 May 1927, an article by Jatindranath Sen Gupta entitled 'Sri Aurobindo's Ashram' was published in *The Hindu,* a Madras newspaper. Sri Aurobindo wrote a paragraph for insertion in this article in which he referred to the community as an 'Ashrama' (CWSA 36:529).

8: The Mother's Creation

1. CWSA 32:3,14. Perhaps the first time Sri Aurobindo said in writing that the Mother of the ashram (that is, Mirra Alfassa) was the Divine Mother was by replying 'Yes' to a question posed by a disciple in 1938: 'Do you not refer to the Mother (our Mother) in your book *The Mother*?' (CWSA 32:31). But the identification was clear to most from the time the book *The Mother* was published.
2. CWSA 32:83.
3. OM 17:3.
4. OM 17:3.
5. Pandit, ed., *Champaklal Speaks,* 29; CWSA 32:568.
6. CWSA 35:331; OM 9:165–66. In this passage, the Mother put her dialogue with Sri Aurobindo in dramatic form without trying to reproduce his exact words.
7. Sen Gupta, 'Sri Aurobindo's Ashram'. Sen Gupta was a friend of Anilbaran Roy, a disciple, and most of the information in the article, and probably much of the wording, came from Anilbaran and other members of the ashram.
8. In letters written to her mother and to Matteo after November 1926, Mirra spelled her forename 'Mira'. To avoid confusion I retain the former spelling. The orthographic change had no affect on her legal name, which, in accordance with French convention, remained Mirra Alfassa or in full Blanche Rachel Mirra Alfassa throughout her life.
9. Daughton, *In the Forest,* 264, 8.
10. Gide quoted in Daughton, *In the Forest,* 78.
11. Letter Matteo Alfassa to Mirra Alfassa, 3 May 1927 (MFP).
12. OM 1:414.
13. CWSA 11:1246–56, 1345–48.
14. CWSA 35:331.

15. OM 17:4.
16. Letters Matteo Alfassa to Mirra Alfassa, 6 September 1927 and 30 December 1927.
17. Letter Matteo Alfassa to Mirra Alfassa, 17 May 1928 (in which Matteo quotes a passage from a letter of Mirra to him dated 25 October [1927]).
18. Vasudha, 'A Talk' [II], 639.
19. Letter Dorothy Hodgson to unnamed friend living in Japan, 23 January 1928. Collection of Roma Hira.
20. CWSA 36:532–33.
21. Tagore, 'Aurobindo Ghose', 60.
22. Lévi had met Tagore a few days earlier in Calcutta and apparently learnt from him of his meeting with Aurobindo. Lévi's own meeting with him took place on 4 August 1927.
23. Venkataraman, 'My Diary Leaves', 363–64.
24. Chaumel, *Premier contact*, 181; OM 14:407–08.
25. Rolland, *La Vie de Vivekananda,* 191. The essay containing this passage first appeared in the monthly review *Europe* in December 1928.
26. 'Madame Morin at Pondicherry'.
27. Magre, *À la Poursuite de la sagesse*, 99, 114.
28. Orban, *Valentine Penrose*, 98–99.
29. Bose, *Selected Speeches*, 47.
30. Roy, 'Notes from a Sadhak's Diary [II]', 58–59; OM 1:415.
31. CWM 3:7.
32. CWM 3:79–80.
33. Rolland, *Inde*, 349; AM 2:405.
34. CWM 3:156–57.
35. OM 17:5.
36. CWSA 32:42.
37. OM 1:416 (translation by Sri Aurobindo CWM 1:381.)
38. CWSA 32:47, 376.
39. Lallubhai Patel, in R. Reddy, 'Evening Meditations', 30.
40. CWM 14:41, 247; 15:269; 16:18; 13:169.
41. CWSA 28:355,84; CWM 3:24,62–63.
42. C. Thémanlys, *Premiers pas*, 53–54.
43. *La Tradition Cosmique*, Tome IV, *Les Chroniques de Chi*, available online at https://incarnateword.in/reference/la-tradition-cosmique-tome-iv-chroniques-de-chi.

44. CWM 3:63.
45. CWSA 28:114. When asked to suggest a Sanskrit equivalent of 'psychic being' Sri Aurobindo proposed *caitya puruṣa* (CWSA 28:62), a term used first in medieval Sanskrit literature, centuries after the Upanishads and other classic Vedantic texts were written.
46. CWSA 35:152.
47. Grégoire, 'Voyage d'un touriste prolétaire', 14.
48. Letter Matteo Alfassa to Mirra Alfassa, 2 June 1929 (MFP).
49. Letter Matteo Alfassa to Mirra Alfassa, 19 February 1934 (MFP).
50. CWSA 36:530; CWSA 35:31.
51. *Étoile de l'AEF* (19 July 1934): 6.
52. See, for example, reports quoted by Martínez, 'Unwanted Scraps', 92, and Daughton, *In the Forest*, 235. In an email to me of 24 September 2021, Daughton wrote: 'Antonetti was such a dominant figure that Alfassa, at least during the period of the construction, played a somewhat obscured role.'
53. AM 10:25, AM 8:180–81
54. See, for example, Vir Gupta and Mueller, 'Golconde'.
55. OM 6:331.
56. CWSA 32:530.
57. CWSA 32:549–50.
58. AM 11:370
59. CWSA 32:596, 659.
60. Monod-Herzen, 'Feeling of Certitude', 706–07.
61. Nirodbaran, 'Talk on Pavitra', 699.
62. CWM 3:25,129; CWSA 35:812.
63. CWSA 35:211.
64. OM 17:10.
65. Nirodbaran, *Twelve Years,* 3–7.
66. Nirodbaran, *Twelve Years,* 7–10, 18.

9: The Ashram and the World

1. Nirodbaran, *Twelve Years,* 11.
2. Nirodbaran, *Twelve Years,* 22.
3. Purani, ed., *Talks,* 571–77.
4. CWSA 36:66.

5. MCW 13:120.
6. CWSA 36:453,463–64.
7. On 25 May 2022, Kalya Lemaire, grandson of André Morisset, told me that Matteo and Mathilde were not harassed by the Vichy government. Neither had to wear the yellow star. André, with his Christian-sounding names, was never taken to be the son of a Jew. Still, when he had to travel from Paris to his factory in Lyon, passing through border controls, he felt a certain amount of anxiety.
8. Klarsfeld and Stroweis, *Le mémorial de la déportation des juifs de France* (search 'Alfassa').
9. Letter British Consul-General, Pondicherry, to Secretary, External Affairs Department, Government of India, 13 July 1940. Collection of Claude Arpi.
10. Nirodbaran, ed., *Talks*, vol. 2, 641.
11. Nirodbaran, ed., *Talks*, vol. 2, 997–98.
12. CWM 13:120–21.
13. *Messages of Sri Aurobindo and the Mother*, Second Series, 6–7.
14. Nirodbaran, *Twelve Years*, 108–15.
15. Nirodbaran, *Twelve Years*, 118.
16. Sarkar, *The Ashram School*, 4–10; Sarkar, *Memorable Years*, vol. 1, 7–10.
17. Sarkar, *Memorable Years*, vol. 1, 13–33; Nirodbaran, *Twelve Years*, 119–20.
18. OM 5:315-16; OM 6:330.
19. Pandit, ed., *Champaklal Speaks*, 54–55; CWSA 32:581.
20. CWSA 35:201–02.
21. CWM 15:44–45.
22. See 'The Mother playing tennis at the Tennis Ground of Sri Aurobindo Ashram, Pondicherry', video available on YouTube at https://www.youtube.com/watch?v=SVyuRP0MuHA.
23. Sarkar, *Memorable Years*, vol. 1: 57.
24. CWSA 35:776–77.
25. CWSA 13:517.
26. OM 12:219.
27. OM 12:5–11.
28. CWM 13:351.
29. Baron quoted in Namakkal, 'Goonda Raj', 11.
30. Appendix to letter Baron to Ministry of Colonies, May 1947 (ANOM via Ajit Neogy).

31. CWSA 36:480-491; Saint Hilaire, *Itinéraire*, 212.
32. Record of meeting between Jawaharlal Nehru, Baron and Henry-Paul Roux (French Chargé d'affairs in India), 27 May 1947, quoted in Arpi, *The Last Months*, 15–16.
33. CWM 13:352.
34. CWSA 36:491–92.
35. Agence France-Presse, press release, 27 September 1947; Schumann, 'Une dette politique', 4–8.
36. Pandit, ed., *Champaklal Speaks*, 91, 93; Morisset, 'A Visit', 264–65.
37. OM 12:397–416.
38. Morisset, 'A Visit', 265.
39. Nirodbaran, *Twelve Years*, 124.
40. Ganguli, 'Pondicherry's Mystic'; Vijayatunga, 'Sri Aurobindo Darshan'; '"Mystery" of Aurobindo's Ashram'; Sheean, 'Kings of the Yogis', 78–79.
41. Cartier-Bresson, notes on visit to Sri Aurobindo Ashram from archives of Magnum Photos, reproduced in 'The Last Photographs of Sri Aurobindo', 208–09.
42. OM 12:87–89.
43. CWM 12:120.
44. Nirodbaran, *Twelve Years*, 275.
45. Sanyal, 'A "Call"', 180–89.
46. CWM 13:7.

10: Alone

1. CWM 13:7.
2. AM 5:107, AM 3:23–24, 459.
3. CWM 13:6.
4. AM 13:331; CWM 13:50.
5. Nirodbaran, *Memorable Contacts*, 48.
6. OM 4:1–2.
7. OM 4:72–73.
8. OM 4:195.
9. OM 4:46,255, 259–60. The twelve senses are listed and explained in C. Thémanlys, *Premiers pas*, 16–17.
10. OM 4:175–76.
11. OM 4:44.

12. CWM 13:8–9.
13. OM 4:9.
14. CWM 12:111. Press release published in *Amrita Bazar Patrika,* 11 January 1951 (datelined 9 January), and subsequently in many other Indian newspapers. Recent purchase of houses mentioned in unsigned document dated 21 March 1951 (ANOM: Fonds local Inde G27, collection of Ajit Neogy).
15. CWM 12:111.
16. CWM 12:112.
17. *Amrita Bazar Patrika,* 25 April 1951.
18. *Sunday Indian Nation,* 22 April 1951.
19. Letter Ménard to Ministre de la France d'Outre-Mer, 19 May 1951. Cf. Letter Ramadier to Ministre F.O.M., 13 May 1951; reply Ménard to Ramadier, 3 July 1951 (ANOM: Fonds local Inde G27, collection of Ajit Neogy).
20. CWM 12:93.
21. Munshi, 'Aurobindo Ashram'.
22. Munshi, 'Aurobindo Ashram'.
23. OM 5:36.
24. OM 5:270.
25. CWM 15:194; OM 14:84.
26. Nehru, *Selected Works,* series 2, vol. 20, 530–31.
27. Landy to Ostroróg, 2 September 1954 (ANOM: cote Inde E32, collection of Ajit Neogy).
28. Ibid.
29. OM 12:103–04. Because the English translation of this text from the *Bulletin* (CWM 12:93–94) has been reproduced so often, I have not retranslated it from the original French; Enginger, 'Pondichéry doit demurer . . .'
30. Press Trust of India, 'Portuguese Should Follow Example of France'.
31. Nehru, *Selected Works,* series 2, vol. 27, 234–38.
32. CWSA 36:484.
33. OM 12:92–98.
34. This motto began to appear on the cover of the *Revue Cosmique* in January 1904, the month the Theons took up the editing of the journal.
35. *Principes généraux,* 21; RC 4 (7) (July 1905): 388–91.
36. See Heehs, 'Sri Aurobindo's Theory of Spiritual Evolution', 169–79.

37. CWSA 28:275.
38. OM 16:308–09; CWM 13:7.
39. OM 16:309–10.
40. CWSA 13:553.
41. CWSA 35:368.
42. CWSA 13:590.
43. CWM 15:91.
44. OM 14:84.
45. CWM 15:94. I cite the widely circulated English version. The text was first made public when it was distributed as a message on 29 February 1960. It was dated '29 February 1956/During the common meditation of Wednesday' and apparently was written on the evening of that day, although the facsimile distributed four years later (CWM 13:95) has the look of a fair copy written especially for the purpose.
46. Sethna, 'Some Diary Notes', 197.
47. CWM 15: 96 (first published in the *Bulletin*, April 1956, p. 67); cf. CWM 1:252.
48. OM 8:142.
49. OM 8:359.
50. AM 2:413
51. AM 6:104 (trans. cf. AM 6:103).
52. OM 8:181–82.
53. AM 1:192 (trans. cf. MA 1:185)
54. OM 9:303–10.
55. AM 1:159–60.
56. AM 1:166; The film the Mother saw was *Bhakta Dhruva*, which was shown in the ashram playground on 28 April 1958. In the film, Dhruva, played by a very young Shashi Kapoor, repeats the mantra 'Om namo bhagavate Nārāyaṇāya' (Om salutation to Lord Narayana) while performing tapasya in the forest. The film is available on YouTube at https://www.youtube.com/watch?v=gep332HFEUI.
57. CWM 15:361–65.

11: New Directions

1. See for instance the Mother's description of a 'practically hellish' visit to a new sugar factory (AM 1:437), an 'appalling' calendar distribution (AM

1:523), and her reactions to the hordes of people who crowded around her as she walked from one room in the ashram to another (AM 2:125, 138).

2. 'Sri Aurobindo International Centre', 134–40.
3. CWM 12:118-19; 117–18.
4. 'Sri Aurobindo International Centre', 140–42.
5. CWM 12:171–73.
6. CWM 12:351–52.
7. *The Hindu*, 21 August 1961.
8. CWSA 35:71.
9. AM 2:118; CWM 15:63.
10. AM 2:118–20, 203; CWM 15:49.
11. AM 1:201.
12. AM 1:341, 368, 406, 462; AM 2:58, 427; AM 3:86.
13. Note in AM 3:133.
14. Note in English reproduced in AM 3:134.
15. OM 12:97.
16. If the Mother had a full cardiac arrest—in other words, if her heart stopped beating—it is all but certain she recovered after being given cardiopulmonary resuscitation by her doctors.
17. AM 2:126–27.
18. AM 3:138–39.
19. Letter Mother to Alexandra David-Neel, 3 May 1962 (MADN).
20. AM 3:146.
21. AM 4:59.
22. AM 4:183.
23. AM 4:17.
24. Instrument of clarification and rectification of 10 July 1967, quoted in Madras High Court Judgment in W.P. 27099 of 23 February 2023, available online at https://indiankanoon.org/doc/42926127.
25. *Indian Express*, 12 February 1965 (datelined 11 February).
26. 'Impact of Anti-Hindi Movement', *Indian Nation*, 11 and 12 March 1965.
27. AM 6:31–33.
28. *Hindustan Standard*, 15 June 1965; *Amrita Bazar Patrika*, 29 July 1965.
29. CWM 13:124–25.
30. *Bulletin* 17 (2) (April 1965): unnumbered plate.
31. CWM 13:364; *Bulletin* 34 (4): 76–77.
32. CWSA 35:633; AM 6:148.

33. CWM 15:60–61.
34. *Bulletin* 17 (2) (April 1965):80. A month earlier, the 'Information Letter' of Sri Aurobindo Society mentioned that the Mother had taken up the Auroville project.
35. AM 6:141–53 Cf. *Auroville in the Mother's Words,* vol. 1: 100–14.
36. AM 3:214, 216, 359.
37. AM 4:17, 260–62; AM 5:78, 104, 220.
38. This series of talks first appeared in the *Bulletin* between February 1965 and April 1973. Currently, it is published as volume 11 of CWM. For background, see editorial note in AM 6:184.
39. OM 11:1–3, 8, 21, 32.
40. OM 11:54, 79–80.
41. OM 11:125.
42. *Auroville in the Mother's Words,* vol. 1: 97,120–24.
43. Reproduced in *Auroville: The City of Dawn,* 'Statements of Support—UNESCO', available online at https://auroville.org/contents/538.
44. *Auroville in the Words of the Mother,* vol. 2:64–67.
45. *Auroville in the Words of the Mother,* vol.1:125.
46. Sarkar, *Ashram School,* 46; CWM 12:182–84.
47. OM 11:127–28, 132.
48. OM 11:160, 170, 180, 215, 226.
49. OM 11:240; AM 11:157, 327–38; OM 11:281; 327, 352, 356.
50. AM 10:309.
51. CWM 13:368.
52. CWM 13:369.
53. Indira Gandhi, message of 25 March 1969, reproduced in *Auroville in the Words of the Mother,* vol. 1: 348.
54. CWM 13:201.
55. CWM 13:223.
56. OM 14:379, 258, 379.
57. Letter Indira Gandhi to the Mother and letter the Mother to Indira Gandhi, both reproduced in AM 12:355–56 under date 29 December 1971.
58. CWM 13:383.
59. CWM 11:307 (original in English).
60. AM 13:373–74.

61. AM 13: 395–96. The method the Mother sketched here corresponds closely to the fifth, occult, method of conquering the fear of death she mentioned in her 1954 article on the subject (OM 12:98).
62. AM 13:427.
63. Bhattacharya, 'Pranab's Talk', 1–10.

12: Epilogue

1. Bhattacharya, 'Pranab's Talk', 1–10.
2. Press release, partially reproduced in *Bulletin* 25 (4) (November 1973): preliminary page.
3. *Indian Express*, 20 November 1973; *Weekly Mail*, 24 November 1973.
4. *New York Times*, 19 November 1973; *Le Monde*, 20 November 1973; 'The Mother Departs', 74.
5. Message by Nolini Kanta Gupta dated 17 November 1973, published anonymously in *Bulletin* 25 (4) (November 1973): preliminary page; Gupta, 'A Message', 22.
6. Sethna, 'The Mother's Victory', 15; Pandit, 'The Mother's Withdrawal', 23; Bhattacharya, 'Sri Aurobindo Ashram', 41.
7. Gupta, 'The Mother and Ourselves', 165.
8. Towards the middle of 1974, an erudite disciple published a comprehensive collection of talks by the Mother in which she spoke of the transformation of the body (K. Gandhi, ed., 'Transformation of the Body', 19–50). In none of them, did she suggest she would return in a 'new body'.
9. AM 1:123.
10. CWSA 28:312.
11. CWSA 35:138–39.
12. CWSA 35:390; CWM 13:108.
13. CWSA 35:755.
14. CWM 13:196.
15. CWM 12:118, 351–52.
16. Supreme Court of India, S.C. Mittal etc. etc. v. Union of India and Others, 8 November 1982: 1983 AIR 1 1983 SCR (1) 729, available online at https://indiankanoon.org/doc/312939/.
17. For glimpses of life in Auroville during this period, see Akash Kapur's *Better to Have Gone*.
18. Government of India, The Auroville Foundation Act, 1988, available online at https://legislative.gov.in/sites/default/files/A1988-54.pdf.

19. Since November 2021, Auroville residents have noted a steady assertion by the government of its unqualified control over the project. In December 2023, the newsletter *Auroville Today* reported that the Auroville Foundation Office (AVFO) changed the wording of its official 'visa Letters of Recommendation', replacing the phrase 'Auroville was founded by "The Mother" of Sri Aurobindo Ashram on 28th February 1968' with '[Auroville is] functioning under the administrative control of the Ministry of Education, Government of India'. See also 'Auroville Foundation', https://aurovillefoundation.org.in/, accessed 23 December 2023. Neither the AVFO's visa letter nor the statement on the foundation's official website mentions the Mother or Sri Aurobindo.
20. 'Census October 2024 – Auroville Population', available online at https://auroville.org/contents/3329 (a note on this page states: 'This report includes Aurovilians, Newcomers, To be newcomer, and their children.'); 'Forests and Biodiversity', available online at https://auroville.org/contents/516; 'Awards', available online at https://auroville.org/contents/884; 'List of Social Enterprises in Auroville', available online https://auroville.org/contents/3371; 'Art & Culture', available online at https://auroville.org/categories/26; all web pages accessed 8 August 2024.
21. AM 13:59.
22. See for example Stephen H. Phillips, *Philosophy of Religion: A Global Approach* (1997), and William Edelglass and Jay L. Garfield, *The Oxford Handbook of World Philosophy* (2011).
23. CWM 12:217.
24. CWM 13:154, 91.
25. OM 2:55.
26. OM 14:84 (see chapter 10 for fuller quotation and discussion).
27. AM 7:78.
28. CWM 13:110.

Bibliography

This biography is based on primary sources in public and private archives, and research libraries in France, India and Israel; on the writings of the Mother and Sri Aurobindo; on newspapers and journals in physical and online collections; and on books and articles in physical and digital form. Many of the primary materials were collected by my friend Francis Bertaud from archives, libraries and private collections in France, Israel and India. This material forms the basis of his invaluable database 'Familles Alfassa–Pinto–Ismalun' on Geneanet.org. I often urged him to present his findings in narrative form. He passed away unexpectedly in 2019 before he could do this. His pioneering work has informed my own research and writing. I and all those interested in the Mother's life owe a debt of gratitude to him.

All biographers must deal with problems involved in collecting, collating and analysing material, and finding appropriate ways to present it in written form. A biographer of Mirra Alfassa, the Mother, faces special difficulties, which I discuss in the Prologue, and Chapters 1 and 8. In brief, much of what makes the Mother's life worth telling has to do with inner experiences for which there is no documentation apart from her own oral and written accounts. Difficulties of this sort beset biographers of other mystics, poets and artists, but they are especially acute in regard to the Mother because she viewed her whole life, outer as well as inner, in spiritual and occult terms.

An awareness of these problems kept me from writing about the Mother's life (apart from a few articles on specialized topics) until the end of 2020, when Ramachandra Guha invited me to contribute a volume to his 'Indian Lives' series. Not long before this, I received a mass of documents collected by Francis Bertaud. Going through his material and reviewing the documents that I and others had collected, I concluded that there was enough for me to attempt a biography that would do justice to all aspects of the Mother's life. I therefore accepted Guha's invitation. As it happened, the city I live in was then under partial lockdown (it was between the first and second waves of COVID-19) so I had enough free time to make a start.

I have received much help across the years from colleagues in the archives and research library in Pondicherry I am associated with. I also would like to express my gratitude to Toshio Akai, Claude Arpi, Liviu Bordas, Vinita Damodaran, Clifford Gibson, Gilles Guigan, Boaz Huss, Ajit Neogy, Olivier Pironneau and Ted Ulrich for help in obtaining material.

When citing the Mother's talks and writings I referred to the original texts, most of which are in French. (The balance are in English.) When translating from French to English I often consulted, and sometimes drew upon, earlier translations. Writings and talks by the Mother are © Sri Aurobindo Ashram Trust; talks published in *L'Agenda de Mère* are © Institut de Recherches Évolutives.

ARCHIVES AND LIBRARIES

Archives du Musée Gustave Moreau, Paris

Archives du Musée Nissim-de-Camondo, Paris

Archives Nationales, Paris (Pierrefitte-sur-Seine)

Archives Nationales d'Outre-mer, Aix-en-Provence

Archives de la Ville de Paris

Baha'i Archives, Haifa, Israel

Bibliothèque Nationale, Paris

Maison Alexandra David-Neel, Digne-les-Bains

ONLINE DATABASES

Familles Alfassa–Pinto–Ismalun, a genealogical database created by Francis Bertaud (anupadin), available online at geneanet.org, https://gw.geneanet.org/anupadin_w?lp=0.

Klarsfeld, Serge, and Jean-Pierre Stroweis, *Le Mémorial de la déportation des Juifs de France*, available online at https://stevemorse.org/france/.

[For newspaper databases, see below under Newspapers]

PRIMARY SOURCES

Manuscript materials

Benilan, Jean, *Le Gouverneur Alfassa (1876–1942)*. Privately printed (MFP)

Matteo Alfassa Papers (in the custody of Mme Anne Benilan, via Gilles Guigan)

Mirra Ismalun, 'Mes mémoires', reproduced in Benilan, *Le Gouverneur Alfassa*, pp. 223–28.

Morisset Family Papers (via Francis Bertaud)

Pascal Thémanlys Papers, Jerusalem (via Francis Bertaud and Boaz Huss)

Correspondence between the Theons and Mirra Alfassa (private collection)

Works of the Mother and Sri Aurobindo

L'Agenda de Mère, thirteen volumes, published by Institut de Recherches Évolutives, Paris, between 1978 and 1982.

Auroville in Mother's Words, Gilles Guigan, ed., two volumes, Auroville: Auroville Press Publishers, 2018.

Collected Works of the Mother, second edition, seventeen volumes, published by Sri Aurobindo Ashram Trust between 2002 and 2004. Available online at https://www.sriaurobindoashram.org/mother/writings.php. The French versions, most of which are the original texts, are published as Œuvres de la Mère (see below).

Collected Works of Sri Aurobindo, thirty-six volumes, published by Sri Aurobindo Ashram Trust between 1997 and 2017. Available online at sriaurobindoashram.org, https://www.sriaurobindoashram.org/sriaurobindo/writings.php.

Messages of Sri Aurobindo and the Mother, Second Series. Pondicherry: Sri Aurobindo Ashram, 1952.

Mother's Agenda, thirteen volumes. English translation of *L'Agenda de Mère* (see above), published by Institut de Recherches Évolutives, Paris, between 1979 and 2000.

The Mother: Paintings and Drawings. Pondicherry: Sri Aurobindo Ashram Trust, 1992.

Œuvres de la Mère, eighteen volumes, PDF edition published by Sri Aurobindo Ashram Trust between 2008 and 2009, available online at https://www.sriaurobindoashram.org/mother/oeuvres.php. I cite the volume numbers of this online edition. The physical books do not have volume numbers.

SECONDARY SOURCES

Journals, Magazines, etc.

Annuaire-almanach du commerce, de l'industrie, de la magistrature et de l'administration... Paris: Didot et Bottin (in the text of this biography I refer to this source as 'the Paris Directory')

Archives Israélites (Paris)

The Asian Review (Tokyo)

Bulletin de l'Alliance Israélite Universelle (Paris)

Bulletin of Physical Education/ Bulletin of Sri Aurobindo International Centre of Education (Pondicherry) (in the notes shortened to *Bulletin*)

L'Écho de l'au-delà et d'ici-bas (Paris)

Journal du magnétisme et de la psychologie (Paris)

Journal officiel de la République Française (Paris)

Journal officiel des Établissements Français dans l'Inde (Pondicherry)

Mercure de France (Paris)

The Modern Review (Calcutta)

Mother India (Bombay/Pondicherry)

Prabartak (Chandernagore)

Recueil des actes administratifs de la préfecture du département de la Seine (Paris)

Revue cosmique (Paris/Tlemcen)

Sri Aurobindo: Archives and Research (Pondicherry)

Sri Aurobindo Circle (Bombay/Pondicherry)

Star of the West (Chicago)

Time (New York)

La Tradition cosmique (Paris)

Les Tendances nouvelles (Paris)

La Voile d'Isis (Paris)

Newspapers

Austria (via Österreichische Nationalbibliothek online)

Fremden-Blatt (Vienna), 1862

Neue Freie Presse (Vienna), 1875

Das Vaterland (Vienna), 1875

Weiner Zeitung (Vienna), 1859

France (via BN, Gallica online)

L'Aurore (Paris)

La Démocratie de l'Ariège (Parmiers)

Fémina (Paris)

Le Figaro (Paris)

Gil Blas (Paris)

La Gazette de France (Paris)

Journal des débats (Paris)

La Lanterne (Paris)

Le Monde (Paris)

Le Monde colonial illustré (Paris)

La Revue (Paris)

French colonies (via BN, Gallica Online)

L'Étoile de l'AEF (Brazzaville)

L'Éveil économique d'Indochine (Hanoi)

India

Amrita Bazar Patrika (Calcutta)

The Hindu (Madras)

The Hindustan Times (Delhi)

The Indian Express (Madras)

The Indian Nation (Patna)

Japan

Fujoshimbun (Tokyo)

Japan Chronicle (Kobe)

Japan Gazette (Yokohama)

United Kingdom (via British Library, British Newspaper Archive Online)

Daily Telegraph & Courier (London)

The Era (London)

Lloyd's Weekly London Newspaper (London)

Jersey Evening Post (Saint Helier)

The Morning Post (London)

United States

The New York Times (New York)

Books, Articles and Dissertations

Abumrad, Jad, and Robert Krulwich. 'Why a Brush with Death Triggers the Slow-Mo Effect', *NPR Radiolab*, available online at https://www.npr.org/2010/08/17/129112147/why-a-brush-with-death-triggers-the-slow-mo-effect.

Alexander, Agnes Baldwin. *History of the Bahá'í Faith in Japan 1914–1938*, ed. Barbara Sims. Tokyo: Bahá'í Publishing Trust of Japan, 1977, available online at https://bahai-library.com/alexander_history_bahai_japan&chapter=3/ .

Almyre, M. 'Les Expositions'. *Les Tendances nouvelles* 6 (15 March 1905): 66–68.

Almyre, M. 'Quelques réflexions à propos du salon des Indépendants'. *Les Tendances nouvelles* 7 (15 April 1905): 78.

Arpi, Claude. *Pondicherry: The Last Months before India's Independence: Perspectives of a British Consul General.* Auroville: Auroville Press, 2005.

Arstila, Valtteri. 'Time Slows Down during Accidents'. *Frontiers in Psychology* 3 (June 2012): 1–10.

Banerji, Sanat K. 'Some Notes on the Mother's *Prières et Méditations*'. *Mother India* 30 (9)–31 (4) (September 1978–April 1979).

Bertaud, Francis. 'Some People in the Early Life of the Mother: Marie Potel'. Unpublished manuscript, 1987.

Bhattacharya, Pradyot Kumar. 'Sri Aurobindo Ashram and the Mother's Passing Away'. *Mother India* 26 (1): 41.

Bhattacharya, Pranab Kumar. 'Pranab's Talk of 4–12–1973 on the Mother'. Supplement (separately printed) to *Mother India* 25 (11–12) (December 1973): 1–8.

Binyamin, Asher. '*Fidélité et erreurs:* Louise Duban and Her Contribution to Our Understanding of the History of the Cosmic Movement'. In Chajes and Huss, eds, *The Cosmic Movement: Sources, Contexts, Impact.* Beersheba, Israel: Goldstein-Goren International Center for Jewish Thought, 2021, 353–75.

Bosc, Ernest. Review of *L'Éther vivant. La Voile d'Isis,* Third Series, no. 30 (June 1912): 191.

Bose, Subhas Chandra. *Selected Speeches of Subhas Chandra Bose.* Delhi: Publications Division, 1965.

Bouyer, Raymond. 'Henri Morisset'. *L'Art décoratif* 7 (January–June 1905): 145–55.

'Causerie'. *Le Pays,* 11 February 1905: unpaginated.

Chajes, Julie, and Boaz Huss. *The Cosmic Movement: Sources, Contexts, Impact.* Beersheba, Israel: Goldstein-Goren International Center for Jewish Thought, 2021.

Chakravarti, Gyanendranath. *Spirituality and Psychism.* Madras: Theosophical Publishing House, 1914.

Chakravarti, J. (*sic*), and Annie Besant. *Conférences du congrès théosophique de 1900.* Paris: Publications Théosophique, 1901.

Chanel, Christian. *De la 'Fraternité Hermétique de Louxor' au 'Mouvement Cosmique': l'œuvre de Max Théon: Contribution à l'étude des courants esotériques en Europe à la fin du XIXème siècle et au* début du XXème *siècle.* Dissertation. Paris: École Pratique des Hautes Études, Section des Sciences religieuses, 1994.

Chaumel, Alfred. 'Premier contact avec les Indes'. *Le Monde colonial illustré* (August 1928): 180–81.

Cosma, Viorel. *George Enescu: A Tragic Life in Pictures.* Bucharest: The Romanian Cultural Foundation, 2000.

Cousins, James H. *The New Japan: Impressions and Reflections.* Madras: Ganesh & Co., 1923.

Cousins, James H., and Margaret E. Cousins. *We Two Together.* Madras: Ganesh & Co., 1946.

Daughton, J.P. *In the Forest of No Joy: The Congo-Océan Railroad and the Tragedy of French Colonialism.* New York: Norton, 2021.

David-Neel, Alexandra. 'Auprès du Dalaï-Lama'. *Mercure de France* 99 (367) (1 October 1912): 466–76.

David-Neel, Alexandra (as Alexandra Myrial). 'Le Culte et les croyances populaires des Annamites'. *Bulletin de la société d'ethnographie* 41 (1) (16 July 1899): 76–83.

David-Neel, Alexandra. *L'Inde où j'ai* vécu. Paris: Plon, 1951.

David-Neel, Alexandra. *Journal de voyage: Lettres à son mari.* Paris: Plon, 1975.

David-Neel, Alexandra (as Alexandra David). *Le Modernisme bouddhiste et le Bouddhisme du Buddha.* Paris: Félix Alcan, 1911.

David-Neel, Alexandra (as Alexandra David). 'Quelques écrivains bouddhistes contemporaines'. *Mercure de France* 77 (300) (16 December 1909): 637–47.

Denis, Maurice (as P.-L. Maud). 'L'Influence de Paul Gauguin'. *L'Occident* 4 (July–December 1903): 160–64.

Doizy, Guillaume. 'À l'Origine de la caricature antisémite en France: Le dessinateur Adolphe Willette (1857–1926)'. *Archives Juives* 50 (1) (2017): 103–24.

Drumont, Édmond. *La France juive.* Two volumes. Paris: G. Marpon & E. Flammarion: 1886.

Enginger, Bernard. 'Pondichéry doit demeurer un centre culturel Franco-Indien'. *Le Monde,* 2 October 1954.

Fort, Bernadette. 'Greuze and the Ideology of Infant Nursing in Eighteenth-century France'. In Anja Müller, ed., *Fashioning Childhood in the Eighteenth Century.* Aldershot, Hants: Ashgate, 2006, 117–34.

Gandhi, Kishore, ed. 'Transformation of the Body'. *Sri Aurobindo Circle* 30 (1974): 19–50.

Ganguli, Romesh Chandra. 'Pondicherry's Mystic'. *Amrita Bazar Patrika,* 22 February 1950.

Gary, Marie-Noël de. *The Camondo Legacy: The Passions of a Paris Collector.* Paris: Les Arts Decoratifs, 2008.

Godwin, Joscelyn, Christian Chanel, and John Patrick Deveney. *The Hermetic Brotherhood of Luxor: Initiatic and Historical Documents of an Order of Practical Occultism.* York Beach, ME: Samuel Weiser, 1995.

Gokak, V.K. 'Interviews in Japan'. In Sri Aurobindo Pathamandir, *Loving Homage.* Calcutta: Sri Aurobindo Pathamandir, 1958, 227–52.

Gokak, V.K. 'Three Prose Poems'. *Sri Aurobindo Mandir Annual* 17 (1958): 165–70.

Grandival. 'Courrier des théâtres'. *La Gazette de France,* 22 June 1897: 3.

Grégoire, J. 'Voyage d'un touriste prolétaire, de Bagdad à Bangkok'. *L'éveil économique d'Indochine,* 26 February 1933: 14–16.

Gupta, Nolini Kanta. 'A Message by Nolini Kanta Gupta', *Mother India* 26 (1) (January 1974): 22.

Gupta, Nolini Kanta. 'The Mother and Ourselves', *Mother India* 26 (3) (March 1974): 165–68.

Gupta, Nolini Kanta. *Reminiscences.* Pondicherry, Sri Aurobindo Ashram Trust, 2015.

Hay, Stephen. *Asian Ideals of East and West.* Cambridge, MA: Harvard University Press, 1970.

Hayami, Akira. *The Influenza Pandemic in Japan, 1918–1920: The First World War between Humankind and a Virus.* Nichibunken monograph series 18 (2015). Chapters available for download at http://id.nii.ac.jp/1368/00006047/

Heehs, Peter. The *Lives of Sri Aurobindo.* New York: Columbia University Press, 2008.

Heehs, Peter. 'The Myth of the Theons'. *Aries: Journal for the Study of Western Esotericism.* Advance article published online 7 March 2024, https://doi.org/10.1163/15700593-tat00016

Heehs, Peter. 'Sri Aurobindo's Theory of Spiritual Evolution'. In *Asian Religious Responses to Darwin.* Cham, Switzerland: Springer Nature (2020): 167–84.

Hoffmann, Eugène. 'Comptes rendus des expositions'. *Journal des artistes,* 30 (18) (14 May 1905): 4, 756–758.

Hue, Gustave. 'Le Groupe Idéa'. *Les Tendances nouvelles* 6 (15 March 1905): 59–63.

Huss, Boaz. 'Madame Théon, Alta Una, Mother Superior: The Life and Personas of Mary Ware (1839–1908)'. *Aries* 15 (2015): 210–46.

'Impact of Anti-Hindi Movement on Sri Aurobindo Ashram' (Statement issued by Sri Aurobindo Ashram and reproduced in many Indian newspapers).

Jasion, Jan Teofil. *'Abdu'l-Bahá, en France: 1911 & 1913,* trans. Pierre Spierkel. Paris: Éditions Bahá'íes, 2017.

Jasion, Jan Teofil. *Quelques rencontres importantes entre les communautés protestante et Bahá'íe en France.* Châtenay-Malabry: La Communauté Bahá'íe de Châtenay-Malabry, 2019.

Jaya Devi, 'At the Feet of Sri Aurobindo [II]'. *Mother India* 22 (10–11) (November–December 1970): 623–25.

Jayawardena, Kumari. *The White Woman's Other Burden.* Abingdon, Oxon.: Routledge, 1995.

Jennings, Hargrave, ed. *The Divine Pymander.* London: George Redway, 1884.

Kapur, Akash. *Better to Have Gone.* New York: Simon & Schuster, 2021.

Keesing, Elisabeth. *Hazrat Inayat Khan: A Biography.* New Delhi: Munshiram Manoharlal, 1981.

Kohen, Sara. 'Italian Synagogue—Kal de Los Francos'. *Salom Turkey* (citing 'Italian Synagogue Brochure' by Naim A. Güleryüz), available online at https://www.salom.com.tr/salomTurkey/haber/109527/italian_synagogue__kal_de_los_francos.

Krämer, Hans Martin. 'Euro-Asian Political Activist and Spiritual Seeker: Paul Richard and Theosophy'. In Hans Martin Kramer and Julian Strube, *Theosophy across Boundaries: Transcultural and Interdisciplinary Perspectives on a Modern Esoteric Movement.* Albany NY: SUNY Press, 2020, 314–44.

Kuzuu, Yoshihisa. 'Farewell to Dr. Richard and Prof. Cousins, advisors of the "Asian Review"'. *Asian Review* 1 (3) (April 1920): 281–83.

Langlois, Alexandre. *Le Rig Veda ou livre des hymnes.* Paris: Firmin Didot Frères, 1848.

'The Last Photographs of Sri Aurobindo'. *Sri Aurobindo: Archives and Research* 14 (2) (December 1990): 207–27.

Laé, Jean-François. 'Le Pouvoir des corps et des mots: l'injure grave dans le divorce'. *Revue interdisciplinaire d'*études *juridiques* 36 (1996), 63–97.

'Madame Morin at Pondicherry'. *The Hindu,* 22 May 1934.

Magre, Maurice. À la *poursuite de la sagesse.* Paris: Fasquelle, 1936.

Martínez, Julia. ' 'Unwanted Scraps' or 'An Alert, Resolute, Resentful People'? Chinese Railroad Workers in French Congo'. *International Labor and Working-Class History* 91 (Spring 2017): 79–98.

Medhananda, 'Queen Hatshepsut'. *Mother India* 10 (5) (June 1958): 40.

Méré, Charles. 'Questions d'art'. *XIX Siècle*, 20 February 1905: unpaginated.

Mitra, Sisirkumar. *The Liberator.* Bombay: Jaico, 1954.

Monod-Herzen, Gabriel. 'A Feeling of Certitude, of Stability'. *Mother India* 61 (8) (August 2008): 706–07.

Morisset, André. 'Remembrances'. *Sri Aurobindo Circle* 34 (1978): 64–66.

Morisset, André. 'A Visit to Sri Aurobindo Ashram'. *The Advent* 7 (4) (November 1950): 264–265.

Morse, John T. 'The Dreyfus and Zola Trials'. *The Atlantic Monthly* 81 (5) (May 1898), 589–602.

'The Mother Departs'. *Time* 102 (23) (3 December 1973): 74.

Mrityunjoy, 'A Look Behind'. In Pandit, M.P., ed., *Breath of Grace.* Pondicherry: Sri Aurobindo Ashram Trust, 1973, 55–77.

Mukhopadhyaya, Prabhatkumar, *Rabindrajibani o Rabindrasahitya-prabeshak,* vol. 2. Calcutta: Vishwabharati, 1355 B.S. [1949].

Munshi, K.M. 'Aurobindo Ashram—A Pilgrimage'. *Hindustan Times,* Independence Supplement, 15 August 1952.

'"Mystery" of Aurobindo's Ashram: Pondicherry's Spiritual Empire'. *India,* 12 June 1949.

Nahar, Sujata. *Mirra the Occultist.* Paris: Institut de Recherches Evolutives, 1989.

Namakkal, Jessica. 'The Terror of Decolonization: Exploring French India's "Goonda Raj"'. *Interventions: International Journal of Postcolonial Studies* 19 (3) (2017, published online 17 October 2016): 1–20.

Nauriya, Anil. 'English Anti-Imperialism and the Varied Lights of Willie Pearson'. *NMML Occasional Paper: History and Society,* new series, 57 (2014).

Nehru, Jawaharlal. *Selected Works of Jawaharlal Nehru,* 100 volumes in two series. New Delhi: Jawaharlal Nehru Memorial Fund, 1972–2019.

Nirodbaran. *Memorable Contacts with the Mother.* Pondicherry: Sri Aurobindo Ashram Trust, 2000.

Nirodbaran. 'A Talk on Pavitra'. *Mother India* 21 (7) (August 1969): 698–704.

Nirodbaran, ed. *Talks with Sri Aurobindo,* two vols. Pondicherry: Sri Aurobindo Ashram Trust, 2001.

Nirodbaran. *Twelve Years with Sri Aurobindo.* Second edition. Sri Aurobindo Ashram Trust, 1973.

Orban, Séverine Aline. *Avis de recherche: Valentine Penrose, œuvre et vie d'une artiste surréaliste.* Dissertation. Louisiana State University, 2014.

Pandit, M.P. ed. *Champaklal Speaks.* Pondicherry: Sri Aurobindo Ashram Trust, 1975.

Pandit, M.P. *Mother and I.* Pondicherry: Dipti Publications, 1984.

Pandit, M.P. 'The Mother's Withdrawal', *Mother India* 26 (1) (January 1974): 23–32.

Papus. *Traité élémentaire de science occulte.* Fifth edition. Paris: Chaumel, 1898.

Plender, Richard. 'The New French Nationality Law'. *The International and Comparative Law Quarterly* 23 (4) (October 1974): 709–47.

Popplewell, Richard James. *Intelligence and Imperial Defence: British Intelligence and the Defence of the Indian Empire 1904–1924.* London: Routledge, 1995.

Pournapréma. *Une Drôle de petite fille.* Pondicherry: Sri Aurobindo Ashram Trust, 2015.

Press Trust of India. 'Portuguese Should Follow Example of France'. In *Amrita Bazar Patrika,* 3 November 1954.

Principes généraux de la philosophie cosmique. Paris: Dépot des Publications Cosmiques, 1907.

Purani, A.B., ed. *Evening Talks with Sri Aurobindo.* Pondicherry: Sri Aurobindo Ashram Trust, 2018.

Raimbault, R.-N. 'Le Salon du congrès d'Anger'. *Les Tendances nouvelles* 11 (30 August 1905): 156–66.

Ransom, Josephine. *A Short History of the Theosophical Society.* Madras: Theosophical Publishing House, 1938, available online at https://archive.ph/SxzA4.

Reddy, Chhalamayi. 'My Journey Miraculous'. *New Race* 6 (1) (February–April 2020): 17–33.

Reddy, Raman. 'Evening Meditations from 1932 to 1946'. *Golden Chain,* November 2007: 30.

Richard, Paul. *The Dawn over Asia*, trans. Aurobindo Ghose. Madras: Ganesh & Co., 1920.

Richard, Paul. 'Democracy'. *Asian Review* 1 (3) (April 1920): 272–75.

Richard, Paul. *Les Dieux*. Paris: Fischbacher, 1914.

Richard, Paul. 'Introduction'. In William Winstanley Pearson , *For India*. Tokyo: The Asiatic Association of Japan, 1917, iii–vii.

Richard, Paul. *The Lord of the Nations*, trans. S.E. Stokes. Madras: Ganesh & Co., 1923.

Richard, Paul. *To the Nations*, translated anonymously. New York: James B. Pond, 1917.

Richard, Paul. *Without Passport: The Life and Work of Paul Richard*. New York: Peter Lang, 1987.

Rodrigue, Aron. *French Jews, Turkish Jews: The Alliance Israélite Universelle and the Politics of Jewish Schooling in Turkey, 1860–1925*. Bloomington, IN: Indiana University Press, 1990.

Rolland, Romain. *Inde: Journal (1915–1943)*. Paris: Editions Vinita, 1951.

Rolland, Romain. *La Vie de Vivekananda et l'évangile universel*. Paris: Stock, 1930.

Rollet, Catherine. 'Allaitement, mise en nourrice et mortalité infantile en France à la fin du XIXe siècle'. *Population* 33 (6) (1978): 1189–1203.

Romanet, Emmanuelle. 'La Mise en nourrice, une pratique répandue en France au XIXe siècle'. *Transtext(e)s Transcultures* 8 (2013), available online at http://journals.openedition.org/transtexts/497.

Rossi, Marie-Lucie. 'La Banque Camondo: histoire et fonds d'archives'. Paris: Archives National du Monde Travail, 1996.

Roy, Anilbaran. 'Notes from a Sadhak's Diary (I)'. *Sri Aurobindo Circle* 32 (1976): 39–48.

Roy, Anilbaran. 'Notes from a Sadhak's Diary (II)'. *Sri Aurobindo Circle* 33 (1977): 58–74.

Roy, Anilbaran, ed. *Sri Aurobindo's Talks of 1926*. Pondicherry: Sri Aurobindo Ashram Trust, 2020.

Saaler, Sven, and Christopher Szpilman, eds. *Pan-Asianism: A Documentary History, vol. 1 (1850–1920)*, PDF edition. Lanham, MD: Rowman & Littlefield, 2011.

Saint-Hilaire, Philippe Barbier. *Itinéraire d'un enfant du siècle.* Paris: Buchet Chastel, 2001.

Saint-Hilaire, Philippe Barbier, ed. *Conversations avec Sri Aurobindo.* Pondicherry: Sri Aurobindo Ashram Trust, 205.

Sanyal, Prabhat. 'A "Call" from Pondicherry'. *Mother India* 5 (11) (December 1953): 180–88.

Sarkar, Namita. *The Ashram School: Glimpses of the Early Years.* Pondicherry: Sri Aurobindo Ashram Trust, 2018.

Sarkar, Namita. *Memorable Years with the Mother,* two vols. Pondicherry: Golden Chain Fraternity, 2017.

Satomi, Kishio. *Japanese Civilization: Its Significance and Realization.* London: Kegan Paul, 1923.

Schlieter, Jens. *What Is It Like to Be Dead?: Near-Death Experiences, Christianity, and the Occult.* New York: Oxford University Press, 2018.

Schnapper, Dominique, and Penelope Johnstone. 'Israélites and Juifs: New Jewish Identities in France'. *European Judaism* 28 (1) (Spring 1995): 40–45.

Sen Gupta, Jatindranath. 'Sri Aurobindo's Ashram: Daily Life of Inmates'. *The Hindu,* 6 May 1927.

Sethna, K.D. The *Mother: Our Light and Delight.* Pondicherry: Clear Ray Trust, 2003.

Sethna, K.D. 'The Mother—Some General Truths and Personal Facts'. *Mother India* 10 (1) (February 1958): 1–11.

Sethna, K.D. 'The Mother's Victory', *Mother India* 26 (1) (January 1974), 8–15.

Sethna, K.D. (as Amal Kiran). 'Some Diary Notes'. *Mother India* 27 (3): 193–97.

Shaw, Stanford. *The Jews of the Ottoman Empire and the Turkish Republic.* London: Macmillan, 1991.

Sheean, Vincent. 'Kings of the Yogis'. *Holiday* 6 (3) (September 1949): 73–82.

Shimazu, Naoko. *Japan, Race, and Equality: The Racial Equality Proposal of 1919.* London: Routledge, 1998.

Société des amis des arts de Bordeaux. 'Compte-rendu'. Bordeaux: Imprimerie G. Gounouilhou, 1907.

Société des amis des arts de Seine-et-Oise. 'Description des œuvres . . . exposés . . . du dimanche 3 Juillet au 2 Octobre 1898'. Versailles: Imprimerie cerf, 1898.

Sohrab, Mirza Ahmad. *Abdul Baha in Egypt.* New York: J.H. Sears, 1929.

'Some Talks of Sri Aurobindo before 1926 (From old talks)'. *Mother India* 26 (5) (May 1974): 349–50.

'Sri Aurobindo International Centre'. *Bulletin of Sri Aurobindo International Centre of Education* 9 (2) (February 1959): 134–140.

Tagore, Rabindranath. 'Aurobindo Ghose'. *Modern Review* 44 (1) (July 1928): 58–60.

Tagore, Rabindranath. *The Message of India to Japan.* New York: Macmillan, 1916.

TenBroeck, W. Dallas, ed. 'Helena Petrovna Blavatsky 1831–1891: Chronological Review of Events in Her Life', available online at https://www.blavatskyarchives.com/dallasblavatsky.htm.

Teo, Wei Ger. 'The Life and Times of Okada Torajiro and His Seiza Method of Self-Harmonization'. *Kyoto Journal*, 5 June 2020, available online at https://www.kyotojournal.org/spirit/the-life-and-times-of-okada-torajiro-and-his-seiza-method-of-self-harmonization/.

Thémanlys, Claire. *Premiers pas vers la route spirituelle.* Paris: Publications Cosmiques, 1922.

Thémanlys, Claire. *Un* Séjour *chez les grands initiés.* Paris: Publications Cosmiques, 1931.

Thémanlys, Louis. *Exposé sur le mouvement cosmique.* Paris: Dépôt des Publications Cosmiques, 1906.

Thémanlys, Pascal. *Max Théon et la philosophie cosmique.* Jerusalem: Bibliothèque Cosmique, 1955.

Una, *Sayings of the Sibyl Alta Una.* London: Universal Philosophic Society, 1884.

Urban, Hugh. *Magia Sexualis: Sex, Magic and Liberation in Modern Western Esotericism.* Berkeley: University of California Press, 2006.

Vasudha. 'A Talk by Vasudha (II)'. *Mother India* 27 (8) (August 1975): 639–44.

Vauxcelles, Louis. 'Notes d'art'. *Gil Blas,* 12 February 1905: 1.

Vauxcelles, Louis. 'Le Salon des Indépendants'. *Gil Blas,* 23 March 1905: 1.

Vauxcelles, Louis. 'La Vie artistique'. *Gil Blas,* 30 July 1907: 2.

Venkataraman, K.S. 'My Diary Leaves'. In Pandit, M.P., ed., *Breath of Grace.* Pondicherry: Sri Aurobindo Ashram Trust, 1973, 363–68.

Vijayatunga, J. 'Sri Aurobindo "Darshan"'. *India,* 21 March 1948.

Vir Gupta, Pankaj, and Christine Mueller. 'A Look at India's First Modernist Building, Golconde in Pondicherry'. *Architecture and Design,* 14 July 2021, available online at https://www.architecturaldigest.in/story/a-look-at-indias-first-modernist-building-golconde-in-pondicherry/.

Wallis, Lucy. 'The Near-Death Experience That Made Me a Top Musician', available online at https://www.bbc.com/news/stories-58465559.

Warlick, M.E. *Max Ernst and Alchemy.* Austin TX: University of Texas Press, 2001.

Weisberg, Gabriel, and Jane Becker, eds. *Overcoming All Obstacles: The Women of the Académie Julian.* New Brunswick, NJ: Rutgers University Press, 1999.

Winnacker, Rudolph. 'Elections in Algeria and the French Colonies under the Third Republic'. *American Political Science Review* 32 (2) (April 1938): 261–77.

Wu, Yu-chuan. 'Straighten the Back to Sit: Belly-Cultivation Techniques as "Modern Health Methods" in Japan, 1900–1945'. *Culture, Medicine, and Psychiatry* (5 February 2016): unpaginated.

Index

Abdu'l-Bahá, 88–90, 113
Académie Julian, 21–22, 33
Advaita Vedanta, 146
Agenda; see Mother's Agenda
Akita, Ujaku, 113
Alexander, Agnes Baldwin, 112–13
Alexandria, 3, 6–8, 18
Alfassa, Bianca (Blanche), 3–4, 9
Alfassa, Éva, 32–33
Alfassa, Jacques, 4, 10, 11, 12
Alfassa, Léon, 4, 6, 8, 11, 12–13, 18, 185–86
Alfassa, Mathilde, 3, 4, 6, 7–8, 9, 11, 13, 14–16, 17, 18, 19–21, 31–33, 73, 78, 85, 158, 185
  death, 186
Alfassa, Matteo, 6–11, 11, 13–19, 21, 24, 28, 32–33, 47, 74, 87, 92–93, 111, 158–59, 161, 163, 166, 172, 173, 185
  death, 186
  responsibilities, 159
Alfassa, Maurice, 3–12, 33, 40, 89, 185
Alfassa, Mirra; *see* Mother, The (Mirra Alfassa...)
Alfassa, Nissim, 3–7, 18, 185
Alfassa, Samuel, 4, 5, 8, 11–13
Alliance Israélite Universelle, 5
All-India Muslim League, 186
Almyre, M., 40
Alta, or Right against Might, 50
Ambedkar, B.R., 177
ancient texts, 56
Andrews, Charles Freer, 162–63
Anger, Roger, 248
Anglo-American spiritualism, 55
animal magnetism, 54–55
'anthropological exhibition' (1878), 9–10
anticolonial uprisings, 155
anti-divine forces, 179, 185, 191
anti-Dreyfus agitation, 19
'anti-Semitic candidate,' 18
antisemitic rioting in Paris, 34
antisemitism, 19, 34, 35
  in France, 24
Antonetti, Raphaël, 158–9, 173
Arabic, 3, 18, 56–57
Arya, 101–3, 105, 108, 133, 138, 170, 181
Ashram; *see* Sri Aurobindo Ashram
Asian Review, 129, 130
astrology and auras, 57
Atlas Mountains, 53–54
atma-samarpana, 98
atomic power, 192

Auroville, 154, 245, 246, 248
Foundation, 266–7
government control of an 'absolute impossibility', 249, 266
Residents' Assembly, 266–7
avatar, 166
Ayton, A.W., 52

Bahaism, 88
Bailly, Edmond, 54–55
Bannerjee, Upendranath, 140
Baron, François, 196, 237, 248
Battle of Clavijo, 36
BBC broadcasts, 187
beauty and harmony, 195
Belle Époque, 34, 50, 82
Bengalis, atrocities against, 1971, 255
Bernhardt, Sarah, 203
Besant, Annie, 77
Bhagavad Gita, 46, 210
Bharati, Subramania, 97
Bharatiya Jana Sangh, 213
Bharatiya Vidya Bhavan, 215
Bhattacharya, Abinash Chandra, 140
Bhattacharya, Pranab Kumar, 189–90, 242, 257
Bimstein, Max; *see* Theon, Max
Bimstein, Yehudah Leib, 49, 51, 56
Black Dragon Society, 119
Blackwood, Algernon, 54
Blavatsky, Madame Helena, 48, 53
Bluysen, Paul, 100
body consciousness, 226
Bonald, Louis de, 32
Bonnard, Pierre, 35–36, 40, 42, 44–5
Bonvin, Louis, 186
Bose, Rash Behari, 116
Bose, Subhas Chandra, 164–65, 191
Bouyer, Raymond, 33, 39
Bracquemond, Félix, 41, 42
Bracquemond, Marie, 41, 42
Bricka, Mademoiselle, 14, 21
British government, 7, 76, 93, 105, 120, 136, 195
British imperialism, 177–78
Brossé, Julian, 32
Brutinel, Pierre, 187
Buddhism, 78, 79, 90–91, 111, 182, 214
Shingon, 113
Theravada, 146
Tibetan, 81
'Buddhist Catholicism,' 81
Bulletin of Physical Education, 193
Bulwer-Lytton, Edward, 49, 50
Burgoyne, Thomas, 51–52

Cairo, 3, 6, 16, 18
Camondo, Abraham-Salomon de, 5
Camondo Bank, 5, 6, 12, 13
Camondo, Isaac de, 22
Camondo, Moïse de, 18, 185
Cape of Good Hope, 112
Cartier-Bresson, Henri, 203
Chakravarti, Gyanendra Nath, 45–46
Challaye, Félicien, 126
Chamberlain, Neville, 182
Chandernagore, 134, 137, 223
referendum of 1949, 199, 219
Charles, Étienne, 44
Chattopadhyaya, Mrinalini, 140
Chattopadhyaya, Virendranath, 140
Chaudhurani, Sarala Devi, 140
Chaumel, Alfred, 163–64
Christianity, 56, 79
civil disobedience movement, 177
Clemenceau, Georges, 10
Coinage Act, 49
Cold War, 245
colonialism, 173, 196
Colonial Office (Paris), 32, 93, 172
Condorcet, Lycée, 14, 21
Congo-Océan railway, 159, 172–73
consciousness, 45, 146, 229
body consciousness, 226

earth-consciousness, 146–47
and Force, 228
human, 178
material, 156
outer, 147
supramental, 146–47, 211
truth-consciousness, 146
universal, 110
Constantinople, 3–5, 7
contrat de mariage (prenuptial agreement), 24
Conversations with the Mother, 166
corps glorieux, 225, 226
Cosmic Drama, 57
Cosmic fellowship, 57
Cosmic movement, 67–69, 71, 73, 74, 84, 217
and religion, 56, 58
Cosmic Myth, 53
Cosmic Philosophy, 56, 59, 109, 171, 194
Cosmic teachings, 49, 65, 66, 161, 165, 211
Courbet, Gustave, 59
Cousins, James Henry, 127, 129, 130, 136, 140
Cousins, Margaret, 132, 140
Crandon, Mina, 64
Cubism, 44

Dalai Lama, 80–81
Dalton, Thomas, 52
darshans, 142, 146, 162, 167, 168, 176, 198, 202, 203, 216, 240, 255
of April 24, 181
from balcony, 176, 202, 233
on the Mother's birthday, 153, 161, 233, 252, 256
from terrace (1963 and after), 240, 244, 252, 256, 257
three darshans formalized, 161–2
'terrace darshan' (1931), 168
Daughton, J.P., 159
David-Neel, Alexandra, 78–80, 82, 240
attitude towards religion, 78
in Calcutta, 81
relationship with her husband, 80
Davidson, Peter, 51–52
Dawn over Asia, The, 136
Day of Siddhi, 148
Debussy, Claude, 54
Degas, Edgar, 22
Delaunay, Jules-Élie, 33
Denis, Maurice, 22
Derain, André, 42
'descent of force,' 28
Dhammapada, 89
dharma, 93, 98
Dharmapala, Anagarika, 80, 96
Dieux, Les, 82, 86–88, 91, 98
disparity of worship, 24
divine forces, 179, 184, 185
Divine Mother, 153, 203, 269
Divine Truth, 166
Doge's Palace (Venice), 29
Dream, A, 220, 245
Dreyfus, Alfred, 34
Dreyfus, Hippolyte, 88, 90–91
Drumont, Édouard, 18
dual citizenship, 197, 198
Dupleix, Joseph François, 99
Durga Puja in 1954, 217
Dutta (Vasavadutta); *see* Hodgson, Dorothy
Duvent, Charles, 39

earth-consciousness, 146–47
Eastern religions, 80
École Polytechnique, 21, 32, 143, 173, 199
Egypt, Ottoman, 3
Emmanuel II of Italy, 5
Enescu, George, 23
Enginger, Bernard, 220, 237; *see also* Satprem

enthusiasm, 88, 157, 160
and violence, 194–95
Entretiens, 210
Erlanger, Camille, 39
Éther Vivant, L', 75, 81, 88
esoteric sub-disciplines, 54
European imperialism, 120, 155
European imperial powers, 119
European nationalism, 120
European occultism, 109
European socialism, 182
European Yogins, 98
Exposé sur le Mouvement Cosmique, 58
Exposition Universelle of 1878, 9
Expressionism, 44

Faivre, Abel, 35–36, 39
Faraday, Michael, 64
Fascism, 186
fatalism, 57
Fauves, the, 43–44
Fear of Death and the Four Methods of Conquering It, The, 223
filariasis, 238
Fleisher, B.W., 115
Fontainebleau Forest, 26–27
Force, and Consciousness, 228
formidable pulsations of Love, 239
France, Pierre Mendès, 219
Franco-German war, 10
Franz-Ferdinand, Archduke, 102
'free progress' system, 235
French East India Company, 99
French-Indian cultural institution, 213
French India, 75, 76, 93, 163, 180, 196–97, 214, 220, 223; *see also* Pondicherry
cession of, 219
de facto transfer of 1954, 242
elections in,100, 199
referendum in, 199
transfer of power to Republic of India, 221
Treaty of Cession to Republic of India, 222, 241
French National Defence Fund, 184, 186–87
French Resistance, 237
French Third Republic, 3
Futurism, 44

Gagarin-Sturdza, Princess, 42
Ganapati Muni, 163
Gandhi, Devadas, 140
Gandhi, Indira, 221, 222, 252–54
Gandhi, Mohandas Karamchand (Mahatma), 136, 137, 164–65, 177
Gauguin, Paul, 35, 42
Gazette de France, 23
Ghose, Aurobindo; *see* Sri Aurobindo
Ghose, Barindra Kumar, 76, 134–35, 139–40, 141, 143–44, 148
Giri, V. V., 253
Gnosticism, 53, 56, 171
Gnostic mythology, 111
God of Calvinism, 91
God of Judaism, 30
Golconde, 174, 189, 200, 222
Goldberg, Rachel, 49
Government of France, 199
Government of French India, 101, 196, 214
Grand Hôtel d'Europe, 96, 133
Gupta, Nolini Kanta, 162–63, 165, 241

Hasan, Abid, 191–92
Herbert, Jean, 164
Hermetic Brotherhood of Luxor, 51–52
Hermeticism, 53, 171
Hillel, Rachel, 4
Hindi, protest against, 242–43

Hirasawa, Tetsuo, 118, 127
Hitler, Adolf, 177–78, 183–84
Hitlerism, 187
Hodgson, Dorothy, 12, 112–13, 115, 122, 125, 128–29, 132–33, 148, 162
Hoffman, Eugène, 39
Hohlenberg, Johannes, 81, 89
homogeneity, 165
Hue, Gustave, 40
Hugo, Victor, 23
human
  animality, 32
  consciousness, 178
  personality, 153
Human Cycle, 236
humanity, 10, 16, 49, 52–53, 56–59, 62, 93, 118, 138, 184, 212–13, 220, 227, 249, 256, 267–68, 288
Hydari, Akbar, 173, 244
hyper-nationalism, 34
immobility, 161, 243
immortality, 225–26
  integral, 57, 161, 225
Impressionism, 22, 35, 39–40
Independent Group of Esoteric Studies, 55–56
India/Indian
  and China, 123–24
  freedom movement, 186
  independence, 197
  nationalism, 177
  revolutionary movement, 76
Indian National Army (INA), 191
Indian National Congress, 136, 164, 177, 186, 191
India–Pakistan wars
  of 1965, 244
  of 1971, 255
Infinity and Eternity, 113
inner aspirations, 84
inner development, 91, 154
inner experiences, 26–27, 45, 65, 76, 117, 154, 193, 237, 261
inner life, 25–26, 28, 46, 100, 103, 108, 110–11, 122, 124, 139, 154, 160, 257
integral yoga, 170–71, 176, 263
International Union of Fine Arts and Letters, 40–42, 58, 90
International Centre of Education; *see* Sri Aurobindo International Centre of Education
International University Centre; *see* Sri Aurobindo International University Centre
Intimism, 39–40
Isha Upanishad, 102
Ismalun, Mathilde; *see* Alfassa, Mathilde
Ismalun, Matteo, 6–8
Ismalun, Mirra (grandmother of Mirra Alfassa), 6–7, 13–14, 15, 18, 23–25, 73
Israélite (term), 18

Jainism, 146
Japan/Japanese, 114
  forces in Burma, 188
  and India relation, 116, 120
  intelligence service, 116
jasmine flower, 142, 156–57
Jaya Devi, 147
Jayatilaka, Don Baron, 90–91
Jinnah, Muhammad Ali, 177
Journal du Magnétisme, 54–55
Joyce, James, 54
Judaism, 17–18, 56
Juif (term), 18
Julian, Rodolphe, 21

Kabbalah, 48, 52–54, 56
Kabbalists, 224
Kamaraj, K., 222, 253
Kandinsky, Wassily, 54

Kanjilal, Hrishikesh, 140
Karaikal, 100
Karpelès, Suzanne, 214
Khan, Inayat, 87–88
Klint, Hilma af, 54
'Knowing How to Suffer,' 75
Kobayashi, Nobuko, 122–23, 125, 139, 140
Kobayashi, Sanzaburo, 118
Krishnamurti, J., 77

La Console, 39
Ladino, 4
Lama, Dalai, 80–81
Landy, Pierre, 219
Laporte, J., 100
League for Racial Equality, 125–26, 136
Lemaire, Philema, 100–101
Lemercier, Rue, 31, 37, 45, 70, 73
Lévi, Sylvain, 163
Life Divine, The, 102, 181
Lord of the Nations, The, 123
Lyons, Eve, 49

MacLeod, Margaretha (Mata Hari), 87
Madame Tussauds, 12
Madras War Fund, 184
Maeterlinck, Maurice, 89
magnetism (occult idea), 54–55
magnetizer, 54–55
Magre, Maurice, 164
Mahakali, 153
Mahalakshmi, 153
Mahasaraswati, 153
Mahayana philosophy, 81
Maheshwari, 153
Maitland, Olive, 165
Mallarmé, Stéphane, 54
Manet, Édouard, 22
manifestation of divinity, 59
Marx, Roger, 41, 42
massière, 22
Master of spiritual philosophy, 172, 209
Mata Hari, 87
material consciousness, 156, 248
material vital plane, 59, 60
Matisse, Henri, 35, 40, 42–44
Matrimandir, 254–55, 265, 267
McPheeters, Jeanette, 165–66
Medium and Daybreak, 51–52
Ménard, André, 214, 218
mental
    construction, 98
    and physical imbalance, 119
Mercadier, Auguste, 19–20
Méré, Charles, 40
Mesmer, Franz, 54–55
metaphysical synthesis, 53
Miaja, José, 182
mind and supermind, 146, 149
Mind of Light, 227
Mirbeau, Octave, 89
Misinterpretation of spiritual experiences, 26
Modèle, Le, 39
Modernism, 35, 44
Monde, Le, 163, 220, 237, 259
Mondrian, Piet, 54
Monet, Claude, 22, 59
Monod-Herzen, Gabriel, 164, 176
Moonje, B.S., 140
Moreau, Gustave, 24, 33
Morin, Louise, 164
Morisset, André, 31, 70, 82, 92, 156, 160–61, 167, 178, 199, 200, 201, 257
    custody, 71
    to Normandy, 58
    to Paris, 38
    primary caregivers, 38
Morisset, François Henri ('Henri'), 23–24
    bronze medal at 1900 Exposition Universelle, 37

custody of André, 71
divorce from Mirra, 70–71
paintings, 37–38, 61
murals in church at Pau, 36
Morisset, Henri Georges, 23
'Mother', as name for female spiritual figures, 149
Mother, the (Mirra Alfassa, Mirra Morisset, Mirra Richard)
aloneness, 208
art classes, 21
attitude towards religion, 45, 46, 90–91, 94–95, 217, 243, 269
at ashram playground, 230
attitude of French Indian officials towards, 214, 219
to Beaugency (1907), 70
birth, 3, 9
birthday celebrations (1927), 153
break with Theon, 73–74
cardiac arrest, 238–39
childhood experiences, 28
in Colombo, 96
completed few paintings between 1899 and 1902, 36–37
in Cosmic movement, 57–69
darshan day, 161–62
darshans and meditations, 168
declaration (public statement) of 1954, ix, 219
divorce from Henri Morisset, 70–71
as divine Shakti, 153
eye problem, 176
French classes to children, 209
health, 107, 143, 167–68
holiday to Cluses, 81
inner development, 154
inner life, 25–26, 110–11
inner resilience, 75
kundalini power, 104
meeting with Aurobindo, 96
meeting with Henri Morisset, 24
origin of appellation 'Mother', 149
paintings and sketches while in Japan, 122, 124
paintings while at Académie Julian, 23
paintings of 1906, 44–45
portrayed in paintings between 1900 and 1902, 37–38
in Paris, 65
relationship with Paul Richard, 78, 135–36
reunion with Aurobindo, 134
sense of security, 208
sensitive to music, 29
social life in Paris, 92
soup ceremony, 152, 156, 157, 162, 168
and Sri Aurobindo Ashram (1929), 172
Sri Aurobindo's spiritual successor, 209
spiritual energy, 174–75
stay-at-home mother, 38
supramental force passed to, 209
Sunday meetings, 165
'terrace darshan,'168
occult writings ('Visions'), 65–67
in touch with Aurobindo in 1915, 108
material consciousness, 248
Mother, The (book), 153
Mother's Agenda (Agenda of the Supramental manifestation), 237, 246, 247
Mountbatten, Louis, 195
Mount Koya, 113
Moyse, Louis, 47; *see also* Thémanlys, Louis
Mukherjee, Syama Prasad, 213–14
Munshi, K.M., 215–16, 218, 222–23
Musée de Versailles, 23
mysticism, nebulous, 78

Nag, Bijoy, 105
Naidu, Sarojini, 140
Nakashima, George, 173–74
Napoleon I, 99, 123
Napoleon III, 9–10
Narayan, 135
Navajata (Keshav Dev Poddar), 246
Nazis/Nazism, 184, 186, 188
Néel, Philippe, 79
'Negro village,' 10, 16–17
Nehru, Jawaharlal, 197–99, 213, 218, 221–23, 241
Nehru–Liaquat Pact, 1950, 213
neoclassical sculpture, 43–44
Neoplatonism, 53
New Idea, The/*L'Idée Nouvelle,* 101
nirvana, 115, 146
Normandy, 15, 39, 58–60, 72, 84

occultism, 47, 48, 50, 53, 61–62, 63–64
occultisme, 48
Occult Magazine, 52
Okada, Torajiro, 118
Okakura, Kakuzo, 120–21
Okawa, Shumei, 116, 120–21, 124, 126, 128–29, 131
Om namo bhagavate, 231
Oostveen, Wilhelmina van, 68
Orphism, 171
Ostroróg, Stanislas, 219
Ottoman Empire, 3–5, 125
Ottoman Jewish network, 6
outer consciousness, 147
overmind, 148–49

Pan-Asianism, 119, 126
Pan-Asiatic movement, 124
pantheism, 88–89
Parekh, Manilal, 179
Paris
    Charity Bazaar fire, 211
    during the Belle Époque, 33–34
    monopoly on cultural events, 41
Paris Commune, 8
Paris Peace Conference, 125
pathétisme, 55, 64
pavilion of Divine Love, 246; *see also* Matrimandir
Pavitra; *see* Saint-Hilaire, Philippe Barbier
Pearson, William Winstanley, 118–19, 120–21, 140, 141
Penrose, Valentine, 164
perfection, individual and social, 59
Petite Salle Pleyel, 23
philosophical meditation, 80
physical transformation, 226
Picard, Georges, 89
Pinto, Giacomo, 13–14
Poddar, Keshav Dev (Navajata), 246
Pondicherry, 75–76, 93, 96, 163–64, 172, 252–54; *see also* French India
    French quarter, 141
    political refugees, 104–5
    referendums in, 199
    revolutionaries based in, 93
Porto-Riche, Georges de, 23
Potel, Léon, 143
Potel, Marie, 85–87, 92, 143
power
    and personalities, 153
    and strength, 195
Prabartak, 134–35
practical occultism, 53
Prakriti of Ignorance, 171–72
pranam, 99, 147, 156–57, 162, 167, 174, 176, 181, 202, 216, 217
    procedure, 174
Prayers and Meditations, 165, 210, 228, 268
Provisional Government of Free India, 191
psychic being , 171, 226

opening, 194
the Mother's identification with, 261
psychological monographs, 89
Purusha (soul, spirit), 144
Pythagoreanism, 171

Questions and Answers, 210

racial equality, 125–26, 136
Rahman, Sheikh Mujibur, 255
Raimbault, René-Noël, 41
Ramadier, Paul, 198, 214
Rameshwaram, 96
Raymond, Antonín, 173–74
Realism, 39–40
recollections of past births, 28
Reddy, Neelam Sanjiva, 253
Redon, Odilon, 54
Reinach, Béatrice, 185
Reinach, Théodore, 90–91
religion
attitude of Madame David-Neel towards, 78
attitude of Mirra/the Mother towards, 45, 46, 90–91, 94–95, 217, 243, 269
and the Cosmic Movement, 56, 58
Sri Aurobindo's aim not to propagate, 242
religious solemnity, 92
Renaissance in India, 213
Renoir, Pierre-Auguste, 22
revolutionaries in Bengal, 105
Revue Cosmique, La, 47, 56–57, 72, 225
rheumatism, 143
Richard, Paul, 67–69, 72, 73–74, 75, 76, 167, 208
attends Hari Prasad Shastri lecture, 116
and Baha'i faith, 89
death, 137
health conditions, 108
intellectual knowledge, 74–75
married with Ethel Linda Todd, 137–38
in Nagpur, 136–37
in Tokyo, 113, 121–22, 125, 128–29
in touch with Aurobindo, 93, 108–9
vacation in Normandy, 84
Riddle of This World, The, 170, 172
Rodin, Auguste, 35–36
Rolland, Romain, 137, 141, 164, 166
Romanet, Emmanuelle, 38
Rosicrucianism, 54
Rossetti, Dante Gabriel, 50
Roy, Anilbaran, 165
Roy, Dilip Kumar, 165, 166, 191, 193, 218
Roy, Motilal, 134, 137
Rue Buffault Synagogue, 9, 17
Rue Saint Gilles house, 155, 216

sadhaks, 216, 269
sadhana
subjective, 138
of transformation, 248
sadhikas, 147
Saint-Hilaire, Philippe Barbier (Pavitra), 143, 147, 165, 196, 203
Saint-Saëns, Camille, 29
Salon des Artistes Français, 33
Salon of the Société Nationale, 33
salvation, 149
Sammer, František, 174
Sanatana Dharma, 93
Sanyal, Prabhat, 204–5
Satie, Erik, 54
Satprem (Bernard Enginger), 220, 237, 238–40, 246, 257
Savitri, 181, 241

Sayings of the Sibyl Alta Una, 51
Scourge of Christ, The, 127
Second World War, 155, 182–85, 187–88, 191–92
battles of Kohima and Imphal, 191
self-abnegation, 108
self-analysis, 84
self-awareness, 211–12
self-discipline, 8
self-effacement, 80
self-help works, 89
self-knowledge, 83
self-maintenance, 160
self-mastery, 83
self-observation, 84
Sen, Indra, 213
Sen, Satyabrata, 204–5
Sen Gupta, Jatindranath, 157–58
sensual indulgence, 158
Sephardim, 3
Sévigné, Madame de, 12
sex-magic rituals, 52
shakti (force, power), 144
Shakyamuni Buddha, 117
Shastri, Hari Prasad, 116
Shastri, Lal Bahadur, 222, 244
Sheean, Vincent, 202–3
shefali flower, 156–57
Shingon Buddhism, 113
Shiva and Shakti, 144–45
Shraddhanand, Swami, 137
'Sibylline lectures,' 50
Sixth International Congress of Progress in Religion, 90
social contagion, 83
social legitimacy, 79
Sohrab, Ahmad, 88
Spanish flu, 130–31, 145
Spanish Jews, 3
Spiritism, 54, 55
spiritual education, 245
spiritualism, 50, 55, 63–64, 221
spiritualists, 55, 64, 90, 224
professional, 64
spiritual/spirituality, 28, 98, 132
common sense, 167
development, 30, 97
equality, 115
flag of India, 221
initiation, 86
interpretation, 178
knowledge, 75–76, 144
and occult thinkers, 28
protection, 187–88
and psychism, 45–46
responsibility, 86
seeking, 98
things, 28, 210–11
Sri (Sanskrit term), 149
Sri Aurobindo (Aurobindo Ghose)
accident, 180–82
aim not to propagate any religion, 242
birthday celebrations, 142
connection with Paul Richard, 93
darshan days, 161–62
death, 207–8
early life, 76
final illness, 204–5
friendship with Tagore and Richards, 114
imprisonment, 76
meeting with Paul Richard (1910), 77
meeting with Mirra and Paul Richard (1914), 96–98
path of yoga, 140
political journalism, 76
public appeal for funds (1927), 158
relationship with the Mother, 136, 145
retirement, 161

sadhaks and visitors, interactions with, 189
sadhana, 138
siddhi, 149
use of name 'Sri Aurobindo', 149
visits from Mirra and Paul Richard in Pondicherry, 101, 133
Sri Aurobindo Ashram
attack on (1965), 242–43
'birthday' of, 149
collective gatherings, 156–57
community, 155
conversation classes, 217
financial difficulties, 190
group (collective) meditations, 156, 162, 176, 189
organization of, 154
school, 192, 212; *see also* Sri Aurobindo International Centre of Education
soup ceremony, 152, 156–57, 162, 168
Sunday meetings (1929), 165
uniform for girls' sports, 190
Sri Aurobindo Ashram Trust, 222, 241
Sri Aurobindo International Centre of Education, 154, 213–15, 233–36, 250, 256, 262, 264–65
Sri Aurobindo International University Centre, 212–15, 233, 244, 264
funding drive for, 218
Sri Aurobindo Memorial Convention, 213
Sri Aurobindo Society (SAS), 236, 245
Suez Canal Company, 7
suffering, 24, 62, 72, 75, 83, 107, 160, 169, 205, 227, 238, 262
sufism, 87–89
supermind, 130, 146
supramental being, 130
supramental consciousness, 146–47, 211
supramental force, 15, 153
supramentalisation of the Overmind, 227–29
supramental manifestation, 229–30, 238
supramental transformation, 226–28, 239
surhomme, 229, 251
surrender, 88, 98–99, 110, 153, 169, 174, 188, 191, 224, 269
Suzanne, Mademoiselle, 14, 15
Synthesis of Yoga, The, 102, 241

Tagore, Rabindranath, 17, 113–14, 117–18, 162
tantra, 144–45
tantric sadhana, 157–58
Tendances Nouvelles, Les, 40-41, 43, 47, 62
terrestrial immortality, 59
territorial holdings, 177, 183
Thémanlys, Claire, 62, 63, 68, 72
Thémanlys, Louis, 47, 57, 58–60
Theon, Madame (Mary Ware), 50–51, 53, 56–58, 60–61, 62, 63, 64, 67, 68–69
death, 72–73
Theon, Max (Maximillian Bimstein), 47, 48–49, 51–57, 60–65, 68–69, 71–73
connection with Mirra, 72
integral immortality, 225
teachings of Theon and Madame Theon, 73, 211
to Tlemcen, 73
Theosophical Society, 45, 50, 52, 54-55, 73, 77, 79, 80, 143
French, 55–56
Theosophists, 51, 224–25
Theravada Buddhism, 146

Tibetan Buddhism, 81
title to property, 209
Tlemcen, 47, 53, 55, 60-63, 65, 68, 69, 73
Todd, Ethel Linda, 137
To India: The Message of the Himalayas, 137
Tradition Cosmique, La, 57, 171
transformation, 145–46, 148, 162, 170–71, 176, 194, 212, 226, 227, 230, 231, 246–248, 252, 256, 260–263
translating works by Sri Aurobindo into French, 216–17
Trouville-sur-Mer, 15, 59, 84
truth-consciousness, 146
twelve senses, 211

uniformity, economic and cultural, 109
Union for Feminine Thought, 83
Union Générale bank, 11
United Nations Educational, Scientific and Cultural Organization (UNESCO), 248–49
unity, 165
  complete, 64
  deeper meaning, 109
  Divine, xi
universal consciousness, 110
Universal Philosophic Society, 50
'Unpublished Study from an Ancient Source,' 57–58
Upanishads, 101, 103

Vauxcelles, Louis, 40
Vedantism, 171
Vedas, 49, 72, 101, 103–4
Vedic and Puranic Earth, 110
Verlaine, Paul, 54
vibration of truth, 247
Viceroy of Egypt, 7
Viceroy's War Fund, 184, 186–87
Vijayatunga, Jinadasa, 202
Villa Zarif, 61
violence, 100, 159, 179
  and bloodshed, 195
Visakhapatnam, 188
Vishva Hindu Parishad, 215
vital power, 63, 183
Vivekananda, Swami
  writings of, 89
Vuillard, Édouard, 35, 40, 42, 44–45

Walsh, Walter, 90–91
Ware, Mary; *see* Theon, Madame
Whistler, James McNeill, 49
women's empowerment, 140
World Union, 236
Wylm, Antoine, 89

xenophobia in France, 19

Yeats, William Butler, 54
yoga
  integral, 179
  of the World, 239
  Sri Aurobindo's path of, 140
yogic psychology, 210
Yogic sadhana, 93
Yokohama, 112, 114, 117
Ysaÿe, Eugène, 29

Zola, Émile, 34–35

About the Author

Peter Heehs was born and educated in the United States. He came to India during the 1970s and settled in Pondicherry, where he works as a research scholar and writer. He is the author/editor of twelve books, including *The Bomb in Bengal, The Lives of Sri Aurobindo, Writing the Self: Diaries, Memoirs and the History of the Self* and *Spirituality without God: A Global History of Thought and Practice.* His articles have appeared in journals such as *History and Theory, Modern Asian Studies* and *Postcolonial Studies,* and magazines such as *History Today* and *Art India.*

HarperCollins *Publishers* India

At HarperCollins India, we believe in telling the best stories and finding the widest readership for our books in every format possible. We started publishing in 1992; a great deal has changed since then, but what has remained constant is the passion with which our authors write their books, the love with which readers receive them, and the sheer joy and excitement that we as publishers feel in being a part of the publishing process.

Over the years, we've had the pleasure of publishing some of the finest writing from the subcontinent and around the world, including several award-winning titles and some of the biggest bestsellers in India's publishing history. But nothing has meant more to us than the fact that millions of people have read the books we published, and that somewhere, a book of ours might have made a difference.

As we look to the future, we go back to that one word—a word which has been a driving force for us all these years.

Read.